PHILIP'S

STRE

Shropshire

C000066356

First published in 2003 by

Philip's, a division of
Octopus Publishing Group Ltd
2–4 Heron Quays, London E14 4JP

First edition 2003
Third impression with revisions 2006
S RAC

ISBN-10   0-540-08339-9 (pocket)
ISBN-13   978-0-540-08339-8 (pocket)

© Philip's 2006

Ordnance Survey®

This product includes mapping data licensed from Ordnance Survey® with the permission of the Controller of Her Majesty's Stationery Office. © Crown copyright 2006. All rights reserved. Licence number 100011710.

Printed and bound in Spain
by Cayfosa-Quebecor

Contents

III **Key to map symbols**

IV **Key to map pages**

VI **Route planning**

X **Administrative and Postcode boundaries**

1 **Street maps** at 2½ inches to 1 mile

167 **Street maps** at 1¼ inches to 1 mile

216 **Street maps** at 2½ inches to 1 mile

221 **Town map** of Wrexham

222 **Index** of towns and villages

226 **Index** of streets, hospitals, industrial estates, railway stations, schools, shopping centres, universities and places of interest

Digital Data

The exceptionally high-quality mapping found in this atlas is available as digital data in TIFF format, which is easily convertible to other bitmapped (raster) image formats.

The index is also available in digital form as a standard database table. It contains all the details found in the printed index together with the National Grid reference for the map square in which each entry is named.

For further information and to discuss your requirements, please contact Philip's on 020 7644 6932 or james.mann@philips-maps.co.uk

Key to map symbols

III

(22a)	Motorway with junction number
	Primary route – dual/single carriageway
	A road – dual/single carriageway
	B road – dual/single carriageway
	Minor road – dual/single carriageway
	Other minor road – dual/single carriageway
	Road under construction
	Tunnel, covered road
	Rural track, private road or narrow road in urban area
	Gate or obstruction to traffic (restrictions may not apply at all times or to all vehicles)
	Path, bridleway, byway open to all traffic, road used as a public path
	Pedestrianised area
DY7	Postcode boundaries
	County and unitary authority boundaries
	Railway, tunnel, railway under construction
	Tramway, tramway under construction
	Miniature railway
Walsall	Railway station
	Private railway station
South Shields	Metro station
	Tram stop, tram stop under construction
	Bus, coach station

◆	Ambulance station
◆	Coastguard station
◆	Fire station
◆	Police station
✚	Accident and Emergency entrance to hospital
H	Hospital
✛	Place of worship
i	Information Centre (open all year)
P	Parking
P&R	Park and Ride
PO	Post Office
Ӿ	Camping site
⊞	Caravan site
▶	Golf course
✕	Picnic site
Prim Sch	Important buildings, schools, colleges, universities and hospitals
River Ouse	Tidal water, water name
	Non-tidal water – lake, river, canal or stream
	Lock, weir, tunnel
	Woods
	Built up area
Church	Non-Roman antiquity
ROMAN FORT	Roman antiquity
87	Adjoining page indicators and overlap bands
220	The colour of the arrow and the band indicates the scale of the adjoining or overlapping page (see scales below)

Acad	Academy	Inst	Institute	Recn Gd	Recreation Ground
Allot Gdns	Allotments	Ct	Law Court		
Cemy	Cemetery	L Ctr	Leisure Centre	Resr	Reservoir
C Ctr	Civic Centre	LC	Level Crossing	Ret Pk	Retail Park
CH	Club House	Liby	Library	Sch	School
Coll	College	Mkt	Market	Sh Ctr	Shopping Centre
Crem	Crematorium	Meml	Memorial	TH	Town Hall/House
Ent	Enterprise	Mon	Monument	Trad Est	Trading Estate
Ex H	Exhibition Hall	Mus	Museum	Univ	University
Ind Est	Industrial Estate	Obsy	Observatory	Wks	Works
IRB Sta	Inshore Rescue Boat Station	Pal	Royal Palace	YH	Youth Hostel
		PH	Public House		

■ The small numbers around the edges of the maps identify the 1 kilometre National Grid lines

■ The dark grey border on the inside edge of some pages indicates that the mapping does not continue onto the adjacent page

The scale of the maps on the pages numbered in blue is 3.92 cm to 1 km • 2½ inches to 1 mile • 1: 25344

0 ¼ ½ ¾ 1 mile
0 250m 500m 750m 1 kilometre

The scale of the maps on pages numbered in green is 1.96 cm to 1 km • 1¼ inches to 1 mile • 1: 50688

0 ¼ ½ ¾ 1 mile
0 250m 500m 750m 1kilometre

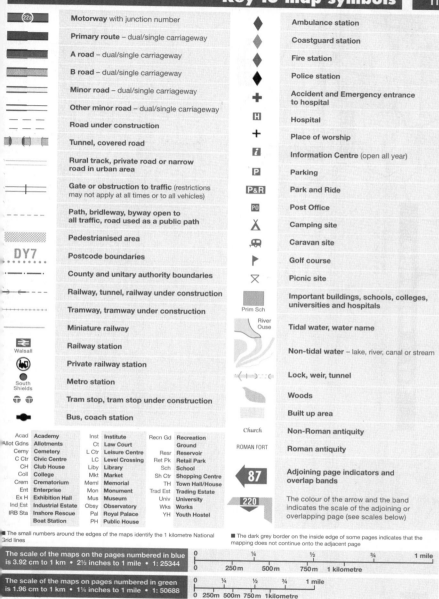

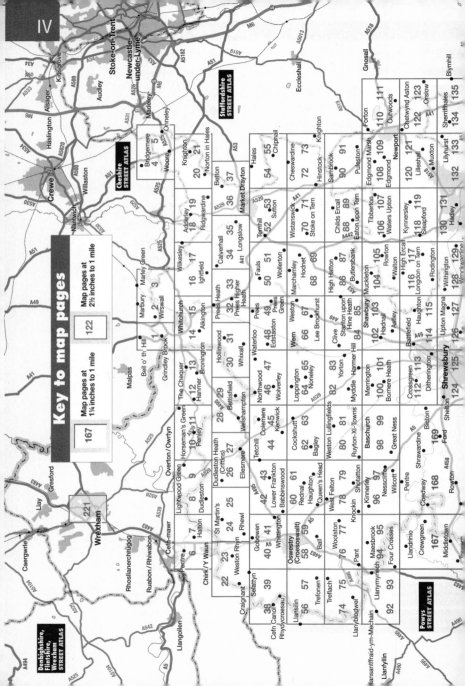

Key to map pages

IV

Map pages at 1¼ inches to 1 mile **167**

Map pages at 2½ inches to 1 mile **122**

Bishops Wood 148
M54
Codsall
Nurton
M6
A41
Shifnal 157
Albrighton 156
Boningale 166
Pattingham
Seisdon 190
Wombourne
Swindon
A449
A458
Kinver
Kidderminster
A442
A449
A451

Tong 147
M54
146 145 144 Telford
Strixley
Shifnal
A464
A5
Kemberton 155
Madeley 153
Ryton
Grindle
Burnhill Green 164
Beckbury
Ackleton
A454
Worfield 189
Claverley
Bobbington
A442
Trimpley
Bewdley
Stourport on Severn
A451
A443
A442

Lawley 143
Little Wenlock 142
Wyke
Sheinton 151
A4169
Broseley 152
Ironbridge
A442
Norton 162
Crowgreaves 163
Astley Abbotts 188
Stanmore 219
Eardington
Bridgnorth 218
Chelmarsh
Hampton
Quatt 201
Alveley
Romsley
Shatterford
Buttonoak 210 211
Lem Hill
Woodhill 200

Worcestershire STREET ATLAS

Uppington 141
Donnington 140
Buildwas 150
Harley 159
Much Wenlock 158
Willey 161
Broseley
Acton Round 187
Morville
Chetton
Neenton
Sidbury 199
Burwarton 198
Cockshutford
Stottesdon
Kinlet
Orleton 209
Cleobury Mortimer
Lindridge 215
Newnham Bridge
Tenbury Wells
A4117

Uppington
Cressage 149
Longnor
Leebotwood
Plaish
Shipton
Holdgate
Munslow 197
Clee St Margaret
Bromdon
Cleeton St Mary 208
Doddington
Cleehill
Nash 214
Boraston
A456
A4112

Atcham 138 139
Cross Houses
Pitchford 179
Acton Burnell
Ruckley
Cardington
Wall under Heywood 185
Diddlebury
Alcaston
Seifton 196
Stanton Lacy
Bitterley 207
Caynham 213
Ashford Bowdler 212
Brimfield
Richards Castle
Orleton
A49

Bayston Hill 136 137
Annscroft
Dorrington 178
Stapleton
A49
All Stretton
Church Stretton 184
Little Stretton 216
Onibury 206
Ludlow 217
Ludford
Batchcott
A4117
A4110

Harwood
Longden 173
Pontesbury
Habberley
Picklescott
Rattlinghope 177
Minton 183
Marshbrook
Craven Arms 195
Broome
Clungunford
Sheinton 205
Leintwardine
Adforton
A4113

Westbury
Aston Rogers 172
Minsterley
Snailbeach
Stiperstones
Hope
Wentnor
Lydham 182
Totterton
Hopesay
Kempton 194
Clunbury
Clunton
Hoptonheath
Bucknell 204
Brampton Bryan
A4110

Rowley 171
Worthen
Marton
Rorrington
Chirbury 174
A490
A488
The Marsh 175
Priest Weston
Snead
Pentre
Bishop's Castle
Acton
Whitcott Keysett 193
Clun
Churchbank
Purlogue
Stowe 203
Knucklas
Knighton/Tref-y-Clawdd

Welshpool (Trallwng) 170
Kingswood
Forden/Ffodun
Montgomery 180
City 181
Pentrehelying
Mardu
Newcastle 192
Llanfair Waterdine
Knucklas 202
Llangunllo
A488

Anchor 191
Felindre
Beguildy
A483

Presteigne
Herefordshire, Monmouthshire STREET ATLAS

Scale
0 5 10 15 km
0 5 10 miles

Scale

0 5 10 km

0 1 2 3 4 5 6 miles

Administrative and Postcode boundaries

County and unitary authority boundaries
District boundaries
Postcode boundaries
Area covered by this atlas

Scale

| 0 | 5 | 10 | 15 | 20 | 25 km |
| 0 | | 5 | | 10 | 15 miles |

Cheshire

SY14

CW5
Woore
CW3

Overton
Whitchurch

LL20
LL14
Chirk
LL13
Penley

SY13

Norton in Hales
St Martin's
Ellesmere
Prees Heath
Calverhall

Wrexham

Gobowen
Bettisfield
Prees
Market Drayton

Staffordshire

Whittington
SY12
Tetchill
Ternhill
TF9
Chipnall

North Shropshire

Oswestry
SY11
Cockshutt
Loppington
Hodnet
Hinstock

Trefonen
Morda
Haughton
Wem
Weston
Child's Ercall
Puleston

SY10 **Oswestry**
Pant
Weston Lullingfields
Clive
ST20

Llanymynech
Knockin
Ruyton-
XI-Towns
Baschurch
Shawbury
Tibberton
Outwoods

Four Crosses
SY22
Wilcott
Newport

Powys

Crewgreen
Harlescott
Crudgington
TF6
Telford and Wrekin
Lilleshall
TF10

Buttington
Ford
SY1
SY3
Shrewsbury
Withington
Admaston
TF5
Donnington
Sheriffhales

Welshpool
Westbury
Bayston Hill
Wellington
TF1
TF2
Bishops Wood

SY21
Minsterley
Pontesbury
Condover
Uppington
Dawley
Telford
TF11
Shifnal
ST19
WV8

Kingswood
Marton
SY5
Cressage
TF4
TF3
Madeley
Albrighton
WV7

SJ
SO

Chirbury
Ratlinghope
Picklescott
SY5
Harley
Coalbrookdale
TF7
Broseley
Norton

Montgomery
Church Stoke
Norbury
Church Stretton
Cardington
Much Wenlock
TF12
Ackleton
WV6
Pattingham
WV4

SY15
Shipton
TF13
Morville
Worfield
Claverley
Wombourne

Shrewsbury and Atcham

SY9
Marshbrook
Bridgnorth
WV15
WV5
DY7
DY3

SY16
Bishop's Castle
South Shropshire
SY6
Bridgnorth

Newcastle
SY7
Craven Arms
Selton
Ditton Priors
WV16
Chelmarsh
Alveley

Clun
Broome
Munslow
Burwarton
Highley
Shatterford

Beguildy
Purlogue
Stottesdon
Kinlet

Leintwardine
Bromfield
Bitterley
Oreton
DY14
DY12
DY11

LD7
Knighton
Ludlow
Cleehill
Doddinton
Cleobury Mortimer
Bewdley

Llangunllo
Adforton
SY8
Caynham

Tenbury Wells
Lindridge

HR6
Orleton
WR15

Herefordshire

Worcestershire

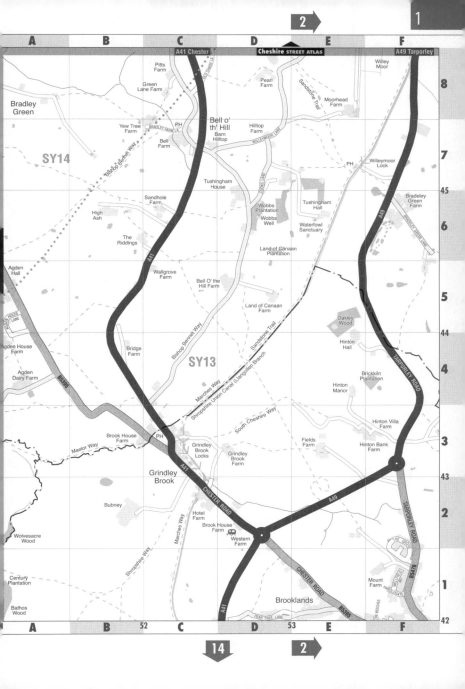

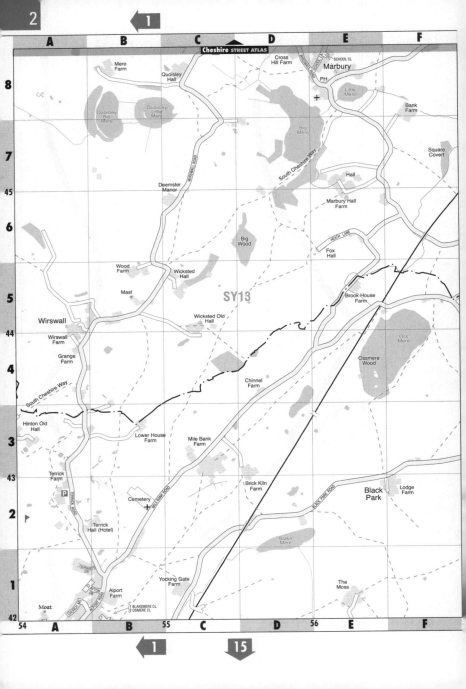

Cheshire **STREET ATLAS**

A   B   C   D   E   F

8

Mere
Farm

Quoisley
Hall

Cross
Hill Farm

Marbury

SCHOOL CL

PH

Little
Mere

Bank
Farm

Quoisley
Big
Mere

Quoisley
Little
Mere

7

Big
Mere

South Cheshire Way

Square
Covert

45

Deemster
Manor

WIRSWALL ROAD

Hall

6

Marbury Hall
Farm

HEATH LANE

Big
Wood

Fox
Hall

Wood
Farm

Wicksted
Hall

SY13

Brook House
Farm

5

Mast

Oss
Mere

Wirswall

Wicksted Old
Hall

Ossmere
Wood

44

Wirswall
Farm

Grange
Farm

4

Chinnel
Farm

South Cheshire Way

Hinton Old
Hall

3

Lower House
Farm

Mile Bank
Farm

BLACK PARK ROAD

Terrick
Farm

P

TERRICK ROAD

43

Cemetery

Brick Kiln
Farm

Black
Park

Lodge
Farm

2

Terrick
Hall (Hotel)

MILE BANK ROAD

Blake
Mere

1

TRAPWAYS DR

Alport
Farm

Yocking Gate
Farm

The
Moss

Moat

CHURCH CL

1 BLAKEMERE CL
2 OSMERE CL

42

54   A   B   55   C   D   56   E   F

1

15

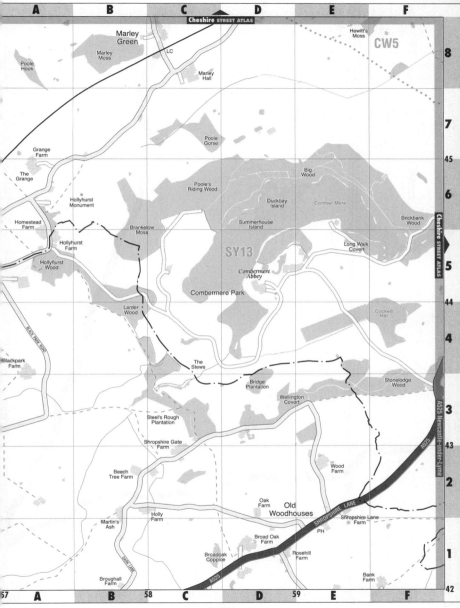

Marley
Green

Marley
Moss

LC

Marley
Hall

Poole
Hook

Poole
Gorse

CW5

Hewitt's
Moss

Grange
Farm

The
Grange

Poole's
Riding Wood

Big
Wood

Hollyhurst
Monument

Duckbay
Island

Comber Mere

Homestead
Farm

Brankelow
Moss

Summerhouse
Island

Brickbank
Wood

Hollyhurst
Farm

SY13

Long Walk
Covert

Hollyhurst
Wood

Combermere
Abbey

Larder
Wood

Combermere Park

Blackpark
Farm

The
Stews

Bridge
Plantation

Wellington
Covert.

Stonelodge
Wood

Cocked
Hat

Steel's Rough
Plantation

Shropshire Gate
Farm

Beech
Tree Farm

Wood
Farm

Martin's
Ash

Holly
Farm

Oak
Farm

Old
Woodhouses

Shropshire Lane
Farm

PH

Broad Oak
Farm

Broadoak
Coppice

Rosehill
Farm

Bank
Farm

Broughall
Farm

A525

A525 Newcastle-under-Lyme

8

7

45

6

5

44

4

3

43

2

1

42

A   B   C   D   E   F

57   58   59

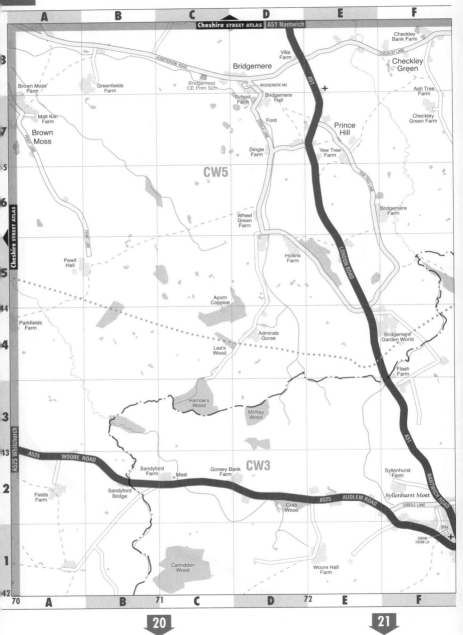

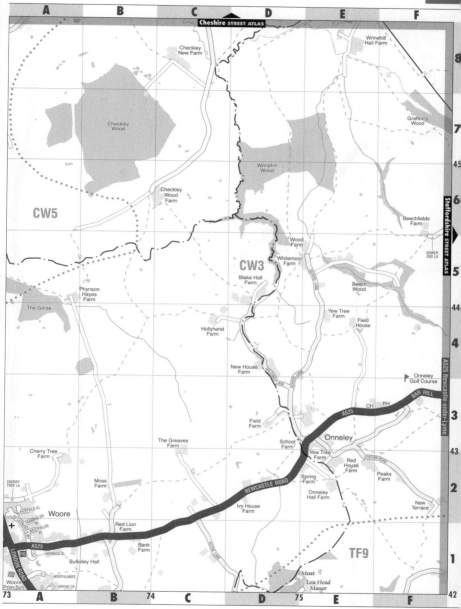

8

7

45

Wrinehill
Hall Farm

Grafton's
Wood

Checkley
New Farm

Checkley
Wood

Wrinehill
Wood

6

Staffordshire STREET ATLAS

CW5

Checkley
Wood
Farm

Beechfields
Farm

BOWER
END LA

Wood
Farm

Whitemoor
Farm

CW3

5

Phynson
Hayes
Farm

The Gorse

Blake Hall
Farm

Beech
Wood

44

Hollyhurst
Farm

Yew Tree
Farm

Field
House

4

New House
Farm

Onneley
Golf Course

A525 Newcastle-under-Lyme

Field
Farm

CH PH

A525

BAR HILL

3

Cherry Tree
Farm

The Greaves
Farm

School
Farm

Onneley

STATION ROAD

43

CHERRY
TREE LA

Moss
Farm

Yew Tree
Farm

Red House
Farm

Peaks
Farm

GLAZEFIELD CL

Woore

NEWCASTLE ROAD

Spring
Farm

Onneley
Hall Farm

New
Terrace

2

WESTFIELDS

Red Lion
Farm

Ivy House
Farm

A525
LONDON ROAD

PO

KENRICK CL

Bank
Farm

ASTON LANE

TF9

1

NORTHLANDS

Bulkeley Hall

GROVE CR

Woore
Prim Sch

Moat
Lea Head
Manor

42

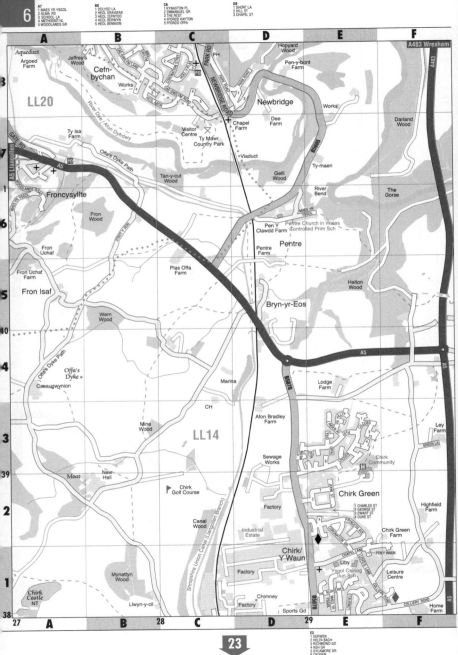

A7
1 MAES YR YSGOL
2 ALMA RD
3 SCHOOL LA
4 METHODIST HL
5 WOODLANDS GR

B6
1 DOLYDD LA
2 HEOL GRAIGFAB
3 HEOL CEFNYDD
4 HEOL BERWYN
5 HEOL BENNION

C8
1 KYNASTON PL
2 EMMANUEL GR
3 THE REST
4 FFORDD KAYTON
5 FFORDD OFFA

D8
1 SHORT LA
2 HILL ST
3 CHAPEL ST

A483 Wrexham

Aqueduct
Argoed
Farm

Jeffrey's
Wood

Cefn-
bychan

Works

Hopyard
Wood

Pen-y-bont
Farm

LL20

River Dee / Afon Dyfrdwy

Newbridge

Works

Darland
Wood

Ty Isa
Farm

Visitor
Centre

Chapel
Farm

Dee
Farm

Ty Mawr
Country Park

Offa's Dyke Path

Tan-y-cut
Wood

Viaduct

Gelli
Wood

Ty-maen

River
Bend

The
Gorse

Froncysyllte

Fron
Wood

Pen Y
Clawdd Farm

Pentre Church in Wales
Controlled Prim Sch

Pentre

Fron
Uchaf

Pentre
Farm

Fron Uchaf
Farm

Plas Offa
Farm

Halton
Wood

Fron Isaf

Bryn-yr-Eos

Wern
Wood

A5

Offa's Dyke Path

Offa's
Dyke

Marina

Lodge
Farm

Caeaugwynion

CH

Afon Bradley
Farm

Ley
Farm

Mine
Wood

LL14

Chirk
Community

Chirk Green

Moat

New
Hall

Sewage
Works

Chirk
Golf Course

1 CHARLES ST
2 GEORGE ST
3 EWART ST
4 DUKE ST

Highfield
Farm

Mynattyn
Wood

Canal
Wood

Factory

Chirk Green
Farm

Pen y Waun

Industrial
Estate

Chirk/
Y Waun

Liby

Leisure
Centre

Chirk
Castle
NT

Llwyn-y-cil

Factory

Chimney

Ygsol Ceiriog
Jun Sch

Factory

Sports Gd

Home
Farm

Shropshire Union Canal (Llangollen Branch)

1 DERWEN
2 HELFA BACH
3 RICHMOND GD
4 ASH GR
5 SYCAMORE DR
6 CROGEN

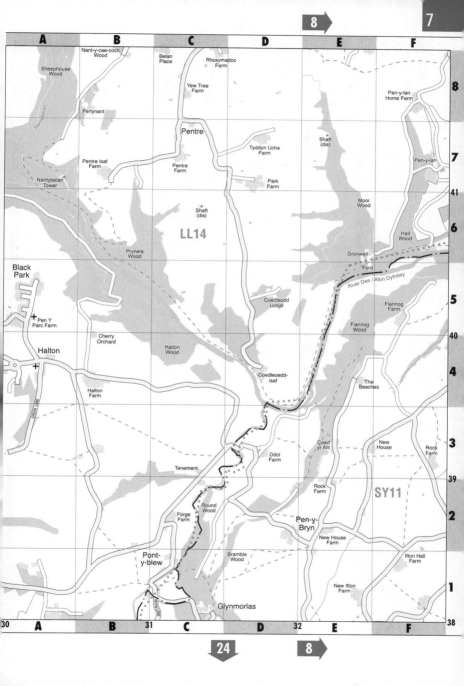

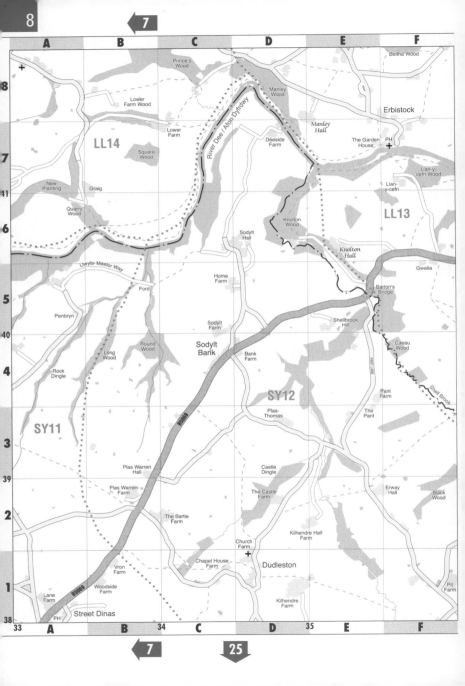

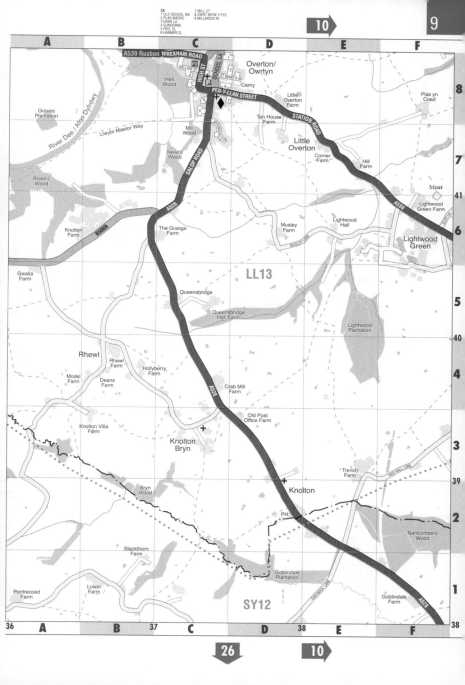

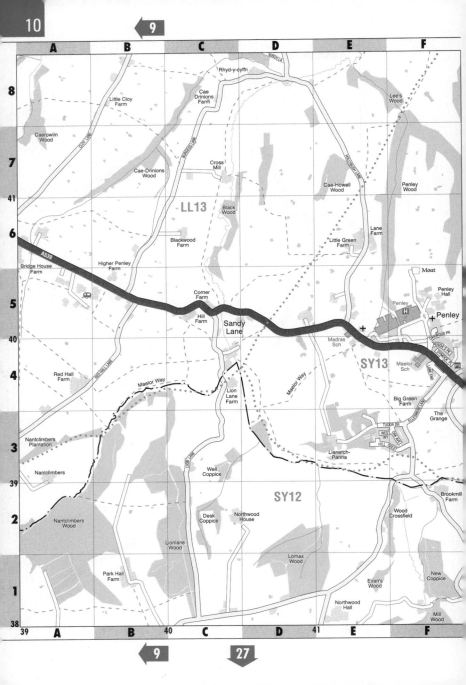

Cheshire STREET ATLAS

A525 Wrexham

A525

A B C D E F

Rock Lane
Bryn Newydd Farm
Bryn Lane
Haughton Lane
Peartree Lane
Peartree House
Moat
Horsemans Green Farm

Horseman's Green

Bryn Wood

Dukes Farm
The Dukes
Glebe Farm
PO

The Bryn
Bryn Farm
Peartree Lane

The Dingles Farm
Rhostre Farm

Penley Wood

Bryn Lane

Pigeon Lane

New Gorse Covert

Brook Lane

Maelor Way

SY13

Pant Farm
Lower House Farm
Wen

PH

Street Lydan

Cumber's Bridge

A539

Park Lane
The Farm
Stryt Lyddan Farm
Crewe's Wood
Cumber's Wood

Cumber's Bank

A539

New House Farm
Park Lane Farm
Cumbers Farm

Gravel Pit Plantation

Small Farm
Taits Farm
Tarts Farm

GRANGE ROAD

Tarts Hill
Wyen Wenn Farm
Gredington Park

Crynos Farm
Tarts Hill Farm

SY12

Scrape Wood
Gredington

Cambrian Wood
Tarts Hill Wood

New House Farm

Bishop's Wood

Hampton Wood
Long Wood

Glade Wood
Wood Farm

Bishops House
Knolls Wood

8

7

41

6

5

40

4

3

39

2

1

38

A   B   C   D   E   F

Three Fingers

Hillside Farm

Cranberry Moss

The Hully

Bank House Farm

Yew Tree Farm

A525

Croxton Farm

New Hall Farm

Brook Farm

Bryn Rossett Farm

London Apprentice Farm

Mount Cop (Motte)

Top House Farm

A525

Mill Bridge

Tumulus

A539

Eglwys Cross

Eglwys Cross Farm

Little Green Farm

Hanmer Mill Farm

Little Arowry Farm

Little Arowry

Croxton Pool

Cae-Shonnett Wood

New House Farm

St Chad's Well

Peter's Coppice

Brook Lane Farm

Hanmer Hall Farm

Black Wood

Brook House Farm

SY13

Maesllwyn Farm

Crabmill Farm

Maelor Way

Hanmer Prim Sch

PH

Earthwork

Hanmer

MAESLLWYN LANE

A539

Home Farm

BEECH CL

PO

STREET LANE

GLEBE COWPER PL

Gredington Park

Hanmer Mere

Top House Farm

Arowry

Arowry Moss

Llyn Bedydd

Maelor Way

NEW ROAD

Arowry Farm

New Road Farm

Park Meadow Farm

Big Arowry Farm

Glebe Farm

MOSS LANE

Holebrook Farm

Moss Lane Farm

Mossfields Farm

A495

NOOK LANE

GRANGE ROAD

New Plantation

NEW ROAD

Smithy Farm

Stimmey Farm

Bettisfield Park

45   A   B   46   C   D   47   E   F

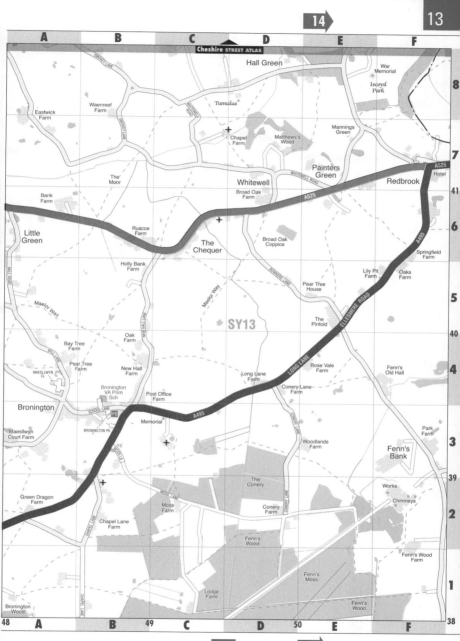

A B C D E F

8

Eastwick
Farm

Waenreef
Farm

Hall Green

War
Memorial

Iscoyd
Park

Tumulus

Chapel
Farm

Matthews's
Wood

Mannings
Green

7

The
Moor

Whitewell

Painters
Green

Redbrook

A525
Hotel

Bank
Farm

Broad Oak
Farm

A525

41

Little
Green

Ruscoe
Farm

The
Chequer

Broad Oak
Coppice

A495

6

Holly Bank
Farm

Maelor Way

Pear Tree
House

Lily Pit
Farm

Oaks
Farm

Springfield
Farm

Bay Tree
Farm

Oak
Farm

SY13

The
Pinfold

ELLESMERE ROAD

5

40

Pear Tree
Farm

MAESLLWYN
CL

New Hall
Farm

Long Lane
Farm

Long Lane

Rose Vale
Farm

Fenn's
Old Hall

4

Bronington
VA Prim
Sch

Post Office
Farm

Conery Lane
Farm

Bronington

SCHOOL LANE

A495

Memorial

Woodlands
Farm

Park
Farm

Fenn's
Bank

3

Maesllwyn
Court Farm

BRONINGTON PK

MOSS LA

Works

Chimneys

39

Green Dragon
Farm

Moss
Farm

The
Conery

Conery
Farm

2

Chapel Lane
Farm

Fenn's
Wood

Fenn's Wood
Farm

Bronington
Wood

Lodge
Farm

Fenn's
Moss

Fenn's
Wood

1

48 A 49 B C 50 D E 38 F

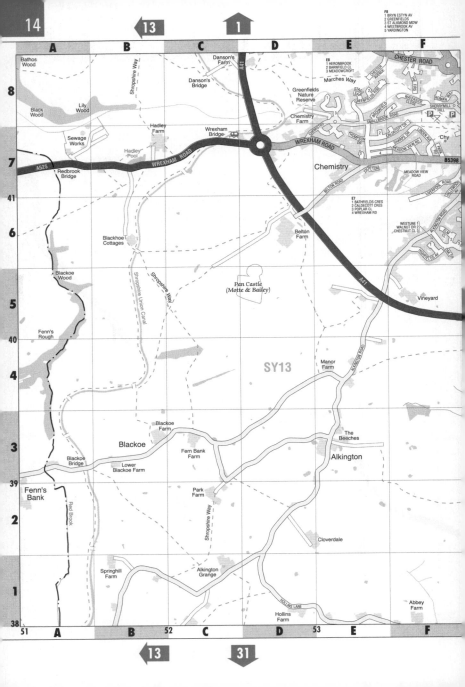

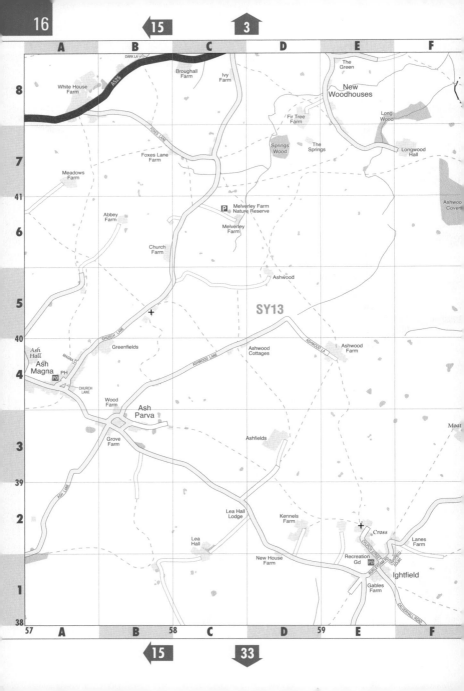

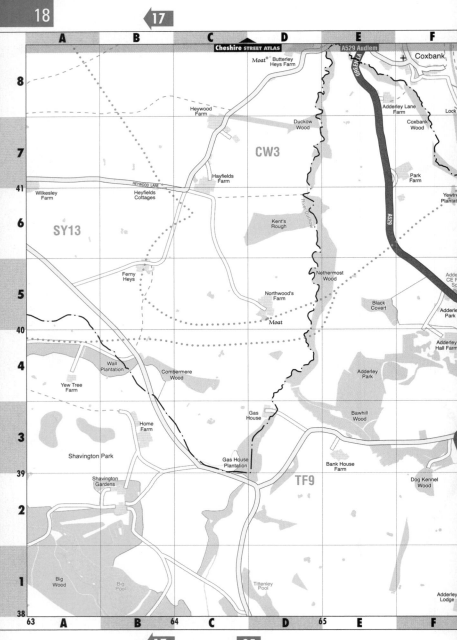

Cheshire STREET ATLAS

A529 Audlem

A B C D E F

8

Moat Butterley
Heys Farm

Coxbank

Heywood
Farm

Duckow
Wood

7

CW3

Adderley Lane
Farm

Lock

Coxbank
Wood

Hayfields
Farm

41

HEYWOOD LANE

Park
Farm

Yewtre
Plantatio

Wilkesley
Farm

Heyfields
Cottages

River Duckow

6

SY13

Kent's
Rough

5

Ferny
Heys

Nethermost
Wood

Adde
CE P
Sch

Northwood's
Farm

Moat

Black
Covert

Adderley
Park

40

Adderley
Hall Farm

4

Wall
Plantation

Combermere
Wood

Adderley
Park

Yew Tree
Farm

3

Home
Farm

Gas
House

Bawhill
Wood

Shavington Park

Gas House
Plantation

Bank House
Farm

39

TF9

Dog Kennel
Wood

Shavington
Gardens

2

1

Big
Wood

Big
Pool

Tittenley
Pool

Adderley
Lodge

38

63 A B 64 C D 65 E F

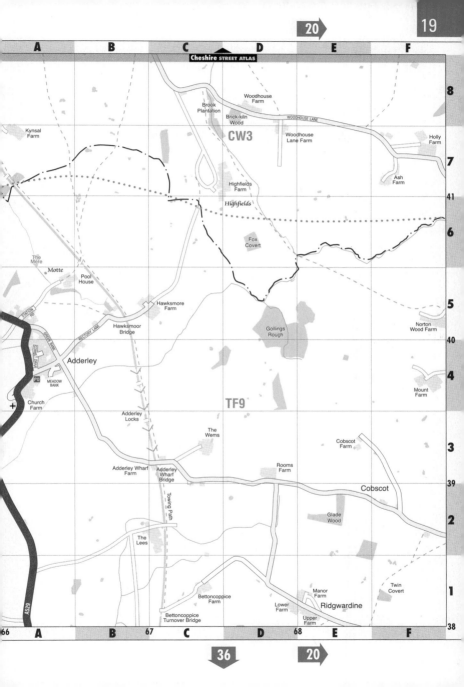

A   B   C   D   E   F

8

Woodhouse
Farm

Brook
Plantation

Brick-kiln
Wood

WOODHOUSE LANE

CW3

Woodhouse
Lane Farm

Holly
Farm

7

Kynsal
Farm

Highfields
Farm

Ash
Farm

41

Highfields

6

Fox
Covert

The
Mere

Motte

Pool
House

5

Hawksmore
Farm

Gollings
Rough

STATION RD

Hawksmoor
Bridge

Norton
Wood Farm

40

CHURCH BANK

WESTBURY LANE

Adderley

4

PO

MEADOW
BANK

Mount
Farm

Church
Farm

TF9

Adderley
Locks

The
Wems

3

Cobscot
Farm

Adderley Wharf
Farm

Adderley
Wharf
Bridge

Rooms
Farm

Cobscot

39

Towing
Path

Glade
Wood

2

A529

The
Lees

1

Bettoncoppice
Farm

Manor
Farm

Twin
Covert

Ridgwardine

Lower
Farm

Bettoncoppice
Turnover Bridge

Upper
Farm

38

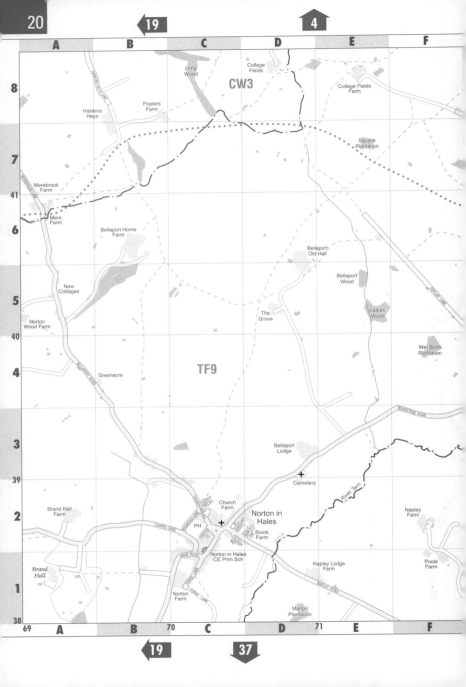

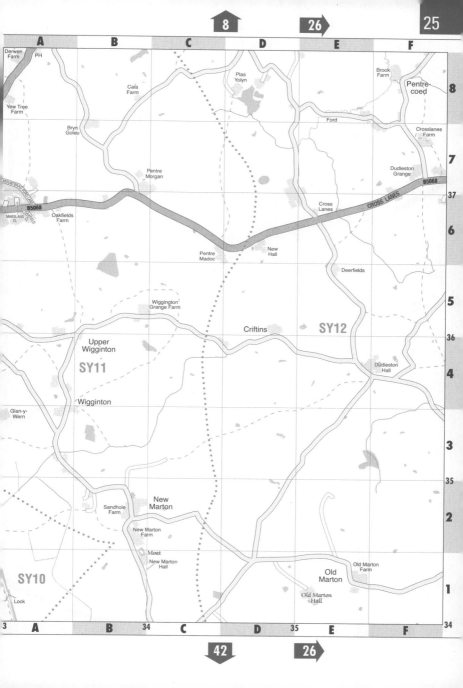

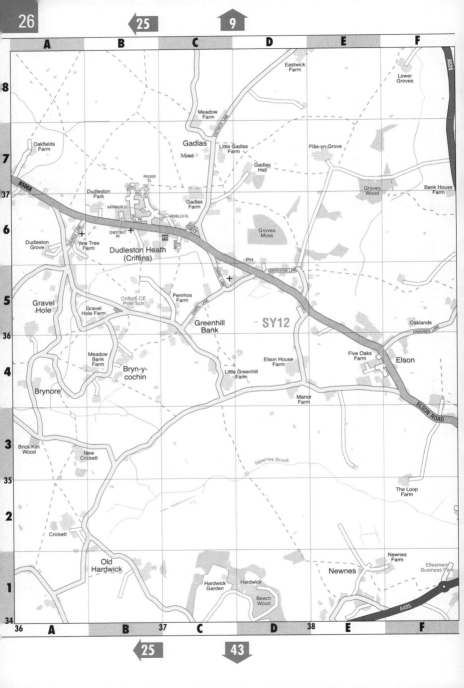

A B C D E F

8

Eastwick
Farm

Lower
Groves

Meadow
Farm

7

Oakfields
Farm

Gadlas

Little Gadlas
Farm

Plâs-yn-Grove

Moat

37

Dudleston
Park

PEEVER
CL

KAYMAUR CL

Gadlas
Hall

Groves
Wood

Bank House
Farm

Gadlas
Farm

REVELLS CL

6

Dudleston
Grove

Yew Tree
Farm

CHESTNUT
AV

PO

Groves
Moss

Dudleston Heath
(Criftins)

PH

HORSESHOE LANE

5

Gravel
Hole

Gravel
Hole Farm

Criftins CE
Prim Sch

Penrhos
Farm

Greenhill
Bank

SY12

Oaklands

CAEGODDY LANE

36

Meadow
Bank
Farm

Bryn-y-
cochin

Little Greenhill
Farm

Elson House
Farm

Five Oaks
Farm

Elson

4

Brynore

Manor
Farm

ELSON ROAD

3

Brick Kiln
Wood

New
Crickett

Newnes Brook

35

The Loop
Farm

2

Crickett

1

Old
Hardwick

Hardwick
Garden

Hardwick

Newnes

Newnes
Farm

Ellesmere
Business Park

Beech
Wood

A495

34

36

A

B

37

C

D

38

E

F

Mill Wood

Trench

Hollyhurst Farm

Trench Wood

Trench Farm

Spout Wood

Spout Farm

Sandhole Plantation

Gamebuck Rough

Stocks Farm

Coptiviney

8

7

37

6

Seven Sisters

Oak Bank Farm

Meridan Farm

Cross

Birch Hill Farm

Green Banks

Inglewood Farm

Sandyhill Farm

The Jonalls

SY12

5

36

Higher Grange

Lodge Farm

Haughton Farm

Crimps Farm

Lea Wood

4

The Grange

GRANGE ROAD

A528

HIGHER WYCH

ROBIN CL 1
KINGFISHER WK 2
CYGNET CL 3
GROSVENOR CTS 4

Works

Cemy

Paddock Wood

Oteley

3

35

B5068

Ellesmere Prim Sch

TRIMPLEY STREET

BROWNLOW ROAD

VICTORIA ST

WILLOW ST

TALBOT ST

CHURCH STREET

The Mere

Meres Visitor Centre

The Rookery

2

Ellesmere

SCOTLAND STREET

Arboretum

Recreation Ground

Motte & Bailey

Monument

Lakelands Sch

Factory

SANDY LANE

The Plantation Nature Reserve

Mereside Farm

A495

George's Wood

Kettle Mere

1

Sewage Works

Marina

A495

34

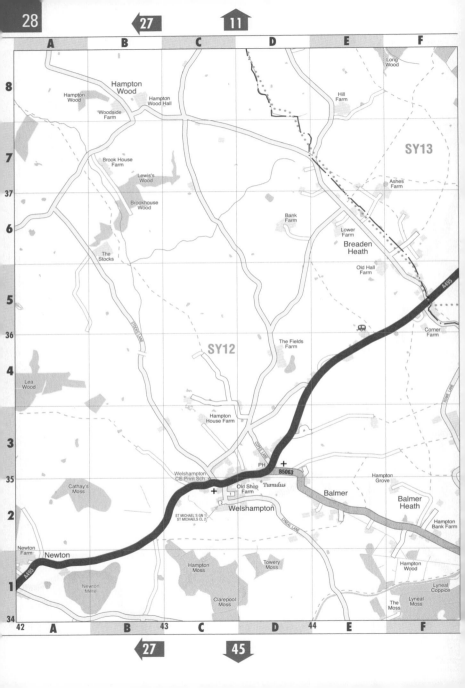

12
30
46
30

A   B   C   D   E   F

8
7
37
6
5
36
4
3
35
2
1
34

Park Pool

Bettisfield Park

Deerbarn Wood

Werrion Slope

Little Hall Farm

Lane Farm

Haulton Ring (moat)

Fields Farm

Nook Lane Farm

Avenue Farm

Cambrian Cott

Fenn's Moss

Church Farm

SY13

Bettisfield Hall Farm

ROWE LANE

Bettisfield Bridge

Shropshire Union Canal (Llangollen Branch)

Clapping Gate Bridge

SNIPES LANE

CHAPEL VW

Bettisfield

Corner House Farm

New House Farm

CADNEY LANE

Cadney Farm

Bettisfield Windmill

Coppice House

MOSS LA

SY12

Cadney Bank

Cadney Moss

Canalside Farm

Hampton Bank

Hampton Bank Bridge

Yetchleys Farm

B5063

Moss Farm

Wem Moss Nature Reserve

Hornspike Farm

NEW ROAD

A495

45   46   47

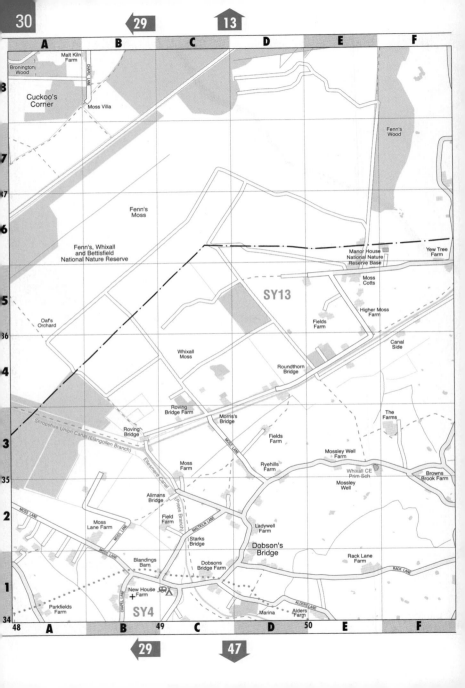

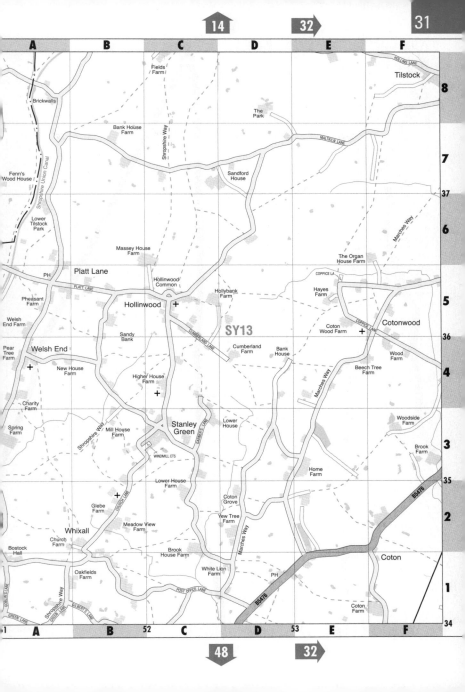

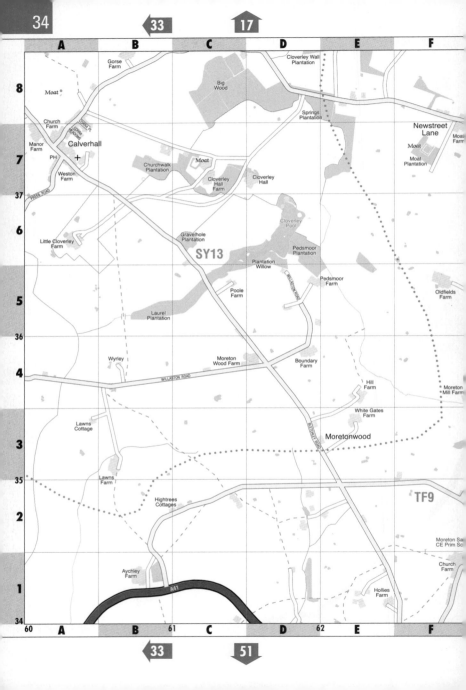

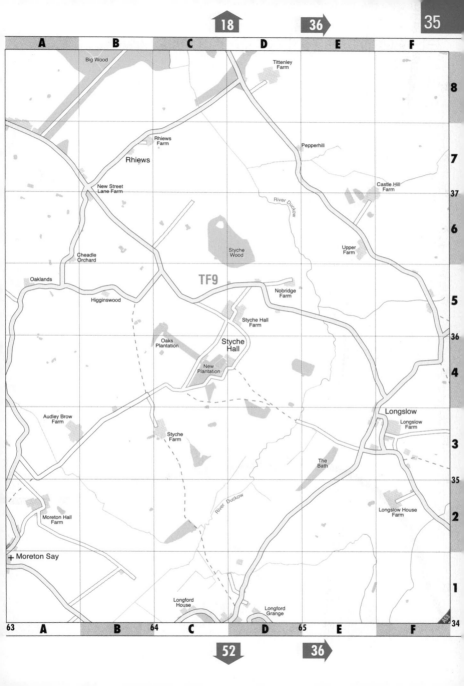

A B C D E F

8

Big Wood

Tittenley
Farm

Rhiews
Farm

7

Rhiews

Pepperhill

New Street
Lane Farm

Castle Hill
Farm

37

River Duckow

6

Cheadle
Orchard

Styche
Wood

Upper
Farm

Oaklands

TF9

Nobridge
Farm

5

Higginswood

Styche Hall
Farm

36

Oaks
Plantation

Styche
Hall

4

New
Plantation

Longslow

Audley Brow
Farm

Longslow
Farm

3

Styche
Farm

The
Bath

35

River Duckow

Longslow House
Farm

2

Moreton Hall
Farm

+ Moreton Say

1

Longford
House

Longford
Grange

8

7

37

6

5

36

4

35

3

2

1

34

66 67 68

TF9

Brownhills

MARKET
DRAYTON

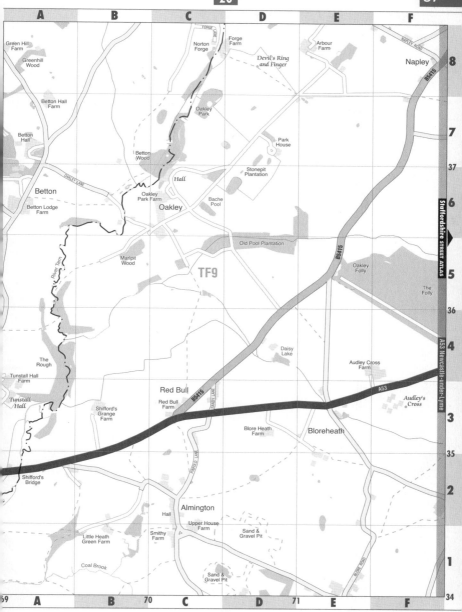

| A | B | C | D | E | F |

Green Hill Farm

Greenhill Wood

Betton Hall Farm

Betton Hall

Betton

Betton Lodge Farm

FORGE LANE

Norton Forge

Forge Farm

Devil's Ring and Finger

Arbour Farm

Napley

B5415

8

Oakley Park

Betton Wood

Park House

7

37

OAKLEY LANE

Hall

Oakley Park Farm

Oakley

Stonepit Plantation

Bache Pool

6

River Tern

Marlpit Wood

Old Pool Plantation

B5415

Oakley Folly

The Folly

TF9

5

36

Staffordshire STREET ATLAS

A53 Newcastle-under-Lyme

The Rough

Tunstall Hall Farm

Tunstall Hall

Daisy Lake

Audley Cross Farm

Audley's Cross

4

Red Bull

Red Bull Farm

B5415

PINFOLD LANE

A53

Blore Heath Farm

Boreheath

3

35

Shifford's Grange Farm

Shifford's Bridge

Almington

Hall

Upper House Farm

Smithy Farm

Sand & Gravel Pit

2

Little Heath Green Farm

Coal Brook

Sand & Gravel Pit

BLORE ROAD

1

34

| A | B | 70 | C | D | 71 | E | F |

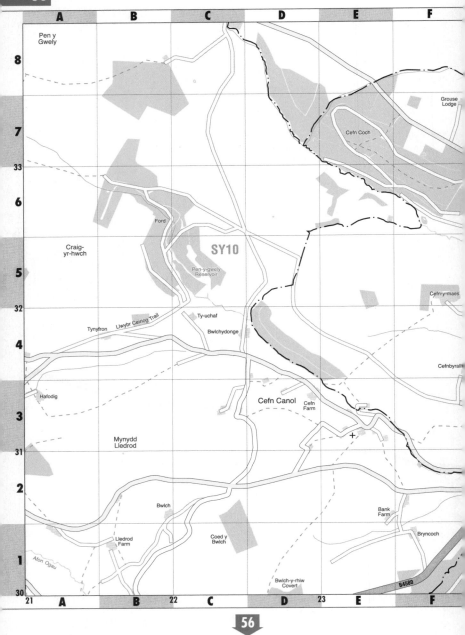

Pen y Gwely

Grouse Lodge

Cefn Coch

Craig-yr-hwch

SY10

Ford

Pen-y-gwely Reservoir

Cefn-y-maes

Tynyfron

Llwybr Ceiriog Trail

Ty-uchaf

Bwlchydonge

Cefnbyrallt

Hafodig

Cefn Canol

Cefn Farm

Mynydd Lledrod

Bwlch

Bank Farm

Lledrod Farm

Coed y Bwlch

Bryncoch

Afon Ogau

Bwlch-y-rhiw Covert

B4580

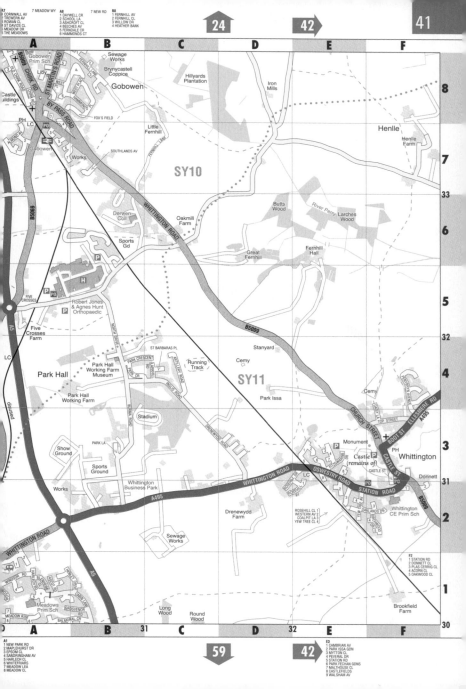

A7
4 CORNWALL AV
5 TREWERN AV
6 ROWAN CL
7 ST DAVIDS CL
8 MEADOW DR
9 THE MEADOWS

7 MEADOW WY

A8
1 DAYWELL CR
2 SCHOOL LA
3 ASHCROFT CL
4 BEECHES AV
5 FERNDALE CR
6 HAMMONDS CT

7 NEW RD

B8
1 FERNHILL AV
2 FERNHILL CL
3 WILLOW DR
4 HEATHER BANK

24   42   41

A   B   C   D   E   F

8

Sewage Works
Gobowen Prim Sch
Libu
Brynycastell Coppice
Hillyards Plantation
Iron Mills
Castle Buildings
Gobowen
Henlie
Henlie Farm

7

PH
LC
PO
BY PASS ROAD
FOX'S FIELD
Little Fernhill
SOUTHLANDS AV
Works
Gobowen
FERNHILL LANE

SY10

WHITTINGTON ROAD

Oakmill Farm
Butts Wood
River Perry
Larches Wood

33

6

Derwen Coll
Sports Gd
Fernhill Hall
Great Fernhill

5

Robert Jones & Agnes Hunt Orthopaedic
Five Crosses
Five Crosses Farm
NORTH DRIVE
B5009

32

LC

St Barbaras Pl
PARK CRESCENT
ARTILLERY ROAD
Stanyard
Cemy

4

Park Hall Working Farm Museum
Running Track
Park Hall
Park Hall Working Farm
PEELS ROAD
SY11
Cemy
Park Issa

EASTERN AVENUE
TOP STREET
CHURCH STREET
BOOT ST
ELLESMERE RD
A495

3

Stadium
PARK LA
Show Ground
Sports Ground
Whittington Business Park
Monument
Castle (remains of)
CASTLE ST
PH
Whittington
Donnett
CASTLE ST
PO
LC

31

Works
A495
WHITTINGTON ROAD
OSWESTRY ROAD
STATION ROAD
B5009
Whittington CE Prim Sch

2

WHITTINGTON ROAD
A5
Sewage Works
Drenewydd Farm
ROSEHILL CL 1
WESTERN AV 2
COALPIT LA 3
YEW TREE CL 4
FAIRLANDS DR

F2
1 STATION RD
2 DONNETT CL
3 PLAS CERRIG CL
4 ACORN CL
5 OAKWOOD CL

Meadows Prim Sch
WINDSOR RD
BALMORAL RD
MEADOW RISE
Long Wood
Round Wood
Brookfield Farm

1

30

A   B   31   C   D   32   E   F

A1
1 NEW PARK RD
2 MAPLEHURST DR
3 EPSOM CL
4 SANDRINGHAM AV
5 HARLECH CL
6 WHITEFRIARS
7 MEADOW LEA
8 MEADOW CL

59   42

E2
1 CAMBRIAN AV
2 PARK ISSA GDN
3 MYTTON GD
4 PEVERAL DR
5 STATION RD
6 PARK FECHAN GDNS
7 MALTHOUSE CL
8 CASTLEFIELDS
9 WALSHAM AV

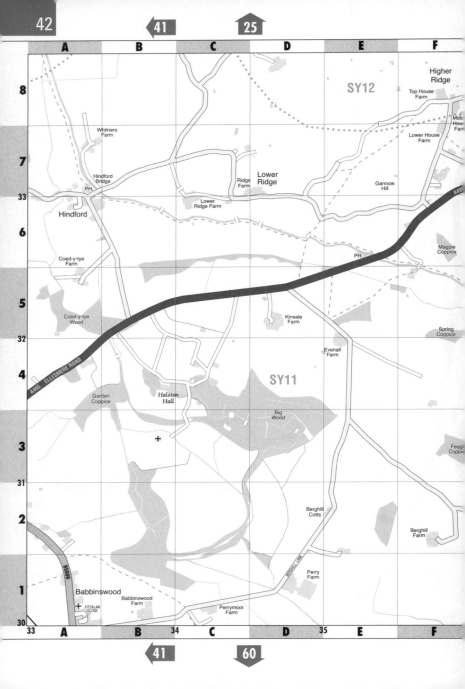

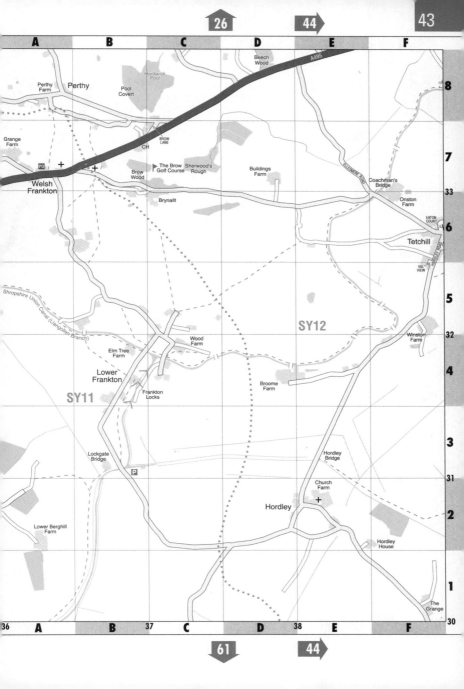

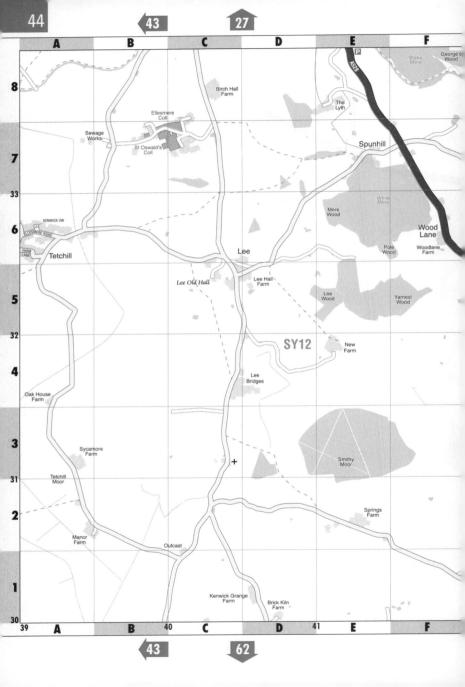

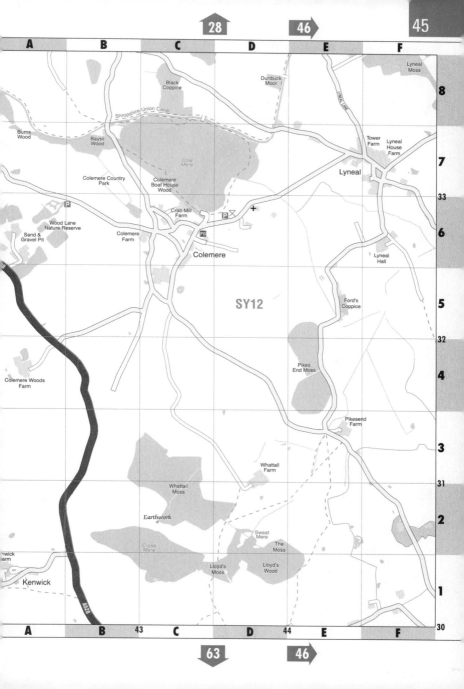

A **B** **C** **D** **E** **F**

8

Lyneal
Moss

Dunbuck
Moor

Black
Coppice

Burns
Wood

Shropshire Union Canal

Baysil
Wood

Tower
Farm

Lyneal
House
Farm

7

Cole
Mere

Colemere Country
Park

Colemere
Boat House
Wood

Lyneal

33

P

Crab Mill
Farm

P

+

Wood Lane
Nature Reserve

P0

6

Sand &
Gravel Pit

Colemere
Farm

Colemere

Lyneal
Hall

SY12

Ford's
Coppice

5

32

Pikes
End Moss

4

Colemere Woods
Farm

Pikesend
Farm

3

Whattall
Farm

31

Whattall
Moss

Earthwork

2

Sweat
Mere

The
Moss

Crose
Mere

Lloyd's
Moss

Lloyd's
Wood

nwick
arm

Kenwick

1

A528

A **B** 43 **C** **D** 44 **E** **F**

30

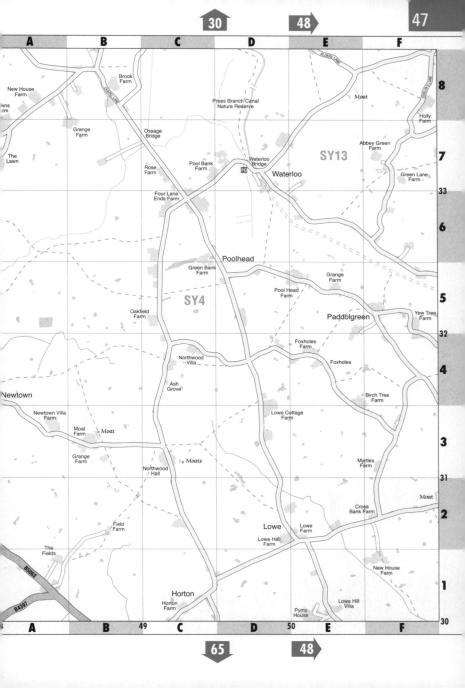

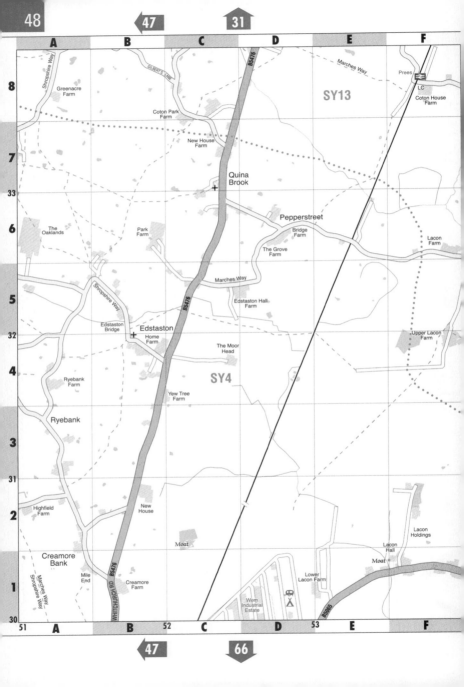

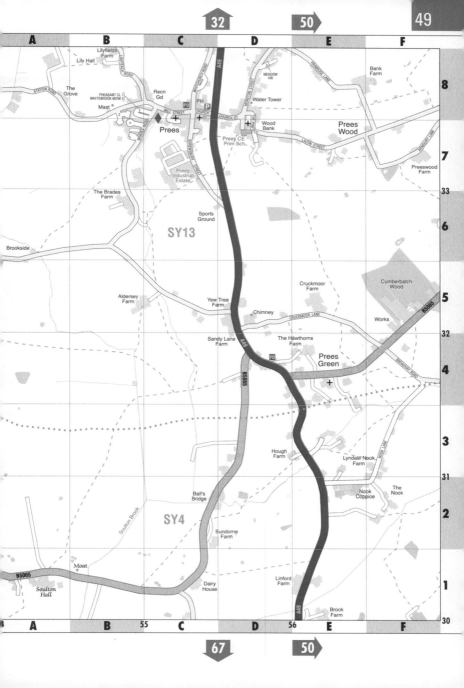

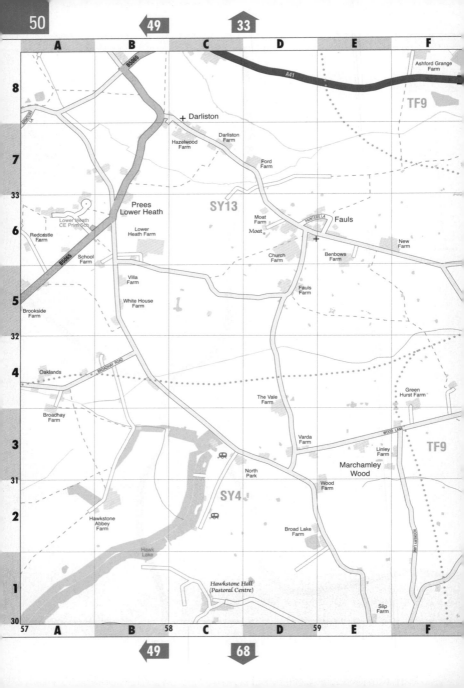

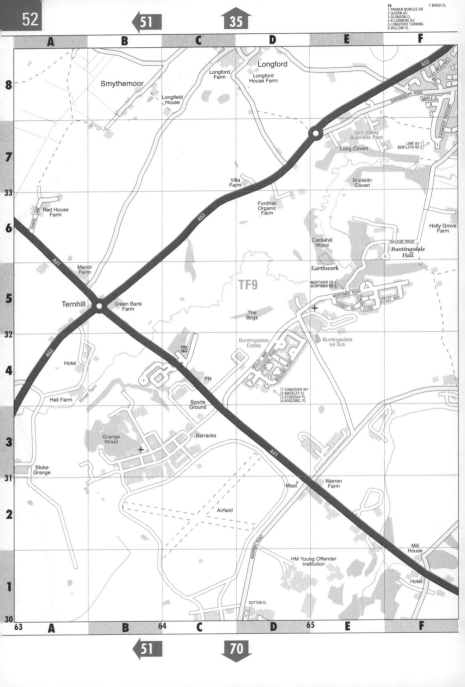

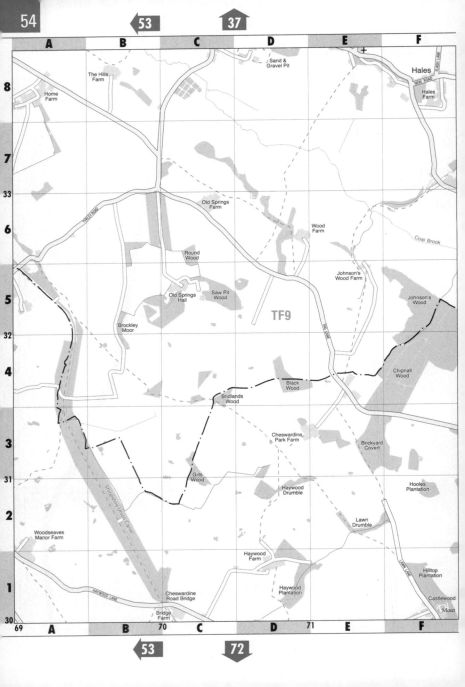

Staffordshire STREET ATLAS

Staffordshire STREET ATLAS

A   B   C   D   E   F

8
7
33
6
32
5
4
31
3
2
1
30

ROMAN VILLA
(Site of)

Lloyd
Drumble

Lloyd
Farm

Park
Springs

Park Springs
Farm

The Nook
Farm

Dales
Wood

Burnt
Wood

Burntwood
Farm

Knowleswood

Smith's
Rough

Badger
Wood

Bishop's
Wood

Goldenhill
Farm

Glass House
Farm

Mill Pool
Plantation

The Lees

Chipnal
Mill Farm

Heatherdale
Farm

TF9

Coalpit
Plantation

Rookery
Wood

Chipnal Hall
Farm

Chipnal
Farm

Rushymoss
Wood

Lipley
Farm

Lipley
Heath
Farm

Chipnall

Yew Tree
Farm

Taglane
Plantation

TAG LANE

MOSS LANE

Moss Lane
Farm

Oldgorse
Plantation

Cheswardine
Hall

Gorsyhill
Plantations

Lipley

ST21

Bishop's
Wood

Pinetum
Plantation

Lipley Hall
Farm

Lipley
Villa Farm

Greaves
Plantation

72   73   74

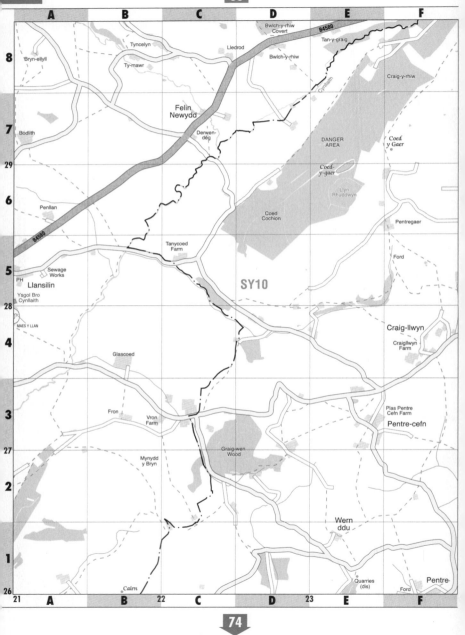

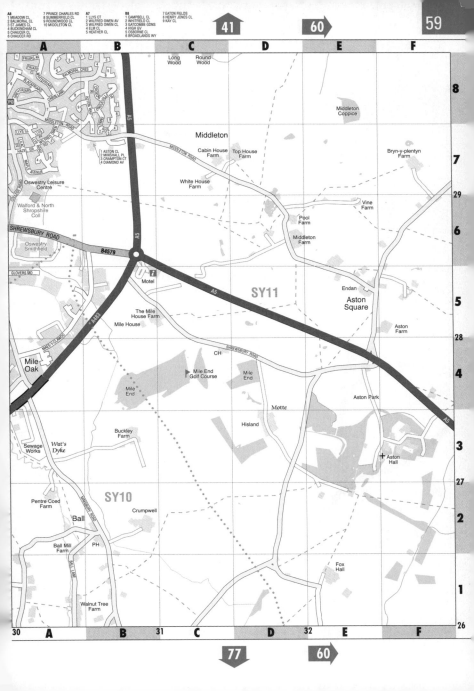

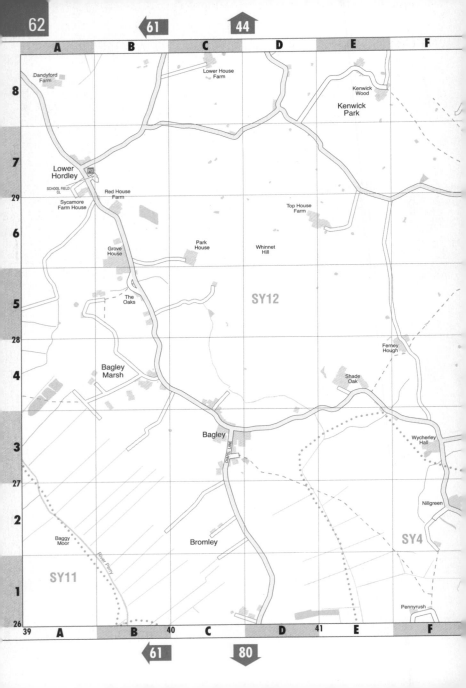

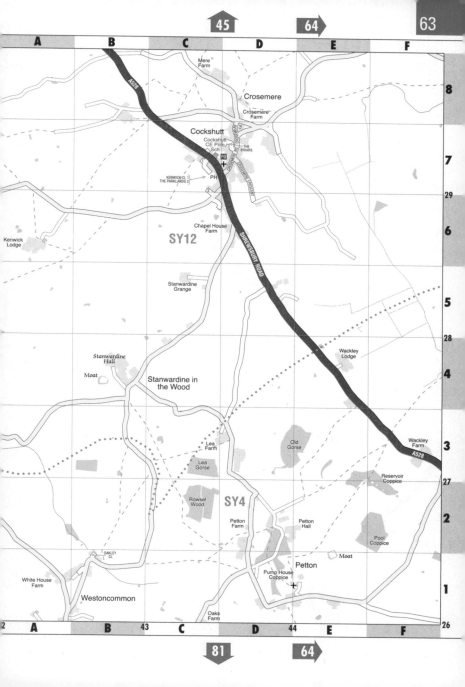

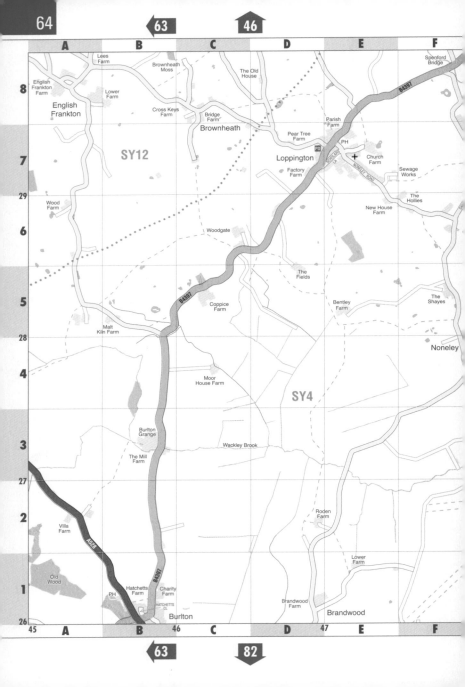

A B C D E F

8

Horton

Yew Tree
Farm
Horton
House Farm
Horton
Hall Farm

LONG HILL ROAD

TRENTHAM
RD

B5063

Ditches
Farm

Factory

The Ditches
Hall

Thomas
Adams Sch

Chy

7

ELLESMERE ROAD

Wem

B5063

29

Slangs
Plantation

River Roden

The Pools
Farm

LOWER HEATH
RD

HIGH ST

6

Green
Hill

BARNARD
ST

Marches Way

5

Manor
Farm

Commonwood
Farm

Pearl Farm

SY4

BROOK DR 1
RODEN GR 2
ALVIN CL 3

Tilley
Bridge

Brook
Farm

28

Grafton
Farm

Ruewood Meadow
Nature Reserve

PH

Tilley

Forrester
Farm

Tilley
Farm

LC

4

B5476

Sleap Brook

Sleap
Bridge

Rue Wood
Farm

3

27

Airfield

Sleap
House Farm

New House
Farm

Tilley
Park Farm

2

Sleap

Sleap
Gorse

The
Drumble

1

LC

B5476

26

A B C D E F

49 50

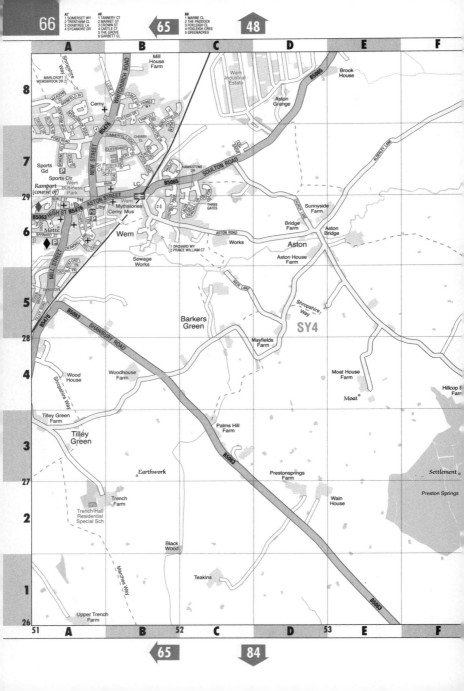

A **B** **C** **D** **E** **F**

Hawk Lake

Grotto Hill

8

Red Castle

St Joseph's Coll

The Terrace

Well House Farm

Chirbury Farm

Hawkstone Farm

Marchamley

7

Obelisk

Tower

Terrace Plantation

Shaft (dis)

29

Hawkstone Park

Elysian Hill

Visitor Centre

Terrace Plantation

Marchamley Hill

6

Rake Park

Rakepark Lodge

Bank Farm

Menagerie Pool

Kenstone

The Citadel

Bury Park

CLIFFE LANE

5

Bury Farm

SY4

Hopley Farm

28

Moat Bank

4

Bury Walls (fort)

Daneswell Farm

Danes Well

TF9

Bury Wood

Spinnel Wood

3

Hermitage Farm

Chirbury Wood

Hopley Coppice

27

Top Moss

2

Quarry Farm

Stone House Farm

Hopton

DARE LANE

1

Quarry Coppice

Morgans Coppice Farm

Old Shop Farm

Morgan's Coppice

A53

26

57   **A**   **B**   58   **C**   **D**   59   **E**   **F**

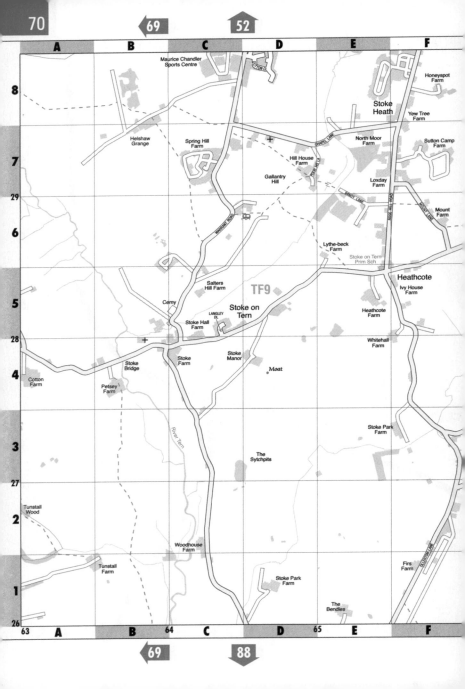

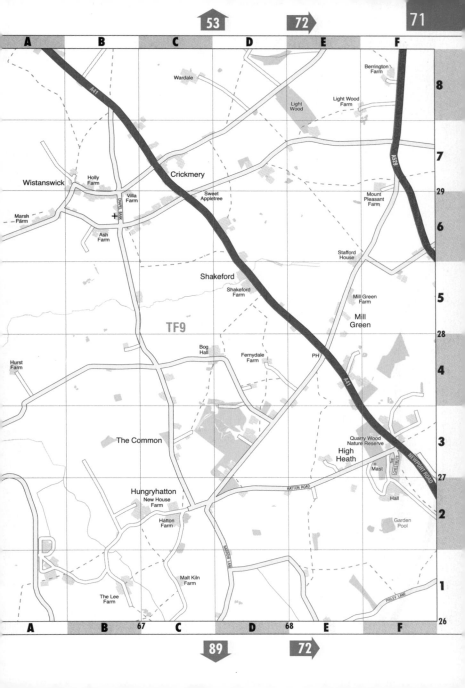

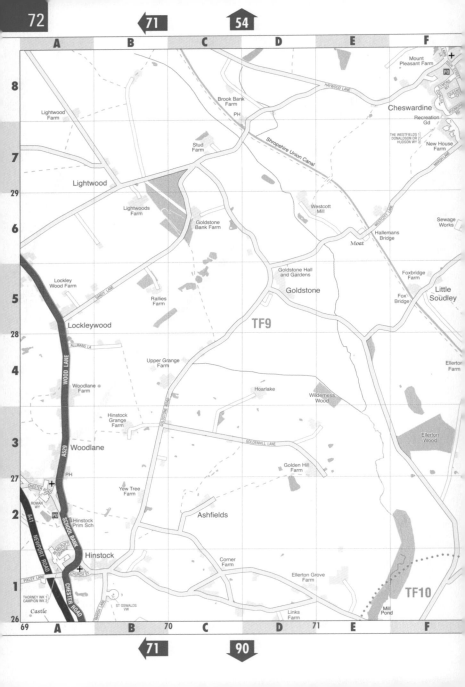

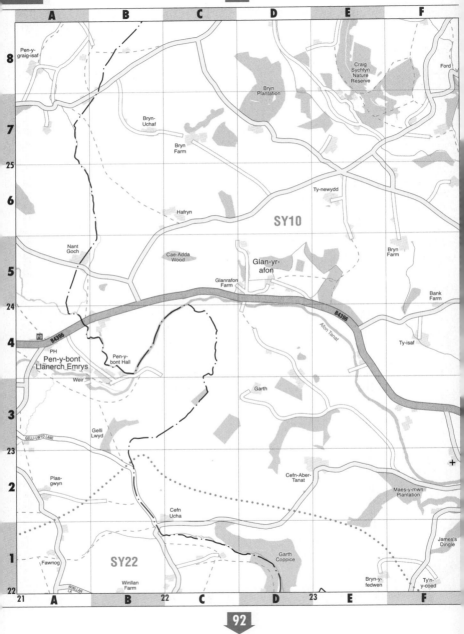

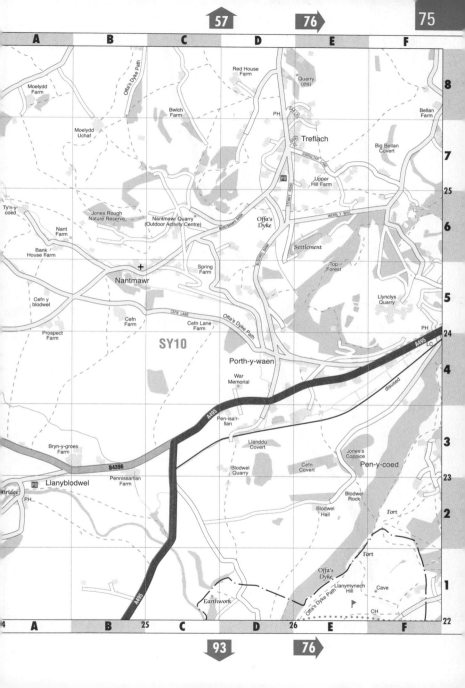

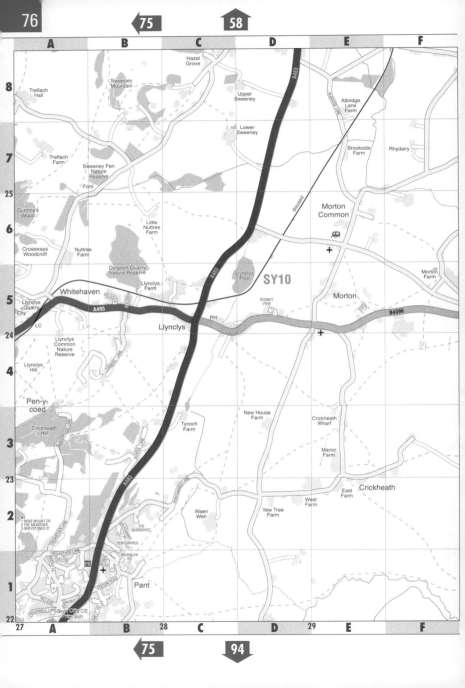

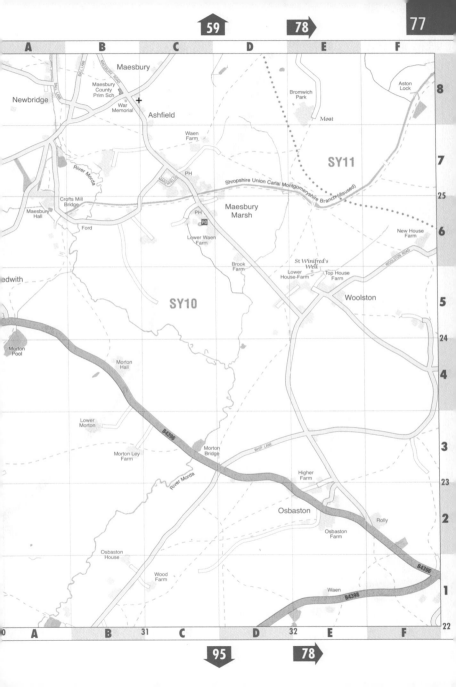

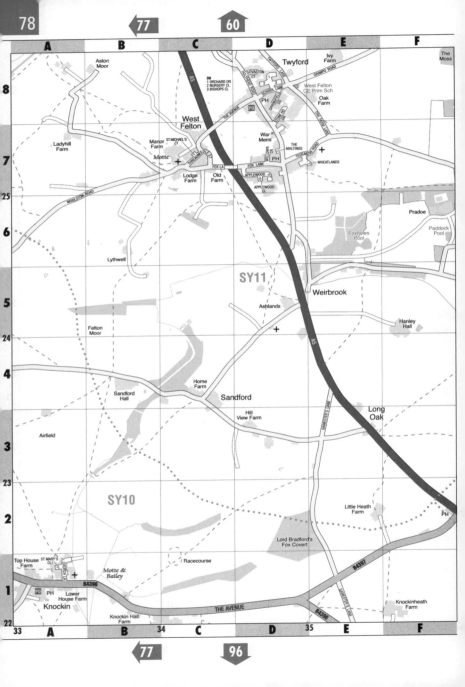

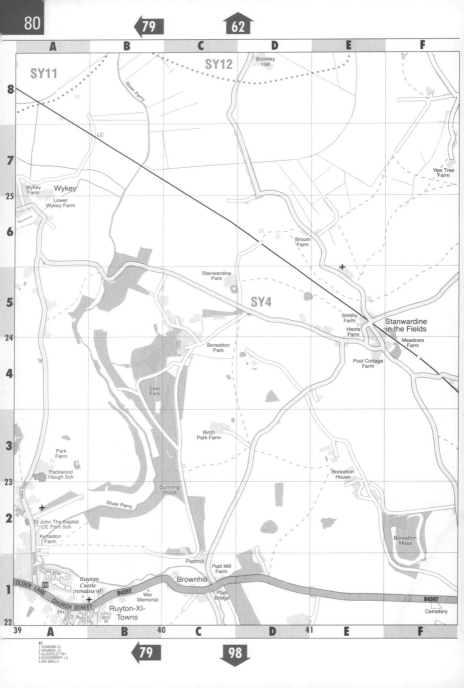

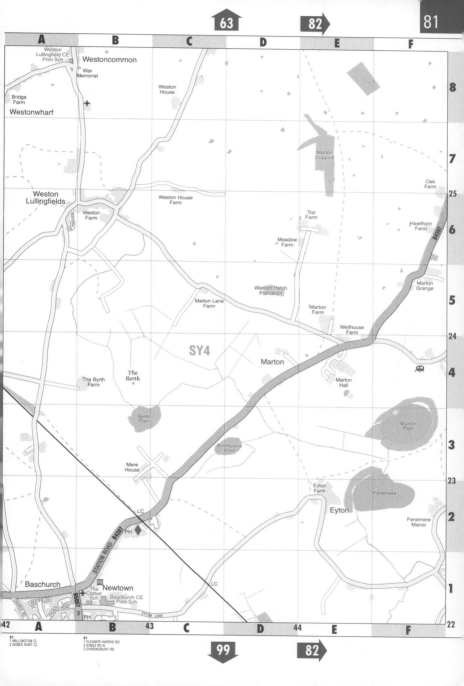

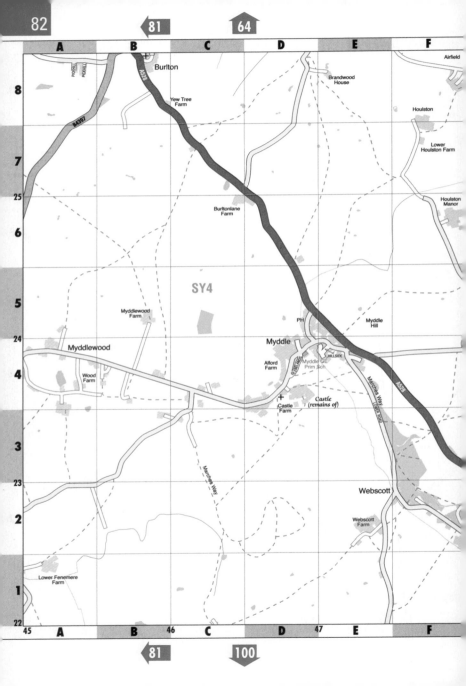

Airfield

Burlton

Brandwood
House

Houlston

Yew Tree
Farm

Lower
Houlston Farm

Burltonlane
Farm

Houlston
Manor

SY4

Myddlewood
Farm

PH

Myddle
Hill

Myddlewood

Myddle

Wood
Farm

Alford
Farm

HILLSIDE

Myddle CE
Prim Sch

Castle
Farm

Castle
(remains of)

Marches Way

Webscott

Marches Way

Webscott
Farm

Lower Fenemere
Farm

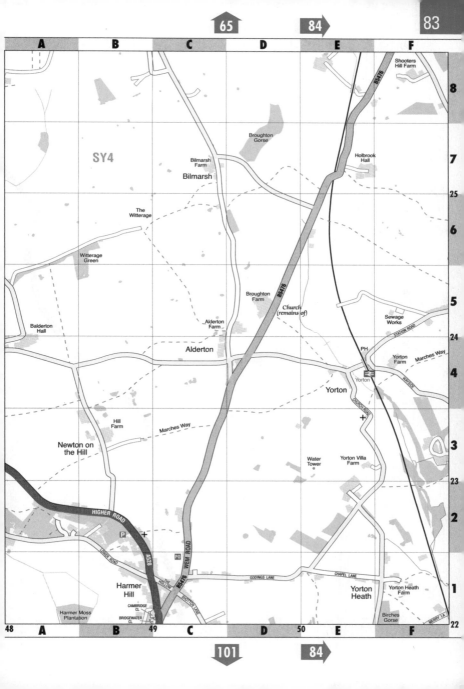

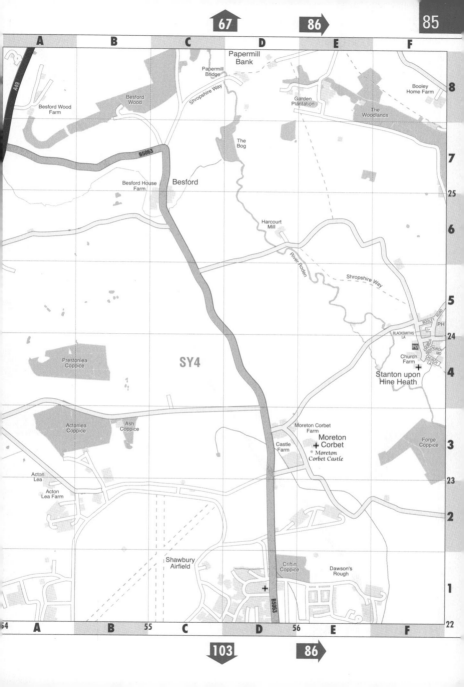

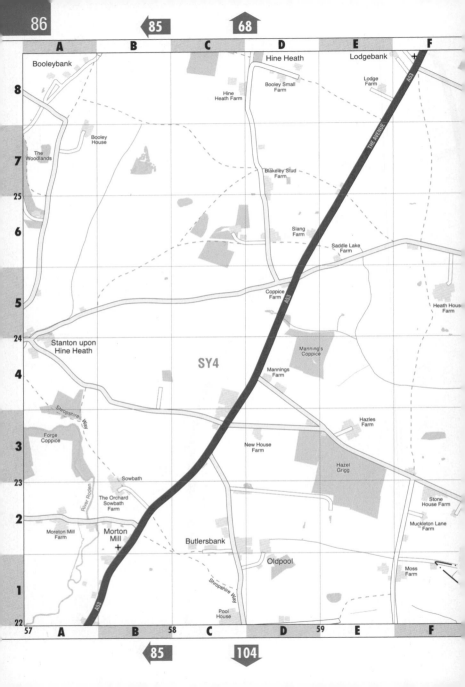

8

A B C D E F

Hineheath Covert

Green Lane Farm

GREEN LANE

Hodnet Heath

Avenue Farm

Avenue Small Farm

Bowling Green

Haw Green Farm

Hawgreen

Bowling Green Farm

TF9

High Hatton Hall

Hall Coppice

High Hatton Farm

High Hatton

25

Radmoor

A442

THE BUTTERY

6

SY4

Drakeley Heath Farm

Station Coppice

SHUKER'S LA

5

GREENHURST LANE

Brick-kiln Coppice

24

New Coppice

Penwood Farm

4

Greenhurst

TF6

Wood Farm

Little Coolmoor

Coolmoor

Windy Oak

3

Wood Mill Farm

23

Longley

PH

Oak House Farm

Pratt Brook

2

Moss Farm

New House Farm

Sunnyside Farm

PO

Ellerdine Heath

1

CITY RD

22

A B 61 C D 62 E F

0

A B C D E F

8

Deakin's
Wood

Oak
Coppice

OLLERTON LANE

Ollerton
Lane

Old Pool
Coppice

Ollerton
Park

7

Willow
Coppice

Elms
Farm

Ollerton

25

River Tern

Home
Farm

6

Peplow

+

Peplow
Hall

Mill
Coppice

TF9

Blakeway

5

Shuker's
Coppice

Mill
Farm

24

Brick-kiln
Coppice

Highway
Farm

Bacon
Hall

Bacon
Hall Farm

A442

4

Grange
Farm

Eaton
upon Tern

3

Hollycroft
Farm

River Tern

MILL LANE

Village
Farm

23

Potford Brook

2

Whitegates
Farm

TF6

Mount
Farm

Alford Brook

1

Sandyford
Bridge

A442

Little
Bolas

The
Pool

22

Sandyford
Farm

63 A B 64 C D 65 E F

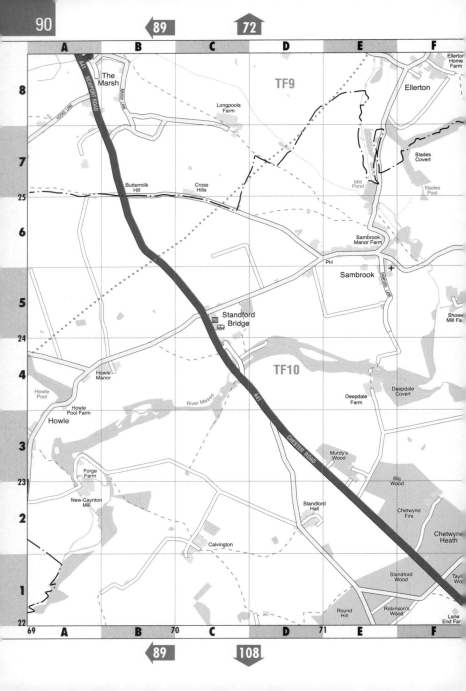

Grange Wood

Ellerton Grange Farm

TF9

Flashbrook Manor

Lower Camp Farm

8

7

25

Camp Farm

Showell Grange

Banqueting Farm

Flashbrook Wood

6

Mow Cop Farm

TF10

5

Chetwynd Airfield

Heliport

24

Puleston Common

Whitleyford Bridge

4

Old Farm

Wellbank Farm

Whitley Manor Farm

3

Cross

Pickstock

23

Brook Farm

Manor Farm

Whitley Moss Covert

2

River Meese

Big Wood

Puleston Hill

Puleston Hill Covert

Puleston House Farm

Puleston

1

Moss Covert

22

ROBEY LANE

A B 73 C D 74 E F

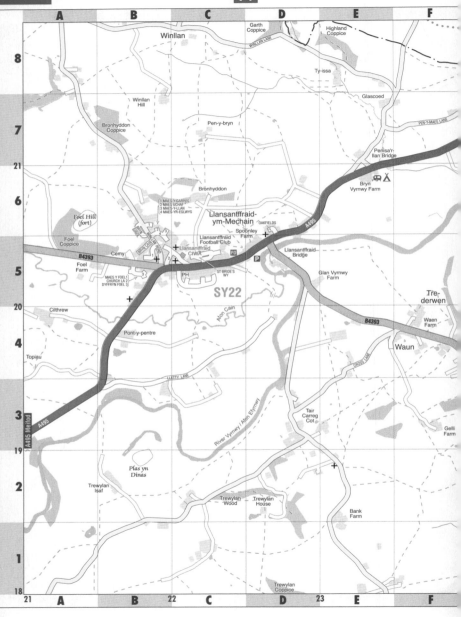

SY22

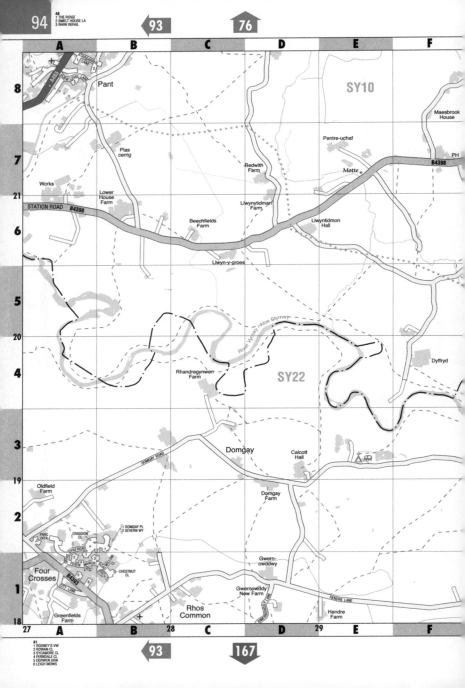

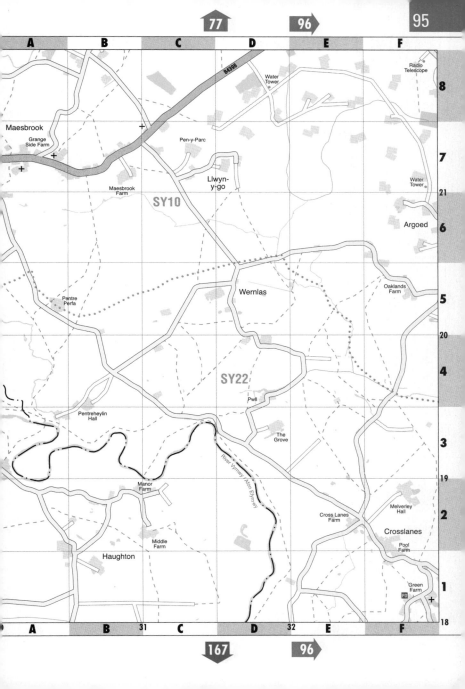

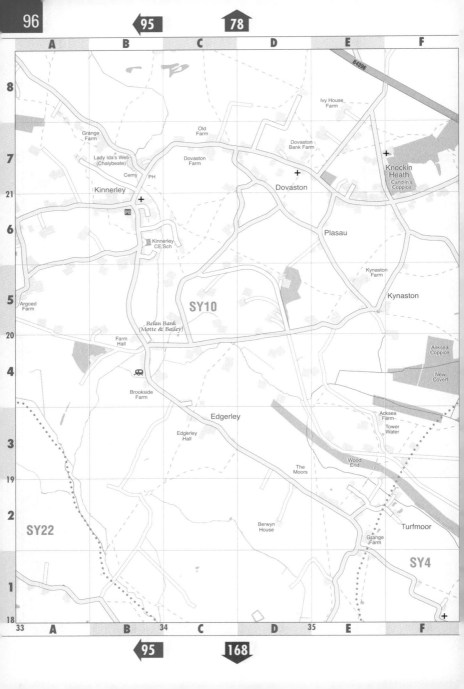

A B C D E F

8

Cranmoor Gorse
Little Heath Plantations
Coton Farm
Low Bank Farm

Common Plantation

Coton Side

7

Wood Farm

Ruyton Moss

21

B4396

Lin Can Coppice

New Heath Farm

Lower Hopton

Cranberry Moss

Heath Farm

Wolfshead Farm

Mount Pleasant Farm

6

SY10

SY4

Hopton Hill

A5

Hopton Farm

Hopton

5

Kinton Moss

The Prill

St Chads Farm

WELL LANE

20

Top Farm

St Andrews CE Prim Sch

P

Fort

P

4

Grove Farm

Kinton

Nesscliffe Hill Country Park

Kinton Farm

Nesscliffe

PH

Kynaston's Cave

Holly House Farm

Old Post Office Farm

PO

PH

3

Military Training Area

Oak Farm

19

WILCOT AVENUE KINGSWAY

QUEENSWAY

A5

Wilcott

2

Motte

Mast

Rushy Leasowes

Haughmond Farm

1

A B C D E F

18

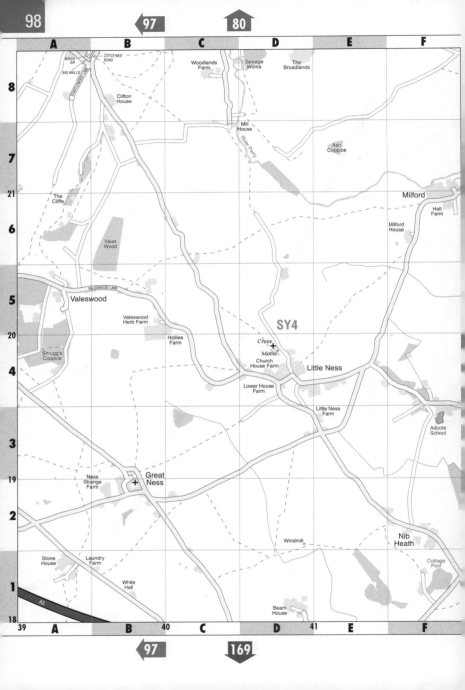

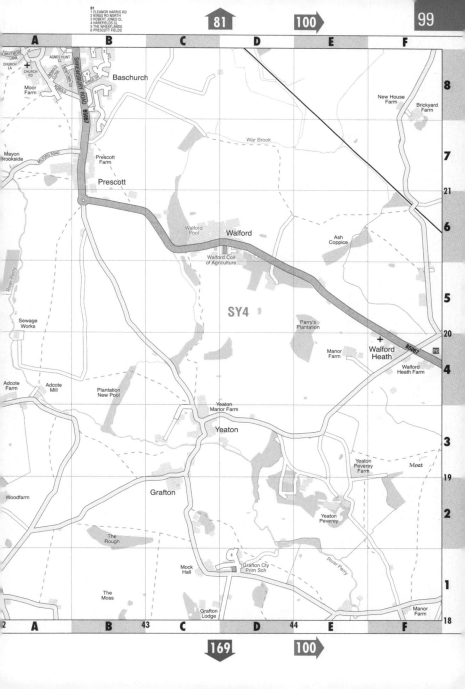

101
84

A B C D E F

8

Hardwicke
Stables

New House
Farm

Hardwicke
Home
Farm

Heath
Farm

7

Hardwicke
Grange
Farm

Shropshire Way

21

Painsbrook
Farm

EATON ROAD

MILL LANE

6

Villa
Farm

SHREWSBURY ROAD

A49

SY4

5

CHAPEL RD
CHURCH CL

Hall
Farm

Church
Farm

PH

WALL DRIVE

20

Moat

Hermitage
Farm

PO Hadnall

Hadnall
Wood

STATION ROAD

4

POOL
DRIVE

Hadnall CE
Prim Sch

Astley
Lane Farm

Littlewood
Farm

PH

1 WILLOW CT
2 WEDGEFIELDS CL

Wood
Farm

WOOD ROAD

Shropshire Way

ASTLEY LANE

3

Astley
Lodge

HATCH LANE

HAWKSMOOR LN

19

Hawksmoor
Coppice

Church
Farm

Astley

2

Waits
Coppice

ASTLEY
CT

Beaconsfield
Farm

Holly
Farm

Bings
Farm

Braidway
Farm

Shropshire Way

Bow
Bridge

A53

1

Kesters
Coppice

A49

Upper
Astley

18

PH

Astley
Grange
Farm

101
114

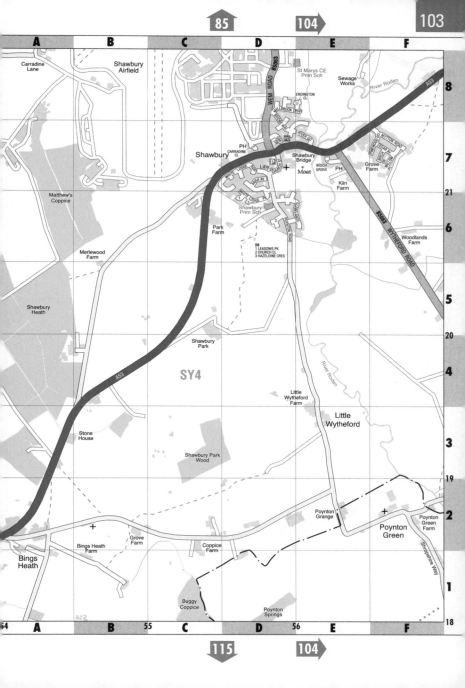

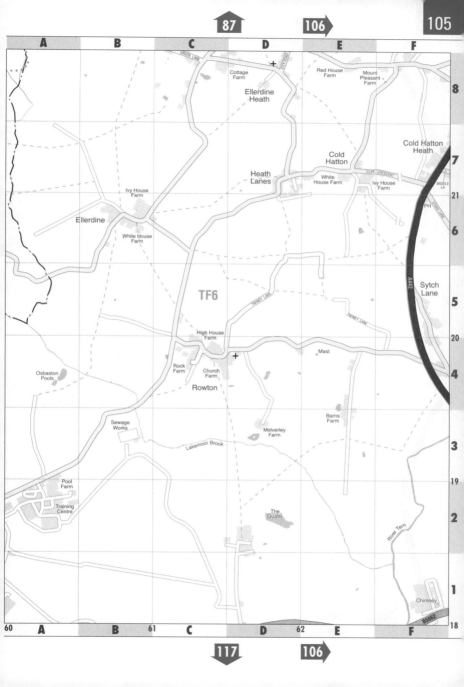

A B C D E F

8

Green Lane
City Road
Cottage Farm
Red House Farm
Mount Pleasant Farm
Ellerdine Heath

Cold Hatton Heath

7

Cold Hatton
Cliff Crescent
Middle La
Heath Lanes
White House Farm
Ivy House Farm
PH

21

Ivy House Farm

Ellerdine

6

White House Farm

A442

Sytch Lane

TF6

5

Twiney Lane
Twiney Lane

20

High House Farm
Mast

+

Rock Farm
Church Farm

4

Rowton

Barns Farm

Osbaston Pools

Melverley Farm

3

Sewage Works

Lakemoor Brook

19

Pool Farm

2

Training Centre

The Quabs

River Tern

1

Chimney

B5062

60 A B 61 C D 62 E F 18

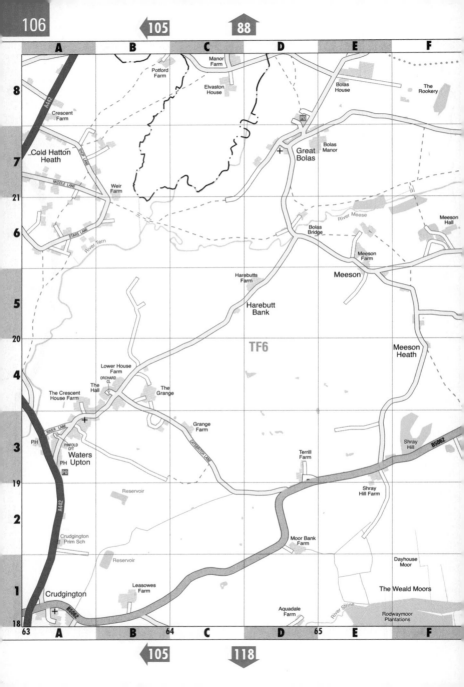

A   B   C   D   E   F

8

Crescent
Farm

Manor
Farm

Potford
Farm

Elvaston
House

Bolas
House

The
Rookery

7

Cold Hatton
Heath

Great
Bolas

Bolas
Manor

21

MIDDLE LANE

Weir
Farm

River Meese

Meeson
Hall

6

STANS LANE

River Tern

Bolas
Bridge

Meeson
Farm

Meeson

5

Harebutts
Farm

Harebutt
Bank

20

TF6

Meeson
Heath

4

Lower House
Farm

ORCHARD
CL

The
Hall

The
Grange

The Crescent
House Farm

Shray
Hill

B5062

3

RIVER LANE

PINFOLD
CFT

PH

Waters
Upton

Grange
Farm

DEBENHILL LANE

Terrill
Farm

Shray
Hill Farm

PH

PD

19

A442

Reservoir

2

Crudgington
Prim Sch

Moor Bank
Farm

Reservoir

Dayhouse
Moor

1

Crudgington

Leasowes
Farm

The Weald Moors

Aquadale
Farm

River Strine

Rodwaymoor
Plantations

B5062

18

63   A   64   B   C   D   65   E   F

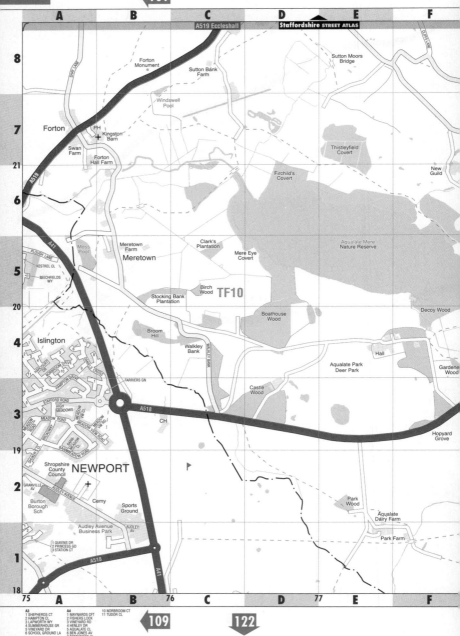

A B C D E F

8

7

21

6

5

20

4

3

19

2

1

18

Forton Monument

Sutton Moors Bridge

Sutton Bank Farm

Windswell Pool

Forton

PH
Kingston Barn

Thistleyfield Covert

Swan Farm

Forton Hall Farm

New Guild

Firchild's Covert

Moss Pool

Meretown Farm

Meretown

Clark's Plantation

Mere Eye Covert

Aqualate Mere Nature Reserve

KESTREL CL
BEECHFIELDS WY
PLOUGH LANE

Stocking Bank Plantation

Birch Wood

TF10

Decoy Wood

Islington

Broom Hill

Boathouse Wood

Walkley Bank

WALKLEY BANK

Hall

Aqualate Park Deer Park

Gardene Wood

FARRIERS GN

A518

Castle Wood

CH

Hopyard Grove

Shropshire County Council

NEWPORT

Shropshire County Council

GRANVILLE AV

Burton Borough Sch

Cemy

Sports Ground

Park Wood

Aqualate Dairy Farm

Audley Avenue Business Park

AUDLEY AV

1 QUEENS DR
2 PRINCESS GD
3 STATION CT

Park Farm

A518

A41

A518

75 A B 76 C D 77 E F

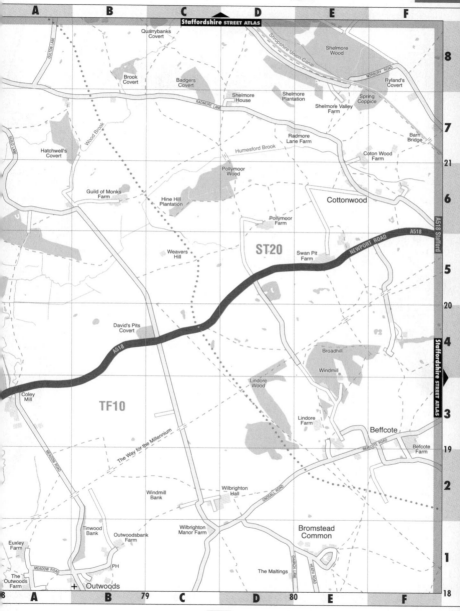

Quarrybanks Covert

Shelmore Wood

Brook Covert

Badgers Covert

RADMORE LANE

Shelmore House

Shelmore Plantation

Shelmore Valley Farm

Shropshire Union Canal

NORBURY ROAD

Ryland's Covert

Spring Coppice

Barn Bridge

Hatchwell's Covert

Radmore Lane Farm

Humesford Brook

Coton Wood Farm

Wood Brook

Pollymoor Wood

Guild of Monks Farm

Hine Hill Plantation

Cottonwood

Weavers Hill

Pollymoor Farm

ST20

Swan Pit Farm

NEWPORT ROAD

A518

A518 Stafford

David's Pits Covert

A518

Broadhill

Windmill

Lindore Wood

Coley Mill

TF10

Lindore Farm

Beffcote

Staffordshire STREET ATLAS

The Way for the Millennium

BEFCOTE ROAD

Befcote Farm

Windmill Bank

Wilbrighton Hall

DROSGAL ROAD

Euxley Farm

Tinwood Bank

Outwoodsbank Farm

Wilbrighton Manor Farm

Bromstead Common

MEADOW ROAD

PH

The Outwoods Farm

Outwoods

The Maltings

CHURCH LANE

HEATH ROAD

8

7

21

6

5

20

4

3

19

2

1

18

Upper Battlefield

Battlefield Farm

Ball's Coppice

A49

A53

Wheatley Farm

Shropshire Way

A5124

A53

Albrightlee Villa Farm

Kendricks Rough

A5112

Sunderton Farm

PH

Battlefield

A3P

Chy

Sunderton Pool

SY4

Colins Rough

HOLT END

SHILLINGTON DRIVE

Superstore

HALLAM DR

TEXBAR

RASHFORD

Albrightlee Hall Farm

The Dell Farm

B4
1 GREATFORD GN
2 LAWSON GDNS
3 HALLAM DR
4 PEACEHAVEN
5 GOWAN CT
6 RAMSEY MDWS
7 MALLARD CL
8 SWALLOW DR
9 WOODPECKER CL
10 KESTREL DR

P&R

A5112

ARLINGTON WY

Works

Harlescott

Superstore

WHITCHURCH ROAD

A49

SY1

ROBIN CL

Sunderme Farm

WHITCHURCH ROAD

A5112

HARLESCOTT LANE

FIELD CRESCENT

FEATHERBED LANE

Harlescott Jun Sch

CORNDON CRESCENT

PO

ALLERTON RD

BEVERLEY RD

ASTER RD

C3
1 WREN CL
2 KESTREL DR
3 CURLEW CL
4 CHAFFINCH WY
5 WOODLARK CL
6 KINGFISHER CL
7 QUATFORD CL
8 NORTHSIDE CL

Sundorne Castle Farm

Hillside Farm

Abbi Fa

Sundorne Sch

Liby

EBURY AVENUE

1 WHITTINGTON CL
2 HOLGATE DR
3 OVERTON CL
4 FARMOOR

Meadows Farm

B5062

SUNDORNE ROAD

B5062

SUNDORNE ROAD

TA Centre

1 FERNDALE RD
2 HOPTON DR

Sports Ground

Sundorne Pool

Severn Way

Recreation Ground

Pimley Manor

SHREWSBURY

Shropshire Way

SY2

A49

Gables Farm

Shropshire Way

The Hollies

CHURCH RD

A2
1 SUNDORNE CR
2 CORNDON CL
3 CORNDON ROAD
4 MEADOW CL
5 MONTGOMERY WY
6 WELLINGTON CL
7 MARLBOROUGH CT

A3
1 DOUNTON CL
2 HARLESCOTT CL
3 HAUGHMOND AV
4 ROSEWAY
5 CORNDON DR
6 MOSTON GN
7 ROSEDALE

A4
1 WHITCHURCH RD
2 HAWKESTONE RD

B3
1 THE BRADLEYS
2 THE SPRINGS
3 THE HIG
4 HASSACKS THE
5 CRAIG CL
6 ALLERTON RD

113 126

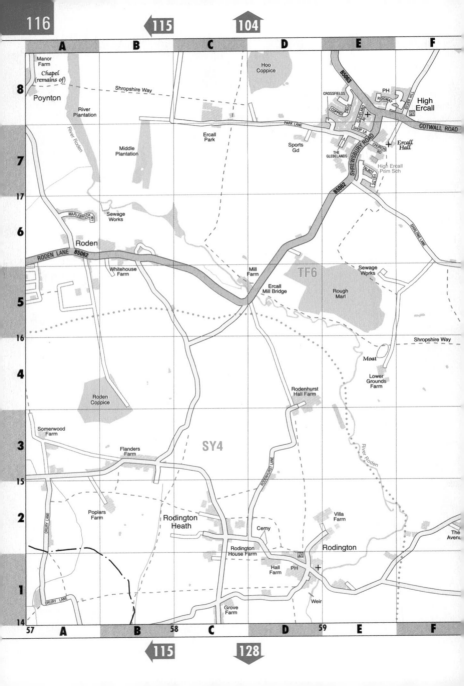

A **B** **C** **D** **E** **F**

8

Manor
Farm
Chapel
(remains of)
Poynton
Hoo
Coppice
River
Plantation
Shropshire Way
PARK LANE
CROSSFIELDS
PH
High Ercall
COTWALL ROAD
Ercall
Park
Sports
Gd
THE
GLEBELANDS
CHURCH RD
Ercall
Hall
SHREWSBURY ROAD
BRIDGE HILL

7

Middle
Plantation
High Ercall
Prim Sch
TALBOT FIELDS
B5062
BRIDLE LANE

17

MARLBROOK LANE
Sewage
Works
Roden
Whitehouse
Farm
Mill
Farm
Ercall
Mill Bridge
TF6
Sewage
Works

6

Roden Lane
B5062
B5062

5

RODEN LANE

16

Shropshire Way
Moat
Rough
Marl
Lower
Grounds
Farm

4

Roden
Coppice
Rodenhurst
Hall Farm
River Roden

3

Somerwood
Farm
Flanders
Farm
SY4
RODENHURST LANE

15

DRURY LANE
Poplars
Farm
Rodington
Heath
Cemy
Villa
Farm
The
Avenu

2

Rodington
House Farm
Rodington
PH

1

DRURY LANE
Hall
Farm
PH
Weir
Grove
Farm

14

57 **A** **B** 58 **C** **D** 59 **E** **F**

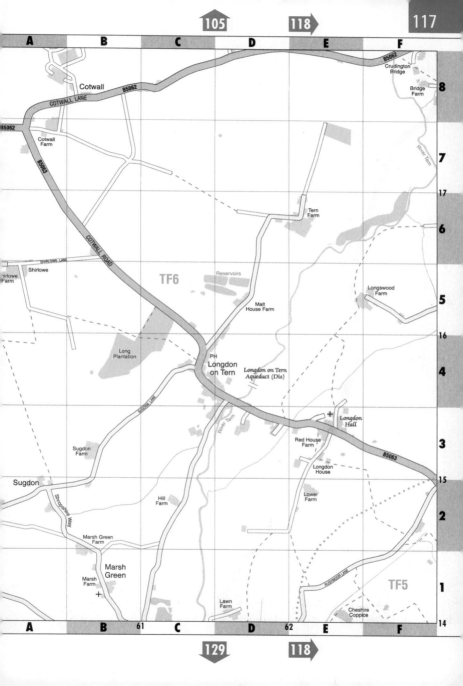

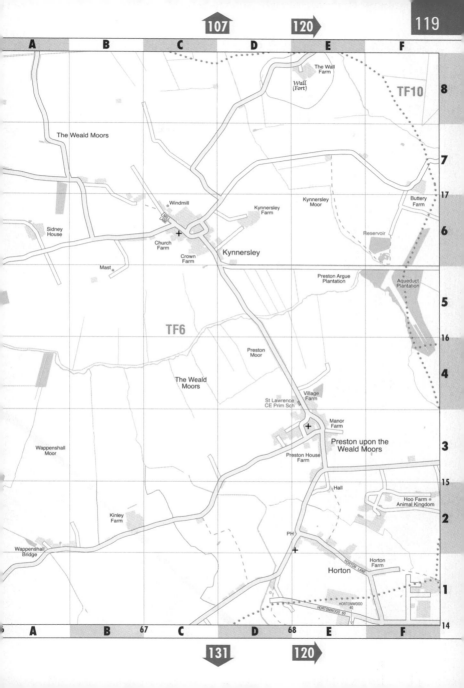

109
122
121
E8
1 MOORFIELD LA
2 PINEWOODS
3 PEMBRIDGE CL
4 ST ANDREW'S WY
5 WALLSHEAD WY

A B C D E F

8
7
17
6
5
16
4
3
15
2
1
14

Church Aston
Church Aston Cty Inf Sch
HIGHFIELD
THE CRESCENT
Aston Hill Covert
Aston Hill
THE CLOSE
PD
A518
WELLINGTON ROAD
PH
PITCHCROFT LANE
Watkins Covert
War Memorial
Brockton
PITCHCROFT LANE
PH
A518
BARNSLEY LANE
LIMEKILN LANE
Brockton Leasows
Newhouse Farm
TF10
Shaft (dis)
Little Hales Manor Farm
TITTENLEY ROAD
PRESWELL DRIVE
WELLINGTON ROAD
WILLMOOR LANE
Lilleshall Hill
Lilleshall Prim Sch
Lilleshall
LIMEKILN LANE
OLD FARM LANE
Mon
Hill Farm
Old Farm
CHURCH RD
ST MICHAEL CLOSE
PEMBRITTS
CLOSE
HILL
Honnington
PD
Cemy
The Incline
Incline Plantation
Home Farm
YEW TREE DR
Old Hall
Lilleshall Grange
15
Lilleshall National Sports Centre
National Recreational Centre
TF2
The Oaks
LILLESHURST ROAD
Grange Plantation
Remains of Abbey (Augustinian)
Abbey Wood
Gorse Covert
Sulphur Piece Plantation

The Outwoods Farm

8

Moreton Gorse

Bromstead House Farm

Walton Grange

WALNUT TREE LA

Moreton Park

Hill Plantation

DYKES LA

CHURCH LANE

Dale End Farm

New House Farm

Moreton Hall Farm

Moreton

POOLEY LANE

Moreton

7

POST OFFICE LANE

Bromstead Heath

17

HEATH ROAD

Walton Wood

Moreton Brook

CHURCH EATON ROAD

Bromstead Hill Farm

6

Chapman's Wood

Orslow Spinney

TF10

Sandbank Plantation

Little Wood

5

Bleak Hill

16

North Lynn Manor

Lynn

Mill Hill

Coneygreaves Plantation

4

Lynn Mill Farm

Mill Plantation

Orslow

Lynn Wood

Guy's Bank

3

15

Bithams Plantation

2

The Bates

Chadwell Mill

Great Chatwell House Farm

Winford Mill Farm

KING'S STREET

Great Chatwell

Chadwell

PH

BURN LANE

CHATWELL LANE

Uplands Farm

1

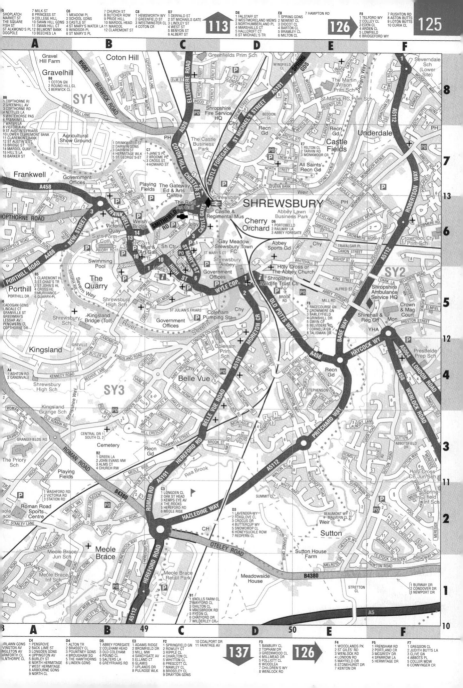

A5
1 BARDSLEY DR
2 WINIFRED CL
3 PATRICIA DR
4 REYNAULDS CL

A6
1 CONNYNGER CR
2 FLAGWALL
3 LAWLEY GDNS
4 BELVIDERE LA

A7
1 HAYWOOD CT
2 UPTON LA
3 WEALD DR
4 SHAW RD
5 TWYFORDS WY

A8
1 RUSHBROOKE WY
2 GLENBURN GDNS
3 MIDDLETOWN SQ
4 HEARNE WY
5 VENNINGTON WY
6 RUSHTON RD

7 MONKMOOR RD
8 JUDITH BUTTS GDNS

B7
1 ALLNESS CL
2 CARTLAND AV
3 FRANKTON CL
4 GALTON DR
5 TWYFORDS WY
6 LONGBRIDGE CL

7 FEARN DR
8 FAIRNESS CL
9 BELGRAVE PL

114   125

RIVERDALE RD
Severndale Sch (Upper Site)
Chy
The Wilfred Owen Prim Sch
Monkmoor Industrial Estate
Chy
BEWDLEY
Monkmoor
Sewage Works
PH
Belvidere Primary Sch
Belvidere Sch
Chy
Mynde Caradoc Cty Prim Sch
Playing Field
Shirehall
St Giles CE Prim Sch
CRANFIELD DR
CARMEN AVENUE
SY2
Weir Hill Farm
Weir
Steadmans Plantation
SHREWSBURY
PRESTON STREET
Sports Ground
Shrewsbury Coll of Arts and Tech
Emstrey Crematorium
Shrewsbury Cricket Club
Holy Cross CE Jun Sch
Springfield Inf Sch
LONDON ROAD (EMSTREY)
Shrewsbury Business Park
1 SALTDEAN CL
2 HOLBORN DR
Mere Pool
THIEVES LANE
SOUTHGATE DR
Garden Centre
ROWTON RD
B4380
OTELEY ROAD
B4380
A5
Weeping Cross
SY5
EMSTREY BANK
Lower Farm
Emstrey
B4380
Quarry Wood
Burnton's Tomb
Longner Hall
Moat Wood
Preston Farm
Preston Boats Farm
Preston on Severn Farm
Preston
SY4
A5
The Manse
Bridge Farm
Abbeywood Tower Farm
PH
Uffington
Shropshire Way
Fort
Queen Eleanor's Bower
Douglas's Leap
Monkmoor Pool Nature Reserve
Severn Way
River Severn
Big Wood
The Oaks
River Severn
Severn Way
Berwick Grove Farm
The Rumbles
A49

125   138

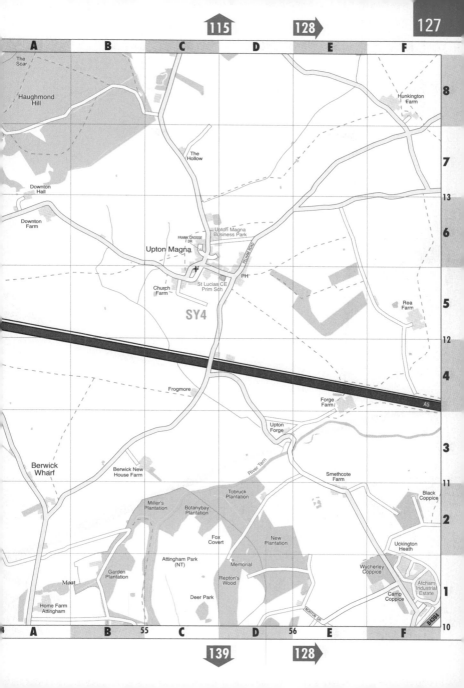

The Scar

Haughmond Hill

Downton Hall

Downton Farm

The Hollow

FRANK CROSSE / DR

Upton Magna

Upton Magna Business Park

Church Farm

St Lucias CE Prim Sch

PH

SY4

Rea Farm

Frogmore

Forge Farm

Upton Forge

Berwick Wharf

Berwick New House Farm

River Tern

Smethcote Farm

Black Coppice

Tobruck Plantation

Miller's Plantation

Botanybay Plantation

Fox Covert

New Plantation

Uckington Heath

Wycherley Coppice

Attingham Park (NT)

Garden Plantation

Memorial

Repton's Wood

Deer Park

Home Farm Attingham

Moat

Camp Coppice

Atcham Industrial Estate

Hunkington Farm

A5

B4394

13

6

5

12

4

3

11

2

1

10

8

7

127
116

A **B** **C** **D** **E** **F**

8

Villa
Farm

Barker's
Square

7

Manor
Farm

WOODLANDS
CE

Sunnyside
Farm

Gate House
Farm

PH

Withington

SY4

13

Walcot Road
Farm

6

The
Lees

Bridge

5

Walcot

MEADOW
DR

River Tern

PH

B4394

12

Duncote
Mill

4

A5

TF6

Duncote
Farm

Charlton

Moat

3

11

2

Ravenshaws
Gorse

BLUEBELL ROAD

A5

1

B4394

Wheathill
Farm

Bluebell

B5061

10

127
140

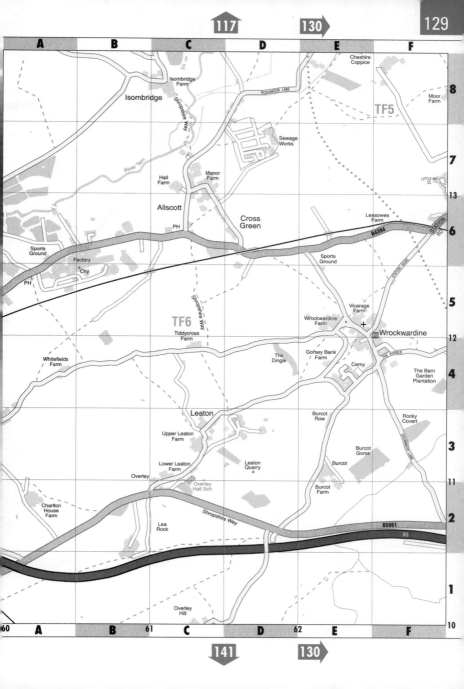

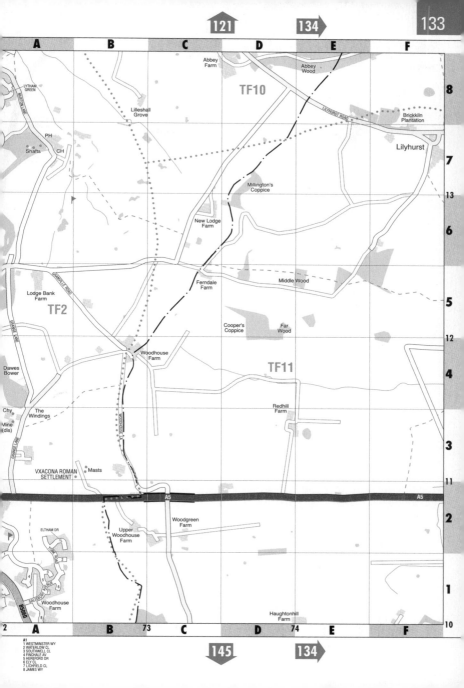

TF10

Abbey Farm

Abbey Wood

LILYHURST ROAD

Brickkiln Plantation

Lytham Green

Lilleshall Grove

Lilyhurst

8

PH

Shafts

CH

Millington's Coppice

7

13

New Lodge Farm

6

GRANVILLE ROAD

Middle Wood

Lodge Bank Farm

TF2

Ferndale Farm

5

GRANGE LANE

Cooper's Coppice

Far Wood

12

Dawes Bower

Woodhouse Farm

TF11

4

Chy

The Windings

Redhill Farm

Mine (dis)

WOODHOUSE LANE

3

VXACONA ROMAN SETTLEMENT

Masts

11

A5

A5

2

ELTHAM DR

Upper Woodhouse Farm

Woodgreen Farm

SALISBURY AVENUE

B5060

Woodhouse Farm

1

Haughtonhill Farm

10

A
B
73
C
D
74
E
F

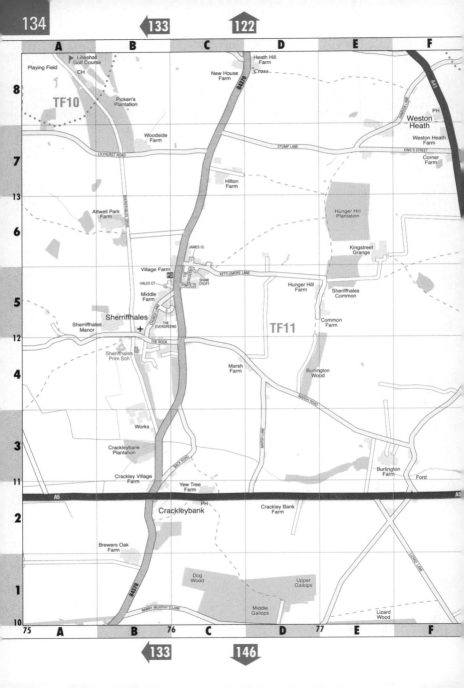

A B C D E F

Playing Field

Lilleshall
Golf Course
CH

8

TF10

Picken's
Plantation

New House
Farm

Heath Hill
Farm
Cross

B4379

Weston
Heath

PH

A41

Woodside
Farm

Stump Lane

Weston Heath
Farm

KING'S STREET

7

LILYHURST ROAD

Corner
Farm

13

Attwell Park
Farm

SHERRIFFALES DRIVE

Hilton
Farm

Hunger Hill
Plantation

6

JAMES CL

Kingstreet
Grange

Village Farm
PO

THE HOLLIES

KETTLEMORE LANE

HALES CT

SHAW
CROFT

Hunger Hill
Farm

Sheriffhales
Common

Middle
Farm

PINFOLD

CHURCH LANE

5

Sherriffhales
Manor

Sherriffhales

THE
EVERGREENS

TF11

Common
Farm

12

THE ROCK

Sheriffhales
Prim Sch

Marsh
Farm

Burlington
Wood

4

MARSH ROAD

MARSH LANE

Works

Crackleybank
Plantation

3

BACK ROAD

Burlington
Farm

Ford

Crackley Village
Farm

Yew Tree
Farm

11

A5

A5

PH

Crackleybank

Crackley Bank
Farm

2

LODGE LANE

Brewers Oak
Farm

Dog
Wood

Upper
Gallops

1

B4379

NANNY MURPHY'S LANE

Middle
Gallops

Lizard
Wood

10

75

A

B

76

C

D

77

E

F

A | B | C | D | E | F

Hoole's
Planting

TF10

Chatwell Park
Farm

Blymhill
Common

Crossroads
Farm

Newhouse
Farm

Gorsey
Bank
Farm

White Sitch

Lodge
Mount

TF11

Picmoor
Wood

The Big
Hythes

Burlington
Pool

Woodside
Farm

Lizard Grange
Farm

Lodge
Farm

The Mount

CHATWELL LANE

BICKFORD LANE

Brockton
Grange

GATHERWYND LANE

Gatherwynd

Lower
Beighterton
Farm

Brineton

Terrace
Farm

GREEN VW

Villa
Farm

Blymhill
Marsh

Holywell
Plantation

Blymhill

Beighterton
Plantation

Beighterton
House Farm

Weston
Under Lizard

BRIDGEMAN
CT

RECTORY DRIVE

A5

Pendrill's
Cave

West
Plantation

SHREWSBURY DRIVE

Weston
Hall

Town
Pool

Temple
Wood

Woodlands
Farm

Weston Park
(Deer Park)

Park
Pool

Mill
Plantation

MILL LANE

MILL LANE

BS514

A41

A41

A5 Cannock

TONG DRIVE

A5 Cannock

Staffordshire STREET ATLAS

8

13

7

6

13

5

12

4

3

11

2

1

10

A | B | 79 | C | D | 80 | E | F

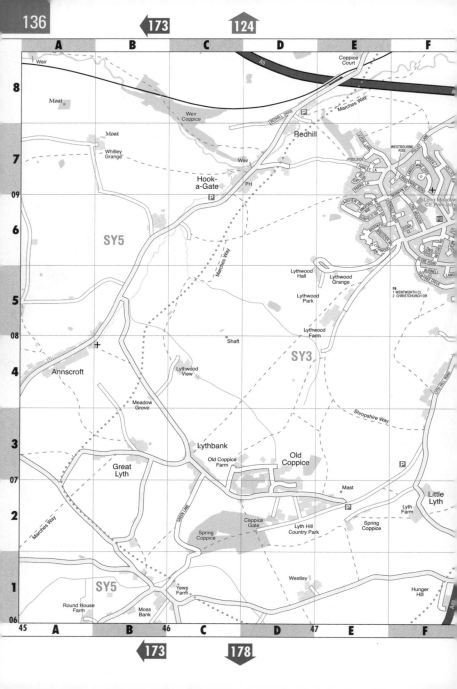

A B C D E F

8

SY2

Pulley

Motel

Sharpstone
Hill

Stone
Quarry

Betton Alkmere
Farm

Betton
Strange

7

Lower Pulley
Farm

Shropshire Way

A5 *
1 BUTCHER'S LA
2 CHESTNUT DR
3 THE MALTINGS

ayston
Hill

Moat

09

HEREFORD ROAD

SHARPSTONE LANE

SHARPSTONE LA

The
Burgs

6

BROCK OAK DR

LYTHWOOD ROAD

Library

CROSS LANE

CROSS LANE

LODGE
DR

The Burgs
(Fort)

A49

KENDRICK'S
BANK

Oakland Cty
Prim Sch

WELLBURY

RUSSEL LANE

SEARRIS LA

Betton
Coppice

Bomere
Farm

SY3

Bayston
Farm

Bomere
Wood

5

ERIC LOCK RD W

Grove
Farm

A5
1 LYNDHURST DR
2 NEWBROOK DR
3 ERIC LOCK RD
4 AMBLECOTE DR

Bomere
Pool

08

Shomere
Pool

Betton
Pool

4

Sand & Gravel
Pit

Allfield
Farm

3

Norton
Farm

Cound Brook

07

SY5

2

Stud
Farm

STATION ROAD

Ford

LYONS LANE

Glebe
Villas

Shrewsbury
Golf Course

THE
FAIRWAYS

Condover

Condover CE
Prim Sch

1

CH

GRANGE
COURT

GRANGE LANE

GROVE LANE

DARLEY RD

PO

BROOK CL

49

C

50

D

E

06

A B C D E F

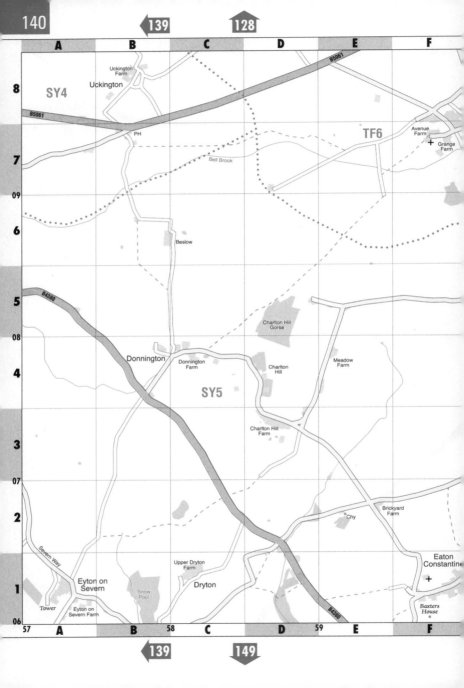

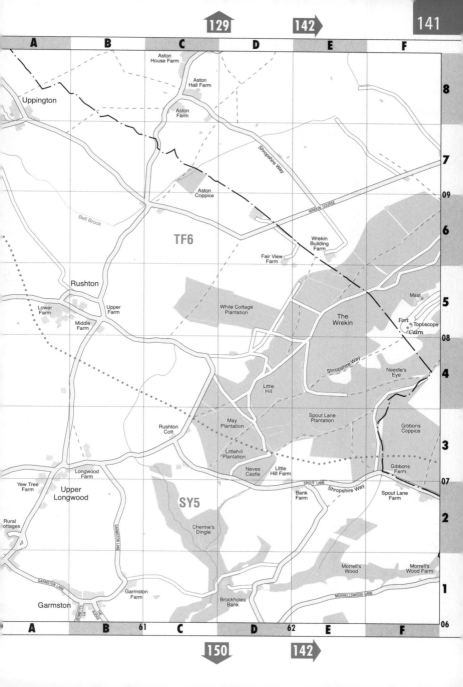

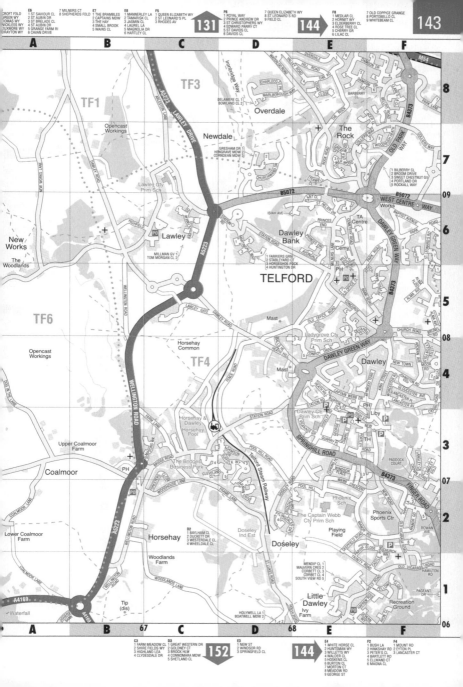

F5
1 WOOLPACK CL
2 NEWFIELD CL
3 ORCHARD RD
4 HIGH STREET
5 BROOKDALE
6 SYCAMORE CL

7 LABURNUM CL
8 PICKWICK CT
9 ST ANDREWS CL
10 BROADWAY CL
11 HAUGHTON DR

8

7

Haughton Hill
Farm

Castle Farm Way B5060

Factories
TF2

Priorslee
Lake

M54

09

Stafford Park 7

Castle Farm
Interchange

Stafford Park 8

Knowlbank

Wesley Brook

Haughton

Village
Farm

6

Works
TF3

Taggs
Rough

A464

Leisure
Park

Knowles Bank
Farm

Haughton
Bridge

HAUGHTON ROAD

BROOKSIDE
CL

Recreation
Ground

Stafford Park 10

Stafford
Park

Knowl
Wood

PRIORSLEE ROAD

Woodgrove

BROADWAY HIGH ST

5

Obelisk
NAIRN
ROUNDABOUT

Blythbury
Farm

Haughton
Farm

Haughton
House Farm

Shifnal

Libry

08

Cemy

SHREWSBURY RD

VICTORIA ROAD

B4379

4

TF11

THIRD LANE

Sunnymead
Farm

Castle

THE LINDENS

TALBOT CL 1
INNAGE CROFT 2

WYKE WY
CARESSWELL
CL

Shifnal
Sports Ctr

INNAGE ROAD

PARK ST

A464

Tower

Shaw
Farm

SHAW LANE

SCHOOL CL

A4169

St Andrews
CE Prim Sch

07

3

The
Wyke

Lodgehill
Farm

2

Dodmoors

Upper
Wyke Farm

Manor
House

1

A4169

Sewage
Works

06

F3
1 MOAT CROFT
2 SILVERMERE PK
3 BROOKLANDS AV
4 TANGLEWOOD CL
5 COTTAGE DR

F4
1 THE PADDOCK
2 CHEAPSIDE
3 JOHN'S ST

2 A B 73 C D 74 E F

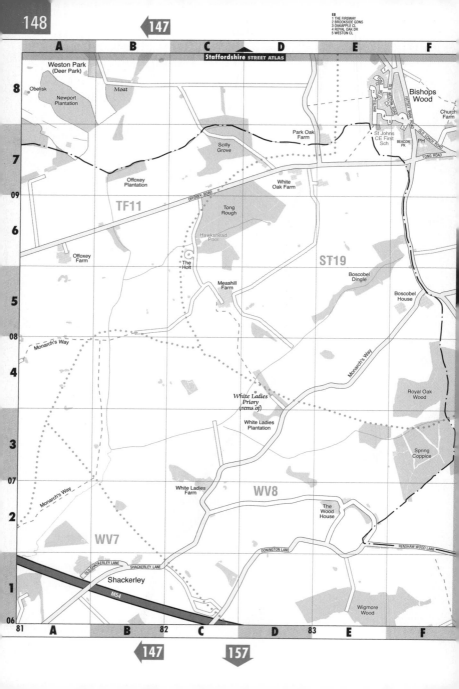

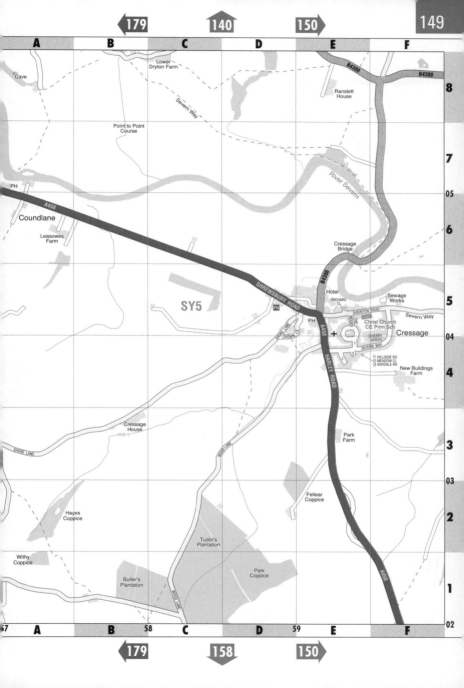

8
"Cave
Lower Dryton Farm
Ranslett House
B4380

Severn Way
Point to Point Course
7

River Severn
05

PH
A458
Coundlane
6
Leasowes Farm

Cressage Bridge

SHREWSBURY ROAD
B4380
Hotel
ORCHARD CL
Sewage Works
SY5
5
Severn Way
SHEINTON ROAD
PO
PH
Christ Church CE Prim Sch
Cressage
CROWN
SHORE LANE
CHERRY ARBOR
04
A458
Severn Way

1 HILLSIDE RD
2 MEADOW CL
3 ASHDALE RD
New Buildings Farm
4

HARLEY ROAD
Cressage House

Park Farm

SHORE LANE
WOOD LANE
3
03

Fellear Coppice
Hayes Coppice
2

Withy Coppice
Tudor's Plantation
Park Coppice
A458

Butler's Plantation
1

WOOD LANE
57
58
59
02

A B C D E F

8

Saplings
Farm

Devil's
Dingle

Mast Braggers
Hill

TF6

Leasows
Farm

Harris's
Coppice

The Moors
Farm

7

Holbrook
Coppice

05

The Holt

Church
Farm

TF8

Roundbank
Coppice

Birches
Coppice

Timber
Wood

6

Buildwas
Prim Sch

Buildwas

BUILDWAS ROAD

Home
Farm

BUILDWAS BANK

Marnwood
Hall

BUILDWAS ROAD

Severn Way

River Severn

Severn Way

5

Buildwas
Abbey

Sand
Pit

04

Buildwas
Park Farm

Severn Way

Brook's
Hill

Hill View
Farm

Power
Station

4

Blue
Pool

Chimney

Brookshill
Coppice

Tick
Wood

Pool
House

Banghams
Wood

Shropshire Way

3

Flats
Coppice

Lawless Cross
Coppice

Hungerdale
Farm

03

Lawley's Cross
Bridge

Tickwood
Hall

Spratts
Coppice

TF12

Hall
Farm

2

Farley
Coppice

TF13

Acklands
Coppice

Benthall
Hall
(NT)

THE AVENUE

Farley

A4169

Woodhouse
Farm

Audience
Wood

Wyke

1

Bradley
Coppice

Shropshire Way

Manor
Farm

WYKE LANE

02

3 A B 64 C D 65 E F

F5
1 MILTON DR
2 MITCHEL WY
3 MASON DR
4 BRIDLERD
5 WEST VW TR
6 WESTERKIRK DR

7 CANONBIE LEA

Aqueduct

Croppings
Farm

Shropshire Way

Wynne's
Coppice

Lightmoor

TF4

F8
1 AVON CL
2 BROADSTONE MS
3 WIDEWATERS CL
4 SCEPTRE CL
5 SHUTFIELD RD

Moors
Farm

Vane
Coppice

Shaft
(dis)

Works

Shaft
(dis)

CASTLEFIELDS WAY

Woodbine
Cabin

Chimney
Works

COALBROOKDALE ROAD

THE
CLOSE

Recreation
Ground

Greenbank
Farm

Coalbrookdale Open Air
Museum of Steel Sculpture

CHERRY TREE HILL

A4169

BRICK KILN BANK

Lightmoor
Junction

MINTON
CL

LORD
MURRAY
DR

Rosehill
House

SCHOOL ROAD

Oilhouse
Coppice

TF7

WAVERLEY

Mus Library &
Ironbridge Institute

Coalbrookdale

THE CROFTS 1
FERRIDAY CL 2
LONG LA DR 3
ROBINS DR 4

BRIERY BANK

Woodside

Westminster
Farm

Museum
of Iron

Dale
Coppice

WOLVERLEY
CT

TREVITHICK

Enginuity

Rough
Park

DRUMMOND
CL

GRESLEY
CL

WALNEY
CT

WENLOCK
CT

PARK LANE

MOUND WAY

STRETHILL RD

TF8

Captain's
Coppice

YHA

Cemy

ARMSTRONG
CL

William Reynolds
Cty Inf &
Jun Sch

Woodside Cty
Inf & Jun Sch

PARKWAY

Playing
Fields

BEECH ROAD

BEECH ROAD

Hill
Top

Abraham
Darby Sch

IRONBRIDGE ROAD

B4373

STRETHILL
RD

BUILDWAS ROAD

PH

Albert
Edward Bridge

Coalbrookdale
CE Prim Sch

Dale
Coppice

Ironbridge

MADELEY ROAD

WICKIN VIEW

HERMITAGE

SAGGARS
CL

Dale End
Riverside Park

Shafts
(dis)

SEVERN
BANK

WOODLAND

CHAPEL
RD

Madeleywood

Lloyd's
Coppice

Mus of the Gorge

BELLE VUE RD

BELMIN RD

JOCKEY
BANK

Benthall
Edge Wood

Shropshire Way

Iron
Bridge &
Toll House

Supper
Theatre

ST LUKE'S RD

WATERLOO STREET

Severn Way

Bedlam
Furnaces

WATERLOO STREET

Mast

River Severn

Jackfield
Bridge

THE LLOYDS

Broad Acres
Farm

Easthope
Coppice

IRONBRIDGE RD

LLOYD HEAD

CHAPEL LANE

GEORGE RD

Workhouse
Coppice

Easthope
Coppice Farm

BALL'S LANE

Jackfield
Tile Museum

TF8

SPOUT LANE

TF12

ST MARY'S
CL

CALCUTTS
ROAD

Chy

Works

Cty

Benthall

Pipe
Mus

CHANTRY

COCKSHUTT LA

REDCHURCH
CL

Broseley

Broseley CE
Prim Sch

B4373

BELVEDERE
RD

IRONBRIDGE ROAD

Woodhouse
Farm

TF12

Leo
Farm

THE AVENUE

BENTHALL LANE

B4375

QUEEN'S

New Rd

Benthall Villa
Farm

Barratts Hill
Farm

C1
1 PADMANS AL
2 CUMBERLAND CL
3 JACKSON AV
4 BIRCHMEADOW RD

F4
1 HOLM LANGGREEN
2 SOMERSET CL
3 HARRISON CL
4 MELLOR CL
5 ROWLEY CL
6 UPPER DINGLE
7 LOWER DINGLE
8 CHESHIRE CL
9 EARLSWOOD DR

10 MADELEYWOOD VW

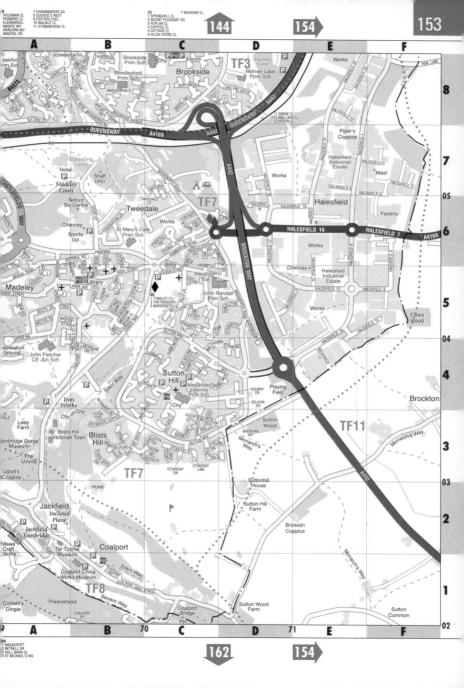

153
145

A **B** **C** **D** **E** **F**

8

Old Mill Pond

Hem Lane

Hem Mill

Hem Manor Farm

HEM LANE

The Hem Farm

The Hem

Lodge Hill

A4169

7

Weir

Evelith

EVELITH LANE

05

PADDOCK LA.

HALESFIELD 7

High Farm

Kemberton

EVELITH LANE

Evelith Manor

6

Monarch's Way

Charles's Wood

Church Farm

MILL LANE

PO

PRIORY RD.

HALL LANE

+

PH

5

MILL LANE

TF11

Hinnington Grange

B4379

04

Monarch's Way

Lowes Farm

Kemberton Gorse

4

Brockton

GRINDLE ROAD

3

03

Field House

Mad Brook Farm

Brockton Bridge

2

Haven Hills Farm

B4379

Weir

Weir

Mad Brook

1

Harrington Hall

Ford

A442 BRIDGNORTH RD

B4176

02

72 **A** **B** **73** **C** **D** **74** **E** **F**

A5
1 ST MARY'SCL
2 THE GLEBE
3 BARRINGTON CL
4 MAYFAIR CL
5 BRINDLEY CL
6 ARROW DR
7 REDFORD DR
8 WOLVERLEY CT
9 MANOR GD
10 WHISTON CL

A   B   C   D   E   F

Wigmore Wood

M54

WV8

8

Lower Wood Farm

High Holborn

DONINGTON LANE

Harriot's Hayes

7

Donington House

Lower Dairy House Farm

New Plantation

05

Harriotts Hayes Farm

DONINGTON LANE

BLUE HOUSE LANE

Albrighton Trust
Moat

Humphreston Hall

HARRIETTS HAYES ROAD

6

ALBRIGHTON BY-PASS

A41

Albrighton

Stockings Rough

Birchfield Prep Sch for Boys

St Mary's Prim Sch

WV7

BEAMISH LANE

Beamish Farm

COUNTY LANE

5

Library PO

Albrighton Cty Inf & Jan Schs

HIGH STREET

MEADOW RD
MEESON CL

04

BARRIDGE

High House Farm

Millfields Farm

HIGH HOUSE LANE

High House Farm

Oaken Park Farm

4

NEWPORT LANE

KINGSWOOD ROAD

Woodhouse Farm

WOODHOUSE LANE

County Lane Farm

Kingswood Common

03

New Houses

KINGSWOOD ROAD

White Gate Farm

3

P

A41

NEWPORT ROAD

A41 Wolverhampton

Boningale

The Old Farm

2

CHURCH LANE

PH

Parkside Farm

HOLYHEAD ROAD

Boningale Manor

PH

A464

Kingswood Sch
P

nurch
arm

Reservoir

INK BROOK LANE

Kingswood Bank Farm

1

Brook Plantation New

PATTINGHAM LA

Kingswood Bus Park

02

A   B   82   C   D   83   E   F

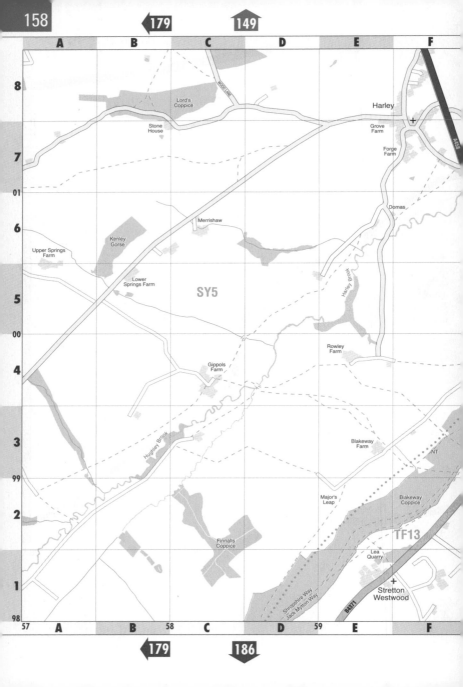

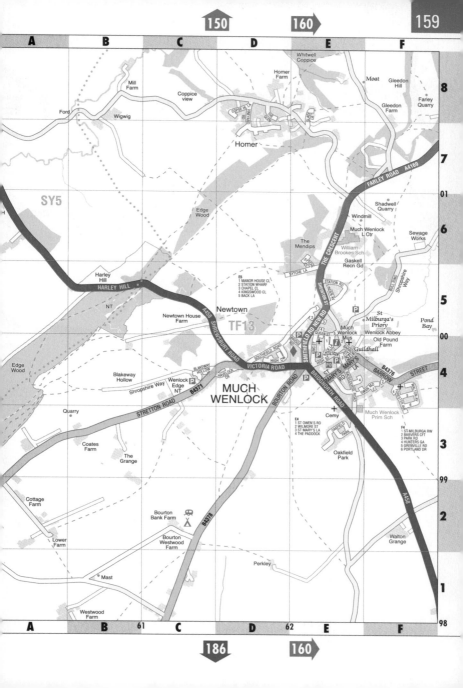

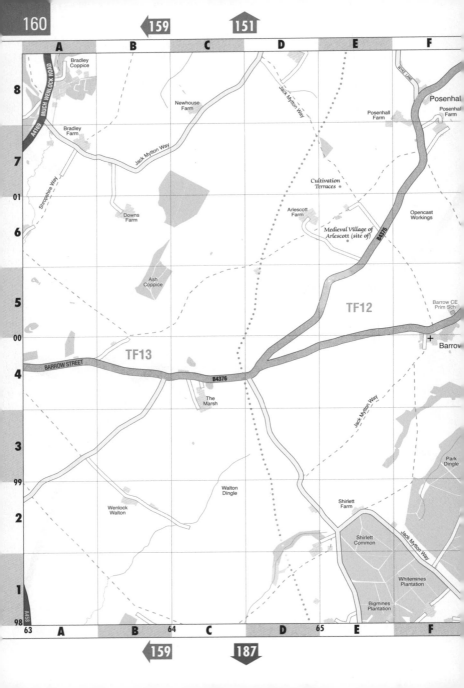

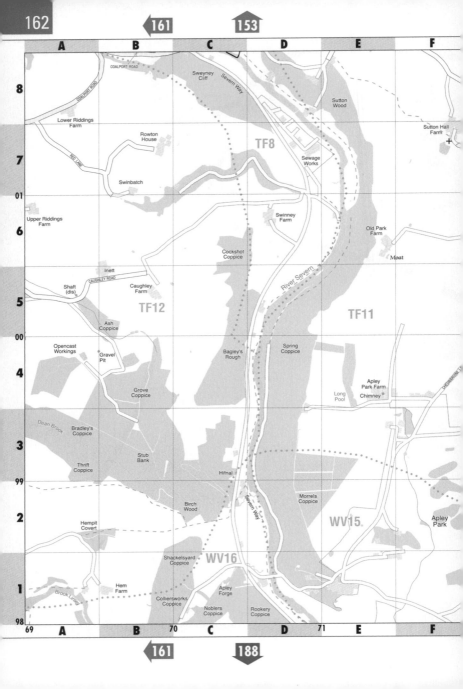

A   B   C   D   E   F

8

7

01

6

5

00

4

3

99

2

1

98

A442

Sutton House

Monarch's Way

Sutton Maddock

BRIDGNORTH ROAD

Vicarage Lane

B4176

New House

Cotsbrook Farm

TF11

WINDMILL LANE

VILLAGE ROAD

Hotel

Norton

Football Ground

Yew Tree Farm

DISENHALL LANE

A442

Monarch's Way

Astol

B4176

Crowgreaves

Stockton Buildings

Stockton

Echoes Hill

The Knolls Coppice

The Leavenhalls

Birches Coppice

Crowgreaves Farm

Acorn Hill

Bayley's Corner

WV15

Patmarsh

Ewdness House

Ewdness Farm

Common Farm

A   B   C   73   D   74   E   F

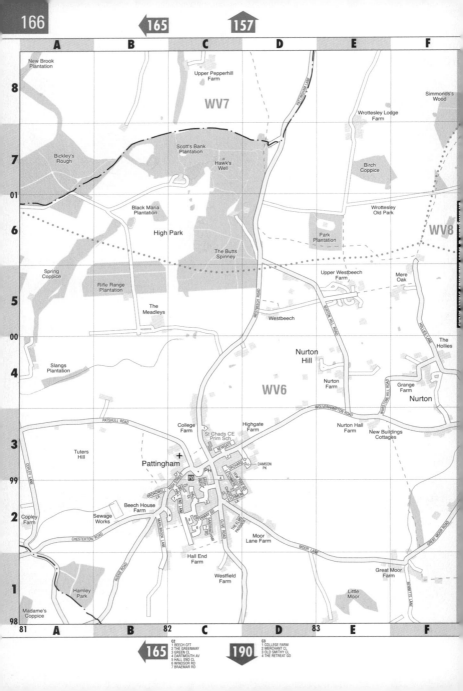

165
157

A   **B**   **C**   **D**   **E**   **F**

8

New Brook
Plantation

Upper Pepperhill
Farm

WV7

Simmonds's
Wood

Wrottesley Lodge
Farm

7

Bickley's
Rough

Scott's Bank
Plantation

Hawk's
Well

Birch
Coppice

01

Black Maria
Plantation

Wrottesley
Old Park

WV8

6

High Park

The Butts
Spinney

Park
Plantation

Spring
Coppice

Rifle Range
Plantation

Upper Westbeech
Farm

Mere
Oak

The
Hollies

5

The
Meadleys

Westbeech

Nurton
Hill

00

Slangs
Plantation

WV6

Nurton
Farm

Grange
Farm

Nurton

4

PATSHULL ROAD

College
Farm

St Chads CE
Prim Sch

NEWGATE

Highgate
Farm

Nurton Hall
Farm

New Buildings
Cottages

3

Tuters
Hill

Pattingham

PH

DAMSON
PK

WOLVERHAMPTON ROAD

99

PO

Beech House
Farm

Sewage
Works

THE ELMS
PADDOCKS

2

Copley
Farm

CHESTERTON ROAD

Moor
Lane Farm

MOOR LANE

Great Moor
Farm

Hall End
Farm

Westfield
Farm

Little
Moor

1

Hamley
Park

Madame's
Coppice

98

A   82   **C**   **D**   83   **F**

81   **B**   **C**   **D**   **E**   **F**

165
190

C2
1 BEECH CFT
2 THE GREENWAY
3 GREEN CL
4 DARTMOUTH AV
5 HALL END CL
6 WINDSOR RD
7 BRAEMAR RD

C3
1 COLLEGE FARM
2 MERCHANT CL
3 OLD SMITHY CL
4 THE RETREAT GD

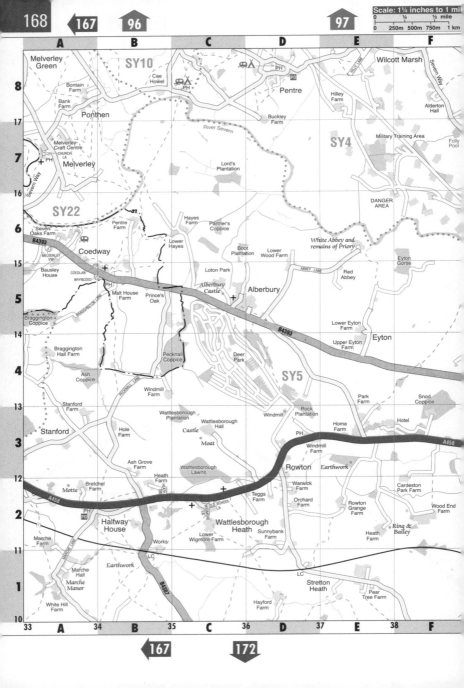

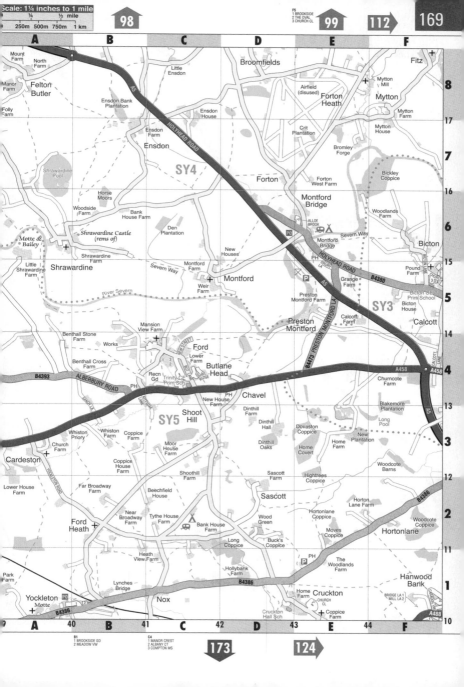

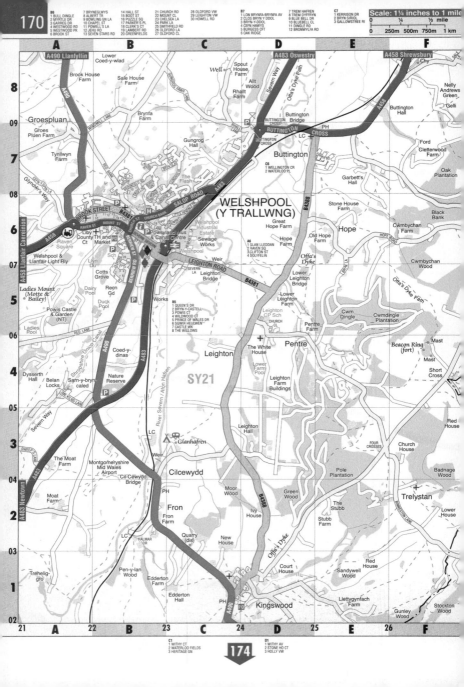

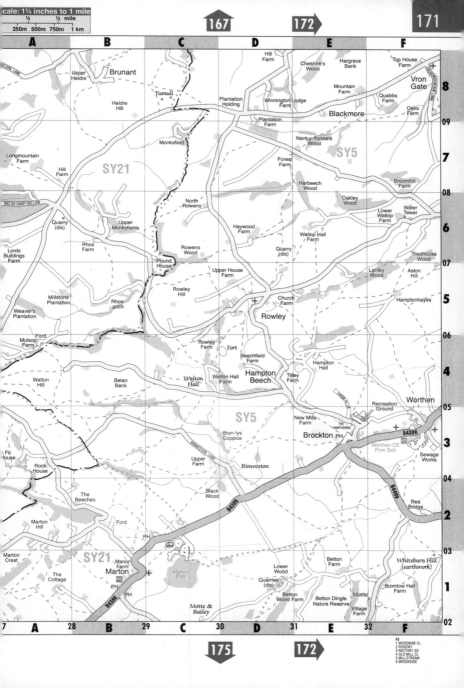

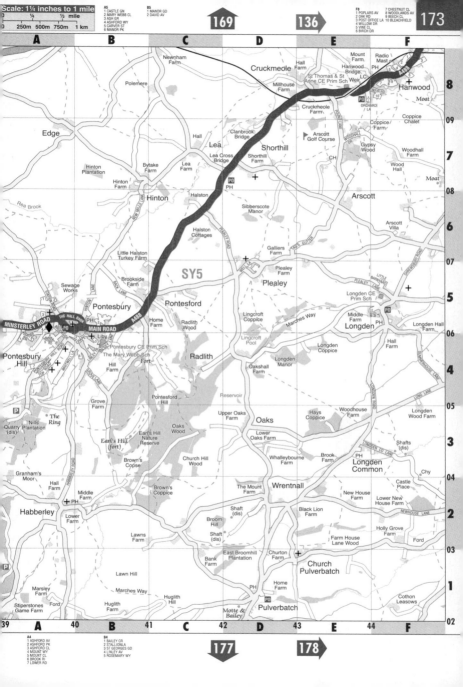

Scale: 1¼ inches to 1 m

| 0 | ¼ | ½ mile |
| 0 | 250m | 500m | 750m | 1 kr |

A B C D E F

8

Pen-y-lan

The Grove

Gunley Wood

Kingswood Farm

Ackley Farm

Gunley Hall

Stockton

Motte & Bailey

Offa's Dyke Path

B4388

Forden C in W Prim Sch

Nantcribbau Farm

Lower Munlyn

Church Farm

01

Forden/ Ffodun

SY21

Rhyd-y-groes

7

LC

PH

Cwm Farm

Carnied

Keith Davis Farm

Great Hem Farm

Upper Hem Farm

Lower Hem Farm

Brynhyfryd

H

Quarry (dis)

00

[CAMLAD DR 1]
MAES-Y-FELIN 2]

Hem Moor

Pit (dis)

Shiregrove Bridge

Walcot Farm

Salt Bridge

6

B4386

99

Stalloe

Earthwork

Chirbury CE Prim Sch

PH

5

Rownal

Crankwell Farm

Winsbury Farm

HORSESHOE RD

LC

Hendomen

Quarry

B4388

Chirbury

Motte & Bailey

Hendomen Farm

B4386

98

B4385

Sewage Works

Dudston

Motte

Lower Lane

4

STATION RD

FORDEN ROAD

NEW ROAD

1 VERLON CL
2 ARTHURS GATE

County Boundary Bridge

Ffridd Wood

CHIRBURY ROAD

POOL RD

97

Ffridd Faldwyn (fort)

Castle

Great Moat Farm

Moat

Timberth

The Old Bell Mus

P

Upper Pool

SY15

Sidnal Farm

3

Montgomery

TH
PH

BISHOPS CASTLE STREET

PRINCESS ST

Lymore Park

Timberth Wood

Broad Street Farm

P

Lower Pool

96

Hill Top Farm

Boardyhall Wood

Whitley Wood

Rockley Wood

Caeprior

War Memorial

2

Llwynobin

New Covert

Motte

Offa's Dyke Path

Gwarthlow

Rhiston

95

Pant-y-maen Wood

Rockley Farm

Rockley

Coed Farm

1

Upper Pantre

Weston Madoc

Pen-y-bryn Hall

Church Stoke

Little Brompton Farm

B4385

A489

94

21 A 22 B 23 C 24 D 25 E 26 F

B3
1 GAOL RD
2 CHIRBURY GATE
3 SCHOOL BANK
4 ARTHUR ST
5 LYMORE VIEW
6 LIONS BANK
7 TAN Y MUR
8 CHURCH BANK
9 BROAD ST
10 KERRY ST
11 BACK LA
12 MALDWYN WY
13 CORNDON DR
14 WELL ST
15 KERRY RD

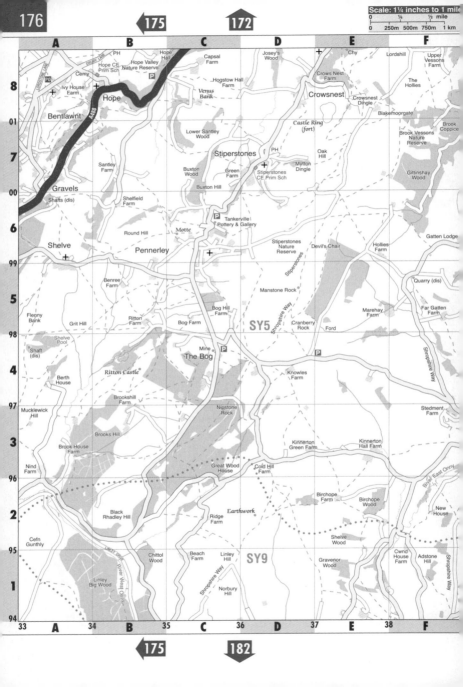

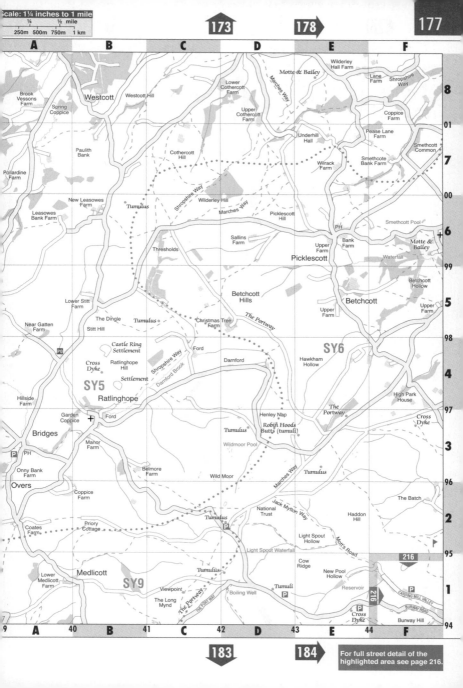

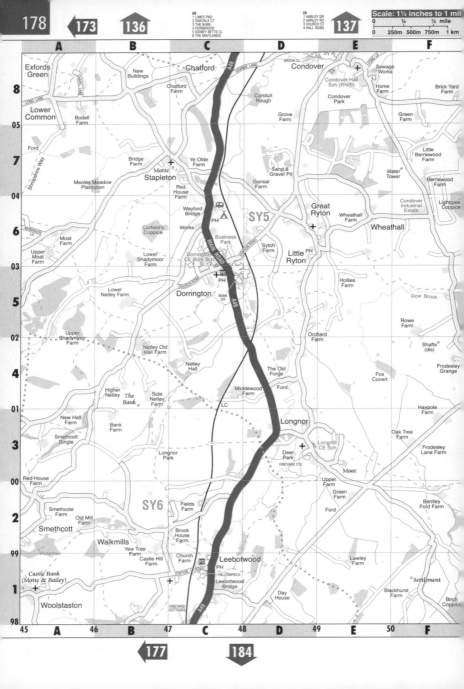

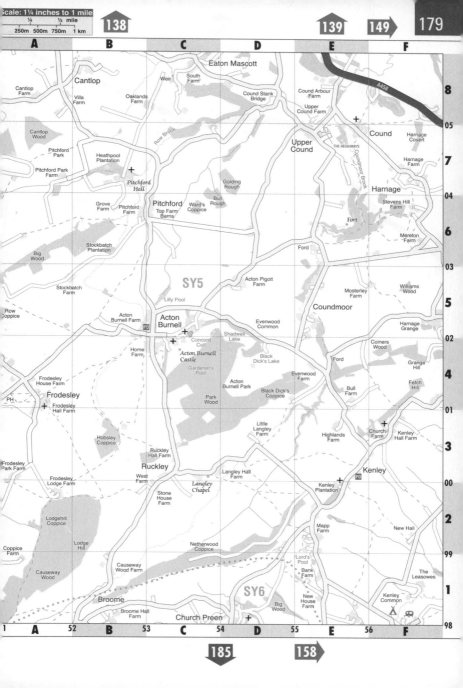

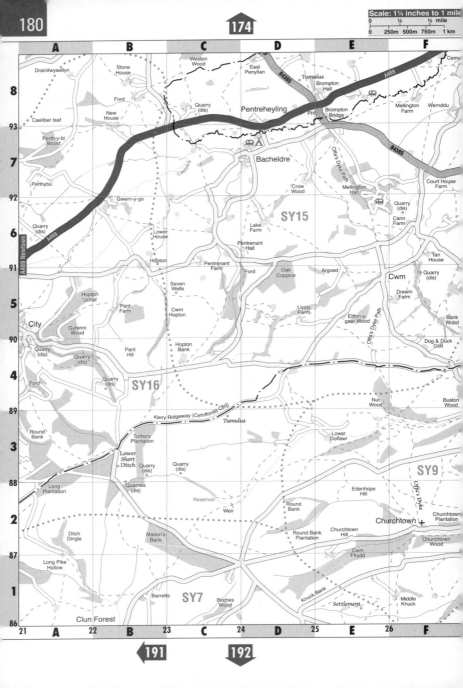

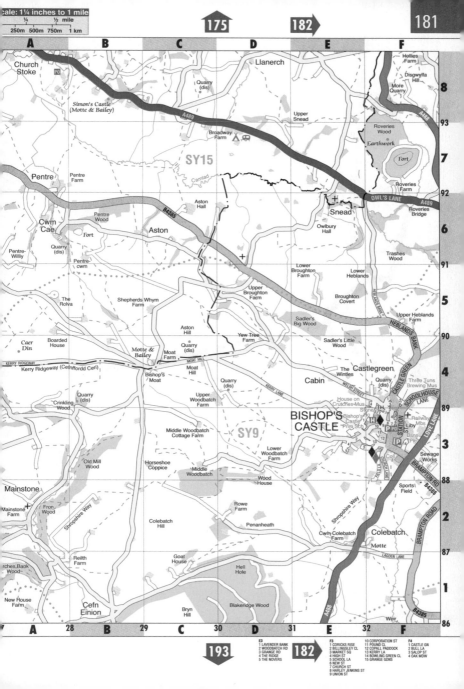

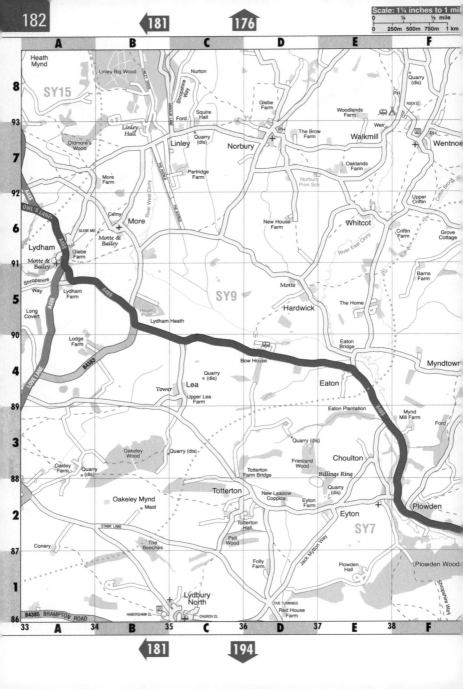

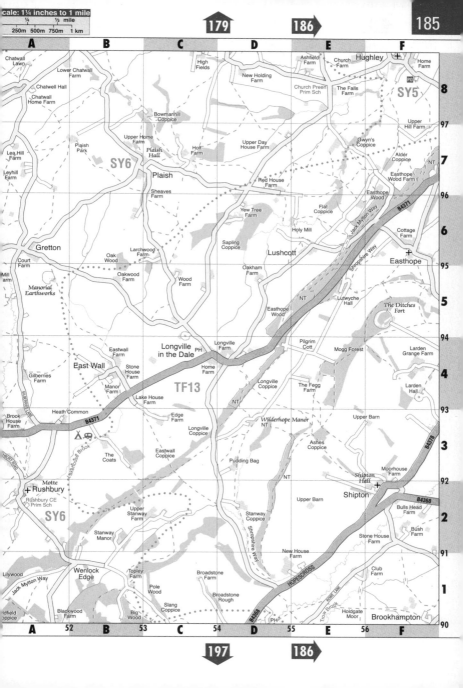

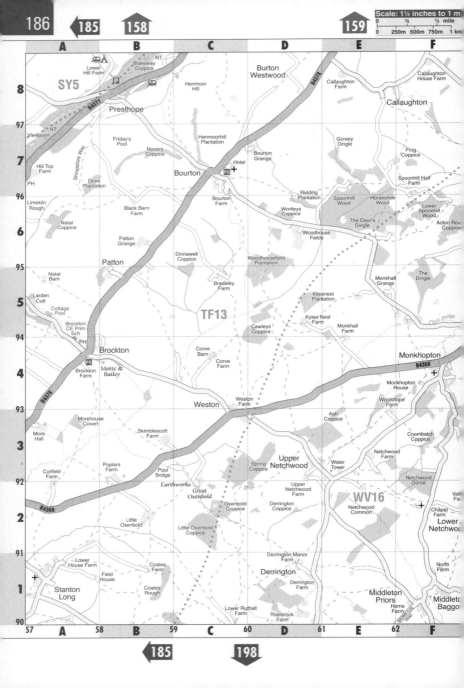

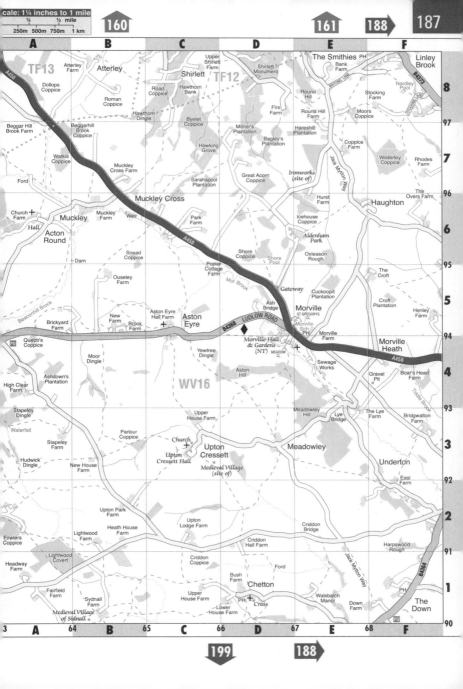

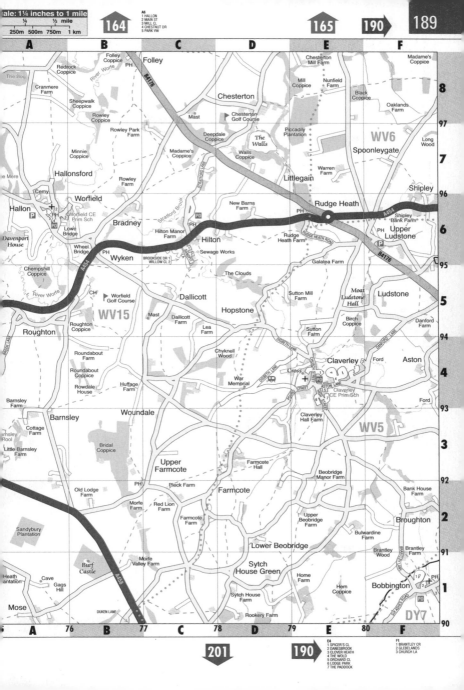

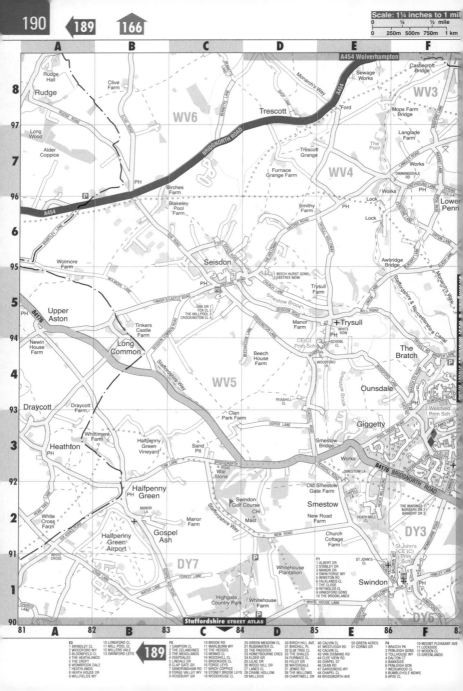

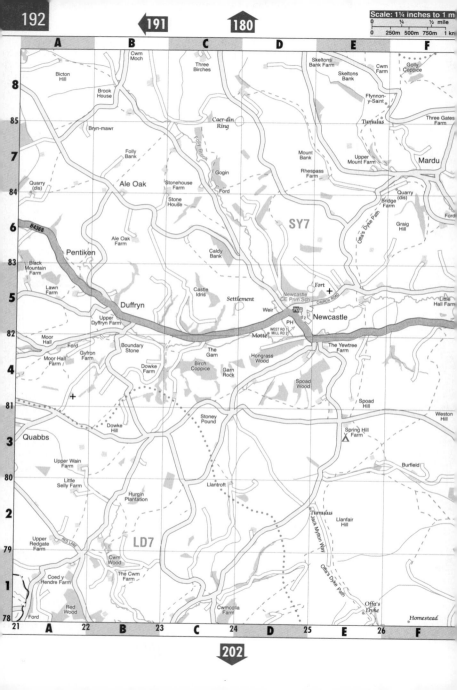

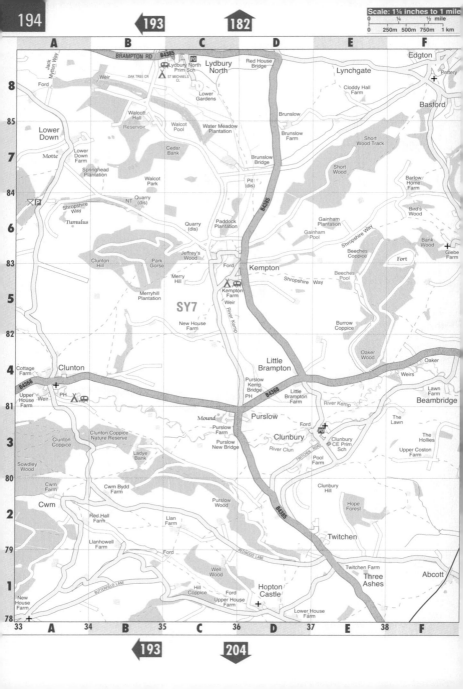

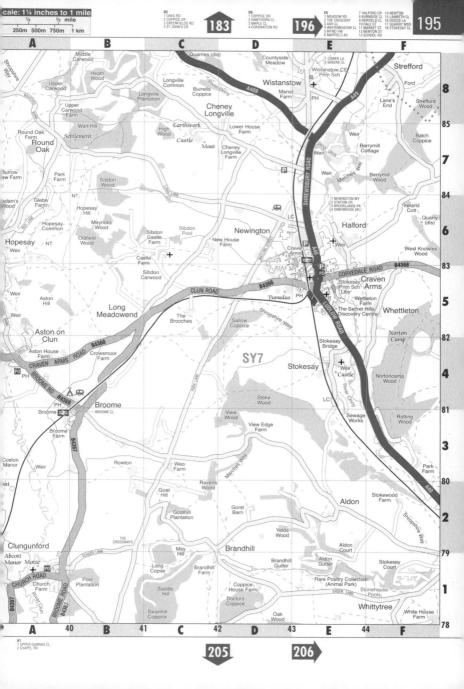

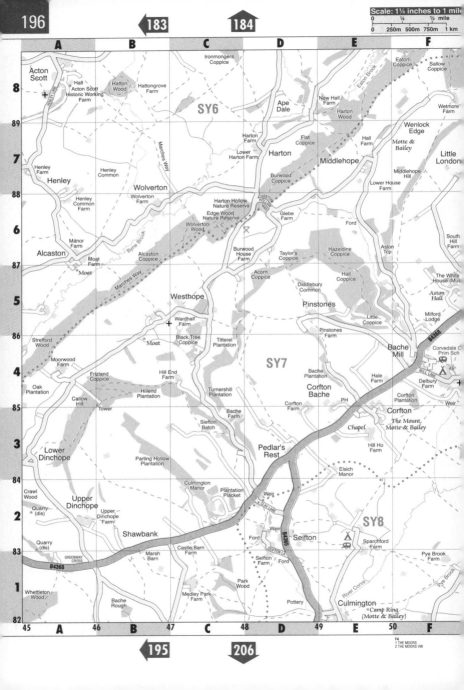

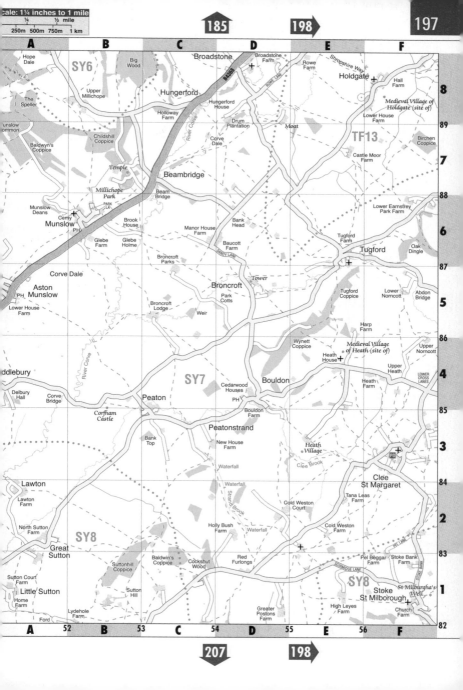

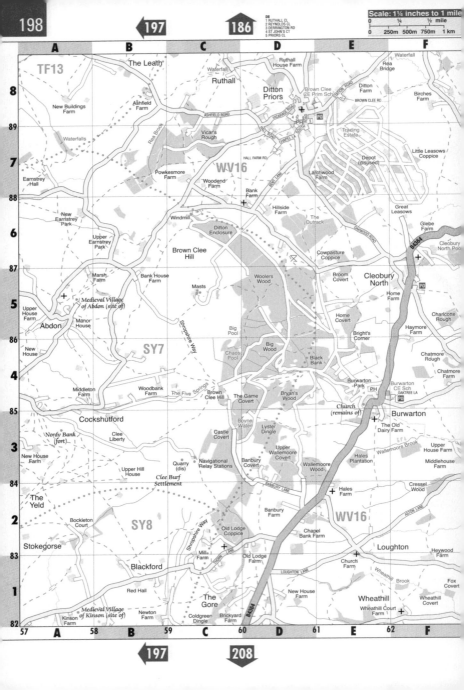

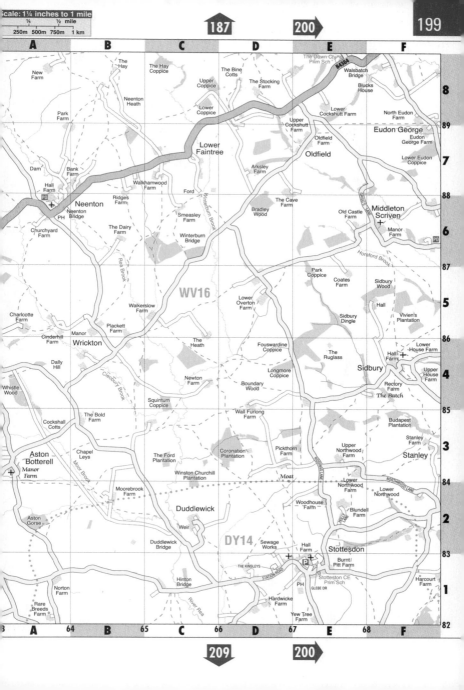

Scale: 1¼ inches to 1 mile

¼   ½ mile

250m 500m 750m 1 km

WV5

Corner Wood

Seggy Pool

Wall Pool

Quatt Bridge

The Dower House Sch

Quatt

Quatt Farm

Wallrea Coppice

Long Covert

Works

Hampton Loade

Burntcroft Coppice

Butter Cross

Lake House

Waterfall

New Barns Farm

Turleygreen

Alveley Industrial Estate

Alveley Prim Sch

Severn Valley Country Park

Visitor Centre

Little London Coppice

Stanley

Butts Farm

May House Farm

Hextons Farm

Ear Things

Wooton

Ford

PH

Bine Farm

Broad Lanes Farm

Wooton Dingle

Ridnehill Wood

Birchen Coppice

Kings Nordley Farm

Coton Farm

Coton Hall

Green House

Allum Bridge

PH

Birdsgreen

PH

Astley Farm

WV15

Filletts

Perryhouse Dingle

Bowhills Farm

Meat

High House Farm

Ladypitt Farm

Fenn Green

Lowe Farm

Pool House Farm

PH

Rookery Farm

Works

Broad Oak Wood

Broad Lanes

Tuckhill

Tuckhill Farm

The Lodge Farm

Keeper's Covert

Lindridge Farm

Lanegreen Farm

Astley

Astley

Beauty Bank Farm

Bowhills Dingle

Square Coppice

Cross Farm

Hartsgreen Farm

Lower House Farm

Romsley

Tudor House

Brittle's Farm

Gatacre Park Farm

Broad Oak

Gatacre Park

Six Ashes

New Plantation

Crump Hillocks Farm

Bradbury's Farm

Chidleys Farm

Moat

Leybrook Coppice

Cains Coppice

No Man's Green

Hartsgreen

Heath House Farm

Arley Wood

Reservoir

Alder Farm

Bobbington Hall

College Farm

Hay Farm

Grove Farm

Four Ashes

White Well

Coxgreen

DY7

The Hollies

Top Gorse

Compton Park Farm

Hightrees Farm

Starr's Green Farm

DY11

Coldridge Wood

DY12

Staffordshire STREET ATLAS

A458 Stourbridge

8

89

7

88

6

87

5

86

4

85

3

84

2

83

1

82

B3
1 MAPLE CRES
2 LIME CL
3 CEDAR CL
4 HONEYBOURNE RD
5 THE LEA
6 ROMSLEY VW
7 ORCHARD HOLMES
8 HAZELGROVE
9 MALLARDS CL
10 GREEN LEYS CRES
11 ARDEN WY
12 MEADOWBROOK CL
13 CHURCH RD
14 WHITTAL CL
15 CHAPEL RD
16 SEABRIGHT WY
17 GOLDEN ACRES

A   76   B   77   C   78   D   79   E   80   F

192

Scale: 1¼ inches to 1 mil

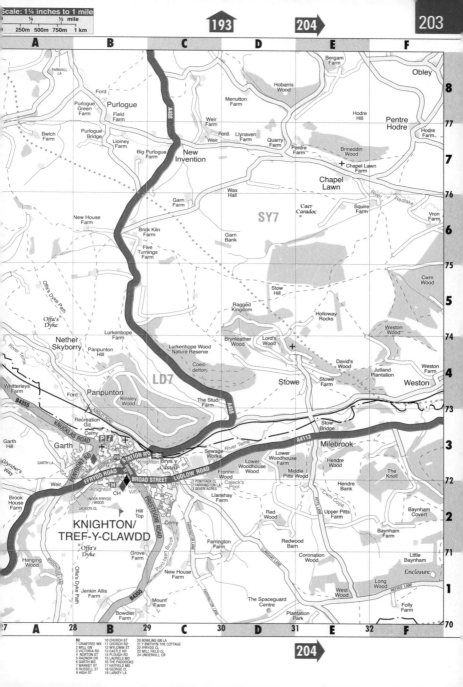

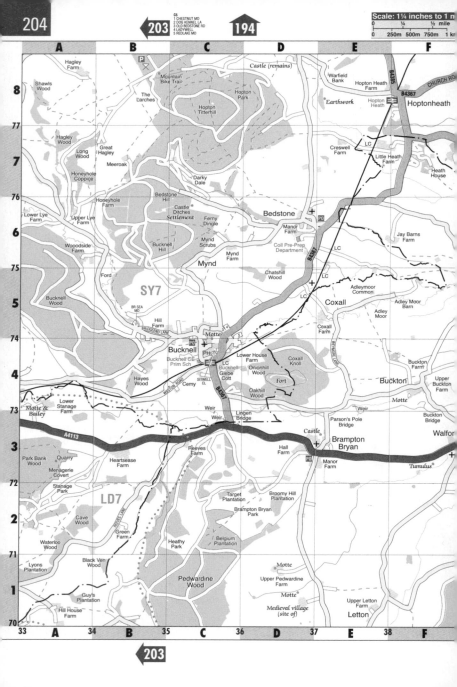

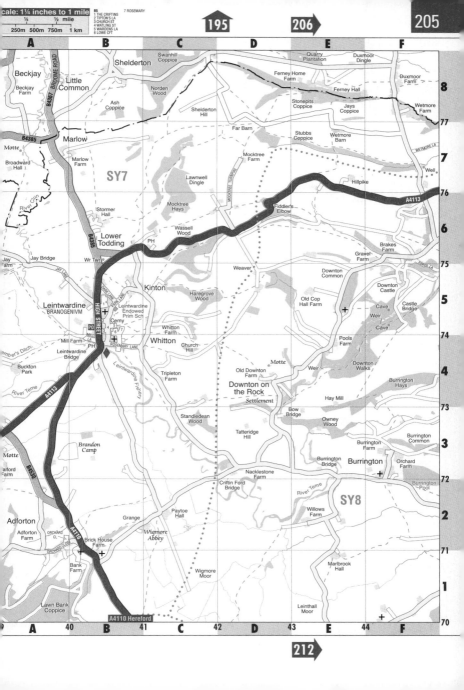

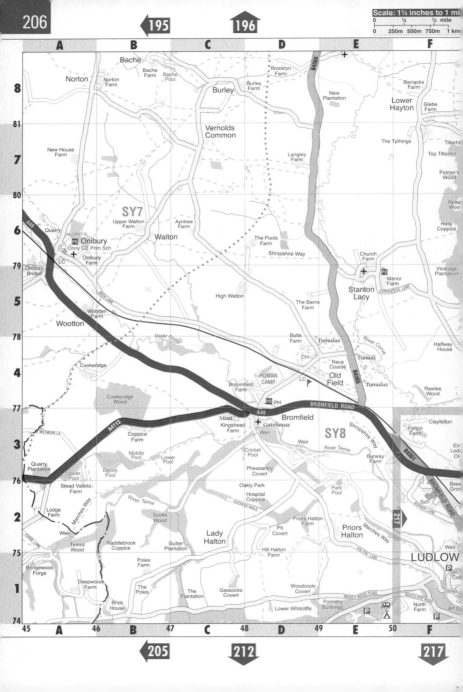

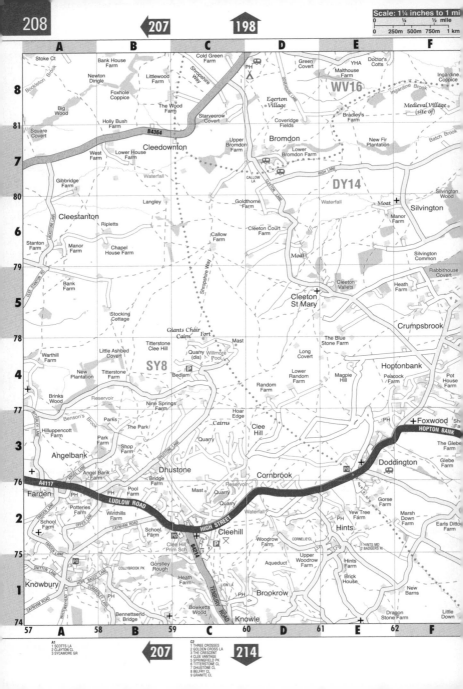

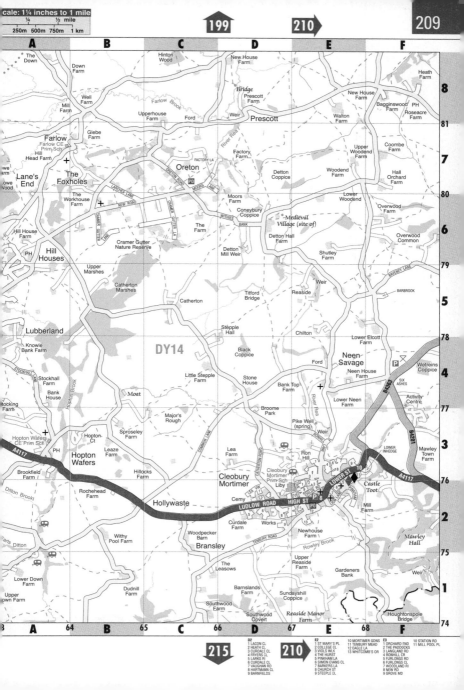

Scale: 1¼ inches to 1 mile

¼   ½ mile
250m 500m 750m 1 km

A B C D E F

For full street detail of Bewdley see Philip's
STREET ATLAS of Worcestershire

A442 Kidderminster
Worcestershire STREET ATLAS
A456 Kidderminster
HABBERLEY ROAD

C2
1 RUSSETT WY
2 LAXTON DR
3 LAMBOURNE DR
4 NEWTON CL
5 DERWENT DR
6 MERTON CL
7 ELTON RD
8 LLESMERE DR
9 BRAMLEY WY
10 CONISTON WY
11 YEW TREE CL
12 MUSKOKA
13 THE LAKES RD
14 YORK RD
15 TUDOR RD
16 WATERLOO RD
17 ELTON RD
18 GROSVENOR WD
19 WHITE HEART CL
20 FORT-MAHON PL
21 OAKWOOD RD
22 FOREST CL
23 HALES PK
24 IRONSIDE CL
25 CHERRY CL
26 SEVERN WY

D2
1 WOODTHORPE DR
2 LANCASTER RD
3 COBHAM CRES
4 CHURCH VW
5 GREENACRES LA
6 SABRINA DR
7 NURSERY RD
8 RIVERWAY DR
9 DOG LA

12 SEVERN SIDE N
13 SEVERN SIDE S
14 PRITCHARD CT
15 GARDNERS MDW
16 PARK CL
17 ORCHARD RD
18 TELFORD DR
19 CLARENCE WY

20 GLOUCESTER WY
21 MARCH GR
22 MORTIMER GR

C1
1 PARK DINGLE
2 VALLEY VW
3 HAWTHORNS CRES
4 PINETREE RD
5 BRANCHES CL
6 BIRCH TREE RD

D1
1 HIGHCLERE DR
2 HERNE S NES
3 SNUFF MILL WKT

E3
1 CORDLE MARSH RD
2 RIDDINGS CL
3 WASSELL DR
4 HOARSTONE CD
5 BELVEDERE CRES
6 DUNMORE RD
7 LINGFIELD RD
8 WYNN CL
9 MEADOW WY
10 CAMPION WY

E2
1 DAMSON WY
2 SPRINGHILL RD
3 AEL SAINTS AVE
4 DELAMERE RD
5 HILLTOP WD
6 THREE OAKS DR
7 IVY RD
8 LODGE CL
9 SPENCER AVE
10 MAYPOLE CL
11 SEVERN CL
12 STATION RD
12 WESTBOURNE ST
13 ACACIA AVE
14 BROOK VALE
15 SANDBOURNE DR

LINCOLN CRES 1
SEVERY CL 2
SALISBURRORD 3
SELBA DR 4

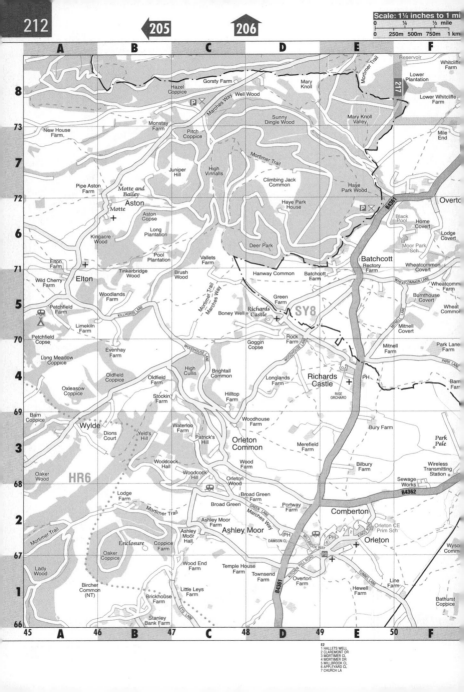

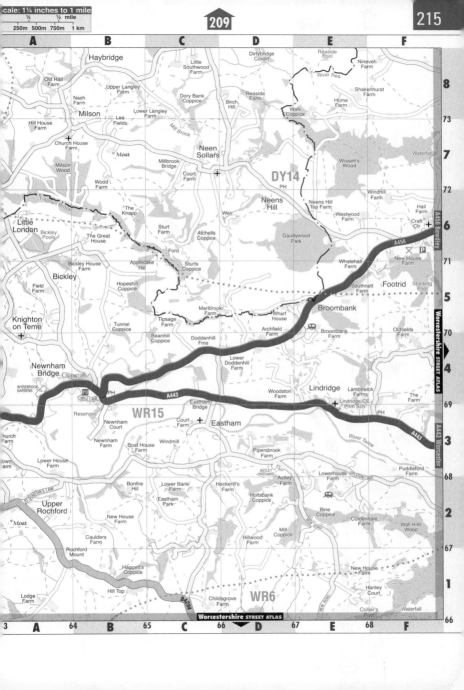

A B C D E F

8

Felton Farm
Clayfelton

Fishmore Farm

Wigley Farm

7

B4361 BROMFIELD ROAD
A49

River Corve

Elm Lodge
CH

Elm Farm

Hilltop Sch

Burway Farm

KEEPSIDE CL

CASTLEFORD RD

South Shropshire Leisure Centre

Ludlow CE Sch

76

SY8

Dun Cow Farm

ROCKS GREEN

A4117

Rock Farm

6

Rockgreen

Burway Farm

Shropshire Way

Sports Ground

C6
1 SUMMERFIELDS
2 MAYFIELDS
3 STANTON DR
4 BRINGEWOOD CL
5 FISHMORE CL
6 WHITBATCH CL

D6
1 BEECH CL
2 MAPLE CL
3 HOPTON CL
4 LIME CL
5 SYCAMORE CL
6 HENLEY ORCHARDS

7 POTTER CL
8 HAYTON VW
9 HAMLET RD
10 HAMLET CL

E5
1 CLEE GD
2 CLEE VW CL
3 WHEELER RD
4 THE PADDOCKS
5 DAHN CL
6 THE WILDINGS

Rock Farm

BITTERLEY CL

5

River Teme

C5
1 ST MARY'S LA
2 ST MARY'S MS
3 QUARRY GD
4 PORTCULLIS CL

NEW ROAD

Ludlow Com Office & Registry Office

Ludlow Inf Sch

Holy Well

Ludlow Jun Sch

Ludlow Inf Sch

Sports Gd

Business Park

BAKER CL

75

Marches Way

Burway Bridge
Weir

LUDLOW +

LANGFORD

Marches Way
MIDDLE WOOD ROAD

HALTON LANE

The Linney Riverside Park

Superstore CAB

Lib

Feathers Art Gall

Castle
Ludlow Coll
Ludlow Mus
Assembly Rooms

City Cy

BRAND

DARK LANE

HONEY MDW

KENNET BANK

CHARLTON

4

North Farm

Tree Tops
Ludlow Coll
Weir

Minter Kemp Art Gallery

Ludford Cemetery

Barns Wood

Temeside Estate

Weir

Temeside Mills

Green Acres

FOLDGATE VW

SHEET RD

3

D3
1 KEYSTONE GD
2 CHURCHILL CL
3 STEVENTON GD
4 JOCKEY FIELD
5 TEME AV
6 TEMESIDE GD
7 STEVENTON CR

Temeside Mills

E3
1 ASH CL
2 MARY ELIZABETH RD
3 OVERTON VW
4 LUDFORD VW

Foldgate Farm

74

Whitcliffe Farm

Ludford

The Moss House

Sheet Pond

2

Lower Plantation

OVERTON ROAD
B4361

Teme Bridge

Lower Barn Farm

Lower Whitcliffe Farm

Sewage Works

Steventon

STEVENTON ROAD

A49

1

73

0 A 51 B C D 52 E F

C3
1 LOWER RAVEN LA
2 SILK MILL LA
3 ST JOHN'S RD
4 LOWER BROAD ST

C4
1 UPPER LINNEY
2 UPPER GALDEFORD
3 ST STEPHEN'S CL
4 TOWER ST
5 KING ST
6 COLLEGE ST
7 HARP LA
8 CHURCH ST
9 CASTLE SQ

10 MARKET ST
11 PEPPER LA
12 FRIARS GD
13 BROAD ST
14 RAVEN LA
15 CASTLE ST
16 HIGH ST

D3
1 ST JULIAN'S AV
2 MORTIMER PL
3 ROCK LA
4 SPRINGFIELD CL
5 CHANDLERS CL

E4
1 BALLARD CL
2 VASHON CL
3 RIDDINGS MD
4 SANDFORD RD
5 MILTON RD
6 JAMES CL
7 KEYSE CL
8 HOUSMAN CL
9 NORMANDIE CL

10 SHEARMAN RD
11 BOWDLER CL
12 SHROPSHIRE WY
13 BLASHFIELD RD
14 CHESTNUT GR
15 SIDNEY RD

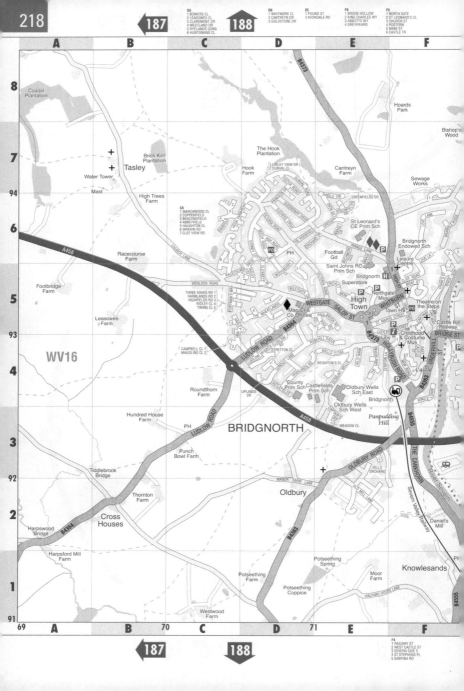

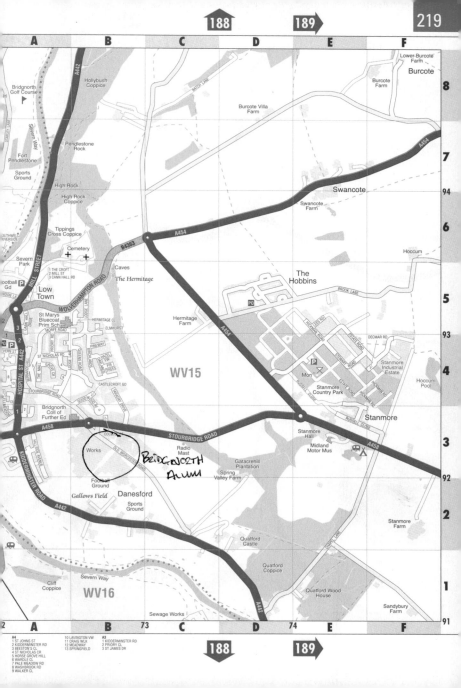

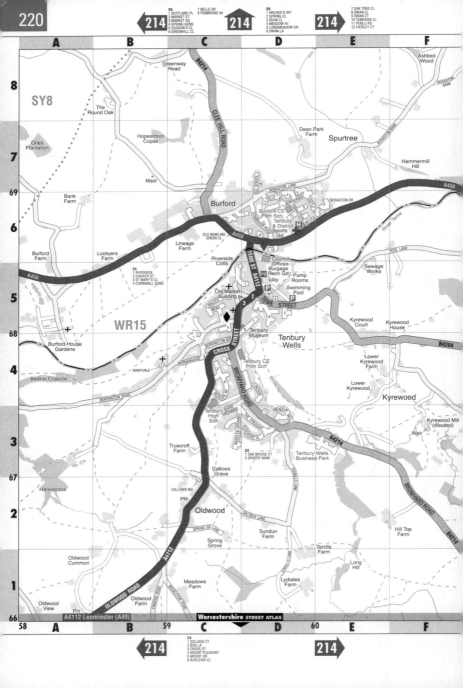

D5
1 SCOTLAND PL
2 MARKET ST
3 MARKET SQ
4 SPRING GDNS
5 GODSON'S CL
6 GREENHILL CL

D6
1 ARCHER'S WY
2 SPRING CL
3 DEAN CL
4 MEADOW RI
5 LONGMEADOW DR
6 SWAN LA

7 OAK TREE CL
8 SWAN CL
9 SWAN CT
10 TEMESIDE CL
11 PENLU RD
12 IVERLEY CT

SY8

The Round Oak

Greenway Head

Orles Plantation

Hopesmoor Copse

Mast

Dean Park Farm

Spurtree

Hammermill Hill

Bank Farm

Burford

Boraston Dr

Burford CE Prim Sch

Tenbury & District Sports Gd

River Teme

Burford Farm

Lockyers Farm

Lineage Farm

OLD BOWLING GREEN CL

Riverside Cotts

Sewage Works

RIGE LANE

C5
1 RIVERSIDE
2 CHURCH ST
3 ST MARY'S CL
4 CORNWALL GDNS

WR15

Old Market Building

Council Offices

Burgage Recn Gd

Liby

Pump Rooms

Swimming Pool

Kyrewood Court

Kyrewood House

B4204

Burford House Gardens

Tenbury Museum

Tenbury Wells

Lower Kyrewood Farm

Bednal Coppice

MARYVALE

Tenbury CE Prim Sch

CROSS STREET

Lower Kyrewood

Kyrewood

BERRINGTON ROAD

Tenbury High Sch

Truecroft Farm

Gallows Grave

Tenbury Wells Business Park

B4214

Kyrewood Mill (disused)

Weir

D3
1 OAK BRIDGE CT
2 GRASSY BANK

Haresbrook

CALLOWS MD

PH

Oldwood

CALTROX LANE

Sundun Farm

Terrills Farm

Hill Top Farm

Long Hill

BROADYARD ROAD

B4214

Oldwood Common

SPRING GR LANE

Spring Grove

Meadows Farm

Lydiates Farm

Oldwood View

PH

Oldwood Farm

A4112

C4
1 COLLEGE CT
2 BOG LA
3 CROSS ST
4 MOUNT PLEASANT
5 MOUNT DR
6 BURLEIGH CL

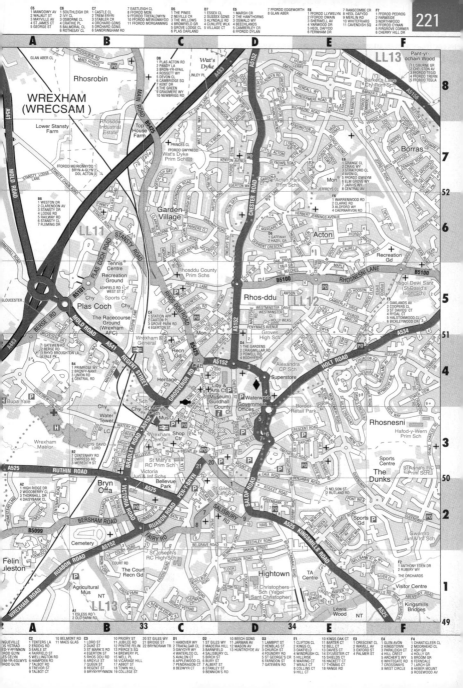

Index

Church Rd **6** Beckenham BR2..........**53** C6

Place name	Location number	Locality, town or village	Postcode district	Page and grid square
May be abbreviated on the map	Present when a number indicates the place's position in a crowded area of mapping	Shown when more than one place has the same name	District for the indexed place	Page number and grid reference for the standard mapping

Public and commercial buildings are highlighted in magenta. Places of interest are highlighted in blue with a star ★

Abbreviations used in the index

Acad	**Academy**	Comm	**Common**	Gd	**Ground**	L	**Leisure**	Prom	**Promenade**
App	**Approach**	Cott	**Cottage**	Gdn	**Garden**	La	**Lane**	Rd	**Road**
Arc	**Arcade**	Cres	**Crescent**	Gn	**Green**	Liby	**Library**	Recn	**Recreation**
Ave	**Avenue**	Cswy	**Causeway**	Gr	**Grove**	Mdw	**Meadow**	Ret	**Retail**
Bglw	**Bungalow**	Ct	**Court**	H	**Hall**	Meml	**Memorial**	Sh	**Shopping**
Bldg	**Building**	Ctr	**Centre**	Ho	**House**	Mkt	**Market**	Sq	**Square**
Bsns, Bus	**Business**	Ctry	**Country**	Hospl	**Hospital**	Mus	**Museum**	St	**Street**
Bvd	**Boulevard**	Cty	**County**	HQ	**Headquarters**	Orch	**Orchard**	Sta	**Station**
Cath	**Cathedral**	Dr	**Drive**	Hts	**Heights**	Pal	**Palace**	Terr	**Terrace**
Cir	**Circus**	Dro	**Drove**	Ind	**Industrial**	Par	**Parade**	TH	**Town Hall**
Cl	**Close**	Ed	**Education**	Inst	**Institute**	Pas	**Passage**	Univ	**University**
Cnr	**Corner**	Emb	**Embankment**	Int	**International**	Pk	**Park**	Wk, Wlk	**Walk**
Coll	**College**	Est	**Estate**	Intc	**Interchange**	Pl	**Place**	Wr	**Water**
Com	**Community**	Ex	**Exhibition**	Junc	**Junction**	Prec	**Precinct**	Yd	**Yard**

Index of localities, towns and villages

A

Abcott 194 F1
Abdon 198 A5
Ackleton 164 D2
Acton Lydbury North ...193 E7
Acton Wrexham 221 E6
Acton Burnell 179 C5
Acton Reynald 84 F3
Acton Round 187 A6
Acton Scott 196 A8
Adderley 19 A4
Adeney 108 C1
Adforton 205 A2
Admaston 130 B6
Albrighton 168 D5
Albrighton Donington ..157 A6
Albrighton Pimhill 101 D1
Alcaston 196 A6
Alderton 83 C4
Aldon 195 E2
Ale Oak 192 B7
Alkington 14 E3
Allscott 188 E7
Allscott 129 C6
All Stretton 184 B6
Almington 37 C2
Alport 175 A1
Alveley 201 A3
Anchor 191 C7
Angelbank 208 A3
Annscroft 136 A4
Aqueduct 152 F8
Argoed Clun 193 C7
Arleston 131 B1
Arowry 12 C3
Arscott 173 E6
Ashbrook 216 B6
Ashfield 77 C8
Ashfields 72 C2
Ashford Bowdler 213 A5
Ashford Carbonell 213 B5
Ashley Moor 212 C2
Ash Magna 16 A4
Ash Parva 16 B3
Asterley 172 E6

Asterton 183 A6
Astley 102 E2
Astley Abbotts 188 C7
Aston Churchstoke 181 C6
Aston Claverley 189 F4
Aston Pipe Aston 212 B6
Aston Wem Rural 66 D6
Aston Bank 214 F5
Aston Botterell 199 A3
Aston Eyre 187 C5
Aston Munslow 197 A5
Aston on Clun 195 A5
Aston Pigott 172 A4
Aston Rogers 172 A5
Aston Sq 59 E5
Atcham 139 A7
Atterley 187 B8
Attingham 139 B8

B

Babbinswood 42 A1
Bache 206 B8
Bacheldre 180 D7
Bache Mill 196 F4
Badger 164 C4
Bagley 62 C3
Bagley Marsh 62 B4
Ball 59 A2
Balmer 28 E2
Balmer Heath 28 F2
Barkers Green 66 C5
Bark Hill 211 D2
Barnsley 189 A3
Barrow 160 F4
Baschurch 81 A1
Basford 194 F8
Batchcott 212 E6
Battlefield 114 A5
Bayston Hill 137 A7
Beach Hay 210 C1
Beambridge Abdon 197 C7
Beambridge Hopesay 194 F4
Bearstone 21 A4
Beckbury 164 D8
Beckjay 205 A8
Bedstone 204 D6

Beguildy 191 E1
Belle Vue 125 C4
Bell o' th' Hill 1 C7
Benthall 152 B1
Bentlawnt 176 A8
Berrington 138 D2
Berrington Green 214 A1
Berwick Wharf 127 A3
Besford 85 C7
Betchcott 177 E5
Bettisfield 29 C3
Betton 37 A6
Betton Strange 137 F7
Bettws-y-crwyn 191 F3
Bewdley 211 D1
Bickley 215 A5
Bicton 169 F6
Bicton Clun 193 C5
Bicton Heath 124 A7
Billingsley 200 C3
Bilmarsh 83 C7
Bings Heath 103 A1
Birdsgreen 201 C4
Birtley 184 C1
Bishop's Castle 181 E3
Bishops Wood 148 F8
Bitterley 207 F4
Blackford 198 B1
Blackmore 171 E8
Blackoe 14 B3
Black Park Chirk 7 A5
Black Park Whitchurch Urban 2 E2
Bletchley 51 E8
Blists Hill 153 B3
Bloreheath 37 E3
Bluebell 128 F1
Blymhill 131 F3
Bobbington 159 F1
Bolas Heath 107 B8
Bomere Heath 100 F4
Boningale 158 C7
Booleybank 86 A8
Boraston 214 E4
Boraston Dale 214 D5
Borras 221 F7
Bouldon 197 D4
Bourton 186 C7
Bowbrook 124 B5

Bowling Green 87 F8
Bradley Green 1 A8
Bradney 189 B6
Brampton Bryan 204 E3
Brandhill 195 D2
Brandwood 64 E1
Bransley 209 C2
Bratton 130 A8
Breaden Heath 28 E6
Bridgemere 4 D8
Bridges 177 A3
Bridgnorth 218 D3
Brimfield 213 B2
Brineton 135 F8
Broad Lanes 201 D7
Broadoak 113 D7
Broad Oak 201 D7
Broadstone 197 C8
Brockton Church Aston .121 B6
Brockton Lydbury North .193 F8
Brockton Stanton Long .186 B4
Brockton Sutton Maddock .153 F4
Brockton Worthen with Shelve ..171 E3
Brogyntyn 40 A2
Bromdon 208 D7
Bromfield 206 D3
Bromley Hordley 62 C2
Bromley Worfield 188 E6
Bromlow 175 F8
Brompton 139 B5
Bromstead Common 111 E1
Bromstead Heath 123 D6
Broncroft 197 D5
Bronington 13 A3
Bronygarth 22 E7
Brookhampton 185 E1
Brooklands 1 E1
Brookrow 208 D1
Brookside 144 C1
Broome 215 E5
Broome Cardington 179 B1
Broome Hopesay 195 B4
Broomfields 169 D8
Broseley 152 D1
Broughall 152 D1
Broughton 189 F2
Brownheath 64 C7

Brownhill 80 C1
Brownhills 36 D4
Brown Moss 4 A7
Brunant 171 B8
Bryn 193 C8
Bryn Mawr 93 C2
Bryn Offa 221 B2
Brynore 26 A4
Bryn Tanat 93 A7
Bryn-y-cochin 26 B4
Bryn-yr-Eos 6 D5
Bucknell 204 C4
Buckridge 210 D1
Buckton 204 F4
Buildwas 151 B6
Bulthy 167 D4
Burcote 219 F8
Burford 220 C6
Burley 206 C8
Burlton 64 B1
Burnhill Green 165 B6
Burrington 205 F3
Burton Westwood 186 D8
Burwarton 198 F3
Bushmoor 183 E2
Butlane Head 169 C4
Buttersbank 86 C2
Buttington 170 D7
Buttonbridge 210 E6
Buttonoak 210 F5
Bwlch-y-Plain 202 D6

C

Cabin 181 E4
Cadney Bank 29 C2
Calcott 169 F5
Callaughton 186 F8
Calverhall 34 A7
Cantlop 179 B8
Cardeston 169 A3
Cardington 184 F6
Castle Fields 125 C2
Castlegreen 181 F4
Catchems End 211 E3
Catstree 188 F7
Catteralslane 15 E6

Caynham	213	E8
Cefn	167	A1
Cefn-bychan	6	B8
Cefn Canol	38	D3
Cefn Einion	181	B1
Chadwell	123	A1
Chapel Lawn	203	E7
Charlton	128	E3
Chatford	178	C8
Chavel	169	D4
Checkley Green	4	F8
Chelmarsh	200	C6
Chelmick	216	F1
Chemistry	14	E7
Cheney Longville	195	D8
Cherrington	107	B4
Cherry Orchard	125	D6
Chesterton	189	D8
Cheswardine	72	F8
Cheswell	120	F6
Chetton	187	D1
Chetwynd Aston	122	A8
Childs Ercall	89	A7
Chipnall	55	A3
Chirbury	174	E5
Chirk Bank	23	E6
Chirk Green	6	E2
Chirk/Y Waun	6	D1
Chorley	200	A2
Choulton	194	D1
Church Aston	121	D8
Churchbank	193	C2
Church Preen	179	C1
Church Pulverbatch	173	E1
Church Stoke	194	F6
Church Stretton	216	D7
Churchtown	180	F2
Cilceywydd	170	C3
City	180	A5
Claverley	189	E4
Cleedownton	208	B7
Cleehill	208	C2
Cleestanton	208	A6
Clee St Margaret	197	F3
Cleeton St Mary	208	D5
Cleobury Mortimer	209	D3
Cleobury North	198	E5
Clive	84	B5
Cluddley	130	A1
Clun	193	D3
Clunbury	194	D3
Clungunford	195	A2
Clunton	194	A4
Coalbrookdale	152	C6
Coalmoor	143	A3
Coalport	153	B2
Cobscot	19	B3
Cockshutford	198	B3
Cockshutt	63	C7
Cockshutt Highley	200	E2
Coedway	168	A6
Coed y go	58	B4
Cold Hatton	105	E7
Cold Hatton Heath	105	F7
Colebatch	181	F2
Colemere	45	C6
Colemore Green	188	C8
Comberton	212	E2
Comley	184	D7
Condover	178	D8
Coppicegate	210	E7
Copthorne	115	A8
Coptiviney	27	F6
Coreley	214	E8
Corfton	196	F3
Corfton Bache	196	E4
Corra Common	17	C1
Coton	31	F1
Coton Hill	125	B8
Cotonwood	31	F5
Cotonwood	111	E6
Cotwall	117	B8
Cound	179	F7
Coundlane	149	A6
Coundmoor	179	E5
Coxall	204	E5
Coxbank	18	F8
Coxgreen	201	F5
Crackleybank	134	C2
Craig-llwyn	56	D4
Craignant	22	D3
Crateford	200	D7
Craven Arms	195	F5
Creamore Bank	48	A1
Cressage	149	F5
Cresgreen	167	F6
Crickheath	76	E2
Crickmery	71	C7
Criftins	235	E6
Crigion	167	C5
Croesau Bach	57	B4
Crosemere	63	D8
Cross	27	A6
Crossgreen	112	E5
Cross Green	129	D6
Cross Houses Berrington	138	F3
Cross Houses Bridgnorth	218	B2
Crosslanes	95	F2
Crowgreaves	163	F3
Crowsnest	176	E8
Cruckmeole	173	D8
Cruckton	169	E1
Crudgington	106	A1
Cuckoo's Corner	36	A8
Crumpsbrook	208	F5
Culmington	196	E1
Cumber's Bank	11	F3
Cwm Churchstoke	180	F5
Cwm Clunbury	194	A2
Cwm Cae	181	A6
Cwm Head	183	D3

D

Dallicott	189	C5
Danesford	219	B2
Darley	161	E3
Darliston	50	C8
Dawley	143	F4
Dawley Bank	143	D6
Daywall	40	E8
Derrington	186	D1
Deuxhill	200	A6
Dhustone	208	C3
Diddlebury	197	A4
Ditherington	113	F1
Ditton Priors	198	D8
Dobson's Bridge	30	D2
Doddington	208	F3
Doley	73	E8
Domgay	94	C3
Donington	156	F6
Donnington Lilleshall and Uppington	132	E7
Donnington Wroxeter and Uppington	132	E7
Donnington Wood	132	E5
Dorrington Condover	178	C5
Dorrington Woore	21	C7
Doseley	143	D2
Dothill	130	D7
Dovaston	96	D7
Dowles	211	C3
Downton on the Rock	205	D4
Draycott	190	A4
Dryton	140	C1
Duddlewick	199	C2
Dudleston	8	D1
Dudleston Heath (Criftins)	26	B6
Duffryn	192	B5
Dunnsheath	112	F8

E

Eardington	188	D1
Eardiston	75	C6
Eastham	215	D3
Easthope	185	E6
East Wall	185	B4
Eaton Eaton-under-Heywood	184	E1
Eaton Lydbury North	182	E4
Eaton Constantine	140	F1
Eaton Mascott	179	D8
Eaton upon Tern	88	F3
Ebreywood	115	A8
Edge	173	A7
Edgebolton	104	A8
Edgeley	15	D5
Edgerley	96	C3
Edgmond	109	A3
Edgmond Marsh	108	F6
Edgton	194	F8
Edstaston	48	B5
Eglwys Cross	12	E6
Elbridge	79	A5
Ellerdine	105	B6
Ellerdine Heath	87	D1
Ellerton	90	F8
Ellesmere	27	A2
Elson	26	E4
Elton	212	A5
Emstrey	126	D1
Enchmarsh	184	F7
English Frankton	64	A8
Ensdon	169	C7
Erbistock	8	F8
Etsell	172	C3
Eudon Burnell	200	A8
Eudon George	199	F7
Exfords Green	178	A8
Eyton Alberbury with Cardeston	168	E4
Eyton Baschurch	84	B2
Eyton Lydbury North	182	E2
Eyton on Severn	140	A1
Eyton upon the Weald Moors	118	E2

F

Farden	208	A2
Far Forest	210	D1
Farley Much Wenlock	151	A1
Farley Pontesbury	172	F6
Farlow	209	A7
Farmcote	189	D2
Fauls	50	E6
Felhampton	183	F2
Felindre	191	B3
Felin Newydd	56	C7
Felin Puleston	221	A1
Felton Butler	169	A8
Fenn Green	201	C2
Fenn's Bank	13	F3
Fingerpost	210	E1
Fitz	169	F8
Folley	189	C8
Footrid	215	F5
Ford	169	C4
Forden/Ffodun	174	B7
Forton Montford	169	D7
Forton Heath	169	E8
Four Ashes	201	F6
Four Crosses	94	A1
Foxwood	208	F3
Frankwell	125	A7
Frochas	167	C1
Frodesley	179	A4
Fron Forden with Leighton and Trelystan	170	C2
Fron Weston Rhyn	22	F4
Froncysyllte	6	A6
Fron-goch	93	E8
Fron Isaf	6	A5

G

Gadlas	26	C7
Garden Village	221	C6
Garmston	141	A1
Garth	203	A3
Giggetty	190	E3
Glan-yr-afon	74	D5
Glazeley	200	B7
Glynmorlas	7	D1
Gobowen	41	B8
Goldstone	72	D5
Good's Green	201	D8
Gosford	213	C3
Gospel Ash	190	B2
Grafton	99	C2
Gravelhill	125	A8
Gravel Hole	26	A5
Gravels	176	A7
Great Bolas	106	D7
Great Chatwell	123	D1
Great Lyth	136	B3
Great Ness	98	B3
Great Ryton	178	E6
Great Sutton	197	A2
Great Wytheford	104	A3
Greenhill Bank	26	C5
Greete	214	A5
Gretton	185	A6
Grimpo	61	A2
Grindle	155	A2
Grindley Brook	1	C3
Grinshill	84	C3
Groespluan	170	A8
Gronwen	58	B1
Gwernyfed	191	C2
Gwern y brenin	58	F1

H

Habberley	173	A2
Hadley	131	D5
Hadley Castle	131	D7
Hadley Park	131	C8
Hadnall	102	C4
Hales	54	F8
Halesfield	153	E6
Hales Park	211	C2
Halford	195	E6
Halfpenny Green	190	B2
Halfway House	168	B2
Hall Green	13	D8
Hallon	189	A6
Hallonsford	189	B7
Halton	7	A4
Hamperley	183	D4
Hampton	200	E5
Hampton Bank	29	A2
Hampton Beech	171	D4
Hampton Loade	201	A5
Hampton Wood	28	B8
Handless	183	A5
Hanmer	12	B4
Hanwood	173	F8
Hanwood Bank	169	F1
Hardwick	182	D5
Harebutt Bank	106	D5
Harlescott	113	E4
Harley	158	E8
Harmer Hill	83	B1
Harnage	179	F7
Hartlebury	188	F8
Harton	196	D7
Hartsgreen	201	E2
Haston	101	F7
Hatton	184	B1
Haughton Llandysilio	95	B1
Haughton Morville	187	B8
Haughton Shifnal	145	E6
Haughton Upton Magna	115	C5
Haughton West Felton	61	D2
Hawgreen	87	E7
Hawkswood	200	A3
Haybridge Hadley	131	B4
Haybridge Milson	215	B8
Haygate	130	B2
Hayton's Bent	207	F6
Hazler	216	E5
Heathcote	70	F5
Heath Hill	122	D1
Heath Lanes	105	D7
Heathton	190	A3
Hemford	175	F7
Hendomen	174	A5
Hengoed	40	E7
Henley Acton Scott	196	A7
Henley Ludford	207	C3
Henlle	41	F7
Heyop	202	D5
Higher Ercall	116	F8
Higher Ridge	42	F8
High Green	200	B2
High Hatton	87	C6
High Heath	71	E3
Highley	200	F2
Hightown	221	D1
High Town	218	E5
Hillfields House	131	F8
Hill Houses	209	A6
Hillwicket	89	F6
Hilton	189	C6
Hindford	42	A6
Hine Heath	86	D8
Hinstock	72	A1
Hinton	173	C6
Hints	208	E2
Hobarris	193	E1
Hodnet	69	D6
Hodnethanks	69	E4
Holbeache	211	D5
Holdgate	197	E8
Hollinswood	144	C6
Hollinwood	31	C5
Hollyhurst	184	C8
Hollywaste	209	C2
Homer	159	D7
Honnington	121	A3
Hook-a-Gate	136	C1
Hope Trewern	170	E6
Hope Worthen with Shelve	176	B8
Hope Bowdler	184	C3
Hopesay	195	A6
Hopstone	73	B5
Hopstone	189	D5
Hopton Great Ness	97	F5
Hopton Hodnet	68	E2
Hoptonbank	208	F4
Hopton Cangeford	207	D7
Hopton Castle	194	D1
Hoptongate	207	B7
Hoptonheath	204	F8
Hopton Wafers	208	E5
Horsehay	143	D2
Horseman's Green	11	F7
Horton Hadley	131	C3
Horton Wem Rural	47	C1
Hortonlane	169	F2
Hortonwood	131	F7
Howle	90	A3
Hughley	158	F1
Hungerford	197	C8
Hungryhatton	71	C2
Huntington	142	E4
Hurdley	175	C1
Hyssington	175	D1

I

Ifton Heath	24	F7
Ightfield	16	E1
Ightfield Heath	33	E7
Ireland's Cross	21	D7
Ironbridge	152	C4
Islington	109	F4
Isombridge	129	B8

J

Jackfield	153	A2

K

Kemberton	154	C6
Kempton	194	D5
Kenley	179	F3
Kenstone	68	D5
Kenwick	45	A1
Kenwick Park	62	E8
Ketley	131	C2
Ketley Bank	132	A1
Kingsland	125	A4
Kingslow	170	D1
Kingswood	170	D1
Kingswood Common	157	F2
Kinlet	210	D7
Kinnerley	96	B7
Kinton Great Ness	97	C4
Kinton Leintwardine	205	C5
Knighton Adbaston	73	F2
Knighton Loggerheads	21	B5
Knighton on Teme	215	A5
Knighton/Tref-y-Clawdd	203	B2
Knockin	78	A1
Knockin Heath	96	F7
Knolton	9	D2
Knolton Bryn	9	C3
Knowbury	208	A3
Knowle	208	C1
Knowlesands	218	F1
Knucklas	202	E4
Kynaston	96	F5
Kynnersley	119	D6
Kyrewood	220	F4

L

Lady Halton	206	C2
Ladyoak	172	C2
Lane's End	209	A7
Lawley	143	C6
Lawton	196	A2
Lea Lydham	182	C4
Lea Pontesbury	173	C7
Leaton Pimhill	100	D2
Leaton Wrockwardine	129	C3
Leaton Heath	100	C2
Leaton Knolls	112	F6
Lee	44	D6
Leebotwood	178	C1
Lee Brockhurst	67	A3
Leegomery	131	B5
Leigh	172	A2
Leighton Forden with Leighton and Trelystan	170	C4
Leighton Leighton and Eaton Constantine	150	B7
Leintwardine	205	A5
Lem Hill	210	C1
Letton	204	E1
Lightcach	32	A2
Lightmoor	152	E8
Lightwood	72	B7
Lightwood Green	9	F6
Lilleshall	121	C4
Lilyhurst	133	F7
Lindridge	215	E4
Linley Barrow	161	F1
Linley More	182	C7
Linley Brook	187	F8
Linleygreen	161	F2
Lipley	52	D2
Little Arowry	12	B6
Little Bolas	88	C1
Little Brampton	194	D4
Little Common	205	B8
Little Dawley	143	E1
Little Drayton	53	A8
Littlegain	189	E7
Little Green	13	A6
Little Hereford	213	E3
Little London Knighton on Teme	215	A6
Little London Munslow	196	F7
Little Lyth	136	E2
Little Ness	98	E4
Little Overton	9	D7
Little Ryton	178	D6
Little Soudley	72	F5
Little Stretton	216	A3
Little Sutton	197	A1
Little Wenlock	142	C3
Little Worthen	172	A4
Little Wytheford	103	E3
Llandrinio	167	C8
Llandysilio	93	C3
Llanerch	181	D8
Llanfair Waterdine	202	D7
Llangunllo	202	A2
Llanllwyd	191	D3
Llansantffraid-ym-Mechain	92	C6
Llansilin	56	A5
Llanybodwel	35	A5
Llanymynech	93	E6
Llawnt	39	C2
Lloyney	202	D6

Llwyn 193 B3
Llwyn-y-go 95 D7
Llynclys 76 C5
Lockleywood 72 A5
Lodgebank 86 E8
Long Bank 211 B1
Long Common 190 B4
Longden 173 E5
Longden Common 173 E3
Longdon on Tern 117 D4
Longford Church Aston ... 109 A1
Longford Moreton Say 52 D8
Long Lane 118 B3
Long Meadowend 195 B5
Longnor 178 D3
Long Oak 78 E3
Longslow 35 F3
Longville in the Dale 185 C4
Loppington 64 D7
Lostford 51 E3
Loughton 198 F2
Lowe 47 D2
Lower Allscot 188 E7
Lower Beobridge 189 D2
Lower Common 178 A8
Lower Dinchope 196 A3
Lower Down 194 A7
Lower Faintree 199 C7
Lower Forge 200 E8
Lower Frankton 43 B4
Lower Hayton 206 F8
Lower Hengoed 40 F6
Lower Hopton 97 D6
Lower Hordley 62 A7
Lower Ledwyche 207 C1
Lower Netchwood 186 F2
Lower Penn 190 F6
Lower Ridge 42 D7
Lower Todding 205 B6
Low Habberley 211 F5
Low Town 219 A5
Lubberland 209 A5
Ludford 217 D2
Ludlow 217 D4
Ludstone 189 F5
Lushcott 185 D6
Lydbury North 194 C8
Lyde 175 E8
Lydham 182 A6
Lynchgate 194 E8
Lyneal 45 E7
Lynn 123 B4
Lythbank 136 C3

M

Madeley 153 A5
Madeleywood 152 E4
Maesbrook 95 A7
Maesbury 77 B8
Maesbury Marsh 77 D6
Mainstone 181 A2
Malehurst 172 F5
Malinslee 144 A4
Marbury 22 E8
Marchamley 68 F7
Marchamley Wood 50 E3
Mardu 192 F7
Marey 23 C1
Market Drayton 36 B2
Marley Green 3 B8
Marlow 205 B7
Marshbrook 183 E4
Marsh Green 117 B1
Marton
  Chirbury with Brompton 171 B1
Marton
  Myddle and Broughton .. 81 D4
Meadowley 187 E3
Meadowtown 175 E8
Medlicott 177 B1
Meeson 106 E5
Meeson Heath 106 F4
Melverley 168 A7
Melverley Green 167 F8
Meole Brace 125 E2
Meretown 110 B5
Merrington 100 E6
Mickley 51 C6
Middlehope 196 E7
Middleton Bitterley ... 207 C4
Middleton Little Hereford 213 D4
Middleton Oswestry Rural . 59 C7
Middleton Baggot 186 F1
Middleton Priors 186 E1
Middleton Scriven 199 F6
Middletown 167 C3
Milebrook 203 E3
Mile Oak 59 A4
Milford 98 F6
Mill Green 71 E5
Milson 215 B8
Minsterley 172 D4
Minton 183 D5
Mondaytown 172 B6
Monkhopton 186 F4
Monkmoor 126 B7

Montford 169 D5
Montford Bridge 169 E6
Montgomery 174 A3
Morda 58 D4
More 182 B6
Moreton 123 D7
Moreton Corbet 83 E3
Moreton Say 35 A1
Moretonwood 34 E3
Morton 76 E5
Morton Common 76 E6
Morton Mill 86 B2
Morville 187 E5
Morville Heath 187 F4
Mose 189 A1
Moston 67 E2
Mount Pleasant 113 D2
Much Wenlock 159 D4
Muckleton 104 E7
Muckley 187 B6
Muckley Cross 187 C6
Munslow 197 A6
Muxton 120 E1
Myddle 82 D4
Myddlewood 82 A4
Mynd 204 C6
Myndtown 182 F4
Mytton 169 F8

N

Nant 22 F1
Nantmawr 75 B5
Nant y Caws 58 D2
Nant-y-gollen 57 B7
Napley 37 F8
Napley Heath 21 A1
Nash 214 D6
Nedge Hill 144 F3
Neen Savage 209 E4
Neen Sollars 215 C7
Neenton 199 B6
Nefod 24 B5
Nesscliffe 97 E3
Nether Skyborry 203 A4
Netherton 200 E1
Newbridge Cefn 6 D8
Newbridge
  Oswestry Rural 77 A8
Newcastle 192 E5
Newdale 143 C7
Newington 195 D6
New Invention 203 C7
New Marton 25 C2
Newnes 26 E1
Newnham Bridge 215 A4
Newport 109 D3
Newstreet Lane 34 F7
Newton
  Welshampton and Lyneal . 28 A1
Newton Worfield 188 D8
Newton on the Hill 83 B3
Newton Much Wenlock ... 159 D5
Newtown Much Wenlock .. 159 B5
Newtown Wem Rural 47 A4
New Woodhouses 16 E8
New Works 143 A6
Nib Heath 98 F2
Nobold 124 E1
Noneley 64 F4
Norbury 182 D8
Nordley 188 A8
Northwood 46 C7
Norton Culmington 206 A8
Norton Stockton 163 B5
Norton
  Wroxeter and Uppington . 139 F8
Norton in Hales 20 D2
Nox 169 C1
Nurton 166 F4
Nurton Hill 166 D4

O

Oakengates 132 A2
Oakley 37 C6
Oaks 173 D3
Obley 203 F8
Oldbury 218 D2
Old Church Stoke 175 B1
Old Coppice 136 D3
Oldfield 199 E7
Old Field 206 E4
Old Hardwick 26 B1
Oldington 188 D8
Old Marton 25 E1
Old Park 144 A7
Oldpool 86 D1
Oldwood 220 C2
Old Woodhouses 3 D2
Old Woods 100 B5
Ollerton 88 E7
Ollerton Lane 88 E8
Onibury 206 A6
Onneley 5 E3
Oreton 209 C7

Orleton 212 E2
Orleton Common 212 C3
Orslow 123 E3
Osbaston Ercall Magna . 104 F2
Osbaston Kinnerley 77 E2
Oswestry (Croeswallt) . 58 B8
Oteley 27 E2
Ounsdale 190 E4
Outwoods 111 B1
Overdale 143 D8
Overs 177 A2
Overton 212 F6
Overton/Owrtyn 9 D8

P

Paddolgreen 47 E5
Painters Green 13 E7
Panpunton 203 B4
Pant 76 B1
Pant-glas 40 A5
Papermill Bank 85 D8
Park Hall 41 A4
Park Heath 77 C3
Park Lane 11 A4
Pasford 165 E3
Pattingham 166 B3
Patton 186 B6
Pave Lane 122 B6
Peaton 197 C4
Peatonstrand 197 D3
Pedlar's Rest 196 D3
Pell, ... 10 F5
Pennerley 176 B6
Pentiken 192 A6
Pentre Chirk 6 D6
Pentre Churchstoke ... 181 A7
Pentre Forden with
  Leighton and Trelystan 170 D4
Pentre Montford 168 D8
Pentre Oswestry Rural .. 56 F1
Pentre St. Martin's 24 E8
Pentre-cefn 56 F3
Pentre-clawdd 40 F4
Pentre-coed 25 F8
Pentrehelying 180 C6
Pentre Hodre 203 F8
Pentre-newydd 12 B6
Pen-y-bont Llanerch
  Emrys 74 A4
Pen-y-Bryn 7 E2
Pen-y-coed 75 F3
Pen y Foel 93 E7
Pen-y-wern 193 D2
Peplow 85 D6
Pepperstreet 48 D6
Perthy 43 B8
Petton 63 E1
Picklescott 179 B1
Pickstock 91 B3
Pinstones 196 E5
Pipe Gate 21 D6
Pitchford 179 C6
Pixley 89 E8
Plaish 185 C7
Plasau 96 E6
Plas Coch 221 B5
Platt Lane 31 B1
Plealey 173 D5
Plowden 182 F2
Ploxgreen 172 D2
Pontesbury 173 B5
Pontesbury Hill 173 A4
Pontesford 173 C5
Pont-Faen 23 A6
Ponthen 168 A8
Pont-y-blew 7 C1
Poolhead 47 D6
Porthill 125 A5
Porth-y-waen 75 D4
Posenhall 160 F8
Pound Green 211 A5
Poynton 116 A8
Poynton Green 103 F2
Prees 49 C7
Prees Green 49 E4
Preesgweene 23 F5
Prees Heath 32 D8
Preeshenlle 24 B2
Prees Higher Heath ... 32 E4
Prees Lower Heath 50 B6
Prees Wood 49 E7
Prescott Stottesdon ... 99 B7
Prescott Stottesdon .. 209 D8
Presthope 186 B8
Preston 207 C1
Preston Brockhurst ... 84 E6
Preston Gubbals 101 D4
Preston Montford 169 E5
Preston upon the
  Weald Moors 119 E3
Priest Weston 175 B4
Prince Hill 4 E7
Priors Halton 206 E2
Priorslee 132 E1
Puleston 91 C1
Pulley 137 A8

Pulverbatch 173 D1
Purlogue 203 B8
Purslow 194 D3
Pye Corner 202 A3

Q

Quabbs 192 A3
Quatford 188 F1
Quatt 201 A7
Queen's Head 60 C2
Quina Brook 48 C7

R

Radlith 173 C4
Radmoor 87 F6
Ragdon 216 D1
Randlay 144 E3
Ratlinghope 177 B4
Reabrook 172 D3
Redbrook 13 F7
Red Bull 37 C3
Redhill Bayston Hill . 136 D7
Redhill Lilleshall and
  Donnington 132 E3
Red Lake 131 F2
Rednal 61 A4
Redwith 77 A5
Rhewl Overton 9 B4
Rhewl
  Selattyn and Gobowen . 24 B1
Rhiews 35 B7
Rhos Llandrinio 167 A8
Rhos Weston Rhyn 23 A4
Rhos Common 94 C1
Rhos-ddu 221 D5
Rhosnesni 221 F3
Rhosrobin 221 B8
Rhoswiel 23 E5
Rhosygadfa 24 E1
Rhydycroesau 39 A2
Rhyd-y-cwm 191 C3
Rhyn 24 B7
Richards Castle 212 E4
Ridgwardine 19 E1
Rindleford 188 F6
Rochford 214 F3
Rockgreen 217 F6
Rockhill 193 B2
Roden 116 A6
Rodington 116 E2
Rodington Heath 116 C2
Rodway 107 A1
Romsley 201 D1
Rorrington 175 D7
Rosehill 53 A1
Rossington 189 A5
Round Oak 195 A7
Rowley 171 D5
Rowton Alberbury with
  Cardeston 168 D3
Rowton Ercall Magna .. 105 C4
Ruckley 179 C3
Rudge 190 A8
Rudge Heath 189 E6
Rushbury 185 E7
Rushton 141 B5
Ruthall 198 C8
Ruyton-XI-Towns 80 B1
Ryebank 48 A3
Ryton 155 C2

S

St George's 132 C2
St Martin's 24 F5
St Martin's Moor 24 D4
Sambrook 90 E5
Sandford Prees 33 C1
Sandford Weston Felton 78 C4
Sandy Lane 10 C5
Sansaw Heath 84 A1
Sascott 169 D2
Seifton 196 D2
Seisdon 190 C6
Selattyn 39 F8
Shackerley 148 B1
Shakeford 71 D5
Shatterford 211 E8
Shavington 196 B2
Shawbirch 130 C8
Shawbury 103 C7
Sheet 207 C1
Sheinton 150 C4
Shelderton 205 B8
Shelton 124 B7
Shelve 176 A6
Sherriffhales 134 B5
Shifnal 145 F4
Shipley 189 F7
Shipton 185 E2
Shirlett 187 C8
Shoot Hill 169 C3
Shorthill 173 D7

Shotatton 79 A2
Shrawardine 169 A5
Shrewsbury 125 D6
Sidbury 199 F4
Silvington 208 F6
Six Ashes 201 E7
Skyborry Green 202 F5
Sleap 65 B1
Sleapford 118 B4
Smestow 190 E2
Smethcott 178 A2
Smythemoor 52 B8
Snailbeach 172 E1
Snead 181 E6
Snedshill 144 C8
Snitton 207 E2
Snittongate 207 F2
Sodylt Bank 8 C3
Somerwood 115 E2
Soudley Cheswardine .. 73 B7
Soudley Hope Bowdler . 184 C2
Spoonleygate 189 F7
Spunhill 44 E7
Spurtree 220 E7
Stableford 164 B2
Standford Bridge 90 C5
Stanford 168 A3
Stanley Alveley 201 A1
Stanley Stottesdon ... 199 F3
Stanley Green 31 C3
Stanlow 165 C2
Stanmore 219 F3
Stanton Lacy 206 E5
Stanton Long 186 A1
Stanton upon
  Hine Heath 85 F4
Stanwardine in the
  Fields 80 F5
Stanwardine in the
  Wood 63 C4
Stapleton 178 B7
Steel Heath 32 A5
Steeraway 142 F8
Steventon 217 E1
Stiperstones 176 C7
Stirchley 144 C2
Stockton Chetwynd Aston
  and Woodcote 122 D6
Stockton Chirbury with
  Brompton 174 F8
Stockton 163 B4
Stokegorse 198 A2
Stoke Heath 70 E8
Stoke on Tern 70 C5
Stokesay 195 E4
Stoke St Milborough .. 197 F1
Stonecacton 184 F4
Stoneylane 207 F3
Stoney Stretton 172 F8
Stottesdon 199 E2
Stowe 203 D4
Street Dinas 8 A1
Street Lydan 11 C4
Strefford 195 F8
Stretton Westwood ... 158 E1
Styche Hall 35 D4
Sugdon 117 A2
Summerhill 109 B4
Sutton Chelmarsh 200 D5
Sutton Shrewsbury 125 E2
Sutton Sutton upon Tern 53 B4
Sutton West Felton .. 60 F3
Sutton Hill 153 C4
Sutton Maddock 163 B7
Swancote 219 E7
Swindon 190 E1
Sytch House Green ... 189 D1
Sytch Lane 105 F5

T

Tarts Hill 11 C2
Tasley 218 B7
Tedsmore 79 C7
Telford 144 B5
Tenbury Wells 220 D4
Ternhill 52 A5
Tetchill 43 F6
The Bog 176 C4
The Bratch 190 F4
The Chequer 13 C6
The Common 71 B3
The Down 187 F1
The Dunks 221 F3
The Foxholes 209 B7
The Grove 198 C1
The Green 193 D4
The Hem 154 C8
The Hobbins 219 E5
The Hope 207 A5
The Humbers 120 A2
The Lakes 211 C2
The Leath 198 B8
The Marsh Chirbury with
  Brompton 175 E5
The Marsh Hinstock .. 90 B8
The Quarry 125 B5

The Rock	143 E7	Uffington	126 D8
The Smithies	187 E8	Underdale	125 F7
The Waterwheel	172 D1	Underton	187 F3
The Wyke	145 C2	Upper Affcot	183 F1
The Yeld	198 A2	Upper Arley	211 C7
Three Ashes	194 E1	Upper Astley	102 E1
Three Fingers	12 A8	Upper Aston	190 A5
Tibberton	107 E5	Upper Battlefield	114 B8
Ticklerton	184 D1	Upper Berrington	214 A2
Tilley	65 F4	Upper College	33 A2
Tilley Green	66 A3	Upper Cound	179 E7
Tilsop	214 E7	Upper Dinchope	196 A2
Tilstock	32 A8	Upper Farmcote	189 C3
Tong	147 D3	Upper Forge	200 D8
Tong Forge	147 A5	Upper Hayton	207 A8
Tong Norton	147 C5	Upper Hengoed	23 D1
Totterton	182 C2	Upper Longwood	141 A2
Town Park	144 B4	Upper Ludstone	189 F6
Trederwen	167 A7	Upper Netchwood	186 D3
Tre-derwen	92 F5	Upper Rochford	215 A2
Treflach	75 E7	Upper Treverward	193 A1
Trefonen	57 D2	Upper Wigginton	25 B4
Trelystan	170 F2	Uppington	141 A8
Trench Ellesmere Rural	27 B8	Upton Cressett	187 C3
Trench Oakengates	132 A5	Upton Magna	127 C6
Trescott	190 D8		
Trewern	167 B2	**V**	
Trimpley	211 E5		
Trysull	190 E5	Valeswood	98 A5
Tuckhill	201 D7	Vennington	172 B8
Tugford	197 F6	Vernolds Common	206 C7
Turfmoor	96 F2	Vron Gate	171 F8
Turleygreen	201 B4		
Tweedale	153 B6	**W**	
Twitchen	194 E2		
Twyford	60 D1	Wagbeach	172 D1
Tyn-y-coed	57 E5	Walcot	128 E5
		Walford Baschurch	99 D6
U		Walford	204 F3
		Walford Heath	99 F4
Uckington	140 B8		

Walkmill	182 E7	Whatmore	214 E6
Walkmills	178 B2	Wheathall	178 E6
Wall Bank	184 F4	Wheathill	198 E1
Wall under Heywood	184 F3	Whettleton	195 F5
Walton Ercall Magna	104 D1	Whiston Cross	156 C4
Walton Onibury	206 B6	Whitchurch	15 C8
Waterloo	47 D7	Whitcot	182 E6
Waters Upton	106 A3	Whitcot Keysett	193 A5
Wattlesborough Heath	168 C2	White Grit	175 E4
Waun	92 F4	Whitehaven	76 A5
Waymills	15 C7	Whitewell	13 D7
Webscott	82 E2	Whittingslow	183 E3
Weirbrook	78 E5	Whittington	41 F3
Wellington	130 D4	Whitton Leintwardine	205 C4
Welshampton	28 D2	Whitton	214 A7
Welsh End	31 A4	Whittytree	195 F1
Welsh Frankton	43 A7	Whixall	31 B2
Welshpool (Trallwng)	170 D6	Wigginton	25 B4
Wem	66 B6	Wigmarsh	79 D7
Wentnor	182 F7	Wilcott	97 D2
Wern Carreghofa	93 D5	Wilcott Marsh	168 F8
Wern Weston Rhyn	23 B2	Wilkesley	17 F7
Wern ddu	56 E1	Willaston	33 F4
Wernlas	95 D5	Willey	161 C3
Wernygeufron	202 B7	Willstone	184 D6
Westbury	172 C8	Winllan	92 C8
Westcott	177 B8	Winnington	21 B1
West Felton	78 C7	Winnington Green	167 E2
Westhope	196 C5	Wirswall	2 A5
Westley	172 C5	Wistanstow	195 D8
Weston Monkhopton	186 C4	Wistanswick	71 A7
Weston Oswestry Rural	58 F3	Withington	128 B7
Weston Stowe	203 F4	Wixhill	67 E6
Weston		Wollaston	167 F3
Weston-under-Redcastle	67 F6	Wollerton	51 E1
Westoncommon	63 B1	Wolverley	46 E3
Weston Heath	134 F8	Wolverton	196 B7
Weston Lullingfields	81 A6	Wombridge	132 A3
Weston Rhyn	23 D4	Woodhill	200 E3
Weston Under Lizard	135 F3	Woodlane	72 A3
Westonwharf	81 A8	Wood Lane	44 F6
Wettles	183 E2	Woodside	152 F6

Woofferton	213 B3
Woolstaston	178 A1
Woolston West Felton	77 E5
Woolston Wistanstow	183 D2
Woore	5 A2
Wootton	201 B8
Wootton Onibury	206 A5
Wootton Oswestry Rural	60 B4
Worfield	189 B6
Worthen	171 F4
Wotherton	175 B7
Woundale	189 B3
Wrentnall	173 D2
Wrexham (Wrecsam)	221 A8
Wribbenhall	211 E2
Wrickton	199 B4
Wrockwardine	129 F5
Wrockwardine Wood	132 C4
Wroxeter	139 E5
Wyke	151 D1
Wyken	189 B6
Wykey	80 A7
Wylde	212 A3
Wyson	213 A2

Y

Yeaton	99 D3
Yockleton	169 A1
Yorton	83 E4
Yorton Heath	83 E1

A

Abbey Fields TF3 .....144 D3
Abbey Foregate
 3 Shrewsbury SY2 .....125 D6
 1 Shrewsbury SY1 .....125 D5
Abbey La SY5 .....168 D5
Abbey Lawn Bsns Pk
 SY2 .....125 D6
Abbey Rd TF1 .....131 A2
Abbey Walls **4** TF2 .....132 A4
Abbey Way TF9 .....36 D2
Abbeyfield **4** WV16 .....218 C6
Abbot St **8** LL11 .....221 C3
Abbots Cl TF2 .....132 A3
Abbots Gn SY2 .....126 A6
Abbots Pl **4** SY2 .....125 F7
Abbots Rd SY2 .....125 F7
Abbots Way Hodnet TF9 .....69 C6
 Shrewsbury SY2 .....126 A7
Abbotsfield Dr SY2 .....125 F3
Abbotts Way **3** WV16 .....218 F6
Abdon Cl **6** WV16 .....200 E3
Abdon Cl **1** TF2 .....132 A3
Abelia Way TF1 .....132 F1
Abenbury Rd LL13 .....221 F1
Abingdon Rd
 3 Albrighton WV7 .....156 F8
 Shrewsbury SY2 .....126 A7
Abney Ave WV7 .....156 F5
Abraham Cl **8** TF3 .....144 B1
Abraham Darby Sch
 TF7 .....152 E5
Acacia Ave **18** DY12 .....211 E2
Acacia Dr TF3 .....131 A5
Acer Cl TF1 .....143 D8
Acorn Cl **8** SY11 .....41 F2
Acorn Rise SY21 .....170 B7
Acorn Way TF5 .....130 C8
Acton Burnell Castle*
 .....179 C4
Acton Gate LL11 .....221 D6
Acton Gdns LL11 .....221 E7
Acton Pk Prim Schools
 LL11 .....221 C5
Acton Rd LL11 .....221 C5
Acton Reynald Sch for Girls
 SY4 .....84 E3
Acton Scott Historic Working
 Farm* SY6 .....196 A8
Adams Cres TF10 .....109 E3
Adams Gram Sch
 TF10 .....109 E3
Adams Ridge **8** SY2 .....125 F2
Adamson Dr TF4 .....143 D3
Adcote Sch SY4 .....98 F3
Adderley CE Prim Sch
 TF9 .....18 F5
Adderley Rd TF9 .....36 E4
Addison Rd TF1 .....130 C3
Adelaide Dr SY21 .....170 B7
Adeney Rd TF10 .....108 C1
Admaston Rd TF1 .....130 C5
Admaston Spa Cres **8**
 TF5 .....130 B7
Admirals Cl TF11 .....146 A6
Admirals Way TF11 .....146 A6
Adswood Gr SY3 .....124 F1
Ael-y-bryn LL11 .....221 C7
Aerospace Mus*
 WV7 .....156 F3
Agden House La SY13 .....1 A5
Agnes Hunt Cl **4** SY4 .....81 A1
Agricultural Mus*
 LL13 .....221 B1
Ainsdale Dr
 Dawley TF2 .....144 E8
 Shrewsbury SY3 .....113 E3
Aintree Cl TF1 .....131 A5
Alan Gutridge Dr SY3 .....124 E5
Albacore Rd TF1 .....131 A7
Albany Ct **2** SY5 .....169 C4
Alberbury Castle*
 SY5 .....168 C3
Alberbury Dr SY1 .....114 B3
Alberbury Rd SY5 .....169 B4
Albert Dr SY1 .....190 F1
Albert Gdns **1** DY1 .....190 F1
Albert Gdns **1** SY11 .....113 F2
Albert Mews **1** SY11 .....40 E1
Albert Rd
 Albrighton WV7 .....156 F4
 2 Oswestry SY11 .....58 E8
 Shrewsbury SY1 .....113 F2
 Wellington TF1 .....130 C4
Albert Sq **4** SY1 .....113 F3
Albert St
 8 Oakengates/Donnington
 TF2 .....132 C3
 5 Shrewsbury SY1 .....125 D7
 7 Wrexham LL13 .....221 D2
Albion Hill TF2 .....132 C3
Albion Hill **8** SY11 .....58 E8
Albion St TF2 .....132 C3
Albridge La SY10 .....76 E8
Albrighton By-pass
 WV7 .....157 B6
Albrighton Cty Inf & Jun
 Schools WV7 .....157 A4
Albrighton Sta WV7 .....157 B5
Albrighton Trust*
 WV7 .....157 B7
Alder Dr **1** SY4 .....172 E4
Alder Rd TF9 .....53 A8

Alderley La SY4 .....66 E7
Aldermead Cl TF5 .....130 A7
Alders La SY1 .....30 D1
Alderslee Cl **8** TF2 .....132 E2
Aldersley Way **8** SY4 .....80 A1
Aldford Way **3** LL12 .....221 F6
Aldridge Cl TF2 .....132 F1
Aldwick Dr SY3 .....124 F2
Alexander Fleming Prim Sch
 TF7 .....153 C4
Alexandra Ave SY3 .....125 A2
Alexandra CP Sch
 LL12 .....221 D4
Alexandra Rd
 1 Market Drayton TF9 .....36 B1
 10 Oswestry SY11 .....40 D1
 4 Wellington TF1 .....130 D3
 Wrexham LL13 .....221 B2
Alfred St SY2 .....125 E5
Alison Dr SY6 .....216 E6
Alison Rd SY6 .....216 E6
Alkington Gdns **1** SY13 .....15 A6
Alkington Rd SY13 .....14 D6
All Saints Ave **8** DY12 .....211 E3
Allcroft Cl SY7 .....206 A6
Allerton Rd **8** SY1 .....114 B3
Allertons Mdw **6** TF5 .....130 B8
Allestree Cl **8** SY1 .....113 E5
Alley The TF6 .....142 D2
Allgold Dr SY2 .....126 A5
Allmans La TF9 .....72 A4
Allness Cl **1** SY2 .....126 B6
Alloe Brook SY4 .....169 E6
Alma Ave TF4 .....143 F5
Alma Fields TF4 .....143 F5
Alma Rd **8** LL20 .....6 A7
Almond Ave SY11 .....41 A7
Almond Cl **7** TF2 .....132 E8
Almond Dr **7** SY12 .....27 A2
Almond Gr LL13 .....221 F4
Alms Cl **8** SY3 .....125 B2
Alport Rd SY13 .....2 A1
Alton Gr TF10 .....109 E1
Alton Terr **1** SY3 .....125 D4
Alveston Way SY2 .....126 A8
Alveley Ind Est WV15 .....201 A3
Alveley Prim Sch
 WV15 .....201 B3
Alverley Cl
 4 Shrewsbury SY3 .....124 F6
 7 Wellington TF1 .....130 E4
Alvin Cl SY4 .....65 F5
Alyndale Rd **8** LL12 .....221 D7
Amber Hill SY3 .....124 E4
Amblecote Dr **4** SY3 .....137 A5
Ambleside Rd **18** SY11 .....58 E8
Ambleside Way **8** TF2 .....132 E6
Anchor Cl SY3 .....15 B7
Andreas Dr **8** TF2 .....132 F8
Angel La SY8 .....208 A3
Annefield Cl TF9 .....36 D2
Anslem Cl **2** TF3 .....144 A1
Anson Dr **8** TF1 .....131 B6
Anson Rd WV7 .....156 B7
Anstice Rd TF1 .....153 A5
Anthony Eden Dr **1**
 LL13 .....221 F2
Anvil Cl TF10 .....107 E5
Apley Ave TF1 .....130 E5
Apley Castle
 Hadley TF1 .....130 E7
 Wellington TF1 .....130 F7
Apley Dr TF1 .....130 E5
Apley Wood Prim Sch
 TF1 .....131 A7
Apple Ave SY4 .....66 E7
Applebrook TF11 .....145 F3
Appledore **8** SY3 .....124 D7
Appledore Gdns TF1 .....130 D2
Applewood Cl
 6 Offa LL13 .....221 D1
 West Felton SY11 .....78 D7
Applewood Hts SY11 .....78 D7
Appleyard Cl **6** SY8 .....212 E2
Apse Cl **9** WV5 .....190 F4
Aqualate Cl **8** TF10 .....110 A4
Aqueduct La TF1 .....144 B1
Aqueduct Prim Sch
 TF4 .....153 A8
Aqueduct Rd TF3 .....153 A8
Aragorn Way **8** TF4 .....153 A8
Aralia Cl **8** TF2 .....132 F1
Aran Rd LL12 .....221 E4
Arbour La SY3 .....182 B8
Arbourne Gdns **8** SY3 .....125 C4
Archer's Way
 1 Tenbury Wells WR15 .....220 D6
 5 Wrexham LL13 .....221 E4
Archers Way SY1 .....113 E6
Arden Cl
 8 Shrewsbury SY1 .....125 F8
 Wem SY4 .....66 B8
Arden Way **11** WV15 .....201 B3
Ardern Ave TF4 .....143 F4
Ardmillan Cl **8** SY11 .....58 F8
Ardmillan Cl SY11 .....58 F8
Ardmillan La **8** SY11 .....58 F8
Ardwin Infants Sch
 SY21 .....170 B6
Argyle St **8** LL11 .....221 C3
Argyll Cres **4** TF2 .....120 E1
Argyll St SY1 .....125 D7
Arleston Ave TF1 .....131 B2
Arleston La
 Lawley & Overdale TF1 .....131 B1
 Wellington TF1 .....131 A2
Arley La DY12 .....211 C7

Arley Sta DY12 .....211 B7
Arley View Cl **7** WV16 .....200 F2
Arlington Way SY1 .....114 A4
Armdale SY1 .....125 F8
Armoury Gdns SY2 .....125 F4
Armoury La SY13 .....14 D6
Armstrong Cl TF7 .....152 C5
Arran Way **8** TF2 .....120 F1
Arrow Dr **8** WV7 .....157 A5
Arrow St **5** TF5 .....130 C8
Arthur St
 8 Montgomery SY15 .....174 B3
 Oswestry SY11 .....58 D8
Arthur's Gate SY15 .....174 B4
Arthurs Gate SY15 .....174 B4
Artillery Rd SY11 .....41 C4
Arundel Cl **2** Ruyton SY4 .....80 A1
 Stirchley & Brookside
 TF3 .....144 C3
Arundel Rd **8** SY11 .....58 D8
Ascot Cl SY6 .....216 D6
Ascot Rd SY11 .....41 A1
Ash Cl
 8 Craven Arms SY7 .....195 E5
 8 Ludlow SY8 .....217 E3
 Shrewsbury SY2 .....125 F2
 Weston Rhyn SY10 .....23 D4
Ash Gr Albrighton WV7 .....147 A8
 4 Chirk LL14 .....6 E3
 8 Pontesbury SY5 .....173 A5
 Wem Rural SY4 .....66 C7
 8 Wrexham LL13 .....221 F4
Ash La SY13 .....15 F5
Ash Las SY5 .....172 E3
Ash Mdw **8** SY5 .....172 C8
Ash Rd
 Bridgnorth WV16 .....218 D6
 Oakengates/Donnington
 TF2 .....132 D8
 8 Oswestry SY11 .....58 F8
 Whitchurch Rural SY13 .....15 F2
Ash St **8** WV16 .....200 E3
Ashbourne Cl **9** TF4 .....144 A4
Ashbourne Dr **4** TF9 .....36 C2
Ashbrook Cres **8** SY6 .....216 D7
Ashburn Way LL13 .....221 F1
Ashcroft **8** WV16 .....218 D5
Ashcroft Cl SY3 .....41 A8
Ashdale Rd SY5 .....149 E4
Ashfield Dr **8** SY22 .....93 F6
Ashfield Rd
 Ditton Priors WV16 .....198 C8
 Rhosddu LL11 .....221 B5
Ashfields **7** TF2 .....132 B2
Ashfields Rd SY1 .....113 D6
Ashford Ave **8** SY5 .....173 A4
Ashford Carbonell Prim Sch
 SY8 .....213 B5
Ashford Cl **8** SY5 .....173 A4
Ashford Dr
 Pontesbury SY5 .....173 A5
 9 Shrewsbury SY1 .....113 D4
Ashford Pk **8** SY5 .....173 A4
Ashford Way **4** SY5 .....173 A5
Ashlands Rd SY10 .....23 D4
Ash-lea Dr TF2 .....132 D6
Ashley Rd TF2 .....132 D2
Ashley St SY2 .....125 D7
Ashley View TF9 .....36 C1
Ashmore Cres TF12 .....152 C2
Ashmore Dr TF2 .....132 A6
Ashton Rd **8** SY3 .....125 A4
Ashwood Cl **8** WV5 .....190 F4
Ashwood La SY13 .....16 C4
Ashworth Way **1** TF10 .....109 F1
Aspen Cl SY10 .....23 D4
Aspen Gr **8** SY3 .....124 E4
Aspen Grange SY10 .....23 D4
Aspen Way
 Newport TF10 .....109 F2
 Wellington TF5 .....130 C8
Assembly Cl **8** WV16 .....200 F2
Astley Cv SY4 .....102 D3
Astley La SY4 .....102 D3
Astley Orch WR15 .....215 D3
Aston Butts **8** SY2 .....125 F8
Aston Cl Oswestry SY11 .....59 B7
 8 Wellington TF1 .....130 F5
Aston Dale **8** TF11 .....146 A4
Aston Dr **12** TF10 .....109 F2
Aston Gr LL12 .....221 E4
Aston La Claverley WV5 .....189 E4
 Maer TF9 .....37 F8
 Wheathill WV16 .....198 F2
 Woore CW3 .....5 C1
Aston Rd Shifnal TF11 .....146 A4
 Sun Bank SY4 .....66 C6
Aston St Shifnal TF11 .....145 F4
 Wem SY4 .....66 A6
Aston Way SY1 .....59 B8
Atcham Ind Est SY4 .....127 E1
Athol Dr TF2 .....132 C2
Atlas Gr TF1 .....130 C4
Attingham Cl **7** TF4 .....144 D1
Attingham Pk (NT)*
 SY4 .....127 C1
Attwood Terr TF4 .....143 F4
Audlem CW3 .....4 E2
Audley Ave TF10 .....109 F2
Audley Ave Bsns Pk
 TF10 .....110 A1
Audley Rd TF10 .....109 F3
Aumbry Cl **8** TF9 .....36 A1
Auster Cl **10** TF1 .....131 A7
Avalon Cl **8** LL13 .....221 D1
Avenue Rd
 Broseley TF12 .....161 D7
 Newport TF10 .....109 F2

Avenue Rd S TF10 .....109 F2
Avenue The
 Barrow TF12 .....151 F1
 Hodnet TF9 .....61 A6
 8 Shrewsbury SY3 .....110 C1
 More SY9 .....182 B7
 Stanton upon Hine Heath
 SY4 .....86 E7
 West Felton SY11 .....78 C8
 Wrockwardine TF6 .....129 F4
Avon Cl **18** Dawley TF4 .....152 F8
 4 Wrexham LL12 .....221 E6
Avon Dale TF10 .....109 F4
Avondale TF4 .....143 E6
Avondale Dr SY11 .....125 E7
Avondale Rd
 Bridgnorth WV16 .....218 E5
 Wellington TF1 .....130 C2
Aylwin Cl **8** TF3 .....144 A1
Aynall La SY8 .....213 C2
Aynesworth Gn **2** SY1 .....113 F4
Ayr Cl TF1 .....131 A5
Aysgarth Rd **1** SY3 .....124 F6

B

Back La
 Bausley with Criggion
 SY5 .....167 B6
 Bomere Heath SY4 .....100 E4
 Clive SY4 .....84 A5
 8 Montgomery SY15 .....174 B3
 5 Much Wenlock TF13 .....159 E5
 Onibury SY7 .....206 B5
 Pontesbury SY5 .....173 B5
 Worfield WV6 .....164 E2
Back Lime St **8** SY2 .....125 C4
Back Rd TF11 .....134 C3
Bader Cl **8** TF3 .....144 B1
Bader Cl **2** TF3 .....144 B1
Badger La WV6 .....164 C4
Badgers Rise SY8 .....208 E2
Bage Way SY3 .....125 E4
Bagley Dr
 Shrewsbury SY1 .....113 D1
 Wellington TF1 .....130 C5
Bailey Cl SY4 .....65 F7
Bailey Cres **8** SY1 .....173 B4
Bailey St **8** SY11 .....58 D8
Bainbridge Gn **8** SY1 .....113 E4
Bakehouse La WV16 .....200 D6
Baker Cl SY8 .....217 F5
Bakewell Cl **8** SY1 .....113 D5
Baldwin Way SY3 .....190 F1
Baldwin Webb Ave
 TF2 .....132 C8
Balfour Rd TF11 .....146 A6
Ball La SY10 .....59 A1
Ballard Cl **8** SY8 .....217 E4
Ball's La TF8 .....152 D2
Balliol Way **8** SY3 .....124 E3
Balls Hill TF4 .....143 D4
Balmoral Cl
 4 Oswestry SY11 .....59 A8
 8 Wrexham LL11 .....221 C6
Balmoral Cres SY11 .....41 A1
Balmoral Dr TF9 .....36 E2
Balmoral Rd LL11 .....221 C6
Banbery Dr **8** WV5 .....190 F2
Banbury Cl **8** SY2 .....125 F3
Banbury La WV16 .....198 D2
Bandon La WV15 .....201 A3
Bank Dr Condover SY5 .....178 C5
 Shrewsbury SY3 .....125 A2
Bank D W **8** SY3 .....124 F2
Bank Farm Rd SY3 .....124 F2
Bank Rd Dawley TF4 .....143 E5
 Wellington TF1 .....130 D3
Bank St **8** WV16 .....218 F5
Bank St SY5 .....178 C6
Bank Top Ind Est SY10 .....24 C5
Bank Way TF2 .....132 C3
Bankhouse La SY4 .....65 F6
Bankside **8** WV5 .....190 F4
Baptist Ave TF4 .....143 F6
Bar Hill CW3 .....5 B7
Barber St TF12 .....161 C8
Barberry Cl TF3 .....143 E8
Barbrook DY14 .....209 F5
Barclay Cl WV7 .....157 B8
Barclay Ct TF2 .....132 C8
Bardsley Dr **8** SY2 .....126 A5
Bargates SY1 .....15 A8
Bark Hill **8** SY13 .....15 A7
Barke St WV16 .....200 E3
Barker St SY1 .....125 B6
Barker's La **1** LL12 .....221 E8
Barker's La Cty Prim Sch
 LL12 .....221 F8
Barkers Ct **8** TF7 .....153 B5
Barkers La **7** DY14 .....209 E2
Barkstone Dr **8** SY1 .....113 D2
Barley Mdws **1** SY22 .....93 F6
Barleyfield **8** SY2 .....125 F6
Barleyfields SY4 .....66 E7
Barleywood Cl **1** TF2 .....132 E6
Barlow Cl **8** TF3 .....144 C3
Barn Cl TF2 .....132 E6
Barn Farm Inf Sch
 TF1 .....130 D7
Barn Rd TF11 .....146 A5
Barnard St Wem SY4 .....66 A6
 Wem Urban SY4 .....65 F6
Barnes Wallis Dr TF1 .....131 A7
Barnet Cl **11** TF1 .....130 D5
Barnfield **8** LL13 .....221 D2
Barnfield Ave SY4 .....66 A8

Barnfield Cl
 4 Oswestry SY11 .....58 F7
 2 Whitchurch SY13 .....14 E8
Barnfield Cres TF1 .....130 C1
Barnfield Dr SY1 .....113 D1
Barnfields **8** DY14 .....209 D2
Barnmeadow Dr TF10 .....110 A3
Barnmeadow Rd TF10 .....110 A3
Barns Gn **8** SY3 .....124 F1
Barnyard Cl **8** SY5 .....172 C8
Barons Rd LL13 .....221 E3
Barrack La TF10 .....109 C6
Barracks La SY3 .....124 F1
Barratts Stile La **18**
 DY12 .....211 D2
Barrington Cl **8** WV7 .....157 A5
Barrington Ct **2** TF11 .....146 A5
Barrow CE Prim Sch
 TF12 .....160 F5
Barrow St TF13 .....159 E4
Barter Ct **11** LL13 .....221 E1
Barter Rd LL13 .....221 E1
Bath Rd LL13 .....221 C2
Bath Rd LL13 .....221 C2
Bath St SY13 .....15 B8
Bathfields Cres **8** SY13 .....14 E7
Battle Rd WV7 .....156 B7
Battlefield Ent Pk SY1 .....113 B5
Battlefield Rd SY1 .....114 A5
Battlefield Way SY1 .....113 E5
Baveney La DY14 .....209 F5
Bayford Dr **8** SY1 .....113 D2
Bayley Hills TF10 .....109 A3
Bayley Rd TF1 .....130 F1
Baylham Cl **1** TF4 .....143 D2
Bayswater Cl **8** TF2 .....132 F2
Baytree Cl SY11 .....24 F6
Beacall's La SY1 .....125 D6
Beachley **8** SY3 .....113 F2
Beacon La SY2 .....201 F2
Beacon Pk ST19 .....148 F7
Beaconsfield
 8 Bridgnorth WV16 .....218 C6
 Dawley TF3 .....144 C1
Beaconsfield Pk SY8 .....207 C1
Beames Cl TF4 .....144 A2
Beamish La WV7 .....157 D5
Bearcroft Grange TF9 .....7 A1
Bearstone Rd
 Loggerheads TF9 .....21 B4
 Woore TF9 .....20 F3
Beatrice Gdns **2** SY13 .....15 B8
Beatrice St **8** SY11 .....40 E1
Beatty Cl **4** TF11 .....146 A6
Beaufort Cl **8** TF1 .....131 A7
Beaufort Gn **1** SY11 .....58 E8
Beaumaris Rd TF10 .....109 E3
Beaumont Rd **2** SY6 .....216 C6
Beaumont Way SY2 .....125 C2
Beckbury CE Prim Sch
 TF11 .....164 D7
Beckbury Dr TF3 .....144 B1
Beddoes Dr SY3 .....137 A5
Beddon Cl SY1 .....125 D8
Bedstone Cl **18** TF3 .....144 C1
Bedstone Coll Pre-Prep
 Department SY7 .....204 D6
Bedwyr Cl **8** LL13 .....221 D1
Beech Ave **8** LL13 .....221 D5
Beech Cl Hanmer SY13 .....12 B4
 8 Hanwood SY5 .....173 F8
 1 Ludlow SY8 .....217 D6
 Newport TF10 .....109 F1
 Pattingham WV6 .....166 C2
 8 Wellington TF1 .....130 C5
Beech Croft **1** WV6 .....166 C2
Beech Dr
 Broseley TF12 .....161 D8
 18 Ellesmere SY12 .....27 A2
 Shifnal TF11 .....145 E8
Beech Gdns **10** LL13 .....221 D2
Beech Gr
 Ellesmere SY12 .....27 A2
 Oswestry SY11 .....58 F7
 Shawbury SY4 .....103 E7
Beech Gr CE Jun Sch
 SY11 .....58 E7
Beech Hurst Gdns
 SY11 .....190 D5
Beech Rd
 Bridgnorth WV16 .....218 D6
 Madeley TF7 .....152 E5
Beech St **8** WV16 .....200 E3
Beeches Ave **8** SY11 .....41 A8
Beeches La **18** SY1 .....125 C5
Beeches Rd SY3 .....136 F6
Beeches The
 2 Admaston TF5 .....130 A6
 Whitchurch Urban SY13 .....1 F1
 Wrexham LL12 .....221 D5
Beechfields Way **8**
 TF10 .....109 F5
Beechhouse La WV5 .....190 D4
Beechley Rd **8** LL12 .....221 D2
Beechley Rd LL13 .....221 D2
Beechurst Spring **8** WV7 .....156 F5

Beechwood Cl 2 TF4 144 A2
Beechwood Dr 3 SY1 113 C1
Beechwood Rd TF4 144 A2
Beedles Cl TF4 153 A8
Beehive La SY3 125 B4
Beeston's Cl 3 WV15 219 A4
Beffcote Rd ST20 111 E2
Belfry Cl 8 SY8 208 C2
Belgrave Cres 4 TF3 144 B1
Belgrave Pl 9 SY2 126 B7
Belgrave Rd LL13 221 C2
Bell Ct 12 LL13 221 E1
Bell La Ludlow SY8 217 C3
Shrewsbury SY2 125 E5
Bell Rd WV5 190 E5
Bell St 13 TF1 130 E4
Bellan La SY10 57 D2
Bellaport Rd TF9 20 A4
Belle Orch 7 WR15 220 D5
Belle Vue Gdns SY3 125 C4
Belle Vue Rd
Ironbridge TF8 152 C4
Shrewsbury SY3 125 C3
Belle Vue Terr SY8 217 C5
Bellevue Rd LL13 221 B3
Bellman's Cross DY12 211 D8
Bellman's Yd TF10 109 F2
Bellpit Rd TF3 143 F8
Belmont SY1 125 C5
Belmont Bank 12 SY1 125 C5
Belmont Rd
Ironbridge TF8 152 D4
10 Wrexham LL13 221 C2
Belton Cl SY13 14 E7
Belton Rd SY13 14 E7
Belvedere Cres 5 DY12 211 E3
Belvedere Dr LL11 221 A4
Belvedere Gdns TF12 152 E1
Belvidere Ave SY2 125 F5
Belvidere La 4 SY2 126 A6
Belvidere Prim Sch SY2 126 A7
Belvidere Rd 6 SY2 125 F6
Belvidere Sch SY2 126 B6
Belvidere Wlk SY2 125 F5
Bembridge TF3 144 C1
Ben Jones Ave 6 TF10 110 A4
Benjamin Rd LL13 221 E2
Bennett Rd TF7 153 C5
Bennetts Bank TF1 131 A3
Bennetts La
Leighton & Eaton Constantine SY5 141 B1
Pattingham & Patshull WV6 166 F1
Bennion's Rd 9 LL13 221 D2
Bent La WV16 198 D7
Benthall Hall (NT)* TF12 151 F2
Benthall La
Barrow TF12 161 A8
Broseley TF12 152 B1
Benthall View TF7 152 E4
Bentlands The TF12 152 B1
Bentleys Rd TF9 52 F7
Benyon St 5 SY1 125 D7
Berberis Rd 1 TF1 131 B6
Berghill La SY11 42 D1
Berinsfield Cl 9 SY1 113 C2
Berkeley Cl 1 TF2 132 F2
Berllan 2 SY22 93 F6
Berllan Cl SY10 23 E5
Bernard Rd LL13 221 E3
Bernards Hill WV15 219 A4
Berries La SY3 137 B6
Berriew Rd SY21 170 B5
Berriew St SY21 170 B6
Berrington Dr 3 SY1 113 D3
Berrington Gdns WR15 220 C4
Berrington Rd WR15 220 B4
Berrisford Cl TF9 36 E1
Berrisford Rd TF9 36 E1
Berse Rd LL11 221 A4
Bersham Rd LL13 221 B2
Bert Smith Way TF9 36 C2
Bertie Rd LL13 221 E3
Berwick Ave SY1 125 B8
Berwick Cl SY1 125 B8
Berwick Rd Pimhill SY1 113 A1
Shrewsbury SY1 125 B8
Berwyn Ave LL14 23 E6
Berwyn Cl 1 TF3 144 C3
Berwyn Dr
Bayston Hill SY3 136 F6
St. Martin's SY11 24 E5
Beswicks La TF9 20 C2
Betley La SY3 137 A5
Betnell Gr 2 TF7 153 A5
Betton Dingle Nature Reserve* SY5 171 E1
Betton Rd TF9 36 E2
Betton St SY3 125 D4
Beulah Dr 8 TF9 36 B1
Bevan Cl TF1 131 D4
Beveley Rd TF2 131 E2
Beverley Cl DY11 211 F3
Bewdley High Sch DY12 211 D1
Bewdley Mus* DY12 211 D2
Bewdley Sta DY12 211 E2
Bewdley Wribbenhall Mid Sch DY12 211 E2
Bickleywood Dr 6 LL13 221 F5
Bicton CE Prim Sch SY3 169 F5
Bicton La SY3 169 F6
Bieston Cl LL12 221 F8
Big Walls 5 Ruyton SY4 80 A1
Ruyton-xi-Towns SY4 98 A8
Bilberry Cl TF3 143 F7
Billingsley Cl 2 SY9 181 F3
Bind La WV16 200 C3
Binweston La
Forden with Leighton & Trelystan SY21 170 F2
Worthen with Shelve SY5 171 C3
Birbeck Dr TF7 152 E4
Birch Cl Llandysilio SY22 94 B1
7 Market Drayton TF9 52 F8
Birch Coppice 17 WV5 190 F3
Birch Dale Ave 1 TF2 132 A4
Birch Dr 6 Hanwood SY5 173 F8
Shawbury SY4 103 F7
Birch Gr Alveley WV15 201 B3
Ruyton SY4 80 A1
Birch Hill Ave 30 WV5 190 F3
Birch La LL13 10 D8
Birch Mdw TF12 152 D1
Birch Rd SY12 27 C2
Birch Row TF12 161 C8
Birch St 5 LL13 221 D2
Birch Tree Rd 6 DY12 211 C2
Birchfield Prep Sch for Boys WV7 157 D5
Birchill Pl 31 WV5 190 F3
Birchlands WV15 219 B4
Birchlee Cl 2 TF2 132 E1
Birchmeadow Rd 4 TF12 152 C1
Birchmore 12 TF3 144 B1
Birchwood Cl 5 TF2 132 E8
Birchwood Dr
2 Shrewsbury SY1 113 D2
Whittington SY11 41 F2
Birchwood Gr SY13 32 E5
Bishop St SY2 125 E6
Bishop's Castle Bsns Pk SY9 181 F3
Bishop's Castle Prim Sch SY9 181 E3
Bishopdale TF3 153 B8
Bishop's Castle Rly Mus* SY9 181 F3
Bishops Castle St SY15 174 B3
Bishops Cl 3 SY11 78 D8
Bishops La 8 TF9 36 B1
Bishton Rd WV7 156 F4
Bitterley CE Prim Sch SY8 207 F4
Bitterley Cl SY8 217 F5
Bitterley La SY8 208 A3
Black Gate St 17 SY11 58 E8
Black Pk Rd
Whitchurch SY13 15 B8
Whitchurch Urban SY13 2 E2
Blackbridge La SY10 76 A3
Blackfriars SY11 59 A8
Blackmere Cl TF10 109 D2
Blackmore Gr SY13 15 A8
Blackpit La WV5 190 F5
Blacksmiths Dr 3 TF2 131 F1
Blacksmiths La SY4 85 F5
Blackstone Dr 3 TF2 132 D3
Blackthorn Gr 9 TF5 130 C8
Blaizefield Cl CW3 5 A2
Blakemere Cl 2 SY13 2 B1
Blakemore TF3 153 C8
Blakemore's Bank SY3 137 B6
Blakeway Cl TF12 161 E7
Blakeway Hollow TF13 159 C4
Blakeway Mews 5 SY3 124 A7
Blashfield Rd 13 SY8 217 E4
Bleachfield 10 SY5 173 F8
Blenheim Cl SY11 41 A1
Blenheim Cres 1 WV7 156 F8
Blenheim Rd 11 TF1 131 A7
Blessed Robert Johnson Cath Coll The TF1 130 E6
Bletchley Rd SY13 34 D3
Blists Hill Victorian Town* TF7 153 A3
Blithe Cl TF12 152 D2
Blodwel Bank SY10 75 D5
Bloomfield Cl 3 WV5 190 E3
Bloomsbury Ct 1 TF2 120 D1
Blore Rd TF9 37 E1
Blue Bell Dr 9 SY21 170 B7
Blue House La WV7 157 B7
Bluebell Cl 10 SY21 170 B7
Bluebell Coppice 4 TF1 131 E1
Bluebell Rd TF6 128 F2
Bluegate 2 TF11 146 A4
Blythe Gdns TF2 132 D5
Blything Ct 10 WV16 200 E2
Boatwell Mdw
Dawley TF4 143 D1
Dawley Hamlets TF4 152 D8
Bockleton Rd WR15 220 C1
Bodbury Cl 4 SY6 216 D7
Boddington Cres 1 TF3 144 D4
Bodhyfryd 4 LL12 221 D4
Body Rd TF2 120 D3
Bog La 2 WR15 220 C4
Bogey La SY5 173 B4
Bollingale Ave 5 TF2 132 A4
Bomere Heath CE Prim Sch SY4 100 E3
Boningale Cl 13 TF3 144 C1
Booley Rd SY4 85 F5
Boot St
15 Welshpool SY21 170 B6
Whittington SY11 41 F3
Boraston Bank WR15 220 E7
Boraston Dr WR15 220 E6
Boraston La WR15 220 D6
Border Cl 3 SY11 58 F7
Border Ret Pk LL13 221 E3
Borderway WR15 220 D6
Borfa Gn SY21 170 B7
Borras Pk Rd LL12 221 F6
Borras Rd LL12 221 F5
Boscobel Cl 6 TF3 144 D1
Boscobel Dr 3 SY1 113 D2
Boscobel House* ST19 148 F5
Boscobel Pl TF9 52 D4
Boscobel Rd TF9 52 D4
Bostock Cl 3 TF5 130 A7
Bostock Cres TF3 153 B8
Botany Bay Cl 3 TF4 144 A1
Botfield Cl
Albrighton WV7 157 B6
Telford Dawley TF3 144 C3
Botfield Rd TF11 146 A5
Boughey Rd TF10 109 E2
Bould La TF12 161 D2
Boulmer Ave WV7 156 D8
Boulton Grange 5 TF3 144 D3
Bournbrook Gdns TF3 153 B8
Bournside Dr TF3 153 B8
Bourton Cl 5 TF3 144 C1
Bourton Rd TF13 159 D4
Bow Way SY4 100 F4
Bowbrook Grange SY5 124 B5
Bowdler Cl 11 SY8 217 E4
Bowens Field SY4 66 A7
Bower End La CW3 5 F5
Bowers Cl 1 WV16 218 D5
Bowkers La SY13 13 D5
Bowland Cl TF3 143 D8
Bowling Gn Cl 14 SY9 181 F3
Bowling Gn La
Albrighton WV7 156 D5
20 Knighton LD7 203 B3
9 Welshpool SY21 170 B6
Bowring Gr TF1 130 D2
Box La LL12 221 E8
Bracewell Dr 8 SY3 124 E4
Bracken Gr TF1 131 A3
Bracken Rise 3 SY12 27 A3
Bracken Way 3 TF10 109 F4
Brackenfield TF3 153 B8
Brackley Dr SY3 124 D7
Bradbury La DY7 201 F6
Bradeley Gn La SY13 1 F6
Brades Rd SY13 49 B7
Bradford St
Shifnal TF11 145 F4
Shrewsbury SY2 125 E6
Bradley Ct 4 TF2 132 E6
Bradley Farm La SY14 1 C7
Bradley Fields SY11 58 C8
Bradley Rd
Oakengates/Donnington TF2 132 D6
Wrexham LL13 221 B3
Bradleys The 1 SY1 114 B3
Braemar Rd 7 WV6 166 C2
Braggington La SY5 168 A5
Bramble Ridge WV16 218 F6
Brambles The 1 TF3 143 E7
Bramblewood TF12 152 D1
Bramley Cl 5 SY1 125 E8
Bramley Way 9 DY12 211 C2
Brampton Rd
Bishop's Castle SY9 181 F2
Lydbury North SY7 182 A1
Bramwell Cl 3 TF2 132 C3
Branches Cl 5 DY12 211 C1
Brand La SY8 217 C4
Brandon Ave TF5 130 B7
Brandon Gr 4 TF1 131 A7
Brands Farm Way TF3 144 D4
Brands Mdw 16 TF2 132 F8
Brandywell Rd TF12 152 D1
Brantley Cres 1 DY7 189 F1
Brantley La
Claverley WV5 189 F2
Trysull & Seisdon WV5 190 A6
Brassey Cl 2 SY3 125 D4
Bratch Comm Rd WV5 190 F4
Bratch La WV5 190 F4
Bratch Pk 1 WV5 190 F4
Bratton Rd TF5 130 A7
Bream Cl 5 TF2 132 A6
Brecknock Ct 2 TF1 131 A4
Bredon Cl WV7 157 A5
Breidden Cl 5 SY10 58 C7
Breidden Pl TF1 130 C6
Breidden Way SY3 136 E6
Brereton TF3 153 C8
Brewery Pl 14 LL11 221 C3
Briar Cl 4 SY5 172 E4
Briars The SY12 63 D7
Briarwood 8 TF3 144 B1
Brick Kiln Bank TF7 152 D7
Brick Kiln Way 9 TF2 132 E7
Brickbridge La WV5 190 F3
Brickhill La TF2 131 E3
Bridge Cl 8 TF2 132 A6
Bridge La SY5 169 F1
Bridge Rd
Alveley WV15 201 B3
Broseley TF12 152 B1
Dawley TF4 143 C3
Bridge Rd *continued*
2 Market Drayton TF9 36 A1
Much Wenlock TF13 159 D4
2 Wellington TF1 130 D3
Bridge Sea Mdw SY7 204 B5
Bridge Specl Sch TF3 144 D2
Bridge St
Bridgnorth WV16 218 F4
8 Clun SY7 193 D3
Knighton LD7 203 B3
1 Oakengates/Donnington TF2 132 A2
13 Shrewsbury SY1 125 B6
21 Wrexham LL13 221 C3
Bridge Way
Oakengates/Donnington TF2 120 E1
Shawbury SY4 103 D8
Bridgeend La SY7 204 B5
Bridgeford Way 6 SY2 125 F8
Bridgeman Ct TF11 135 F2
Bridgeman Rd SY11 58 F8
Bridgemere CE Prim Sch CW5 4 C8
Bridgemere Gdn World* CW5 4 F4
Bridgemere Mews CW5 4 D8
Bridgenorth Rd
Bobbington WV5 190 C3
Swindon DY3 190 C3
Bridges Bsns Pk The TF4 143 C3
Bridgewater Cl SY4 83 B1
Bridgewater St 7 SY13 15 A7
Bridgnorth Ave 49 WV5 190 F3
Bridgnorth Castle* WV16 218 F4
Bridgnorth Coll of Further Ed WV15 219 A3
Bridgnorth Endowed Sch WV16 218 F6
Bridgnorth Hospl WV16 218 E5
Bridgnorth Rd
Broseley TF12 161 D7
Dawley Hamlets TF3 153 B8
Highley WV16 200 E2
Madeley TF7 153 C7
Much Wenlock TF13 159 E4
Stockton TF11 163 B5
Sutton Maddock TF11 154 A1
Trysull & Seisdon WV6 190 C7
Wolverley & Cookley DY11 211 F7
Wombourne WV5 190 F3
Bridgnorth Sta WV16 218 F4
Bridgwater Cl 6 TF4 144 A2
Bridgwood 16 TF3 144 C1
Bridle Ct TF7 153 A6
Bridle Rd 4 TF7 152 F5
Bridle Terr TF7 153 A5
Bridleway The 5 TF9 36 B1
Bridleways The SY6 216 D5
Briery Bank TF7 152 D6
Briery La SY3 124 A6
Briggs La SY10 76 A1
Briggs Way TF2 132 C4
Bright St LL13 221 B3
Brimstree Dr TF11 145 F3
Brindley Cl
5 Albrighton WV7 157 A5
1 Wombourne WV5 190 E3
Brindleyford TF3 153 B8
Brindleyford Prim Sch TF3 153 B8
Bringewood Cl 4 SY8 217 C6
Bringewood Rd SY8 217 C6
Bringewood Rise SY8 217 C6
Britannia Way TF1 131 C5
Britons La WV16 187 E8
Brixton Way SY1 113 F4
Brixton Way Ret Pk SY1 113 F4
Bro Gwilym LL14 6 B8
Broad Mdw La TF7 152 D6
Broad Oak Cres SY3 137 A6
Broad Oaks 7 TF3 144 D3
Broad St Knighton LD7 203 B2
13 Ludlow SY8 217 C4
9 Montgomery SY15 174 B3
Broadhaven Cl 1 SY1 113 C2
Broadhay Rd SY13 49 F4
Broadlands Way 6 SY11 59 B8
Broadstone Mews 2 TF4 152 F8
Broadway Hadley TF1 131 D3
Newport TF10 110 A3
Shifnal TF11 145 F5
Broadway Ave TF2 132 A6
Broadway Cl
10 Shifnal TF11 145 F5
Shrewsbury SY2 125 F1
Broadwell La WV6 166 B2
Broadwell The 13 SY3 124 F3
Brock Hollow 3 TF4 143 D3
Brockford Glade TF5 130 B7
Brockton CE Prim Sch TF13 186 A5
Brockton Way TF7 153 D6
Brockwood Copse 7 TF1 130 B7
Bromfield Dr 2 SY3 125 E3
Bromfield Gr 4 LL12 221 D5
Bromfield Rd SY8 217 A7
Bromley Rd
Ludlow SY8 217 D5
Shrewsbury SY3 124 A7
Bromley Way 5 TF2 132 C2
Bromyard Rd WR15 220 F2
Bronington Pk SY13 13 B3
Bronington VA Prim Sch SY13 13 B4
Bronwylfa SY22 93 F8
Bronwylfa Rd 12 SY21 170 B7
Bron-y-dre LL13 221 B1
Bronygarth Rd SY10 23 C4
Bron-y-nant 2 LL13 221 B4
Bron-yr-efail 3 LL12 221 D8
Brook Cl SY5 137 B1
Brook Dr SY4 65 F5
Brook Hollow 1 WV16 218 F6
Brook La Hanmer SY13 11 F5
Worfield WV15 219 E5
Brook Mdw 5 TF5 130 B8
Brook Rd
Bomere Heath SY4 100 F4
Craven Arms SY7 195 D6
Madeley TF7 153 C6
Pontesbury SY5 173 A4
Shrewsbury SY3 125 D5
Whitchurch SY13 15 B7
10 Wombourne WV5 190 F3
Brook Rise 6 SY5 173 A4
Brook St
Shrewsbury SY3 125 C3
6 Welshpool SY21 170 B6
Wrexham LL13 221 C3
Brook Vale 14 DY12 211 E2
Brook Vessons Nature Reserve* SY5 176 F7
Brookdale 3 Hadley TF1 131 C5
2 Hadley TF1 131 B4
5 Shifnal TF11 145 F5
Brookes Rd 6 TF12 161 E7
Brookfield
Bayston Hill SY3 136 E6
Whitchurch SY13 14 E8
Brookfield Cl SY10 23 D4
Brookfield Rd SY21 170 B7
Brookfields SY10 23 C4
Brookhouse Rd SY11 58 E8
Brookhurst Way 2 TF2 132 F8
Brooklands Ave 3 TF11 145 F3
Brooklands Pk SY7 195 E6
Brooklands Rd WV7 157 B5
Brooklands The 10 DY3 190 F1
Brooklea Cl SY10 57 E2
Brooklyn Rd SY10 76 B1
Brooksbury SY6 216 C6
Brookside Bicton SY3 112 A2
2 Oakengates/Donnington TF2 120 E1
Pontesbury SY5 173 A5
6 Worthen with Shelve SY5 171 F3
Brookside Ave
Dawley TF3 153 B8
Newport TF10 109 E1
Stirchley & Brookside TF3 144 D1
Brookside Cl
Shifnal TF11 145 F6
15 Wombourne WV5 190 F3
Brookside Dr WV15 189 C6
Brookside Gdns
2 Brewood ST19 148 E8
1 Westbury SY5 169 B1
Brookside Prim Sch TF3 153 B8
Brookvale Rd 13 TF2 132 F1
Broom Dr
2 Minsterley SY5 172 E4
The Rock TF3 143 F7
Broom Gr 5 LL13 221 F4
Broome Cl SY7 195 B3
Broome Pl 2 SY1 125 C7
Broome Rd
Clungunford SY7 195 A1
Hopesay SY7 195 A4
Broome Sta SY7 195 A3
Broomfield Cl TF10 109 D3
Broomfield Pl TF10 109 D3
Broomfield Rd
Admaston TF5 130 A6
Newport TF10 109 D3
Broomhall Cl SY11 58 C6
Broomhall La
Oswestry Rural SY10 58 B7
Pimhill SY4 101 B2
Broomhurst Way 7 TF2 120 F1
Broseley CE Prim Sch TF12 152 D1
Broseley Cl 8 SY2 125 F2
Broseley Pipe Mus* TF12 152 C1
Brougham Sq 4 SY3 125 D4
Broughton Rd SY1 114 A3
Brow La SY12 43 C7
Brown Clee CE Prim Sch WV16 198 E8
Brown Clee Rd WV16 186 F1
Brown Moss Nature Reserve* SY13 15 E3
Brownlow Cres 1 SY12 27 B2
Brownlow Pk 2 SY12 27 B2
Brownlow Rd SY12 27 B2
Brownlow St SY13 15 A8
Broxton Rd LL13 221 F4
Broxtons Wood 4 SY5 172 C8
Brunel Rd Dawley TF4 143 F5
Great Dawley TF3 144 A5
Brunel Way SY3 125 D4
Brunlees Dr 4 TF3 144 C3

Bryn Cain SY22 .... 92 B5
Bryn Estyn Ave 1 SY13 ... 14 F8
Bryn Glas SY21 .... 170 B7
Bryn Gryffudd SY22 .... 221 F7
Bryn La Hanmer SY13 .... 11 B6
  Trewern SY21 .... 170 E5
Bryn Mawr (Fort)*
  SY22 .... 93 C3
Bryn Mawr SY5 .... 167 F6
Bryn Offa CE Prim Sch
  SY10 .... 76 A1
Bryn Rd SY3 .... 124 F7
Bryn Rise 1 SY10 .... 58 C7
Bryn Siriol
  Llansantffraid SY22 .... 92 B6
  2 Welshpool SY21 ...... 170 C7
Brynafon Cl SY20 .... 24 B1
Bryn-a-glyn LL11 .... 221 B7
Bryncoed SY5 .... 168 A5
Bryndraw Terr 22 LL13 .. 221 C3
Bryneglwys 1 SY21 ...... 170 B6
Brynhafod Dr 6 SY11 .... 58 C8
Brynhafod La SY11 ...... 58 C8
Brynhafod Rd SY11 ...... 58 C8
Brynhafren Cty Prim Sch
  SY5 .... 167 F6
Brynhyfryd Hospl
  SY21 .... 174 A7

Bryn-y-Cabanau Rd
  LL13 .... 221 D2
Bryn-y-Castell 2 SY21 .. 170 B5
Bryn-y-Ddol 1 SY21 ..... 170 B7
Brynyffynnon 9 LL11 .... 221 C3
Bryn-y-Grog Hill LL13 ... 221 F1
Bryony Rise 11 SY3 ..... 144 D3
Bryony Way TF2 .... 132 E1
Buchan Ave WV7 .... 156 D8
Buckingham Cl 4 SY11 ... 59 A8
Buckingham Cres 7
  TF3 .... 144 B1
Buckingham Rd LL11 .... 221 C6
Buckland Wlk 5 TF10 ... 109 F5
Bucknell CE Prim Sch
  SY7 .... 204 C4
Bucknell Sta SY7 .... 204 C4
Buffalo La 1 SY7 .... 193 C3
Buildwas Bank TF8 ..... 151 D6
Buildwas La
  Buildwas TF8 .... 151 C7
  Little Wenlock TF6 .... 142 D1
Buildwas Prim Sch
  TF8 .... 151 B6
Buildwas Rd
  Buildwas TF8 .... 151 C6
  Ironbridge TF8 .... 152 A4
  3 Wellington TF1 .... 130 C5
Bull Dingle 1 SY21 ..... 170 B6
Bull La
  8 Bishop's Castle SY9 .. 181 F4
  Hope Bowdler SY6 .... 216 F3
Bull Ring Ludlow SY8 ... 217 C4
  Much Wenlock TF13 ... 159 F5
Bullrush Glade TF2 ..... 132 E1
Bumblehole Mdws 8
  WV5 .... 190 F4
Bun La TF10 .... 123 C1
Buntingsdale Est TF9 ... 52 D4
Buntingsdale Infants Sch
  TF9 .... 52 E4
Buntingsdale Rd TF9 .... 53 A7
Bupa Yale Hospl LL11 .. 221 A4
Burcot Row TF6 .... 129 E3
Burford 17 Dawley TF3 .. 144 C1
  Dawley TF3 .... 153 C8
Burford CE Prim Sch
  WR15 .... 220 D6
Burgage Cl 2 TF9 .... 36 D1
Burgage The TF9 .... 36 C1
Burgess Croft 5 SY22 .. 170 B7
Burgess La LL13 .... 10 C7
Burgs La SY3 .... 137 B5
Burleigh Cl
  4 Dawley TF3 .... 144 C1
  8 Tenbury Wells WR15 .. 220 C4
Burley St 5 SY3 .... 125 C3
Burleydam Rd SY13 .... 16 E1
Burlington Cl 4 TF4 .... 144 A2
Burma Rd SY11 .... 41 B4
Burnell Cl SY3 .... 136 F5
Burnell Rd TF5 .... 130 A6
Burnham Ave SY2 ..... 126 B6
Burnside 1 TF3 .... 153 B8
Burnside Cl 8 SY7 ..... 195 E5
Burnside Gdns SY3 .... 125 B1
Burnt La SY21 .... 167 A1
Burroughs Bank TF4 ... 152 D7
Burton Borough Sch
  TF10 .... 110 A2
Burton Cl 6 TF4 .... 143 E4
Burton Dr LL12 .... 221 D8
Burton St Dawley TF4 .. 143 E4
  Shrewsbury SY1 ...... 125 D7
Burtondale TF3 .... 153 C8
Burwarton CE Sch
  WV16 .... 198 F4
Burway Cl SY8 .... 217 B6
Burway Dr
  Shrewsbury SY1 ...... 125 F1
  8 Whitchurch SY13 ... 15 B7
Burway La SY8 .... 217 A6
Burway Rd SY6 .... 216 C6
Bury St 8 LL13 .... 221 C2
Bury Walls (Fort)* SY4 .. 68 B4
Bush Cl Albrighton WV7 . 157 A5
  Wellington TF1 ...... 130 D7

Bush La 1 TF4 .... 143 F2
Bushfield Rd WV7 ...... 157 A5
Bushmoor Coppice Nature
  Reserve* SY6 .... 183 D2
But La SY5 .... 169 C4
Butcher Row 8 SY1 .... 125 C6
Butcher's La 1 SY3 .... 137 A6
Butler Rd
  Shrewsbury SY1 ...... 125 B4
  Wem SY4 .... 66 A8
Butlers Ct 8 TF2 .... 132 D3
Buttercup Cl 6 TF3 ..... 144 C3
Buttercup Way 4 SY3 .. 125 D3
Butterfield La SY7 ..... 194 B1
Buttermere Dr 11 TF2 .. 132 C2
Butterwick Dr 2 SY1 ... 113 C2
Buttery Gr TF2 .... 132 B3
Buttington Cross
  SY21 .... 170 D7
Buttington Rd TF2 .... 126 A8
Button Bridge La
  DY12 .... 210 F7
Buttonwood Glade 3
  TF3 .... 131 E2
Butts Rd
  Market Drayton TF9 ... 36 B1
  1 Wellington TF5 .... 130 B8
Buxton Rd TF4 .... 144 A4
By Pass Rd SY11 ...... 41 A8
Byfield 8 SY1 .... 113 F2
Bynner St SY3 .... 125 D4
Byron Cl 2 TF9 .... 53 A7
Bytherig SY5 .... 167 B4

C

Cabin La SY11 .... 41 B1
Cactus Dr 7 TF1 .... 131 B7
Cadfael Dr 8 TF3 ...... 144 A1
Cadman Dr TF2 .... 132 F1
Cadney La SY13 .... 29 C3
Cadogan Gdns 1 SY3 .. 125 A6
Cae Coed SY15 .... 174 F1
Cae Glas Pk* SY11 ... 58 D8
Cae Haidd SY22 .... 93 C6
Caegoody La SY12 ..... 26 F4
Cae-gwilym La LL14 .... 6 B8
Cae-gwilym Rd LL14 ... 6 C8
Cae Rd SY11 .... 40 E1
Caernarvon Cl 2 TF9 .. 36 E2
Caernarvon La SY4 .... 66 A6
Caernarvon Rd 4 LL12 . 221 F6
Caia Rd LL13 .... 221 D3
Calcott 1 TF3 .... 144 D2
Calcott Cres 3 SY2 ... 124 A8
Calcott La SY3 .... 112 A1
Calcutts Rd TF8 ...... 152 E2
Caldecott Cres 2 SY13 . 14 E7
Calder Cl
  Lilleshall & Donnington
  TF2 .... 132 F7
  5 Shrewsbury SY2 ... 126 B7
Caldercrofts 5 TF10 ... 109 F4
Callow Cres SY5 ..... 172 E3
Callow La
  Minsterley SY5 ...... 172 E4
  Wheathill DY14 ...... 208 D7
Callows Mdw WV15 ... 220 C2
Calverhall 1 TF3 ..... 144 D2
Calverhall Rd SY13 .. 16 F1
Calverton Way TF2 ... 132 F3
Calvin Cl 46 WV5 .... 190 F3
Camberley Cres 5 LL12 . 221 E5
Camberley Dr LL12 ... 221 E5
Cambria Ave SY2 .... 27 A2
Cambrian Ave 4 SY1 .. 41 E3
Cambrian Dr SY11 ... 40 E1
Cambrian Pl 8 SY11 .. 58 E8
Cambridge Cl SY4 ... 83 B1
Cambridge Sq 6 LL11 . 221 D8
Camellia Dr 7 TF2 ... 132 F1
Camlad Dr SY21 ..... 174 A6
Camp La SY8 .... 217 B3
Campbell Cl
  Bridgnorth WV16 .... 218 C4
  3 Oswestry SY11 .... 59 B8
Campbell Rd TF9 .... 56 D2
Campion Cl 1 WV5 ... 190 F3
Campion Dr TF2 .... 132 E2
Campion Way 10 SY12 . 211 E3
Camross Dr 8 SY11 .. 113 C2
Canal Rd SY22 ...... 93 F7
Canal Wood Ind Est
  LL14 .... 23 C8
Candle La CW3 ...... 4 F2
Candleberry Mdw 2
  TF1 .... 131 E1
Cankhorn The WV16 .. 218 F3
Cann Hall Dr WV15 .. 219 A5
Cann Hall Rd WV15 .. 219 A5
Canon St SY2 .... 126 C5
Canonbie Lea 8 TF7 .. 152 F5
Canonbury SY1 ..... 125 B4
Canonvale 8 SY3 ... 125 B4
Canterbury Cl 22 TF2 . 132 F8
Cantreyn Dr 8 WV16 . 218 D6
Cape St TF12 .... 152 C1
Capel Cl 2 SY3 ..... 122 D1
Capewell Rd TF2 ... 131 F5
Cappoquin Dr TF2 .. 132 C4
Captain Webb Dr TF4 . 143 E2
Captain's Rd WV16 .. 218 E3
Captains Mdw 2 TF1 . 143 E7
Caradoc Cres SY2 ... 126 A6

Caradoc Dr SY6 ...... 216 E5
Caradoc View SY5 ... 169 F1
Carding Mill Valley (NT)*
  SY6 .... 216 A8
Carding Mill Valley
  SY6 .... 216 C7
Cardington Dr 2 SY11 . 113 D3
Careswell Gdns TF11 . 145 E3
Carling Cl 5 SY1 .... 113 D2
Carlisle Cl 8 TF1 .... 131 B7
Carlson Dr LL11 ..... 221 D8
Carlton Cl SY3 ...... 124 B6
Carlton Dr TF2 ...... 132 B3
Carlton Rise 8 WV16 . 200 E2
Carmarthen Gn 5 TF1 . 131 A4
Carmen Ave SY7 .... 126 A6
Carnforth Cl SY3 .... 125 A1
Carnoustie Dr 7 TF7 . 153 C3
Carpenters La SY8 .. 206 E5
Carradine Cl SY4 .... 103 D7
Carreghofa Cty Prim Sch
  SY22 .... 93 E6
Carreghofa La SY22 .. 93 E6
Carrington Cl 8 SY3 . 124 D7
Cart Gate TF1 ...... 130 D3
Cartland Ave SY22 .. 126 B7
Cartmel Dr SY1 ..... 113 E3
Cartway WV16 ...... 218 F5
Carver St SY5 ...... 173 A5
Carver's Cl TF1 .... 130 D2
Carvers Rd 8 TF12 . 161 C8
Carwood 8 TF3 .... 144 D2
Cashbrook Dr SY13 . 15 B8
Castle Acre Rd 1 SY1 . 131 B7
Castle Bsns Pk The
  SY1 .... 125 C7
Castle Cl
  Tenbury Wells WR15 . 220 D6
  1 Wrexham LL11 .... 221 C7
Castle Cres LL14 ... 23 D8
Castle Ct 4 SY4 .... 66 A6
Castle Farm Intc TF3 . 145 A7
Castle Farm Way
  Dawley TF2 .... 132 F2
  St. Georges & Priorslee
  TF2 .... 145 A8
Castle Foregate SY1 . 125 C7
Castle Gates SY1 ... 125 C6
Castle Gn
  8 Bishop's Castle SY9 . 181 F4
  5 Pontesbury SY5 .. 173 A5
Castle Hill
  Church Stretton SY6 . 184 A6
  Whitchurch SY13 .... 15 A7
Castle Hill View TF9 . 69 C6
Castle House Sch
  TF10 .... 109 F4
Castle La
  Bayston Hill SY3 ... 136 F6
  Hadley TF1 .... 131 D5
Castle Rd
  Bayston Hill SY3 ... 137 A6
  Chirk LL14 .... 23 D7
  Churchstoke SY15 .. 83 E1
  Dawley TF4 .... 143 F1
  10 Knighton LD7 ... 203 B3
Castle Sq 8 SY8 .... 217 C4
Castle St Clun SY7 .. 193 C4
  8 Hadley TF1 ...... 131 D5
  11 Ludlow SY8 ..... 217 C4
  Oswestry SY11 .... 58 E8
  3 Shrewsbury SY1 . 125 C6
  Whittington SY11 .. 41 A5
Castle Terr 8 WV16 . 218 F5
Castle View TF2 .... 131 E2
Castle View Terr 8 SY7 . 217 C6
Castle Wlk 7 SY1 ... 170 B5
Castlecroft 8 TF3 .. 144 D2
Castlecroft Gdns
  WV15 .... 219 B4
Castlefields
  Bridgnorth WV16 ... 218 D4
  8 Whittington SY11 . 41 E3
Castlefields Prim Sch
  WV16 .... 218 E4
Castlefields Way
  Dawley TF3 .... 144 A1
  Dawley Hamlets TF4 . 152 F7
  Madeley TF7 ...... 153 A7
Castleford Rd SY8 .. 217 A6
Catherton 8 TF3 ... 144 D2
Catherton Rd DY14 . 209 D3
Catstritch La TF16 . 106 C3
Catterals La SY3 ... 15 E6
Catterick Cl 8 TF1 .. 131 A5
Caughley Cl TF12 .. 161 E7
Caughley Rd
  Barrow TF12 ...... 162 A5
  Broseley TF12 ..... 161 F6
Caus Castle* SY5 .. 172 A6
Carlton St
  8 Oakengates/Donnington
  TF2 .... 132 E3
  4 Wellington TF1 .. 130 D4
Charnborough Ct 8
  TF2 .... 132 A3
Cavan Dr 8 TF1 .... 143 E6
Cavell Cl 8 TF1 .... 130 F6
Cavendish Cl
  18 Oakengates/Donnington
  TF2 .... 132 A3
  3 Shrewsbury SY2 . 126 B7
Cavendish Sq 11 LL12 . 221 E8
Caxton Pl
  8 Oswestry SY11 .. 58 E8
  2 Wrexham LL11 .. 221 C4
Caynham Cty Prim Sch
  SY8 .... 213 D7
Caynham Rd
  Caynham SY8 ..... 208 B2
  Whitton SY8 ...... 207 F1
Caynton 2 TF3 .... 144 D1

Caynton Rd TF11 .... 164 D8
Cecil Cl TF4 .... 143 E5
Cedar Ave
  6 Ellesmere SY12 ... 27 A3
  Shawbury SY4 ...... 103 F7
Cedar Cl
  8 Alveley WV15 .... 201 B3
  Bayston Hill SY3 ... 136 F6
  7 Market Drayton TF9 . 36 A1
  St. Martin's SY11 .. 54 E5
  The Rock TF3 ...... 143 E8
  Wrexham LL12 .... 221 F7
Cedar Dr WV7 ...... 157 A5
Cedar Gr SY4 ...... 66 A7
Cedars Dr SY1 ..... 113 C1
Cedarwood Dr 8 TF2 . 132 B8
Cefn Hawys 4 SY21 . 170 B7
Cefn La SY10 ...... 75 C5
Cefn-y-spin La SY21 . 170 A7
Ceiriog Cl LL14 .... 23 D8
Celandine Way TF2 . 132 E2
Celandines The 2 WV5 . 190 F3
Cemetery Rd
  Dawley TF4 .... 143 E6
  Market Drayton TF9 . 36 B1
Centenary Rd 1 LL13 . 221 B2
Central Ave
  Church Stretton SY6 . 216 C6
  8 Hadley TF1 ..... 131 C3
  8 Wrexham LL12 .. 221 E6
Central Dr SY3 ..... 123 B1
Central Ordnance Depot
  TF2 .... 120 B1
Central Rd 8 LL11 .. 221 B4
Chaffinch Way 4 SY3 . 114 C3
Chainmakers Gate 7
  TF2 .... 132 C8
Chalice Cl 10 TF2 ... 132 F8
Chancel Dr 4 TF9 .. 36 A1
Chandlers Cl 8 SY8 . 217 D4
Chanticleer Cl 8 LL13 . 221 F4
Chantry Ct TF9 .... 69 C6
Chantry Cl TF12 .... 152 C1
Chapel Bank TF9 ... 71 F6
Chapel Cl
  Bomere Heath SY4 . 100 E4
  8 Much Wenlock TF13 . 159 E5
  48 Woolstaston WV5 . 190 F3
Chapel Gr 4 TF2 ... 132 C5
Chapel Hill 8 SY3 .. 124 A7
Chapel La
  Bridgnorth WV15 .. 219 E2
  Bronington SY13 .. 13 B1
  Broseley TF8 ...... 152 E3
  Chirk LL14 .... 6 E1
  Dawley Hamlets TF3 . 153 A8
  Ditton Priors WV16 . 198 D7
  Ellesmere Rural SY12 . 26 C5
  Hodnet TF9 .... 68 E2
  Hordley SY12 ..... 62 C3
  Loggerheads TF9 .. 21 C5
  Longden SY5 ...... 178 A8
  Moreton Say TF9 .. 52 A6
  Myddle & Broughton SY4 . 83 E1
  Norton in Hales TF9 . 20 B2
  Oswestry Rural SY10 . 57 D3
  Pant SY22 .... 93 F6
  Rock DY14 .... 209 D2
  Stoke upon Tern TF9 . 70 D7
  Whixall SY4 .... 30 B1
  Wombourne SY3 .. 190 E2
Chapel Rd
  18 Alveley WV15 .. 201 B3
  5 Clungunford SY7 . 195 A1
  Hadnall SY4 ...... 102 C5
  The Gorge TF8 .... 152 D4
Chapel St
  8 Carn-mawr LL14 . 6 D8
  Dawley TF4 .... 143 E3
  TF2 .... 132 E3
  8 Oswestry SY11 .. 58 E8
  Pontesbury SY5 ... 173 B4
  2 Welshpool SY21 . 170 B6
  Wem SY4 .... 66 A6
  48 Wombourne WV5 . 190 F3
Chapel Terr 8 TF2 .. 132 D3
Chapel View SY13 .. 29 D5
Chapmans Cl 11 TF3 . 144 B1
Charlecote Pk 8 TF3 . 143 D8
Charles Ave WV7 ... 156 F5
Charles Rd 8 TF1 .. 131 A2
Charlotte St Chirk LL14 . 6 C2
  8 Oakengates/Donnington
  TF2 .... 132 C5
Charlton Ave SY13 .. 16 A7
Charlton Cl 8 SY22 . 126 B7
Charlton Rise 8 SY8 . 217 E4
Charlton Sch TF1 ... 130 D7
Charlton St
  8 Oakengates/Donnington
  TF2 .... 132 D3
  4 Wellington TF1 .. 130 D4
Charnborough Ct 8
  TF2 .... 132 A3
Chartwell 2 SY2 .... 216 D7
Chartwell Dr 30 WV5 . 190 F3
Chartwell Rd TF1 ... 131 A2
Chasepool Rd SY3 .. 190 E1
Chatford 8 TF3 ..... 144 D2
Chatford Dr 6 SY3 .. 125 B1
Chatwell La TF10 ... 123 D1
Chatwood Cl 8 SY3 . 125 A1
Chaucer Cl 8 SY11 .. 59 A8
Chaucer Rd 8 SY11 . 59 A8
Cheapside 2 TF11 .. 145 F4

Checkley La
Checkley cum Wrinehill
  CW5 .... 4 F8
  5 Oakengates/Donnington
  TF2 .... 132 E3
Chelmarsh 8 TF3 ... 144 D1
Chelmarsh Prim Sch
  WV16 .... 200 D6
Chelmick Cl 8 SY6 .. 216 D5
Chelmick Dr SY6 ... 216 D5
Chelsea La 22 SY21 . 170 B6
Chelston Rd LL12 ... 221 F8
Chelwood Dr 8 SY1 . 113 C1
Chemistry SY13 .... 14 D7
Chepstow Dr 8 TF1 . 131 A5
Cherington 8 TF3 .. 144 D2
Cherry Arbor SY5 .. 149 E4
Cherry Dr 8 WV16 .. 200 F2
Cherry Cl
  8 Bewdley DY14 .. 211 C8
  Wem SY4 .... 66 B7
Cherry Dr 2 SY7 ... 27 A2
Cherry Tree 8 TF3 .. 143 F8
Cherry Hill Dr 6 LL12 . 221 F7
Cherry Tree Dr
  Oswestry SY11 .... 34 F6
  St. Martin's SY11 .. 54 E6
Cherry Tree Hill TF8 . 152 C7
Cherry Tree La CW3 . 5 A2
Cherrybrook Dr TF2 . 152 C2
Cheshire Cl 8 TF7 .. 152 F4
Cheshire Gdns 8 TF9 . 36 C1
Cheshire St 8 TF9 .. 36 C1
Cheshire View LL13 . 221 E4
Chester Ave LL13 ... 14 E8
Chester Rd
  Chetwynd TF10 .... 109 B8
  Edgmond TF10 .... 90 D3
  Hinstock TF9 ..... 72 A1
  Whitchurch SY13 .. 1 E1
  Whitchurch Urban SY13 . 1 C2
  Wrexham LL11 .... 221 D6
Chester St
  Shrewsbury SY1 .. 125 C7
  Wrexham LL12 ... 221 D3
Chesterfield Rd 8 TF4 . 144 A4
Chesterton 8 TF3 .. 144 D2
Chesterton Rd WV6 . 166 A4
Chestnut Ave
  Ellesmere Rural SY12 . 26 B6
  Oswestry SY11 ... 58 F7
  Wrexham LL12 ... 221 E6
Chestnut Cl
  7 Hanwood SY5 .. 173 F8
  Llandrinio SY22 .. 94 B1
  8 Shrewsbury SY3 . 124 D6
  Whitchurch SY13 . 14 C3
Chestnut Dr
  8 Bayston Hill SY3 . 137 A6
  8 Oakengates/Donnington
  TF2 .... 132 A6
  1 Trewern SY21 .. 167 D3
  Wellington TF1 .. 130 B5
  4 Worfield WV15 . 189 A6
Chestnut Gr 8 SY11 . 217 E4
Chestnut Rd TF9 ... 53 A8
Chestnuts The TF9 . 71 F3
Cheswardine La TF11 . 162 F4
Cheswardine Prim Sch
  TF9 .... 73 A8
Cheswell Dr TF10 .. 121 A5
Chetwode Cl TF9 .. 21 C6
Chetwynd Cl 8 TF3 . 144 C1
Chetwynd End TF10 . 109 E3
Chetwynd Gr TF10 . 109 F4
Chetwynd Pk TF10 . 109 D8
Chetwynd Pk Deer Park*
  TF10 .... 109 D5
Chetwynd Rd TF10 . 109 E4
Chevin Cl TF1 ..... 113 C5
Chichester Dr TF1 . 131 A7
Chilcombe Dr 10 TF2 . 132 F1
Childe Rd DY14 .... 209 E2
Childhood & Costume Mus*
  WV16 .... 218 F4
Children's Way 8 SY2 . 125 D3
Childs Ercall CE Prim Sch
  TF9 .... 89 A7
Chilton Cl 8 SY3 ... 125 B1
Chirbury 2 TF3 .... 144 D2
Chirbury CE Prim Sch
  SY15 .... 174 F5
Chirbury Rd SY15 .. 174 B3
Chirk Castle (NT)* LL14 . 6 A1
Chirk Cwm Hospl LL14 . 6 A3
Chirk Rd Gobowen SY11 . 41 A8
  Weston Rhyn LL14 . 23 E7
  Chirk Sta LL14 .... 23 C8
Chiswick Cl 8 TF2 . 126 D1
Chockleys Dr 8 TF1 . 131 B5
Chockleys Mdw 4 TF1 . 131 B5
Christ Church CE Prim Sch
  SY5 .... 149 F5
Christ Church La 8 TF2 . 132 F3
Christchurch 8 SY7 . 136 F6
Christine Ave TF1 .. 130 D2
Church Aston Cty Inf Sch
  TF10 .... 111 A1
Church Bank
  11 Clun SY7 ...... 193 C3
  8 Montgomery SY15 . 174 B3
  Welshpool SY21 .. 170 B6
  8 Wem 8 Bicton SY3 . 124 E7
  Forden with Leighton &
  Trelystan SY21 ... 170 D5
  Hadnall SY4 ...... 102 C5

Church Cl continued
Lydbury North SY7 . . . . .182 C1
Madeley TF7 . . . . .153 B5
Pontesbury SY5 . . . . .169 E1
St. Martin's SY11 . . . . .24 E5
Church Eaton Rd
TF10 . . . . .123 D6
Church Fields TF9 . . . . .20 C2
Church Hill
5 Ellesmere SY12 . . . . .27 C2
Ironbridge TF8 . . . . .152 C4
Church La
Baschurch SY4 . . . . .99 A8
Bicton SY3 . . . . .169 C8
Bishop's Castle SY9 . . . . . . .181 F3
3 Bridgnorth DY7 . . . . .189 F1
Boningale WV7 . . . . .157 A2
Elnosall Rural SY12 . . . . .26 A6
Ginosall TF10 . . . . .111 D1
Knockin SY10 . . . . .78 A1
Little Wenlock TF6 . . . . .142 D2
Llansantffraid SY22 . . . . .92 B5
Melverley SY22 . . . . .168 A7
7 Orleton SY8 . . . . .212 E2
Rock DY14 . . . . .210 D2
Sheriffhales TF11 . . . . .134 B5
Shrewsbury SY3 . . . . .125 B2
St. Martin's SY11 . . . . .24 E5
Stanton upon Hine Heath
SY4 . . . . .85 F4
Tasley WV16 . . . . .218 C6
Trysull & Seisdon WV5 . . . . .190 B8
Wem Rural SY4 . . . . .66 D6
Whitchurch Rural SY3 . . . . . . .16 A4
Whixall SY13 . . . . .31 B2
Church Mdw SY13 . . . . .2 A1
Church Par TF2 . . . . .132 A3
Church Preen Prim Sch
SY6 . . . . .185 E8
Church Rd
Albrighton WV7 . . . . .156 F5
10 Alveley WV15 . . . . .201 B3
Barrow TF12 . . . . .161 C3
Baschurch SY4 . . . . .43 B1
Broseley TF8 . . . . .152 F2
Clungunford SY7 . . . . .195 A1
Condover SY5 . . . . .178 C5
Dawley TF4 . . . . .143 F5
High Ercall TF6 . . . . .116 C1
Ironbridge TF8 . . . . .152 C5
11 Knighton LD7 . . . . .203 B3
Lilleshall TF10 . . . . .121 B3
Norton in Hales TF9 . . . . .20 C2
Shifnal TF11 . . . . .145 F4
Stanton upon Hine Heath
SY4 . . . . .85 F4
Swindon DY3 . . . . .85 A8
Uffington SY4 . . . . .114 D1
21 Welshpool SY21 . . . . . . .170 B6
Church Row 4 SY3 . . . . . .125 B2
Church St
7 Bishop's Castle SY9 . . . . .181 F3
3 Bridgnorth WV16 . . . . . . .218 F5
Broseley TF12 . . . . .161 D8
Chirk LL14 . . . . .23 E8
Church Stretton SY6 . . . . . . .216 C6
Claverley WV5 . . . . .189 E4
68 Cleobury Mortimer
DY14 . . . . .209 E2
9 Clun SY7 . . . . .193 D3
3 Condover SY5 . . . . .178 E8
Ellesmere SY12 . . . . .147 F2
Hadley TF1 . . . . .131 D4
11 Highley WV16 . . . . .200 E2
Hinstock TF9 . . . . .72 A1
Hodnet TF9 . . . . .57 B3
Ightfield SY13 . . . . .16 C2
3 Knighton LD7 . . . . .203 B3
Leintwardine SY7 . . . . .205 B5
3 Ludlow SY8 . . . . .217 C4
Madeley TF7 . . . . .153 A5
4 Market Drayton TF9 . . . . . .53 C8
Oakengates/Donnington
TF2 . . . . .132 A2
Oswestry SY11 . . . . .144 C4
Prees SY13 . . . . .49 D8
Ruyton SY4 . . . . .80 A1
Shawbury SY4 . . . . .103 D7
Shifnal TF11 . . . . .145 F3
7 Shrewsbury SY3 . . . . .126 A7
Tenbury Wells WR15 . . . . . .220 C5
9 Wellington TF1 . . . . .130 E4
Welshpool SY21 . . . . .170 B6
2 Whitchurch SY13 . . . . .15 A8
Whittington SY11 . . . . .14 A1
3 Wrexham LL11 . . . . .221 D3
Church Stretton Prim Sch
SY6 . . . . .216 D7
Church Stretton Sta
SY6 . . . . .216 D7
Church Terr 5 SY7 . . . . . . .58 D7
Church View
6 Bewdley DY12 . . . . .211 D2
Tibberton TF10 . . . . .107 E5
Church Walks TF1 . . . . .20 C2
Church Wlk
Dawley TF4 . . . . .143 F2

Church Wlk continued
Little Hereford SY8 . . . . .213 E3
Oakengates/Donnington
TF2 . . . . .132 D2
9 Wellington TF1 . . . . .130 F3
Churchill CI 2 SY8 . . . . . . .217 D3
Churchill Dr
4 Oakengates/Donnington
TF2 . . . . .132 B1
Wem SY4 . . . . .66 C6
Churchill Rd
Church Stretton SY6 . . . . . . .216 D7
Shrewsbury SY3 . . . . .125 B2
Wellington TF1 . . . . .130 E3
Churchward CI 6 TF2 . . . . .132 E2
Churchward Dr TF4 . . . . . . .143 D7
Churchway
3 Church Stretton SY6 . . . . .216 C6
Telford Dawley TF3 . . . . .144 D2
Churncote SY3 . . . . .144 D2
Churton Dr
Whitchurch SY13 . . . . .15 B7
Wrexham LL12 . . . . .221 D4
Cilcen Gr LL12 . . . . .221 D5
Cilcoed LL14 . . . . .6 E3
Cinders Rd WR15 . . . . .220 B1
Circular Rd WV7 . . . . .147 E1
City La SY22 . . . . .94 A1
City Rd TF6 . . . . .87 D1
Civic Gn SY3 . . . . .15 C7
Clanbrooke 1 TF3 . . . . . . .144 D1
Clap Gate Gr 6 WV5 . . . . .190 F4
Clap Gate Rd WV5 . . . . . . .190 F4
Clare's La Cl TF3 . . . . .143 E8
Claremont Bank 11 SY1 . . .125 B6
Claremont Dr 3 SY16 . . . . .218 D5
Claremont Hill 13 SY1 . . . .125 B6
Claremont Orch 3 SY8 . . .212 E2
Claremont St 10 SY1 . . . . .125 B6
Clarence Ave 5 LL11 . . . . .221 B6
Clarence Rd LL11 . . . . .221 B6
Clarence St 10 DY12 . . . . .211 D2
Clarendon Ave 5 LL11 . . . .221 B6
Clarke Rd 2 LL12 . . . . .221 F6
Clarkefields SY3 . . . . .137 A6
Claverley CE Prim Sch
WV5 . . . . .189 E4
Claverley Dr TF3 . . . . .144 B1
Claverley Rd SY1 . . . . .114 B3
Claverly Cres SY1 . . . . .114 B2
Clay La SY6 . . . . .196 A2
Claypit St 1 SY13 . . . . .15 A8
Clays La TF9 . . . . .68 E5
Clayton CI 2 SY8 . . . . .208 A1
Clayton Way SY3 . . . . .124 C2
Clee Gdns 1 SY8 . . . . .217 C4
Clee Hill Prim Sch
SY8 . . . . .208 C2
Clee Hill Rd
Burford WR15 . . . . .220 C8
Nash SY8 . . . . .214 C7
Clee Rise
4 Highley WV16 . . . . .200 E4
Little Wenlock TF6 . . . . .142 D2
Clee Stanton Rd
Bitterley SY8 . . . . .207 F4
Stoke St. Milborough
SY8 . . . . .208 A5
Clee Vantage SY8 . . . . .208 C2
Clee View SY8 . . . . .217 B4
Clee View CI 2 SY8 . . . . . .217 E5
Clee View Rd
7 Bridgnorth WV16 . . . . . . .218 C6
54 Wombourne WV5 . . . . . .190 F3
Cleeton La SY7 . . . . .2 A1
Clematis Dr 6 TF1 . . . . . . .131 B7
Cleobury La LL12 . . . . .202 C4
Cleobury Mortimer Prim Sch
DY14 . . . . .209 D3
Cleobury Rd DY12 . . . . .211 C2
Clerk's Ct 3 SY1 . . . . .170 B6
Cleveland Ave TF4 . . . . .116 E7
Cleveland CI TF4 . . . . .143 C3
Cleveland St SY1 . . . . .125 E6
Cliff Cres TF6 . . . . .105 E2
Cliff Hollow SY8 . . . . .138 C2
Cliff Rd WV16 . . . . .218 F5
Clifford Rd TF9 . . . . .53 A8
Clifford St SY2 . . . . .125 E5
Cliffs La TF10 . . . . .110 F8
Clift Cres 4 TF1 . . . . .130 C4
Clifton CI 1 LL13 . . . . .221 E1
Clifton St 3 SY1 . . . . .170 A6
Clive Ave SY6 . . . . .216 C4
Clive CE Prim Sch SY4 . . . . . .84 B5
Clive Gn 3 SY2 . . . . .125 F7
Clive Rd
8 Market Drayton TF9 . . . . . .53 C8
Pattingham WV6 . . . . .166 C2
Pattingham & Patshull
WV6 . . . . .190 B8
Shrewsbury SY3 . . . . .126 A7
Clive Way SY2 . . . . .125 E5
Clogs Bank DY12 . . . . .210 F5
Cloisters The 3 TF2 . . . . . .132 A4
Clos Bryn Y Ddol 2
SY21 . . . . .170 B7
Clos Ystrad 2 LL13 . . . . . . .221 C1
Close The
Newport TF10 . . . . .121 E8
7 Swindon DY3 . . . . .190 F1
The Gorge TF8 . . . . .152 A7
Clover Gr 2 TF3 . . . . .144 D3
Clover Heath 3 WV5 . . . . . .189 E4
Clover Rd 3 TF3 . . . . .144 D4
Cloy La LL13 . . . . .9 F6
Clun Castle* SY7 . . . . .193 C4
Clun CI TF1 . . . . .130 C6

Clun Mus* SY7 . . . . .193 D4
Clun Rd SY7 . . . . .195 C5
Clunbury CE Prim Sch
SY7 . . . . .194 E3
Clunbury Rd TF1 . . . . .130 C5
Clunton Coppice Nature
Reserve* SY7 . . . . .194 B3
Clwyd Wen LL13 . . . . .221 E2
Clydesdale Dr 4 TF4 . . . . . .143 C3
Coach Central TF3 . . . . .144 B6
Coach Rd
Shrewsbury SY3 . . . . .124 A7
7 The Gorge TF8 . . . . .152 B5
Coachman Mdw 6 TF1 . . . .130 C7
Coachwell CI TF3 . . . . .144 A6
Coalbrookdale & Ironbridge
CE Prim Sch TF8 . . . . .152 B4
Coalbrookdale Mus of Iron*
TF8 . . . . .152 B6
Coalbrookdale Mus of Iron
Library TF8 . . . . .152 B6
Coalbrookdale Open Air Mus
of Steel Sculpture*
TF8 . . . . .152 C7
Coalbrookdale Rd
TF8 . . . . .151 E8
Coalmoor La TF6 . . . . .142 F2
Coalpit La SY11 . . . . .41 E2
Coalport China Works Mus*
TF8 . . . . .153 B1
Coalport CI TF12 . . . . .161 E8
Coalport Dr 10 SY12 . . . . . .125 F2
Coalport High St TF8 . . . . . .153 B1
Coalport Rd
Broseley TF8 . . . . .153 B1
Madeley TF7 . . . . .153 B5
Cob Gr SY4 . . . . .100 E4
Cobden Rd LL13 . . . . .221 B3
Cobham Cres 3 DY12 . . . . .211 D2
Cobwell Rd TF12 . . . . .152 D2
Cockford Bank SY7 . . . . .14 E4
Cockshutt CE Prim Sch
SY12 . . . . .63 C7
Cockshutt La
TF9 . . . . .152 D1
7 Highley WV16 . . . . .200 E4
Cockshutt Rd 2 TF2 . . . . . .132 B4
Coder Rd SY8 . . . . .217 E4
Coed La SY15 . . . . .174 F1
Coedlan SY5 . . . . .168 A5
Coed-y-ffynnon 3
LL13 . . . . .221 C1
Cokayne La SY1 . . . . .113 E4
Coldridge Dr 5 SY1 . . . . . . .113 C1
Coleham Head 6 SY3 . . . . .125 D5
Coleham Prim Sch
SY3 . . . . .125 D4
Colemere Dr 6 TF1 . . . . . . .130 C5
College CI 2 DY14 . . . . . . .209 E2
College Ct
Bridgnorth WV15 . . . . .219 B3
2 Tenbury Wells WR15 . . . . .220 C4
College Farm 1 WV16 . . . . .166 C3
College Fields 9 SY1 . . . . .125 C5
College La 6 TF1 . . . . .130 F5
College St SY9 . . . . .59 A6
College St
6 Ludlow SY8 . . . . .217 C4
19 Wrexham LL11 . . . . .221 C4
Coller Mdw 5 SY2 . . . . . . .125 F7
Coleridge Cl 3 TF9 . . . . . . .53 A7
Collett Way TF2 . . . . .132 E2
Colley CI 2 SY2 . . . . .125 F8
Colliers Way
Dawley TF3 . . . . .144 A7
Lawley & Overdale TF3 . . . . .143 F7
The Rock TF3 . . . . .143 E7
Colliery Rd Chirk LL14 . . . . . .6 E1
Wrexham LL11 . . . . .221 B6
Collford CI 7 TF2 . . . . .132 F2
Collingwood Dr 9 SY3 . . . .124 B6
Collins CI 3 TF12 . . . . .161 E7
Collins St SY11 . . . . .221 E1
Collybrook Pk SY8 . . . . .208 B1
Conflower Gr 4 SY1 . . . . . .113 D2
Colridge CI 2 TF2 . . . . . . .132 E7
Colsty Bank SY7 . . . . .193 D7
Columbine Way 2 TF2 . . . . .132 E7
Colwyn Rd LL13 . . . . .221 E3
Combermere Abbey*
. . . . .3 D5
Combermere Dr
9 Shrewsbury SY3 . . . . . . .113 D5
8 Wellington TF1 . . . . .130 D5
Combsville La 2 SY11 . . . . . .40 F1
Comet Dr SY1 . . . . .113 E1
Comm The
Bomere Heath SY4 . . . . .100 F4
Oakengates/Donnington
TF2 . . . . .132 D7
Commercial Way 6
TF2 . . . . .132 B2
Common La DY14 . . . . .208 A2
Common Rd WV5 . . . . .190 F2
Compton Mews 3 SY5 . . . .169 C4
Comptons The TF9 . . . . .73 A8
Concord Coll SY5 . . . . .179 C4
Concorde TF4 . . . . .143 E5
Condover CE Prim Sch
SY5 . . . . .137 C1
Condover Dr SY2 . . . . .125 F1
Condover Hall Sch (RNIB)
SY5 . . . . .178 E8
Condover Ind Est SY5 . . . . .178 F6
Condover Way TF9 . . . . .52 C8
Conduit La WV16 . . . . .218 D4

Conery La SY13 . . . . .13 D2
Coney Gn
18 Shrewsbury SY11 . . . . . . .58 E8
4 Shrewsbury SY3 . . . . .124 A7
Coney Gn Way TF1 . . . . . . .130 D7
Coneybury View TF12 . . . . . .161 E8
Coningsby Rd WV7 . . . . . . .156 D8
Coniston
5 Dawley TF2 . . . . .132 D1
Telford TF2 . . . . .144 D8
Coniston Rd 2 SY1 . . . . . . .113 F3
Coniston Way 10 DY12 . . . .211 C2
Conners La TF10 . . . . .109 A3
Connormara Mdw 4 TF4 . . .143 D3
Connor Cres LL13 . . . . .221 E2
Conningyer Cres
8 Shrewsbury SY1 . . . . .125 F7
8 Shrewsbury SY2 . . . . .126 A6
Conroy Dr TF4 . . . . .143 C2
Constable Dr 8 TF5 . . . . . .130 B8
Constitution Hill 10 TF1 . . . .130 E4
Conway Dr SY2 . . . . .126 A7
Conway St TF4 . . . . .144 A2
Cooks La SY13 . . . . .1 D6
Cookscross WV15 . . . . .201 B3
Coolock CI 3 SY3 . . . . .124 F1
Cooper CI TF2 . . . . .144 F8
Coopers CI LL13 . . . . .221 F5
Coopers Field 3 SY11 . . . . . .24 F7
Coopers La SY11 . . . . .24 F6
Copall Paddock 12 SY9 . . . .181 F3
Copelea TF9 . . . . .72 A8
Copley La WV6 . . . . .166 A3
Copper Beech Rd 1 TF1 . . .131 C3
Copperfield 8 WV10 . . . . . .218 C6
Copperfield Dr
1 Oakengates/Donnington
TF2 . . . . .132 D8
Shrewsbury SY3 . . . . .124 D5
Coppice CI 4 TF7 . . . . .153 C5
Coppice Dr
Chetwynd TF10 . . . . .109 E5
1 Craven Arms SY7 . . . . . . .195 D5
High Ercall TF6 . . . . .116 E8
Coppice Holt Rd 1 TF5 . . . .130 A7
Coppice Gn SY3 . . . . .124 E3
Coppice Rd 3 SY11 . . . . . . .146 A6
Coppice The 6 TF9 . . . . . . .36 B1
Copse Hill TF13 . . . . .159 D8
Copthorne Cl SY3 . . . . .124 F6
Copthorne Dr 3 SY3 . . . . . .124 F6
Copthorne Gdns 8 SY3 . . . .124 E6
Copthorne Pk SY3 . . . . .124 E6
Copthorne Rd 3 SY3 . . . . . .125 B6
Copthorne Rise 1 SY3 . . . . .125 B6
Corbet CI Dawley TF4 . . . . .143 E1
Shrewsbury SY3 . . . . .113 D5
Corbet Dr TF9 . . . . .19 A4
Corbet Gr TF9 . . . . .52 E5
Corbet Sch The SY4 . . . . . . .81 A1
Corbet CI TF4 . . . . .143 E1
Cordingley Way TF2 . . . . . . .132 C6
Cordle Marsh Rd 2
DY12 . . . . .211 E3
Cordwell Rd SY4 . . . . .66 B6
Cordy La WV7 . . . . .157 B8
Corfham Castle* SY7 . . . . .197 B3
Corfield Cres 3 TF2 . . . . . .132 A3
Coricks Rise 8 SY3 . . . . . . .113 F2
Corinthian Dr SY3 . . . . .125 F8
Cornbrook 5 TF3 . . . . .144 D2
Corndean Mdw TF3 . . . . . . .143 D7
Corndon CI 2 SY1 . . . . .114 A2
Corndon Cres SY1 . . . . .114 A3
Corndon Dr
18 Montgomery SY15 . . . . .174 B3
5 Shrewsbury SY1 . . . . .114 A3
Corndon Rd 8 SY1 . . . . . . .114 A2
Cornelia Cres 2 SY2 . . . . . .125 F6
Cornelie CI SY8 . . . . .208 D2
Corner Farm Dr SY2 . . . . . .124 A6
Cornfield CI SY4 . . . . .100 F4
Cornfiower Gr 8 TF1 . . . . . .131 E1
Cornmell La 2 TF10 . . . . . . .109 F3
Corns Gr 81 WV5 . . . . .190 F2
Cornwall Ave 1 SY1 . . . . . . .41 A7
Cornwall Dr SY3 . . . . .137 A5
Cornwall Gdns WR15 . . . . . .220 C5
Cornwallis Dr 2 TF11 . . . . . .146 A5
Coronation Ave SY8 . . . . . . .217 B6
Coronation Cres TF7 . . . . . .153 B6
Coronation Dr Chirk LL14 . . . . .6 E2
Telford TF2 . . . . .132 D8
Coronation Rd 4 SY7 . . . . .195 D6
Coronation St
Cefn-mawr LL14 . . . . .6 C8
3 Highley WV16 . . . . .200 F3
Corporation La
Pimhill SY3 . . . . .113 B1
Shrewsbury SY1 . . . . .125 B8
Corporation St 10 SY9 . . . .181 F3
Corra Mdws SY13 . . . . .34 A7
Corra PI SY13 . . . . .34 A8
Corsten Dr SY2 . . . . .126 A8
Corve CI SY8 . . . . .217 D5
Corve Wk TF7 . . . . .132 D5
Corvedale Rd SY7 . . . . .195 E5
Coseley Ave SY2 . . . . .126 B7
Cosford Airfield WV7 . . . . . .156 C6
Cosford Sta WV7 . . . . .156 C6
Cote Rd TF5 . . . . .130 C8
Cotes Cres 8 SY3 . . . . .124 A7
Coton Cres 4 SY1 . . . . .125 C8

Chu - Cro 229

Coton Gn SY1 . . . . .125 B8
Coton Hill SY1 . . . . .125 C7
Coton La WV15 . . . . .201 B5
Coton Mount SY1 . . . . .125 B8
Cotshore Dr 18 SY3 . . . . . . .124 F3
Cotswold Dr WV7 . . . . .157 B5
Cotswold CI 8 TF7 . . . . . . .153 C5
Cottage Dr 3 TF11 . . . . . . .145 F3
Cottage Farm CI 7 TF7 . . . .153 B5
Cottage Fields SY11 . . . . . . .24 F6
Cottage Hospl TF9 . . . . .53 C8
Cottage La SY4 . . . . .24 F6
Cotwall La TF6 . . . . .117 A8
Cotwall Rd TF6 . . . . .116 F7
Cound CI TF1 . . . . .130 C5
Country Mdws TF9 . . . . .52 F8
Country Pk Halt Sta
WV16 . . . . .200 F3
County La WV7 . . . . .157 F4
Court Rd Madeley TF7 . . . . .153 B6
Telford TF3 . . . . .144 A8
Courtbond CI TF12 . . . . .152 D3
Courtland SY12 . . . . .221 B1
Court St TF7 . . . . .153 B5
Court The TF7 . . . . .153 B3
Courthouse La SY22 . . . . . . .93 C1
Courtland Dr TF2 . . . . .132 A6
Covert La WV16 . . . . .200 D5
Crab La DY7 . . . . .190 B1
Crabtree La
Ercall Magna TF6 . . . . .104 E1
3 Wem SY4 . . . . .66 A7
Crabtree Wlk 1 LD7 . . . . . .203 B3
Crackshall La TF4 . . . . .152 B8
Craig CI 3 SY1 . . . . .114 B3
Craig Way 8 LL12 . . . . .221 E6
Craig Wlk 10 WV15 . . . . . .219 A4
Craiggmillar Rd 2 LL12 . . . .221 D4
Cralves Mead WR15 . . . . . .220 C5
Cramer Gutter La
DY14 . . . . .209 B6
Cramer Gutter Nature
Reserve* DY14 . . . . .209 B6
Crampton Ct SY1 . . . . .59 B7
Cranage Cres TF1 . . . . .130 C3
Cranbrook Dr 8 SY1 . . . . . . .40 D1
Crane Hollow 28 WV5 . . . . .190 F3
Cranford Rd LL13 . . . . .221 F4
Cranmere TF3 . . . . .144 D2
Cranmore Dr 8 WV6 . . . . . .200 E3
Crathie PI 4 LL11 . . . . .221 C6
Craven Arms Rd SY7 . . . . . .195 A4
Craven Arms Sta SY7 . . . . .195 E6
Crawford Mdw SY12 . . . . . . .12 E4
Crescent CI 1 LL13 . . . . . . .221 E3
Crescent La SY1 . . . . .125 B5
Crescent PI WR15 . . . . .220 D3
Crescent Rd
Hadley TF1 . . . . .131 C4
9 Wellington TF1 . . . . .130 D5
Wrexham LL13 . . . . .221 D3
Crescent The
Bomere Heath SY4 . . . . .100 E4
3 Cleehill SY8 . . . . .208 C2
2 Craven Arms SY7 . . . . . . .195 E5
Much Wenlock TF13 . . . . . . .159 E5
Newport TF10 . . . . .121 F8
Oakengates/Donnington
TF2 . . . . .132 C7
Sheriffhales TF11 . . . . .134 C5
Tenbury Wells WR15 . . . . . .220 D3
Cressage Ave 3 SY1 . . . . . .113 D3
Cresswell Ct SY5 . . . . .124 B5
Crest Rd 8 TF2 . . . . .132 E3
Crest The TF3 . . . . .144 A8
Crewe St SY1 . . . . .125 D8
Cricket Mdw WV16 . . . . . . .218 C5
Cricketers La 8 TF2 . . . . . . .132 E3
Criftins CE Prim Sch
SY12 . . . . .26 B5
Criftins The 8 SY7 . . . . .205 B5
Criggion CI SY12 . . . . .12 E4
Criggion La SY5 . . . . .167 C5
Crispin La LL11 . . . . .221 B5
Crockington La WV5 . . . . . .190 C5
Crockington La WV5 . . . . . .190 D5
Crocus Dr 8 SY3 . . . . .125 D3
Croesnewydd Rd LL13 . . . . .221 B3
Croeswylan CI SY10 . . . . . . .58 D6
Croeswylan Cres 1 SY10 . . .58 D6
Croeswylan La SY10 . . . . . . .58 D5
Croft Fold 11 TF4 . . . . .143 E5
Croft Rd SY21 . . . . .170 B6
Croft The
Bridgnorth WV15 . . . . .219 A5
14 Wombourne WV5 . . . . . .190 E3
Croft Way TF9 . . . . .36 B1
Crofters View TF6 . . . . .142 D3
Crofts The TF7 . . . . .152 D6
Crogen 8 LL14 . . . . .6 A4
Cronk Hill SY4 . . . . .84 D4
Crosemere Cres 3 SY12 . . . .63 D7
Crosemere Rd SY12 . . . . . . .63 D7
Cross Bank SY6 . . . . .216 A4
Cross Hill 8 SY1 . . . . .125 B5
Cross Houses Hospl
SY5 . . . . .138 F4
Cross La
Bayston Hill SY3 . . . . .137 B6
Llansantffraid SY22 . . . . .92 A4
Cross Lanes
Ellesmere Rural SY12 . . . . . . .25 E6
Selattyn & Gobowen SY10 . . .40 A7
Cross Rd
Albrighton WV7 . . . . .156 F4

Cross Rd continued
Bausley with Criggion
SY5 ....167 B6
3 Oakengates/Donnington
TF2 ....132 B4
Cross Roads SY3 ....137 B6
Cross St
3 Ellesmere SY12 ....27 C2
Market Drayton TF9 ......36 D1
Oswestry SY11 ....58 E8
3 Shrewsbury SY1 ....125 C4
3 Tenbury Wells WR15 ...220 C6
Wrexham LL11 ....221 C5
Crossbank TF3 ....144 E2
Crossfields TF6 ....116 E8
Crossways
1 Church Stretton SY6 ...216 D5
7 Wrexham LL13 ....221 E4
Crossways The SY7 .....195 B2
Crow Hill La SY5 ....171 E4
Crow La
Child's Ercall TF10 ....89 B8
Upton Magna SY4 ....115 C3
Crowdale Rd 2 TF5 ....130 B8
Crowmeole Dr SY3 ......125 D5
Crowmeole La SY3 ....124 E4
Crowmere Gn 2 SY2 ....125 F5
Crowmere Rd SY2 ....125 E6
Cromoor Cty Prim Sch
SY2 ....125 F6
Crown Cl SY6 ....216 A2
Crown La
Church Stretton SY6 ....216 A2
Cressage SY5 ....149 D4
Crown St
Great Dawley TF4 ....143 F3
3 Wem SY4 ....66 A6
Croxon Rise SY11 ....59 B8
Cruckmoor La SY13 ....49 D5
Cruckton Cl SY3 ....124 D5
Cruckton Hall Sch
SY5 ....169 D1
Crudgington Prim Sch
TF6 ....106 A2
Crundalls La DY12 ....211 E3
Cuckoo's Rest 8 TF4 .....153 A8
Culmington SY7 ....137 A2
Cumberland Cl 2 TF12 .152 C1
Cumberland La SY11 .....31 C5
Cumberland Mews 4
TF1 ....131 A4
Cumberley La
Caynham SY8 ....208 A1
Hope Bagot SY8 ....214 B8
Cunliffe St LL11 ....221 C5
Cunliffe Wlk 3 LL12 ....221 D7
Cunnery Rd SY6 ....216 B5
Cunningham Way 6
SY1 ....113 D1
Curdale Cl 3 DY14 ......209 D2
Curie Croft 1 TF1 ....130 F6
Curlew Cl 3 SY1 ....114 C3
Curlew Dr TF1 ....131 B5
Curriers La TF11 ....146 A5
Cwms La SY6 ....216 E6
Cwrt Bryn Y Pys 8 LL13 ...9 C8
Cygnet Cl SY1 ....27 B3
Cygnet Dr TF3 ....153 C8
Cypress Cl 6 TF9 ....36 A1
Cyril Hayward Ct 6
TF1 ....131 C5

D

Daddlebrook 3 TF3 .....144 D5
Daddlebrook Rd
WV15 ....201 B3
Dahn Cl 5 SY2 ....217 E5
Daisy Bank Dr TF2 ....132 E4
Daisy La SY11 ....41 F4
Daisybank Cl 4 LL13 ....221 A2
Dalby Cl 8 SY2 ....125 F8
Dale Acre Way 1 TF3 ...144 C6
Dale Rd Ironbridge TF8 .145 C2
Shrewsbury SY3 ....126 A8
Dale St
11 Craven Arms SY7 ......195 E5
Wrexham LL13 ....221 E3
Dalebrook Dr 2 TF2 ....132 E6
Dalefield Dr 4 TF5 ....130 A7
Dalelands
Dalelands Est TF9 ....53 B7
Dalelands W TF9 ....53 B7
Dallamoor TF3 ....144 D5
Dallas La SY10 ....57 D2
Dalton Cl 4 WV5 ....190 F4
Dalton Dr 1 SY3 ....124 D7
Damford La TF10 ....90 E5
Damson Dr SY8 ....212 D2
Damson Dr TF3 ....143 E8
Damson La TF11 ....134 F8
Damson Pk WV6 ....166 D3
Damson Way 1 DY12 ...211 E2
Dana The SY5 ....125 D6
Danesbrook 5 WV5 ......189 F4
Danesford TF3 ....144 D6
Danford La WV6 ....189 F4
Daniels Cross TF10 ......110 A4
Darby La SY6 ....184 F2
Darby Rd TF8 ....152 A7
Darfield 3 SY1 ....113 D1
Dargate Cl 4 SY3 ....124 F1
Dark La Broseley TF12 ...152 D1

Dark La continued
Great Dawley TF4 ....144 B4
Leintwardine SY7 ....205 B5
Ludlow SY8 ....217 E4
Newport TF10 ....109 E1
3 Overton LL13 ....13 C6
Shrewsbury SY3 ....125 F5
Whitchurch Rural SY13 ......3 B1
Dark La Dr 5 TF3 ....144 A5
Dark Orch WV15 ....220 C3
Darliston TF3 ....144 D5
Dartmouth Ave 4 WV6 .166 C2
Darville SY1 ....113 E1
Darwin Gdns SY3 ....125 E2
Darwin Rd 5 TF1 ....130 D5
Darwin St SY3 ....125 B7
Dashwood Dr 2 TF1 .....130 D7
Davenport Dr 2 TF5 .....130 B7
Davenport House *
WV15 ....189 A6
David Ave 2 SY5 ....173 B5
Davids Cl 3 TF4 ....143 F6
Davies Cl 3 LL13 ....221 E1
Davies St SY4 ....66 A8
Davina Gdns 3 SY3 ......136 F6
Dawley CE Prim Sch
TF4 ....143 E3
Dawley Gn Way TF4 .....143 E4
Dawley Rd
Lawley & Overdale TF1 ...143 B7
Wellington TF1 ....131 A2
Daywell 1 TF1 ....144 D6
Daywell Cres
1 Gobowen SY11 ....41 A8
Selattyn & Gobowen SY10 ..24 A1
De Warenne Cl 2 SY13 ...15 B7
Dean Cl Dawley TF2 .....132 C2
3 Market Drayton TF9 .....36 A1
3 Tenbury Wells WR15 ...220 D6
Wrexham LL12 ....221 F6
Dean Rd
48 Wombourne WV5 ......190 F3
Wrexham LL11 ....221 F6
Deane Cl 3 SY3 ....124 B7
Decmar Rd WV15 ....221 F4
Dee Ave LL12 ....221 E6
Dee Cl TF1 ....130 D6
Deedes Ave SY2 ....125 F3
Deepdale 4 TF3 ....144 D6
Deepdales 8 WV5 ....190 F3
Deepfield Rd TF4 ....143 E2
Deepfields 3 SY3 ....124 E3
Deer Pk Dr TF10 ....109 E5
Deer Pk Rd TF1 ....130 D3
Deercote TF3 ....144 C5
Deermoss 7 SY13 ....15 A8
Deighton's Cl WV16 .....218 E4
Delamere Cl 3 TF3 ....143 D8
Delamere Rd 6 TF2 ......132 C2
Delaware Ave WV7 ....156 F5
Delfan SY10 ....76 A1
Dell The SY4 ....124 B6
Delph Side 5 TF12 ....161 C8
Delph The 8 TF3 ....144 C4
Delwood Dr SY1 ....170 B6
Dene Rd WV4 ....190 F6
Denham Dr 3 SY11 ....40 D1
Denning Rd LL12 ....221 E2
Derfald St 81 SY1 ....125 D7
Derrington Rd 3 WV16 .198 D8
Derwen 1 LL14 ....6 E3
Derwen Cl SY11 ....41 A5
Derwen Cres LL11 ....221 C1
Derwen Gn 5 SY22 ....94 A1
Derwent Ave 2 SY1 ......113 C5
Derwent Cres LL11 ....221 D6
Derwent Dr
8 Bewdley DY12 ....211 C2
Telford TF2 ....132 E1
Deuxhill Cl TF4 ....143 E5
Deva Way LL13 ....221 D7
Devil's Spittleful Nature
Reserve * DY12 ....211 F2
Devon Cl 5 TF2 ....221 D8
Dhustone Cl 2 SY8 ......208 C2
Dhustone La SY8 ....208 B3
Diamond Ave SY11 ....59 B7
Dickens Pl 3 SY3 ....124 D5
Dickins Rd TF2 ....132 C6
Didcot Cl 3 SY1 ....125 E8
Digbeth La WV5 ....189 D4
Diglake SY13 ....32 A8
Diksmuide Dr TF3 ....27 B3
Dimmingsdale Rd
WV4 ....190 F7
Dinchope Dr 5 TF3 ......144 D6
Dingle Dr TF11 ....164 C8
Dingle La CW5 ....4 D7
Dingle Rd 5 SY21 ....170 B7
Dingle The LD7 ....203 E2
Dingle View WV16 ....218 E6
Dinham SY8 ....217 B3
Dinthill TF3 ....144 D5
Ditherington Rd SY1 ....113 E1
Dobell La SY4 ....49 B3
Docks Mdw SY4 ....80 A1
Doddington Cl TF3 ....144 D5
Doddlecote Cl TF3 ....144 C2
Dodgson La SY7 ....195 E5
Dodington SY13 ....15 A7
Dodmoor Grange TF3 ...144 D4
Dodmore La SY8 ....217 C6
Dog In the La TF6 ....143 A4
Dog Kennel La
2 Bucknell SY7 ....204 C5
Market Drayton TF9 ....53 D8
Dog La 9 DY12 ....211 D2

Dogpole 6 SY1 ....125 C5
Dol Acton LL11 ....221 B7
Dolgoch SY10 ....76 B5
Dolgoch Quarry Nature
Reserve * SY10 ....76 B5
Dolydd La LL14 ....6 B8
Dolydd Rd LL13 ....221 B3
Dolyfelin SY21 ....170 A6
Domas Way 9 SY22 ....94 B2
Domgay Pl SY22 ....94 B2
Domgay Rd SY22 ....94 B3
Donaldson Dr 2 TF9 .....72 F7
Donington La WV6 ....148 D2
Donkey La (Avenue Road)
SY8 ....213 B5
Donkey La SY8 ....213 B5
Donnerville Cl 2 TF1 ....130 C5
Donnerville Dr TF1 ....130 B5
Donnerville Gdns TF1 ...130 B6
Donnett Cl 2 SY11 ....41 F2
Donnington Dr TF2 ......120 B4
Donnington Way TF2 ....120 C2
Donnington Wood CE Jun
Sch TF2 ....132 E6
Donnington Wood Cty Inf Sch
TF2 ....132 D5
Donnington Wood Way
TF2 ....132 D5
Dorchester Dr TF2 ....132 F7
Dorran Pl 1 TF2 ....132 D1
Dorrington CE Prim Sch
SY5 ....130 D6
Dorset Cl LL12 ....221 D8
Doseley Ind Est TF4 .....143 D2
Doseley Rd TF4 ....143 D2
Dothill Cty Jun Sch
TF1 ....130 D6
Douglas Rd 1 SY3 ....124 C7
Dounton Cl 1 SY1 ....114 A3
Dovaston Cl 1 SY1 ....78 D8
Dovedale Fold 3 TF4 ....144 A6
Dovehouse La WV16 .....208 D8
Dover Dr 2 TF1 ....131 B6
Dower House Sch The
WV16 ....199 E8
Dowles Rd DY12 ....211 C3
Down Cty Prim Sch The
WV16 ....199 E8
Downemead 1 TF3 ....144 D5
Downfield Rd SY3 ....124 E3
Downing Cl 2 SY22 ....94 A1
Downton Viewa SY9 ....217 E5
Drapers Ct 3 TF1 ....130 E4
Drawbridge La WV16 ....208 D8
Drawwell La SY4 ....66 A6
Drawwell St SY3 ....125 C3
Draycott 2 TF3 ....144 D5
Drayton Gdns 9 SY3 .....125 F2
Drayton Gr 8 TF1 ....36 C1
Drayton Rd Hodnet TF9 ..69 D7
Shifnal TF11 ....146 A6
Drayton Way TF4 ....143 E5
Drenewydd Rd 11 SY11 ..41 C3
Drinkwater St SY3 ....124 B7
Drovers Way 4 TF10 ......110 A4
Drummery La TF6 ....125 F7
Drummond Cl 7 TF2 .....152 C6
Drury La Bicton SY4 ......169 E5
Minsterley SY5 ....172 C2
Withington SY4 ....116 A1
Dry Mill La DY12 ....211 B5
Duchess Dr WV16 ....218 D6
Duchess Wlk SY8 ....206 D2
Duckett Dr 2 TF4 ....143 D2
Dudleston Cl 4 SY7 ......195 E5
Dudmaston Hall (NT) *
WV15 ....200 F7
Duffryn TF3 ....144 D6
Duke St Broseley TF12 ...152 C1
Chirk LL14 ....6 E2
Oakengates/Donnington
TF2 ....132 D2
2 Wrexham LL11 ....221 C3
Duke's Dr The TF6 ....118 F5
Duken La WV15 ....189 B1
Dukes Hill 2 TF1 ....132 A2
Dukes Way 8 TF2 ....132 D3
Dumblehole La SY8 ......213 B5
Dumbar 3 SY1 ....125 A6
Dundonald Rd 4 SY3 ....113 C5
Dunedin Dr 4 SY3 ....124 E4
Dungarven Dr TF10 ......109 D2
Dunkeld Dr SY2 ....126 A7
Dunlin Cl 2 TF1 ....131 B5
Dunmaster Way 5 TF1 ...144 B1
Dunmore Rd 8 DY12 .....211 E3
Dunning Cl 1 SY4 ....80 A1
Dunsheath TF3 ....144 C6
Dunstone 2 TF3 ....144 D6
Dunval Cl WV16 ....218 D7
Dunval Rd WV16 ....218 D7
Durrant Rd 2 TF2 ....132 D1
Dutton Cl
Clive Barracks TF9 ....70 D8
Stoke upon Tern TF9 ....52 D1
Dutton Gn 8 SY1 ....113 E4
Duxmoore Way 5 TF3 ...143 E5
Dyas Cl 7 TF11 ....145 A3
Dyas Mews 1 TF11 ....145 F3
Dyffryn Foel SY22 ....92 B5
Dykes La TF10 ....123 D8
Dymock Pl LL13 ....10 F4

E

Eagle La 12 DY14 ....209 E2
Earls Cl SY11 ....221 C2
Earls Dr TF4 ....153 A8
Earl's Hill Nature Reserve *
SY5 ....173 C3
Earls View Hill 2 SY3 ...124 A6
Earlston Pk SY1 ....124 A4
Earlswood 3 SY3 ....124 C6
Earlswood Dr 9 TF2 .....152 F4
East Ave
Oakengates/Donnington
TF2 ....132 C7
Wrexham LL11 ....221 C6
East Castle St WV16 .....218 F4
East Cres SY1 ....114 A2
East Gate 3 SY1 ....125 B3
Eastern Ave WV7 ....156 F8
Easthope Rd
Broseley SY12 ....152 C2
4 Church Stretton SY6 ....216 C6
Eastleigh Cl 2 LL11 .....221 C7
Eastwick La SY12 ....9 E1
Eastwood Dr 6 TF2 ......132 E6
Eaton Cres 2 TF2 ....132 C1
Eaton Fields 3 SY11 .....59 B8
Eaton Rd TF9 ....89 A5
Ebnal Rd SY2 ....126 A3
Ebstree Mdw 3 WV5 ....190 C5
Ebstree Rd WV5 ....190 C5
Ebury Ave 1 SY3 ....114 A2
Eckford Pk SY4 ....66 A6
Eden Cl 8 SY2 ....125 F8
Eden St 8 SY11 ....58 E8
Edge Cl SY3 ....124 A4
Edge Wood Nature Reserve *
SY6 ....196 C6
Edgefield Gn 1 SY3 ......124 B6
Edgelea Cres 3 SY13 ....15 B6
Edgeley Gdns SY13 ....15 B6
Edgeley Rd SY13 ....15 B6
Edgmond Rd TF10 ....109 D4
Edinburgh Rd
Broseley TF12 ....152 C1
Wrexham LL11 ....221 C6
Edith Cl 8 TF3 ....144 A1
Edward German Dr 3
SY13 ....15 A8
Edward Parry Ct 4 TF4 .143 F6
Edward St
Oswestry SY11 ....58 D7
Wrexham LL13 ....221 B2
Egerton Cl 5 SY13 ....15 A8
Egerton Rd SY13 ....15 B8
Egerton St 8 LL11 ....221 C4
Egerton Wlk LL11 ....221 D7
Eglantine Cl 18 TF2 .....132 E8
Eider Dr TF1 ....131 A7
Elan Cl 7 DY12 ....211 C2
Elder Gr 2 WV5 ....190 F3
Elderberry Cl 3 TF3 .....143 F8
Eldon Dr SY3 ....124 E7
Eleanor Harris Rd 1 SY4 ..81 B1
Eleanors Cl 3 TF4 ....143 E8
Elgar Cl SY1 ....58 F8
Eliot Cl TF3 ....144 A2
Elizabeth Ave WV16 .....218 D5
Elizabeth Cres TF12 .....152 C1
Elizabeth Cl 6 TF9 ....36 C1
Elizabeth Gr WV16 ....200 E2
Elizabeth St SY13 ....15 A8
Elkington Cl 10 TF10 ....109 E2
Elland Cl 5 SY2 ....125 F8
Ellerdine Cl 2 TF3 ....143 D8
Ellerton Rd TF9 ....34 E3
Ellesmere Bsns Pk
SY12 ....26 F1
Ellesmere Coll SY12 ......27 A2
Ellesmere Ct 8 TF10 ....109 E2
Ellesmere Dr
8 Bewdley DY12 ....211 C2
6 Shrewsbury SY1 ....113 C1
Ellesmere Gr 4 TF9 ....52 F8
Ellesmere La LL13 ....10 C8
Ellesmere Prim Sch
SY12 ....27 A2
Ellesmere Rd
Bronington SY13 ....13 E5
1 Shrewsbury SY4 ....113 D4
St. Martin's SY11 ....24 E6
Wem Urban SY4 ....65 E7
Whittington SY11 ....41 F3
Ellis Peters Dr TF3 ....144 A1
Ellsmore Cl 4 TF3 ....143 F2
Elm Cl 12 Ellesmere SY12 ...27 A2
Newport TF10 ....109 F1
4 Oswestry SY11 ....59 A7
Elm Dr TF9 ....36 A1
Elm Gr LL11 ....221 E5
Elm Gr Way 6 LL12 ......221 E6
Elm Rd WV7 ....156 C5
Elm St SY1 ....125 C8
Elm Tree Cl 8 SY5 ....190 F3
Elm Way 8 TF7 ....131 F6
Elmfield Rd SY2 ....125 F5
Elmhurst WV15 ....219 B5
Elmpark Dr TF1 ....130 C5
Elms La SY6 ....216 A2
Elms Paddock SY6 ....216 A2
Elms Paddock The
SY6 ....166 C2
Elmsdale Cres 2 TF5 ....130 A7
Elson Rd SY12 ....26 F3
Elstree Cl 5 SY3 ....124 F1

Elswick Cl 6 SY3 ....124 F1
Eltham Dr TF2 ....133 A2
Elton Rd 8 DY12 ....211 C2
Ely Cl 6 TF1 ....133 A1
Emmanuel Ct 2 LL14 .....6 C8
Empress Rd 2 LL13 ....221 B2
Emral Rise TF1 ....130 D6
Emscote 4 SY1 ....113 D1
Emsirey Bank SY5 ....124 C1
Eneurys Rd LL11 ....221 D6
Enfield St 5 SY7 ....193 D3
Enginuity * TF8 ....152 B6
English Walls SY11 ....58 E7
Ennerdale Cl 2 TF2 ....132 E1
Ennerdale Rd SY1 ....113 E3
Epsom Cl 3 SY1 ....124 A4
Epsom Ct 4 TF1 ....131 A5
Ercall Cl TF2 ....132 A5
Ercall Gdns 2 TF1 ....130 D3
Ercall Jun Sch TF1 ....130 F2
Ercall La TF1 ....130 D2
Ercall Nature Reserve The *
TF1 ....142 C8
Ercall View TF1 ....131 D1
Ercall Wood Tech Coll
TF1 ....130 E2
Erddig Rd 8 LL13 ....221 C1
Erdington Cl SY4 ....103 E8
Eric Lock Rd 3 SY3 ......137 A5
Eric Lock Rd W SY3 ......137 A6
Erw Las LL12 ....221 D7
Escent TF9 ....52 E5
Eskdale Rd SY2 ....126 A7
Esless Rd 11 LL14 ....221 A1
Espley 14 TF1 ....130 E4
Espley Robt TF9 ....69 D7
Essex Chase TF2 ....132 F1
Essex Dr 1 LL12 ....221 D7
Essex Rd SY6 ....216 D6
Estate Rd WV15 ....219 E4
Euston Way TF3 ....144 C7
Evelith La TF11 ....154 F7
Everglade Rd
5 Dawley TF2 ....132 E1
Dawley TF2 ....132 D6
Evergreens The TF11 ...134 B5
Everley Cl 1 SY2 ....124 E4
Ewart Rd TF2 ....132 D6
Ewart St LL14 ....6 E2
Exeter Dr TF1 ....130 F5
Eyton La SY4 ....81 B1
Eyton Pl 2 TF4 ....143 F4
Eyton Rd 2 TF4 ....144 A4
Eyton View 1 TF1 ....130 D6

F

Factory La DY14 ....209 C7
Faintree Ave 11 SY2 ....125 F2
Fair Lawn WV1 ....157 A5
Fair Oak TF10 ....109 F4
Fair View SY1 ....167 A3
Fairburn Dr 2 SY3 ....124 F4
Fairburn Rd TF1 ....144 A3
Fairfield WV16 ....218 C6
Fairfield Cl 9 SY7 ....195 E5
Fairfield Ct 2 TF1 ....130 E4
Fairfield St 3 LL13 ....221 C2
Fairlawn Ave SY3 ....125 A1
Fairlawn Gdns 1 SY3 ....125 A1
Fairness Cl 8 SY2 ....126 B7
Fairview Dr 3 SY2 ....136 F6
Fairways Dr
Madeley TF7 ....152 F4
Whitchurch SY13 ....2 A1
Fairways The SY5 ....137 B1
Fairy Rd LL13 ....221 C2
Falcons Way SY5 ....124 C5
Falklands Cl 6 DY3 ....190 F1
Fallow Deer Lawn
TF10 ....109 F5
Fallow Rd 8 SY5 ....130 C8
Fallowfield SY6 ....178 C1
Falstaff St SY1 ....125 D8
Far Forest Lea Meml Fst CE
Sch DY14 ....210 D1
Far Vallens TF1 ....131 D4
Faraday Dr WV15 ....219 B4
Farcroft Dr TF4 ....143 D6
Farden La SY8 ....208 A2
Farfield Cl 5 SY2 ....124 C7
Farfields Rd TF9 ....36 D2
Farley Rd TF3 ....159 F7
Farlow CE Prim Sch
DY14 ....209 A2
Farm Cl TF7 ....153 C5
Farm Gr TF10 ....109 D3
Farm La
All Stretton SY6 ....184 B6
Church Stretton SY6 ....216 D4
Dawley TF4 ....143 C3
Ellesmere Rural SY12 .....44 A6
Farm Lodge Gr 3 TF3 ...144 A5
Farm Mdw Cl 1 TF4 ......143 C3
Farm Rd Barrow TF12 ....161 C3
Telford TF3 ....165 D7
Farmdale Rd WV5 ....165 D7
Farmfields Rise CW3 ......5 A1
Farmlands Rd WV16 .....218 C5
Farmlodge La SY1 ....113 C1
Farmoor SY1 ....114 C2
Farnside 2 LL12 ....221 D7
Farmstead Ct 2 SY3 .....130 C2
Farndon St 6 LL13 ....221 D3
Farr La SY4 ....114 B4
Farriers Gn
Dawley TF4 ....143 D6
Newport TF10 ....110 B3

Farrington La LD7 ....203 C1
Fearn Dr **7** SY2 ....126 B7
Featherbed La
　Bicton SY3 ....112 C1
　Shrewsbury SY1 ....114 B3
Feathers Art Gall*
　SY8 ....217 C4
Feiashill Cl WV5 ....190 D4
Feiashill Rd **7** SY3 ....190 E3
Felcourt Dr **7** SY3 .....124 C7
Fellows Cl TF4 ....143 F1
Fellow Cl **3** SY11 ......125 E7
Fence Rd TF4 ....143 D4
Fenns Cres TF2 ....132 D3
Fenton Cl **1** SY3 ....124 C7
Fenwick Dr LL3 ....124 A7
Fern Lea Croft **16** SY3 .124 A7
Fernbrook **4** SY5 ....178 C6
Ferndale **6** LL13 ....221 F4
Ferndale Cl **4** SY22 ....94 A1
Ferndale Cres **5** SY11 ..41 A8
Ferndale Dr **7** TF2 .....144 E8
Ferndale Rd SY1 ....114 B2
Fernham Dr **6** LL12 .....221 E8
Fernhill Ave
　1 Gobowen SY11 ......41 B8
　Selattyn & Gobowen SY11 .24 B1
Fernhill Cl **2** SY11 .....41 A8
Fernhill La SY11 ....41 B8
Fernwood Cl **3** TF1 .....130 D7
Ferrers Rd SY11 ....58 E7
Ferriday Cl TF7 ....152 D6
Ferry Rd TF8 ....119 A3
Festival Gdns **4** TF1 ...130 F2
Ffordd Alafon LL12 ....221 F8
Ffordd Aled LL12 ....221 E8
Ffordd Alun LL12 ....221 E8
Ffordd Cynan **2** LL12 ...221 E7
Ffordd Dyfed LL12 ....221 E5
Ffordd Dylan **2** LL12 ...221 E5
Ffordd Edgeworth **7**
　LL12 ....221 E5
Ffordd Elan LL12 ....221 E7
Ffordd Elfed LL12 ....221 E5
Ffordd Elwy LL12 ....221 E5
Ffordd Estyn LL11 ....221 C1
Ffordd Glyn LL12 ....221 C1
Ffordd Gwilym **11** LL12 .221 C2
Ffordd Gwynedd LL12 .....221 C7
Ffordd Hooson LL12 ....221 E5
Ffordd Jarvis LL12 ....221 E8
Ffordd Kayton LL14 ....6 C8
Ffordd Lerry LL12 ....221 E8
Ffordd Llywelyn **1**
　LL12 ....221 E8
Ffordd Madoc LL12 ....221 E5
Ffordd Maelor LL12 ....221 E5
Ffordd Meirionnydd **10**
　LL11 ....221 C7
Ffordd Mon **1** LL12 .....221 C2
Ffordd Morgannwg **11**
　LL11 ....221 C7
Ffordd Offa **6** LL14 .....6 C8
Ffordd Owain **2** LL12 ...221 E8
Ffordd Pedrog **1** LL12 ..221 E7
Ffordd Tegid LL12 ....221 E8
Ffordd Tegla LL12 ....221 E8
Ffordd Trefaldwyn **9**
　LL11 ....221 C7
Ffordd Trefin LL12 ....221 E8
Ffordd Tudno LL12 ....221 E7
Ffordd Ystrad LL12 ....203 B3
Ffrydd Cl **12** LD7 ....203 B3
Ffrydd Rd LD7 ....203 B2
Ffynnon Gdns **1** SY11 ...58 F7
Ffordd Cl Dawley TF4 ......143 F6
　Shrewsbury SY1 ....114 A3
Field Cres SY1 ....114 A3
Field Dr SY4 ....84 A5
Field House Dr SY3 ....125 A1
Field La
　Bishop's Castle SY9 ......211 F3
　Kemberton TF11 ....154 C6
　Tenbury SY8 ....213 F2
Field Rd TF2 ....132 C4
Fieldfare Way TF4 ....153 A8
Fieldhouse Dr **4** TF2 ...120 D1
Fielding Cl **1** TF2 ......161 E7
Fifth Ave **16** TF2 ......132 A1
Finchale Ave **4** TF3 ....133 A1
Findon Dr **2** SY11 ......40 D1
Findon Way **5** SY3 .....124 B6
Finger Rd TF4 ....143 F2
Finney Cl LL11 ....221 B6
Finsbury Dr **5** TF2 .....132 F2
Fir Gr SY11 ....58 F6
Fir Trees WV15 ....219 B4
Fireclay Dr TF2 ....132 D3
Firecrest Dr **10** TF1 ....130 F6
Firgrove Cres **5** LL12 ..221 F7
Firs The SY13 ....114 A4
First Ave
　Oakengates/Donnington
　TF2 ....132 B1
　Shrewsbury SY1 ....113 F2
First Terr **2** SY1 ......113 F2
Firsway The **1** ST19 ...148 E8
Firtree Cl **3** SY7 ....27 A2
Fish St **8** SY1 ....125 C5
Fisher Rd SY21 ....170 E7
Fishers Lock **2** TF10 ...110 A4
Fishmore Cl **5** SY8 .....217 C6
Fishmore Rd SY8 ....217 C6
Fishmore View SY8 ....217 C6
Fismes Way SY4 ....66 B8
Fitchett Bsns Pk TF2 .....132 C2
Fitzalan Cl SY11 ....42 A1

Fitzalan Rd
　3 Oswestry SY11 ......58 C7
　Shrewsbury SY1 ....113 E4
Fitzgwarine Dr SY11 ......41 E3
Five Crosses SY12 ....41 A5
Five Turnings SY7 ....182 D1
Flagwall **2** SY22 ....126 A6
Flash La
　Loggerheads TF9 ....54 F8
　Wombourne WV4 ....190 F5
Flatt Rd TF10 ....108 F4
Fleming Ct **4** TF1 ......130 F6
Fleming Cl **7** LL11 .....221 B6
Florence Ct **6** SY3 .....124 C7
Floyer La TF12 ....152 B1
Foel Hill (fort)* SY22 .....92 A6
Foldgate La SY8 ....217 E3
Foldgate View SY8 ....217 F3
Foley Gr **1** WV5 ....190 F3
Folley Rd WV6 ....164 E1
Folliott Cl **5** SY22 .....125 F3
Forbes Cl TF7 ....152 D6
Ford Rd TF10 ....109 E2
Ford St **4** SY7 ....193 D3
Forden in W Prim Sch
　SY21 ....174 B8
Forden Rd SY15 ....174 B4
Forest Cl
　2 Bewdley DY12 ......211 C2
　3 Wellington TF5 .....118 C1
　Wellington TF5 ....130 C8
Forest La DY7 ....190 C1
Forest Rd TF9 ....53 A8
Forest Way SY2 ....126 A7
Forester Ave TF13 ....159 F4
Forester Gr **2** TF1 .....130 F2
Forester Rd TF12 ....161 E7
Foresters Cl TF4 ....143 C2
Forge Gate TF3 ....144 B7
Forge La
　Leintwardine SY8 ....205 F6
　Norton in Hales TF9 .....20 C1
Forge Leys **16** WV5 ....190 F3
Forge Ret Pk TF3 ....144 A8
Forge Valley Way **8**
　WV5 ....190 F3
Forresters Rd WR15 ......220 D6
Forsythia Cl **7** TF2 .....132 F1
Fort View **8** SY11 ......40 A1
Fort-Mahon Pl **20** DY12 .211 C2
Forton Rd TF10 ....109 F4
Foster Rd
　Bridgnorth WV16 ....218 D7
　Wrexham LL11 ....221 B6
Fosters Foel **8** TF4 ....153 A8
Fothergill Way SY4 ....65 F6
Foundry Cl **10** TF2 .....132 B2
Foundry La
　Broseley TF12 ....161 D7
　Welshpool SY21 ....170 B6
Foundry Rd **4** LL13 .....221 D3
Fountain Dr TF2 ....132 C2
Four Crosses SY21 ....170 F3
Fourth Ave TF2 ....132 B1
Fowler Cl **1** TF1 ....130 C5
Fox Ave TF2 ....132 D1
Fox Cl WV5 ....190 C5
Fox La Broseley TF12 .....161 C8
　West Felton SY11 ....78 C7
Fox Rd WV5 ....190 B6
Fox's Covert **1** TF5 ....130 C8
Fox's Field SY11 ....41 A8
Foxen Manor Rd SY22 ....94 A1
Foxes La SY13 ....16 B7
Foxglove Cl **2** SY3 .....125 D3
Foxglove Rise **8** TF3 ...144 D3
Foxleigh Cl **3** SY4 .....66 B8
Foxleigh Cres **4** SY4 ...66 B8
Foxleigh Gr **5** SY4 .....66 B8
Foxley Gr **17** SY3 ......124 A7
Foxwood Dr LL13 ....221 A1
Frame La TF4 ....143 D2
Frances Ave LL13 ....221 D8
Frankton Cl **3** SY22 ....126 B7
Frankwell SY3 ....125 B6
Fraser Ct **5** SY13 ......15 A6
Freeston Ave TF2 ....132 C1
Frensham Rd **1** SY2 ....125 E7
Freshfields **8** SY1 ......113 E5
Friar's La TF11 ....147 D4
Friar's St **1** SY1 ....218 F5
Friars Ave SY1 ....59 A8
Friars Field SY8 ....217 D4
Friars Gdn **3** SY8 ......217 C4
Frith Cl SY2 ....126 A7
Frizes Leasowe **10** TF2 .132 A1
Frog La **5** TF2 ....132 A1
Frogmore Rd TF9 ....36 C1
Fryers Cl **4** DY14 ......209 D2
Fuchsia Cl **3** SY3 ......125 D3
Furbers La SY13 ....32 E5
Furlongs Cl **6** DY14 ....209 E3
Furlongs Rd **8** DY14 ...209 E3
Furnace Cl **4** WV6 .....164 E2
Furnace La TF12 ....132 B7
Furnace Rd TF2 ....132 C1
Fylingdales Dr TF4 ....153 A8

Gainsborough Way
　TF5 ....130 B7
Gallowstree Rise **3**
　SY21 ....170 C2
Galton Dr **2** SY21 .....126 B7
Gamester's La SY10 ....78 E1
Gaol Rd **1** SY15 ....174 B3
Garbett Cl **3** SY4 ......66 A6
Garbett Rd TF4 ....152 F8
Garden Cl TF2 ....132 B5
Garden Ct LL11 ....221 D7
Garden La The* 8 E7
Garden Rd LL11 ....221 C4
Garden Village SY1 ....114 B3
Gardeners Way **17** WV5 .190 F3
Gardners Mdw **13** DY12 .211 D2
Garfield Rd TF3 ....131 E1
Garmston La SY1 ....74 A1
Garmston Rd SY2 ....125 F2
Garner Rd LL13 ....221 E4
Garner's La SY13 ....31 C3
Garreg Bank SY21 ....167 A2
Garreg Cl **2** SY21 ......170 B6
Garridge Cl WV7 ....157 A4
Garth La LD7 ....203 A3
Garth Mdws **6** LD7 ....203 B3
Gatacre Ave SY11 ....40 C1
Gate Rd **1** SY11 ....40 E1
Gatcombe Gdns **3** SY1 ..59 B8
Gatcombe Way TF2 ......132 F2
Gate Rd LL20 ....6 A7
Gate St
　1 Oakengates/Donnington
　TF2 ....132 C2
　Oswestry SY11 ....40 E1
Gatehouse Cl TF6 ....132 B7
Gates La SY7 ....183 F1
Gateway **1** LL12 ....221 D6
Gateway Ed & Arts Ctr The*
　LL12 ....221 D3
Gatherwynd La **7** LL11 .135 E6
Gay Meadow (Shrewsbury
　Town FC) SY2 ....125 D6
Gdns The **1** LL12 ......221 D6
Gelli-lwyd La SY10 ....74 A3
George Chetwood Ct **4**
　TF4 ....144 A4
George Pl TF1 ....130 C4
George Rd LD7 ....203 B3
George St Clark LL14 .....6 E2
　1 Dawley TF4 ....143 E4
　3 Oakengates/Donnington
　TF2 ....132 D2
　5 Wrexham LL11 ......221 C5
Gerald St LL11 ....221 C4
Gibbons Cl **1** TF2 ......132 B6
Gibbons Rd TF2 ....132 B6
Gibraltar La SY10 ....75 E7
Gibson St LL13 ....221 B3
Giggetty La WV5 ....190 F3
Gilberries La SY6 ....185 A4
Gilbert Cl TF10 ....109 D2
Gilbert's La
　Wem Rural SY13 ....48 B8
　Whixall SY13 ....31 A1
Giles Cl **1** TF5 ....130 B7
Gilpin Rd TF5 ....130 A6
Gilwell Dr **1** TF2 ......132 F1
Gittens Dr TF4 ....153 A8
Gittin St SY11 ....40 B3
Glade Way TF5 ....118 C1
Gladstone St TF1 ....131 D4
Gladwyn Rd LL12 ....221 D8
Glamis **3** SY3 ....132 B6
Glan Aber **8** LL12 ......221 E5
Glan Aber Cl LL11 ....221 A8
Glan Garth LL12 ....221 E4
Glan Lleddan **1** SY21 ..170 A6
Glebe Brook Rd TF2 ......132 F1
Glebe Cl SY6 ....184 C3
Glebe Dr DY14 ....199 E1
Glebe Mdw SY9 ....182 A6
Glebe Rd SY3 ....136 F6
Glebe St TF1 ....130 E3
Glebe The
　2 Albrighton WV7 .....157 A5
　Atcham SY5 ....139 A7
　Chelmarsh WV16 ....200 D6
Glebelands
　2 Bobbington DY7 .....189 F1
　Myddle & Broughton SY4 ..82 C4
　Oakengates/Donnington
　TF2 ....132 D2
　Shawbury SY4 ....103 E6
Glebelands The TF6 ......116 E7
Glen Avon **8** LL12 .....221 E4
Glen Brook Rd TF2 ....132 F1
Glen Gr SY13 ....32 E5
Glen The TF13 ....159 D8
Glenburn Gdns **2** SY2 ..126 A8
Glendinning Way TF7 ....152 F4
Glendon Cl **3** TF9 ......36 C1
Glendower Cl SY1 ....125 D8
Glendower Pl LL12 ....221 C2
Gleneagles SY7 ....153 B3
Glentworth Ave SY8 .....58 D5
Glentworth Cl SY10 .....58 D5
Glentworth Dr SY1 ....58 D5
Glentworth Rise SY8 .....58 D5
Gloucester Ave TF4 ......143 F4
Gloucester Cl LL11 ....131 A7
Gloucester Ct LL11 ......221 A1
Gloucester Dr SY1 ....113 D4
Gloucester Way **20**
　DY12 ....211 D2

Glovers Mdw SY11 ....59 A5
Glovers Way **1** TF5 ....130 B8
Glyn Ave LL11 ....221 E7
Glyndwr Rd LL12 ....221 D7
Gnosall Rd TF10 ....111 D2
Goblin's La SY11 ....31 A1
Gobowen Prim Sch
　SY11 ....41 A8
Gobowen Rd SY11 ....40 F1
Gobowen Sta SY11 ....41 A7
Godings La SY4 ....83 D1
Godson's Cl **3** WR15 ...220 D5
Goldcrest Dr SY11 ....114 B3
Goldcrest Gr **1** TF3 ....131 E1
Golden Acres **9** WV15 ..201 B3
Golden Cross La **2** SY8 .208 C2
Goldenhill LD7 ....72 D3
Goldenhill La TF9 ....72 D3
Goldstone Dr **1** WV16 ..218 D6
Goldstone Hall & Gdns*
　TF9 ....72 D5
Goldstone Rd TF9 ....72 B3
Golf House La SY13 ....15 D4
Golf Links La TF1 ....130 E2
Golfa Cl SY21 ....167 D3
Gooch Cl TF7 ....152 D6
Goodrich Cl TF2 ....120 E1
Goodwood Ave WV15 ....219 B4
Goodyear Way TF4 ......132 E7
Gooseberry La
　Grinshill SY4 ....84 C3
　4 Ruyton SY4 ....80 A1
Goosefield Cl **15** TF6 ...36 B1
Goosemoor Cl DY12 ......210 C7
Gorse La
　Bayston Hill SY3 ....136 E7
　Trysull & Seisdon WV5 ...190 D3
Gorse Mdw SY13 ....32 F5
Gorsy La TF10 ....91 F4
Goshawk Dr TF4 ....152 F8
Gospel Ash Rd DY7 ......190 B1
Gough Cl TF2 ....144 F8
Goulbourne Rd **5** TF2 ..132 D2
Gowan Cl **8** SY11 ......114 B4
Gower Cl **2** SY11 ......57 E6
Gower Pl SY11 ....58 F8
Gower St TF7 ....152 A6
Grafton Cty Prim Sch
　SY4 ....99 D1
Grafton Mews SY1 ....113 E4
Grainger Dr TF1 ....131 B5
Grampian Cl **2** TF1 ....120 E1
Grange Ave
　4 Strichley & Brookside
　TF3 ....144 D1
　Wrexham LL11 ....221 C6
Grange Central **2** TF1 ..144 C6
Grange Cl
　Condover SY5 ....137 C1
　4 Strichley & Brookside
　TF3 ....144 D1
　1 Wrexham LL11 ......221 E6
Grange Ct SY5 ....137 B1
Grange Farm Ct
　WV16 ....188 D1
Grange Farm Rise **8**
　TF4 ....143 B6
Grange Farm View
　TF3 ....144 B3
Grange Gdns **13** SY9 ...181 F3
Grange Jun & Inf Sch
　SY1 ....113 E4
Grange La
　Condover SY5 ....137 B1
　Lilleshall & Donnington
　TF2 ....132 A1
　Shrewsbury SY1 ....125 A3
Grange Sch The **1** TF1 ..113 E4
Grange Sports Ctr The
　SY1 ....113 E4
Grangefields **4** SY3 ....124 F3
Grangefields Rd SY3 .....125 A3
Granite Cl **13** SY8 ......208 C2
Gransden Dr **2** SY3 ....124 E4
Grantley Ave **6** SY3 ....124 C7
Granville Ave TF1 ....109 F2
Granville Ct TF10 ....109 D2
Granville Dr **8** TF2 .....132 F1
Granville Rd
　Lilleshall & Donnington
　TF2 ....132 C5
　Newport TF10 ....109 F2
Granville St
　1 Oakengates/Donnington
　TF2 ....132 D2
　Shrewsbury SY1 ....125 A8
　3 Wrexham LL11 ......221 C5
Grasmere Cl **8** SY13 ...14 E8
Grasmere Dr **8** LL13 ...221 D8
Grasmere Rd **11** WV16 ..200 E2
Grasmere Rd SY1 ....113 F3
Grassy Bank **3** LL13 ....221 D8
Gravel Hill SY11 ....40 C4
Gravel Hill La
　Pimhill SY1 ....113 A1
　Shrewsbury SY1 ....125 A8
Gravel Leasowe **8** SY3 ..124 F3
Great Croft Dr TF1 ....143 E7
Great Croft TF10 ....107 D5
Great Hales St TF9 ....36 D1

Great Hay Dr TF7 ....153 B3
Great Moor Rd WV6 .....166 F2
Great Western Dr **1**
　TF4 ....143 D3
Greatford Gn **1** SY11 ..114 B4
Grebe Cl TF3 ....153 D8
Green Acres
　Ludlow SY8 ....217 E3
　20 Wombourne WV5 ...190 F3
Green Bank TF9 ....19 A5
Green Cl **3** WV6 ....166 C2
Green End
　Oswestry SY11 ....40 D1
　1 Whitchurch SY13 ....15 A7
Green La Adderley CW3 ...18 E8
　Albrighton WV7 ....136 F4
　Bayston Hill SY3 ....136 F7
　Bomere Heath SY4 ......100 F3
　Chirk LL14 ....6 F3
　Churchstoke SY15 ......175 B2
　Ercall Magna TF6 ....105 C8
　Longden SY3 ....136 C2
　Newport TF10 ....109 E4
　Onibury SY7 ....195 C1
　Orleton SY8 ....212 D2
　Prees SY13 ....32 E1
　1 Shrewsbury SY3 ....125 B2
　St. Martin's SY11 ....13 E2
　Stanton upon Hine Heath
　SY4 ....69 C1
　Whixall SY13 ....31 A1
Green Leys Cres **10**
　WV15 ....201 B3
Green Mdw Cl **20** WV5 ..190 F3
Green Pk SY11 ....221 B1
Green The **3** LL12 .....221 D8
Green View TF11 ....135 F8
Green Way **3** TF4 ......143 E5
Greenacre Rd SY3 ....124 F6
Greenacres
　4 Oakengates/Donnington
　TF2 ....131 F2
　3 Wem SY4 ....66 B8
Greenacres La **2** TF2 ...211 D2
Greenacres Prim Sch
　SY1 ....113 E5
Greenacres Way TF10 ....109 D3
Greenbank Cl **8** SY1 ...58 E8
Greenbank St LL12 ......221 D2
Greendale Cl **8** WV16 ..200 E2
Greene Cl SY7 ....195 E8
Greenfield Sq SY10 ......58 D4
Greenfield St **2** SY1 ...125 C8
Greenfields
　5 Shifnal TF11 ....146 A4
　12 Welshpool SY21 ....170 B6
　2 Whitchurch SY13 ....14 F5
Greenfields Cres
　Bridgnorth WV16 ....218 E6
　Shifnal TF11 ....146 A4
Greenfields Dr WV16 .....218 E6
Greenfields La SY1 ......125 C8
Greenfields Rd
　Bridgnorth WV16 ....218 E6
　3 Craven Arms SY7 ...195 C5
Greenfields Rise SY11 ....14 E8
Greenfinch Cl **4** TF1 ...130 F3
Greenfoot La SY13 ....15 A5
Greengage Way **11** TF2 .132 E8
Greenhill Ave **2** SY3 ...125 B6
Greenhill Cl **6** WR15 ...220 D5
Greenhurst La TF6 ....87 C4
Greenlands **5** WV5 .....190 F4
Greenlea Rd **7** LL12 ...130 F3
Greenway Ave WV15 ....201 B3
Greenway Cross SY7 ....196 A1
Greenway Gdns WV6 ....166 C2
Greenway The
　11 Ellesmere SY12 ....27 A2
　2 Pattingham WV6 ....166 C2
Greenways **3** SY3 ......125 A6
Greenwood Cl **3** SY7 ...125 F3
Greenwood Ct SY11 .....125 F7
Gregson Cl **1** SY7 .....125 F7
Grenville Ct **3** TF1 .....146 A4
Grenville Rd **8** TF13 ...159 F4
Gresford Way LL12 ......221 D8
Gresham Dr TF3 ....143 D7
Gresley Cl TF7 ....152 D6
Greville Rd SY3 ....125 B4
Grey Bank SY7 ....193 D4
Grey Gn La DY12 ....211 D3
Greyfriars
　8 Bridgnorth WV16 ....218 F6
　Oswestry SY11 ....59 A8
Greyfriars Rd **3** SY3 ...125 D5
Greyhound Hill SY11 .....132 B1
Greyhound La WV4 ......190 F7
Greystones Ct **3** SY10 ..58 F4
Greystones Way SY11 ....58 A1
Griffin Cl SY2 ....126 A7
Grigg's La WV16 ....199 E2
Grimpo Rd SY11 ....78 E8
Grindle Rd TF11 ....164 D4
Grinshill **2** TF1 ....130 D6
Grinshill Dr **4** SY21 ....130 D6
Grizedale Dr TF4 ....143 D2
Groom's Alley **5** TF1 ...130 D4
Grooms La TF12 ....154 C6
Grosvenor Cotts SY12 ...37 A3
Grosvenor Ct **2** TF9 ...36 D2

Grosvenor Gdns TF11 ....146 A4
Grosvenor Gn **5** SY1 ....113 E4
Grosvenor Rd
  Market Drayton TF9 ......36 D1
  Oswestry SY11 ....41 A1
  Wrexham SY11 ....221 C4
Grosvenor Wood 18
  DY12 ....211 C2
Grotto Rd
  15 Market Drayton TF9 ...36 B1
  Market Drayton TF9 .....53 B8
Grove Campus The Grove Sch
  TF9 ....
Grove Cres
  Bridgnorth WV15 ....219 A4
  Woore CW3 ....5 A1
Grove Dr SY7 ....195 E7
Grove Gdns TF9 ....36 D1
Grove La
  Bayston Hill SY3 ....137 A5
  Grinshill SY4 ....84 D4
  Pontesbury SY5 ....173 B4
Grove Lodge Cl 5 LL11 ..221 D5
Grove Mdw 9 DY14 ....209 E3
Grove Pk Rd 5 LL11 ...221 C4
Grove Rd
  Shrewsbury SY1 ....125 C5
  The Rock TF3 ....131 E1
  Wrexham LL11 ....221 C4
Grove St TF2 ....132 D2
Grove The Hadley TF1 ..131 C5
  Hodnet TF9 ....69 D4
  Minsterley SY5 ....172 E4
  Pinhill SY4 ....100 E4
  4 Shifnal TF11 ....146 A4
  5 Wem SY4 ....66 A6
  Whitchurch SY13 ....1 F2
Grovefields SY1 ....131 B5
Groves High Sch LL12 ..221 D4
Grug Hill SY3 ....79 F2
Guest Rd TF12 ....161 E7
Guests Cl 8 TF2 ....132 E2
Guild La TF10 ....111 A7
Guinea Cl 18 TF2 ......132 B2
Guinea La SY4 ....67 E6
Guinevere Cl 3 SY11 ...40 F1
Guisbourne Ave 3 TF5 ..130 C8
Gungrog Fawr La
  SY21 ....
Gungrog Hill SY21 .....170 C8
Gungrog Rd SY21 ....170 B6
Gwelfryn SY22 ....93 D6
Gwenfro Jun & Inf Sch
  LL13 ....221 F2
Gwernowddy La SY22 ...94 D1
Gwern-y-go La SY22 ...167 B8
Gwydyr Way 3 LL13 ....221 D1
Gwyn Cl 5 SY2 ....125 F6

H

Habberley La DY11 .....211 F4
Habberley Rd
  Bewdley DY11 ....211 F3
  Pontesbury SY5 ....173 A2
Habersham Ct SY7 .....182 B1
Hackett Ct 16 LL13 ....221 E1
Hadley Cls Infants' Sch
  TF1 ....131 C4
Hadley Cty Jun Sch
  TF1 ....131 C4
Hadley Gdns TF1 ....131 B7
Hadley Lodge Rd TF1 ..131 E4
Hadley Pk Rd TF1 .....131 B6
Hadley Rd Hadley TF2 ..131 C4
  Oakengates/Donnington
  TF2 ....132 A3
Hadnall CE Prim Sch
  SY4 ....102 C4
Hafod Cl Oswestry SY10 ..58 C8
  2 Pant SY22 ....93 F6
Hafod-y-Wern Prim Sch
  LL13 ....221 F3
Hafren Cl 3 SY3 ....125 A6
Hafren Rd Dawley TF4 ..143 E1
  Shrewsbury SY3 ....125 A6
Haig Rd LL13 ....221 D2
Halcyon Ct 6 TF2 ......132 F8
Hales Ct TF11 ....134 B5
Hales Pk 25 DY12 ......211 C2
Halesfield 1 TF7 ....144 F1
Halesfield 2 TF7 ....153 F7
Halesfield 4 TF7 ....153 E7
Halesfield 5 TF7 ....153 E7
Halesfield 6 TF7 ....153 E7
Halesfield 7 TF7 ....153 E6
Halesfield 8 TF7 ....153 E6
Halesfield 9 TF7 ....153 E5
Halesfield 10 TF7 ......153 E4
Halesfield 11 TF7 ......153 E4
Halesfield 13 TF7 ......153 D5
Halesfield 14 TF7 ......153 D5
Halesfield 15 TF7 ......153 D6
Halesfield 16 TF7 ......153 D6
Halesfield 17 TF7 ......153 D6
Halesfield 18 TF7 ......153 D7
Halesfield 19 TF7 ......153 D7
Halesfield 20 TF7 ......153 E6
Halesfield 21 TF7 ......153 E7
Halesfield 22 TF7 ......153 E8
Halesfield 23 TF7 ......153 E8
Halesfield 24 TF7 ......144 E1
Halesfield 25 TF7 ......144 E1
Halesfield Ind Est TF7 ..153 E5

Halesford Rd TF7 ......153 C6
Halford Cres 7 SY7 ....195 E5
Halfpenny Gn Airport
  DY7 ....190 B2
Halfpenny Gn Vineyard*
  DY7 ....190 B3
Halfway House La
  WV16 ....218 E1
Halghton La SY13 ......11 C8
Halifax Dr **4** TF1 ....131 B6
Halifax Rd WV7 ....147 F1
Hall Bank SY15 ....175 A1
Hall Bank The SY5 .....173 B5
Hall Barn Cl 3 TF7 ....153 A5
Hall Ct WV6 ....166 C2
Hall Dr SY4 ....102 C5
Hall End Cl 8 WV6 .....166 C2
Hall End La WV6 ....166 C2
Hall Farm Rd WV16 ....198 D7
Hall Gdns 3 SY5 ....178 E8
Hall La TF11 ....154 B6
Hall Pk Way TF3 ....144 A6
Hall Sl 18 SY2 ....170 B6
Hallam Dr 3 SY1 ....114 B4
Hallcroft Cl TF10 .....109 E3
Hallcroft Ct SY1 ......125 D8
Hallcroft Gdns TF10 ...109 E3
Halldene 13 TF1 ....131 B4
Hallets Well 1 SY8 ....218 E2
Hallon SY1 ....189 A6
Halls Farm La DY12 ....211 D4
Halmer Dr SY11 ....170 B2
Halston Cotts SY5 .....173 C6
Halstonwood Cl 5 LL13 ..221 F5
Halton La
  Bromfield SY8 ....206 E2
  Ludlow SY8 ....217 A4
Hamilton Dr SY2 ....126 B8
Hamilton Rd TF4 ....143 F1
Hamlet Ct 10 Ludlow SY8 ..217 D6
  Oakengates/Donnington
  TF2 ....132 A3
Hamlet Rd 9 SY8 ......217 D6
Hammersley Ave SY3 ....217 D6
Hammonds Cl 5 SY11 ...41 A8
Hammonds Pl SY11 .....41 B8
Hampden Rd OL13 ......221 C2
Hampshire Dr LL11 .....221 C8
Hampson Ave LL13 ......221 E2
Hampton Cl
  2 Newport TF10 ......110 A3
  Oswestry SY11 ....58 C8
Hampton Dr
  8 Market Drayton TF9 ..36 C2
  Newport TF10 ....110 A3
Hampton Fields SY11 ...58 C8
Hampton Hill TF11 .....130 C1
Hampton Loade Sta
  WV16 ....200 F5
Hampton Rd
  Oswestry SY11 ....40 C1
  7 Shrewsbury SY1 ....125 E8
Hampton Rise SY11 .....40 C1
Hancocks Dr 8 TF2 ....132 B2
Hand La TF11 ....122 D1
Hankins Heys La CW3 ..20 A8
Hanley La SY3 ....136 E7
Hanmer Cl 4 LL13 .....9 C8
Hanmer Prim Sch SY13 ..12 A4
Hanover Ct TF7 ....153 B6
Hanover Way 1 LL13 ...221 D1
Hanwood Rd SY5 ....124 C2
Harcourt Cres SY2 .....126 A6
Harcourt Dr TF10 .....110 A4
Harding Cl 1 TF2 ......132 C7
Hardwick Dr SY3 ....124 D6
Harebell Glade 8 TF3 ..144 D3
Harefields Cl 4 SY4 ....99 B8
Haresfield 8 SY3 ....124 C7
Harlech Cl 5 SY11 .....41 A1
Harlech Rd SY11 ....41 A1
Harlescott Cl 6 SY1 ....114 A3
Harlescott Cres SY1 ...113 E4
Harlescott Ind Est
  SY1 ....113 E3
Harlescott Jun Sch
  SY1 ....114 B3
Harlescott La SY1 .....113 E5
Harley Cl TF1 ....130 C6
Harley Dr
  1 Condover SY5 ....178 E8
  Shrewsbury SY3 ....113 E3
Harley Hill SY5 ....159 B5
Harley Jenkins St 8
  SY9 ....181 F3
Harley Rd
  8 Condover SY5 ....178 E8
  Cressage SY5 ....149 E4
Harley Way WV16 ....218 C5
Haroldgate SY13 ....1 F1
Harp Cl Dawley TF4 ....143 F2
  7 Ludlow SY8 ....217 C4
Harper Adams Agricultural
  Coll TF10 ....108 E5
Harriets Hayes Rd
  WV7 ....157 E6
Harrington Heath 2
  TF5 ....118 C1
Harris's Gn TF12 ......161 C8
Harrison Cl 3 TF2 .....152 F4
Harrison Cl 37 TF2 ....152 F4
Harrow Cres WV7 ......156 B7
Hartley Cl 7 TF3 ......131 E1
Hartmann Cl 8 DY14 ...209 D2
Harton Hollow Nature
  Reserve*** SY6 ....196 C6
Harton Hollow Way
  SY6 ....196 D6

Hartsbridge Rd 3 TF2 ..131 F2
Hartshill
  Oakengates TF2 ....131 F2
  Oakengates/Donnington
  TF2 ....132 A2
Hartshill Ave
  1 Oakengates/Donnington
  TF2 ....131 F2
  7 Oakengates/Donnington
  TF2 ....132 A3
Hartwood Cl 6 TF10 ...109 F5
Harvey Cres TF1 ....131 B2
Harvington Cl 4 TF1 ...130 E5
Haslehurst Cl SY7 .....193 D4
Hassacks The 5 SY1 ...114 B3
Haston Rd SY4 ....101 F6
Hatch La Astley SY4 ...102 E3
  Blymhill & Weston-under-Lizard
  TF11 ....135 D4
Hatchetts Cl SY4 ....64 B1
Hatfield Mdws 17 LD7 ..203 B3
Hatton Rd TF9 ....71 D2
Haughmond Ave 3 SY1 ..114 A3
Haughton Cl 13 WV16 ..218 C6
Haughton Dr 11 TF11 ..145 E5
Haughton La TF11 ......145 E5
Haughton Rd TF11 .....145 F6
Havelock Cres TF13 ....159 D4
Havelock Rd SY3 ....125 D4
Havenwood 7 TF3 ......144 E2
Hawkestone Rd 4 SY1 ..114 A4
Hawkshaw Cl 8 TF2 ....132 B2
Hawksmoor La SY4 .....101 E5
Hawkstone Ave 4 TF10 ..109 E2
Hawkstone Ct SY4 ......67 F6
Hawkstone Dr SY4 ......66 C7
Hawksworth Rd TF2 ....144 C8
Hawshaw Cl 2 TF3 .....144 C3
Hawthorn Cl
  2 Craven Arms SY7 ...195 D6
  St. Martin's SY11 ......24 F6
Hawthorn Cres 3 DY12 ..211 C2
Hawthorn Dr 10 WV16 ..200 E3
Hawthorn Pl TF2 ....132 D8
Hawthorn Rd
  Minsterley SY5 ....172 E4
  3 Oakengates/Donnington
  TF2 ....132 C7
  Shrewsbury SY3 ....125 D4
Hawthorne Cl 4 TF2 ...132 A1
Hawthorne Gr SY11 ....58 F7
Hawthorns The
  Bridgnorth WV16 ....218 E4
  2 Ellesmere Urban SY12 ..27 A3
  3 Shrewsbury SY3 .....125 D4
  Worthen with Shelve
  SY5 ....171 E3
Hay The 3 TF3 ....143 E7
Haybridge Ave TF1 .....131 B4
Haybridge Rd 5 TF1 ...131 C5
Haycock Way SY3 ......153 D8
Hayes La WR15 ....213 F2
Hayes Rd TF1 ....131 A1
Haygate Dr 1 TF1 .....130 C2
Haygate Dr 5 TF1 .....130 C2
Haygate Dr W TF1 .....130 C2
Haygate Rd TF1 ....130 C2
Hayles The SY8 ....213 B5
Hayton View 8 SY8 ....217 D6
Haytor Rd LL11 ....221 C6
Hayward Ave 3 TF2 ....132 D1
Haywood Cl 13 WV2 ....126 A7
Haywood La
  Cheswardine TF9 ....72 E8
  Sutton upon Tern TF9 ...54 B6
Hazel Cl SY21 ....167 A1
Hazel Gr Oswestry SY11 ..58 F7
  2 Wrexham LL12 ......221 D6
Hazel View WV15 ......219 B4
Hazeldine Cres 3 SY3 ..125 A4
Hazeldine Cres 2 SY6 ..103 D6
Hazelgrove 8 WV15 ....201 B3
Hazelwells Rd WV16 ....200 E3
Hazeldine Way SY3 ....125 C2
Hazler Cres SY6 ....196 D5
Hazler Dr SY6 ....216 E6
Hazler Orch SY6 ....216 E5
Hazler Rd SY6 ....216 E5
Hazlitt Pl SY4 ....66 B7
Hearne La TF9 ....69 C6
Hearne Way 4 SY2 .....126 A8
Heath Cl DY14 ....209 D2
Heath Dr SY5 ....168 B2
Heath Hill TF14 ....133 D4
Heath House Dr 8 WV6 ..190 E3
Heath La SY13 ....2 E6
Heath Mill Cl DY3 .....190 E2
Heath Mill Rd DY3 .....190 E2
Heath Rd Gnosall TF10 ..111 A8
  Wellington TF1 ....130 D5
  Whitchurch Rural SY13 ..15 C3
Heathbrook Junc TF9 ...69 F6
Heather Bank 4 SY11 ..41 B8
Heather Cl 5 SY12 .....59 A7
Heather Dr 2 TF1 ......130 F3
Heatherdale TF1 ....131 A5
Heathfield Cl 7 SY11 ..113 D2
Heathfield Rd DY12 ....211 D2
Heathlands 9 WV16 ....190 E3
Heathlands Rd 7 TF2 ..132 C3
Heathlands The 4 WV6 ..190 E3
Heathwood Rd
  Newport TF10 ....109 D2
  Press Higher Heath SY13 ..32 E3
Heaton Cl 2 SY3 ....124 F3
Hebden Gr 10 SY3 .....124 B6

Heber Mount 8 LL13 ...221 F4
Heblands Bank SY9 ....181 F5
Hedges The 17 WV5 ....190 F3
Hedingham Rd TF1 .....131 C7
Hedley Way TF9 ....52 D4
Heightington Rd
  DY12 ....211 D1
Heighways La SY6 .....184 B6
Heighways The SY5 ....179 E7
Heldre La SY21 ....167 A1
Helfa Bach 2 LL14 .....6 E3
Helmeth Rd SY6 ....216 E6
Hem La Shifnal TF11 ...153 F8
  Westbury SY5 ....172 C4
Hemsworth Way
  9 Shrewsbury SY1 ....113 C1
  1 Shrewsbury SY1 ....125 C8
Henblas St 9 LL11 .....221 D3
Hendre La 2 SY22 .....167 A8
Hendrie Cl 1 TF1 ......131 D2
Henfaes La SY21 ....170 C6
Hengrave Mdw 7 SY3 ..143 D7
Henley Dr
  E Newport TF10 ......110 A4
  Oakengates/Donnington
  TF2 ....132 B6
  Oswestry SY11 ....41 A1
Henley La
  Acton Scott SY6 ....196 A8
  Bitterley SY8 ....207 C3
Henley Orchards 8
  SY6 ....217 D6
Henley Rd SY8 ....217 D5
Henlle Cl SY11 ....23 F1
Henlle Gdns SY11 ......23 F1
Henlow Rise 3 SY3 ....124 F2
Henry Jones Cl 6 SY11 ..59 B8
Heol Abon LL20 ....6 B8
Heol Bennion 5 LL20 ...6 B8
Heol Berwyn 4 LL20 ...6 B8
Heol Cefnydd 6 LL14 ...6 B8
Heol Dafydd 8 LL12 ....221 E8
Heol Dinas LL12 ....221 E7
Heol Graigfab 8 LL14 ..6 B8
Herbert Ave TF1 ......130 C2
Herbert Jennings Ave
  LL12 ....221 E6
Hereford Cl 2 WV7 ....156 F8
Hereford Dr 5 TF2 .....133 A1
Hereford Rd
  Bayston Hill SY3 ....137 B7
  5 Shrewsbury SY3 ....125 C3
Heritage Gn 3 SY2 ....170 C1
Hermitage Cl
  Bridgnorth WV15 ....219 B5
  1 Westbury SY5 ......172 C8
Hermitage Dr
  8 Shrewsbury SY3 ....125 F5
  Wrexham LL13 ....221 D1
Hermitage Way TF7 ....152 E4
Hermitage Wlk SY3 ....153 D8
Herne's Nest 2 DY12 ..211 D1
Heron Cl Dawley TF3 ..153 D8
  Ellesmere Urban SY12 ..27 A3
Heron Dr SY1 ....114 B4
Heron Way 8 TF10 .....109 F5
Heronbrook 1 SY13 ....14 E8
Herons Gate Rd DY7 ...201 F3
Hertford Cl 8 TF1 .....130 F5
Hesba Cl TF1 ....130 C3
Hexham Way SY2 ......125 E2
Heyop Rd LD7 ....202 D5
Heywood La SY13 ......217 F7
Hiatt Ave 8 TF1 ....130 E4
Hickman Rd WV15 .....219 E4
Hig The 3 SY1 ....114 B3
Higford La TF11 ....146 B6
High Cross Ave SY5 ...138 F3
High Cswy TF13 ....159 D4
High Ercall Prim Sch
  TF6 ....116 E7
High Fawr Ave SY11 ...58 C8
High Fawr Cl 3 SY10 ..58 C8
High Gr 4 SY11 ....59 B8
High House La WV7 ....157 D4
High La DY14 ....58 C8
High Lea Cl 8 SY11 ....58 C8
High Mdws TF10 ....110 A3
High Mount TF2 ....132 D6
High Oaks 3 SY3 ......124 B7
High Park WV6 ....166 C5
High Point TF6 ....142 C2
High Ridge Dr 1 LL14 ..221 A2
High Ridge Way SY3 ...124 F4
**High St. Albrighton WV7 ..157 A5
**Bewdley DY12 ....211 C6
4 Bishop's Castle SY9 ..181 F3
  Bridgnorth WV16 ....218 F5
  Broseley TF12 ....161 C8
  Cheswardine TF9 ....72 F8
  Church Stretton SY6 ...216 C6
  Claverley WV5 ....199 E4
  Cleehill SY8 ....208 C2

High St continued
  Much Wenlock TF13 ....159 E4
  Newport TF10 ....109 F3
  Overton LL13 ....9 C8
  Pattingham WV6 ....166 C2
  4 Shifnal TF11 ....145 F5
  Shrewsbury SY1 ....125 C5
  Swindon DY3 ....190 F1
  Wellington TF1 ....130 E3
  Wem SY4 ....65 F6
  Weston Rhyn SY10 .....15 A3
  Whitchurch SY13 ......15 A8
  Wrexham LL11 ....221 D3
Highclere Dr 8 DY12 ..211 D1
Higher Rd SY4 ....83 B2
Highfield
  Chetwynd Aston & Woodcote
  TF10 ....121 F8
  Lawley & Overdale TF4 ..143 B6
Highfields 2 SY22 .....126 A5
Highfields Ave SY13 ...14 F6
Highfields Rd WV16 ....218 C5
Highgate SY13 ....15 A7
Highgate Dr 3 SY3 ....124 F3
Highgrove Mdws 8 TF2 ..132 F2
Highland Lea 3 TF4 ....143 C3
Highland Rd 8 TF10 ...109 E2
Highlands Rd WV16 ....218 D4
Highley Prim Sch
  WV16 ....200 E2
Highley Sta WV16 .....200 F2
Hightown Rd LL13 ....221 D3
Highway View TF1 .....131 B2
Hilda Noble Ct 7 TF3 ..153 C5
Hill Cres
  Ellesmere Rural SY12 ...26 B7
  Shrewsbury SY3 ....125 B3
Hill Crest
  Ellesmere Urban SY12 ...27 C3
  Penley LL13 ....10 E3
  6 Wrexham LL12 .....221 E4
Hill Crest Rd 8 TF2 ....132 C2
Hill Ct 9 LL13 ....221 E1
Hill Fold TF4 ....143 E6
Hill La TF11 ....26 B6
Hill Rd
  Oakengates/Donnington
  TF2 ....120 D3
  The Rock TF3 ....143 E8
Hill St 2 Cefn-mawr LL14 ..6 D8
  4 Oakengates/Donnington
  TF2 ....132 C2
  Wrexham LL11 ....221 C3
Hill Top Rd TF9 ....131 F3
Hill's La 18 SY1 ....125 B2
Hilbury Rd LL13 ....221 C1
Hillewood Ave SY13 ...14 F6
Hillrise 3 LL13 ....221 C1
Hills La TF7 ....153 C5
Hills La Dr TF7 ....153 C5
Hillside Edgmond TF10 ..108 F4
  Ironbridge TF8 ....152 D4
  Lilleshall TF10 ....121 B4
  Ludlow SY8 ....217 C5
  Myddle & Broughton SY4 ..82 E4
  Oswestry SY11 ....40 E1
  Pant SY10 ....76 A1
  Shifnal St. Anne WV15 ..219 A3
Hillside Cl SY11 ....131 A1
Hillside Dr SY2 ....126 B6
Hillside Rd
  Cressage SY5 ....149 E4
  3 Oakengates/Donnington
  TF2 ....132 A1
Hilltop Ave 5 DY12 ....211 E3
Hilltop Sch SY8 ....217 D7
Higford La TF11 ....131 F2
Hilltop View Rd LL12 ..221 F7
Hily Bank WV16 ....218 E4
Hilly La SY4 ....168 E8
Hilton Cl 14 TF3 ......144 C1
Himley La DY3 ....190 F1
Hinksford Gdns 9 DY3 ..190 F1
Hinksford La DY3 .....190 F1
Hinkshay Rd
  2 Dawley TF4 ....143 F2
  Great Dawley TF4 ......144 A3
Hinnington Rd TF11 ...155 A3
Hinsley Mill La TF9 ...36 E2
Hinstock Prim Sch TF9 ..72 A2
Hinton La SY5 ....173 B5
Hints Mdw SY8 ....208 E2
Hinwood Rd SY5 ......172 D7
Hoarstone Cl 4 DY12 ..211 E3
Hoarstone La DY12 ....211 E3
Hockley Rd 7 TF12 ....161 C8
Hodgebower TF8 ......152 C4
Hodgkinson Wlk 8 SY5 ..124 C2
Hodnet Hall & Gdns*
  TF9 ....69 B5
Hodnet Link TF9 ......69 C4
Hodnet Prim Sch TF9 ..69 D5
Hoel-y-plas LL14 ......6 C8
Holbache Rd 1 SY11 ...58 D7
Holborn Dr 2 SY2 .....126 A2
Holcroft Way SY5 .....138 F3
Holdgate Dr SY1 ......114 C2
Holdings La CW3 ......5 D4
Holland Dr 7 TF2 .....132 A3
Hollies Dr SY3 ....136 F7
Hollies La Enville DY7 ..201 F4
  Kidderminster Foreign
  DY11 ....211 F6
  Pattingham & Patshull
  WV6 ....166 F5
  Trefonen SY10 ....57 D2
Hollies Rd TF1 ....130 C4
Hollies The SY11 .....24 E5
Hollins La SY13 ....14 D1

Hollinsgate TF3 ... 144 C6
Hollinswood Cty Inf & Jun Sch TF3 ... 144 C6
Hollinswood Rd TF2 ... 132 C1
Hollow Ash La WV15 ... 201 B5
Hollow The SY4 ... 83 C1
Holloway Dr 2 WV5 ... 190 F3
Holloway The DY3 ... 190 F4
Holly Cl Clive SY4 ... 84 B5
  Ellesmere SY12 ... 27 A3
  Market Drayton TF9 ... 53 A8
Holly Gn 6 SY11 ... 58 E7
Holly Gr 2 TF3 ... 221 F4
Holly Grange SY10 ... 23 F5
Holly La DY14 ... 199 E2
Holly Rd Dawley TF4 ... 143 F1
  Tenbury Hamlets TF4 ... 143 D1
  Tenbury Wells WR15 ... 220 D6
Holly View 3 SY21 ... 170 D1
Holly Walks LL12 ... 221 D5
Hollybirch Gr 2 TF9 ... 132 D2
Hollybush La ... 10 E7
Hollybush Rd WV16 ... 218 E4
Hollyhurst Rd TF2 ... 132 A4
Hollyoak Gr 3 TF2 ... 132 E1
Holm Oak 2 WV16 ... 200 E3
Holm Lang Gn 3 TF7 ... 152 E4
Holme Ct 3 TF2 ... 130 E5
Holmer La TF3 ... 144 D1
Holmer Lake Prim Sch TF3 ... 153 D8
Holt End SY11 ... 114 B5
Holt Rd LL12 ... 221 E4
Holt St LL12 ... 221 D3
Holy Cross CE Jun Sch SY2 ... 125 F3
Holyhead Rd
  Albrighton TF11 ... 156 B5
  Bicton SY3 ... 112 B1
  Hadley TF1 ... 131 D2
  Montford SY4 ... 169 C7
  Oakengates/Donnington ... 131 F2
  Wellington TF1 ... 130 E2
  West Felton SY11 ... 78 D8
Holyrood Cres LL11 ... 221 C6
Holywell La
  Dawley Hamlets TF4 ... 143 D1
  Telford TF4 ... 152 D8
Holywell St SY2 ... 125 E6
Home Farm Rd WV6 ... 165 D7
Homestead Av ... 24 F6
Homestead La LL12 ... 221 A2
Homestead The LL13 ... 221 A2
Honey Mdw SY8 ... 217 E4
Honeybourne Cres WV5 ... 190 F3
Honeybourne Rd 4 WV15 ... 201 B3
Honeysuckle Row 6 SY3 ... 125 D3
Honington Ave WV7 ... 156 C8
Hon Farm Animal Kingdom* TF6 ... 119 F2
Hook Farm Rd WV16 ... 218 C6
Hook La The WV7 ... 157 A1
Hookfield The WV16 ... 218 C6
Hooks La TF9 ... 89 F7
Hop Pole La DY12 ... 211 C2
Hope Bagot La SY8 ... 208 A1
Hope CE Prim Sch SY8 ... 176 B8
Hope Rd SY21 ... 170 E6
Hope St LL11 ... 221 C3
Hope Valley Nature Reserve* SY5 ... 176 B8
Hopecrones TF3 ... 185 D1
Hopeshay Cl SY3 ... 144 C1
Hopkins Heath TF5 ... 118 B1
Hopton Bank DY14 ... 208 F3
Hopton Cl 3 SY8 ... 217 D6
Hopton Dr SY1 ... 114 B2
Hopton Heath Sta SY7 ... 204 E8
Hopton Wafers CE Prim Sch DY14 ... 209 A3
Hordley Ave 8 SY1 ... 113 D4
Hordley Rd
  Ellesmere Rural SY12 ... 43 F5
  Wellington TF1 ... 130 C5
Horksley SY1 ...
Hornbeam Cl TF1 ... 131 A3
Hornet Rd TF2 ... 120 D3
Hornet Way 2 TF3 ... 143 F8
Horsa Way SY1 ... 156 B7
Horse Gr Hill 8 WV15 ... 219 A4
Horsebridge Rd SY5 ... 172 E4
Horsechestnut Dr 8 TF5 ... 130 C8
Horsehay & Dawley Sta TF4 ... 143 C3
Horseshoe La SY12 ... 26 D5
Horseshoe Paddock TF4 ...
Horseshoe Rd SY15 ... 174 F8
Horsley Dr LL12 ... 221 D8
Horton Cl TF2 ... 120 A1
Horton La Hadley TF6 ... 119 E1
  Oakengates/Donnington
  TF6 ... 131 F8
Horton Rd 1 TF2 ... 131 F6
Hortonwood 1 TF1 ... 131 E7
Hortonwood 2 TF1 ... 131 E7
Hortonwood 7 TF1 ... 131 E7
Hortonwood 8 TF1 ... 131 F7
Hortonwood 10 TF1 ... 131 F7
Hortonwood 30 TF1 ... 131 E7
Hortonwood 31 TF1 ... 131 E7
Hortonwood 32 TF1 ... 131 F7

Hortonwood 33 TF1 ... 131 F7
Hortonwood 35 TF1 ... 131 F8
Hortonwood 37 TF2 ... 132 A8
Hortonwood 40 TF1 ... 119 E1
Hortonwood 50 TF1 ... 120 A1
Hortonwood 60 TF1 ... 119 E1
Hoskens Cl 5 TF4 ... 143 E4
Hospital La 5 Clun SY7 ... 193 D3
  Market Drayton TF9 ... 53 A8
  Whitchurch Rural SY13 ... 15 D2
Hospital St WV15 ... 219 A4
Hotspur St SY1 ... 125 C8
Houghton Houses TF6 ... 115 C4
Houlston Cl 3 TF2 ... 132 D4
House on Crutches Mus* SY9 ... 181 E4
Housman Cl
  1 Bewdley DY12 ... 153 A8
  2 Ludlow SY8 ... 217 E4
Housman Cres SY8 ... 217 D4
Howard St 4 SY1 ... 125 C4
Howell Rd 20 SY21 ... 170 B6
Howle Cl TF3 ... 144 C2
Hubbal La TF11 ... 147 D3
Hubert Way SY1 ... 113 A4
Hucklemarsh Rd SY8 ... 217 C6
Hudson Rd WV7 ... 156 B7
Hudson Way 3 TF9 ... 72 F7
Hullah La SY1 ... 221 F4
Humber La TF2 ... 120 B3
Humber Way TF2 ... 120 B2
Hunsterson Rd CW5 ... 4 C8
Hunter St SY1 ... 125 B7
Hunters Gate 4 TF13 ... 159 F4
Huntingdon Ave TF4 ... 219 A5
Huntingdon La SY8 ... 213 B5
Huntingdon Dr TF4 ... 143 D6
Huntroyde Ave 4 SY21 ... 170 B6
Huntsman Way 2 TF4 ... 143 E4
Huntsman's Cnr LL12 ... 221 F7
Huntsmans Cl 8 WV16 ... 218 D5
Hurdsman St 8 SY1 ... 40 D1
Hurleybrook Way 1 TF1 ... 131 B4
Hurst Cl 5 TF2 ... 161 E7
Hurst The 4 DY14 ... 209 E2
Hussey Rd SY1 ... 113 E4
Hutchinson Way 3 SY1 ... 131 D2
Huxley Cl SY2 ... 126 A3
Hyde Cl 9 TF2 ... 132 F8

I
Ice House Cl TF6 ... 130 E7
Idsall Cres 1 TF1 ... 146 A3
Idsall Sch TF11 ... 146 A6
Ifton Heath Prim Sch SY11 ... 24 E7
Ightfield Ct SY13 ... 16 E1
Inclinne TF1 ... 131 D2
Inglestre TF1 ... 131 D2
Ingleby Way 4 SY3 ... 124 D7
Inglis Rd SY1 ... 41 C4
Ingram La WV16 ... 200 D5
Innage Cres WV16 ... 218 E6
Innage Croft TF1 ... 145 C4
Innage Gdns WV16 ... 218 E5
Innage La WV16 ... 218 E5
Innage Rd TF1 ... 145 C4
Innes Ave 3 SY1 ... 113 F3
Institute of Iron TF8 ... 152 B6
Iris Cres TF2 ... 132 C4
Iron Bridge & Toll House* TF8 ... 152 C3
Iron Bridge Way The TF4 ... 152 E8
Ironbridge Gorge Mus* TF7 ... 153 A3
Ironbridge Rd TF12 ... 152 E1
Ironmasters Way TF3 ... 144 B7
Ironside Cl 24 DY12 ... 211 C2
Ironstone Cl 4 TF2 ... 132 D3
Isiah Ave TF1 ... 143 D6
Island Gn Sh Ctr LL11 ... 221 C3
Isle La SY3 ... 112 B2
Islington St LL12 ... 109 F4
Ivatt Cl 7 TF4 ... 144 A2
Ivetsey Bank Rd ST19 ... 148 F8
Ivor Thomas Rd TF2 ... 132 D1
Ivy Cl 2 LL11 ... 221 C6
Ivy Gr TF1 ... 130 D3
Ivy Hatch 3 SY1 ... 113 F2
Ivy House Paddocks TF1 ... 131 D3

J
Jabe Davies Cl 6 TF2 ... 132 D1
Jackets Cl LD7 ... 203 B2
Jackfield Tile Mus* TF8 ... 152 F2
Jackson Ave
  1 Broseley TF12 ... 152 C1
  2 Broseley TF12 ... 161 C8
James Cl 5 Ludlow SY8 ... 217 E4
  9 Oakengates/Donnington
  TF2 ... 132 E7
  Sheriffhales TF11 ... 134 C6
James Clay Ct 1 TF1 ... 131 C3
James Nelson Cres 5 TF2 ... 132 C7
James Way
  3 Oakengates/Donnington
  TF2 ... 132 E7

James Way continued
  3 Oakengates/Donnington
  TF2 ... 132 E3
  6 Oakengates/Donnington
  TF2 ... 132 D2
  5 St. Georges & Priorslee
  TF2 ... 132 C7
Jane's Pl 1 SY1 ... 125 C7
Japonica Dr SY1 ... 113 A4
Jarman Ave 11 LL13 ... 221 D2
Jarman St 2 SY1 ... 125 C2
Jarvis Way 1 TF4 ... 143 E5
Jasmin Cl 3 TF3 ... 143 E8
Jasmine Cl 4 SY11 ... 40 F1
Jasmine Gdns 3 TF3 ... 143 E8
Jay Cl SY1 ... 113 B5
Jay La SY7 ... 205 A5
Jeffreys Cl LL12 ... 221 E7
Jeffreys Rd LL12 ... 221 E7
Jehu Rd 2 SY21 ... 170 B6
Jellicoe Cres 8 SY11 ... 146 A6
Jemmett Cl 2 SY1 ... 58 D7
Jenks Rd 7 WV5 ... 190 F3
Jennings Rd SY1 ... 58 C7
Jiggers Bank TF4 ... 143 A1
Jockey Bank TF8 ... 152 D4
Jockey Field 4 SY8 ... 217 D7
John Broad Ave TF1 ... 130 F2
John Evans Mews 2 SY3 ... 125 B2
John Fletcher Ct Jun Sch TF7 ... 153 A4
John Randall Prim Sch TF3 ... 153 C5
John St Chirk LL14 ... 6 E2
  Shrewsbury SY1 ... 125 D7
John Wilkinson Prim Sch TF12 ... 152 E3
John's St 3 SY11 ... 145 F4
Johnston Rd TF4 ... 143 F4
Johnstone Cl 2 TF2 ... 132 C5
Joseph Rich Ave 7 TF12 ... 153 A5
Jubilee Ave TF3 ... 132 D8
Jubilee Dr WV16 ... 200 E2
Jubilee Dr 11 LL13 ... 221 C3
Jubilee St SY4 ... 84 A5
Judith Butts Gdns 8
Judith Butts La 2 SY1 ... 125 F7
Julian Rd TF8 ... 217 D5
Juniper Cl LL12 ... 221 F7
Juniper Dr 3 TF10 ... 111 E4
Juniper Row 6 TF10 ... 109 F1

K
Katesway 3 SY1 ... 113 D1
Kay Cl 9 SY1 ... 59 B8
Kaymaur Cl SY2 ... 26 B6
Keble Way 8 SY3 ... 124 E3
Keelton Cl SY3 ... 124 C6
Keepers Cres 2 TF2 ... 132 E4
Keepside Cl SY8 ... 217 A6
Kelsall Dr 14 SY3 ... 124 A7
Kemberton Dr 7 TF2 ... 132 C6
Kemberton Rd TF7 ... 153 C6
Kemble Dr 3 SY3 ... 124 F3
Kemps Eye Ave 3 SY3 ... 125 C3
Kendal Rd SY1 ... 113 F3
Kendall Way LL12 ... 221 E8
Kendricks Bank SY4 ... 137 B6
Kenfields 3 TF9 ... 89 B6
Kenilworth Cl 4 TF9 ... 36 E2
Kenley Ave SY1 ... 113 D3
Kennedy Cl SY6 ... 216 C7
Kennedy Rd SY3 ... 125 A4
Kennel La WV7 ... 156 D4
Kennel Bank SY7 ... 212 D8
Kenrick Ct CW3 ... 5 A1
Kensington Gr LL12 ... 221 D7
Kensington Way 2 TF2 ... 132 A3
Kent Cl 2 SY11 ... 15 B7
Kent Dr 7 LL12 ... 221 D8
Kenton Dr 2 SY3 ... 125 F6
Kenwenick Cl SY3 ... 63 C7
Kenwood Dr SY3 ... 124 D5
Kenwood Gdns SY3 ... 124 C5
Kenwood Rd SY3 ... 124 C4
Kenwray Dr TF2 ... 132 D4
Kenyon Ave LL11 ... 221 D7
Kerrison Dr SY1 ... 170 C7
Kerry Cl SY1 ... 181 F3
Kerry Pl LL12 ... 221 E4
Kerry Ridgeway SY1 ... 181 A4
Kerry St 10 SY15 ... 174 B3
Kershaw SY1 ... 217 D6
Kestrel Cl SY8 ... 110 A5
Kestrel Ct 3 TF1 ... 130 B6
Kestrel Dr 2 SY1 ... 114 C3
Kesworth Dr 8 TF2 ... 132 F1
Ketley Bsns Pk TF1 ... 131 C2
Ketley Town Jun Sch TF1 ... 131 D1
Kettlemore La TF1 ... 134 C5
Kew Gdns 4 TF2 ... 132 F1
Keston Gdns SY1 ... 113 A6
Keystone Gdns 3 SY8 ... 217 D3
Kid La 8 SY7 ... 193 D3
Kidderminster Rd
  Bewdley DY12 ... 211 E2
  8 Bridgnorth WV15 ... 219 C1
Kilbhorse La SY8 ... 212 F3
Kilnbank Cres 5 TF9 ... 53 C8
Kilnbank Rd TF9 ... 53 C8
Kilvert Cl TF10 ... 108 F3

King Charles Way 2 WV16 ... 218 F6
King St Broseley TF12 ... 152 C1
  Dawley TF4 ... 143 F4
  Much Wenlock TF13 ... 159 C4
  9 Oswestry SY1 ... 58 E8
  Shrewsbury SY2 ... 125 E5
  Wellington TF1 ... 130 E4
  Wrexham LL11 ... 221 C4
King's Haye Rd 8 TF1 ... 130 D3
King's Loade WV16 ... 218 F4
King's St Blymhill & Weston-under-Lizard TF10 ... 123 C1
  Sheriffhales TF11 ... 134 C7
Kingfisher Cl
  6 Newport TF10 ... 109 F5
  6 Shrewsbury SY1 ... 114 C3
Kingfisher Way TF1 ... 130 C6
Kingfisher Wlk SY12 ... 57 B3
Kings Ave TF9 ... 53 A8
Kings Cl 2 LL12 ... 221 D5
Kings Dr SY4 ... 99 B8
Kings Oak Ct 6 LL13 ... 221 C1
Kings Rd SY8 ... 212 E2
Kings Rd N 2 SY1 ... 58 E8
Kingsbury 3 SY1 ... 24 F7
Kingscote Cl SY2 ... 126 A2
Kingsland TF1 ... 131 A2
Kingsland Grange Sch SY1 ... 125 A3
Kingsland Rd SY1 ... 125 A4
Kingsley Dr TF2 ... 120 D3
Kingsmills Rd LL13 ... 221 E1
Kingston Dr SY1 ... 126 A2
Kingston Rd TF2 ... 132 B6
Kingstown 2 TF2 ... 221 E4
Kingsway
  Whitchurch SY13 ... 15 A7
  Wilcott SY4 ... 97 D2
Kingsway Cres 3 SY13 ... 131 A2
Kingsway Dr 10 SY13 ... 15 A7
Kingswood Bsns Pk WV7 ... 157 F1
Kingswood Cl TF3 ... 159 C5
Kingswood Cres SY3 ... 124 C4
Kingswood Rd
  Albrighton WV7 ... 157 C4
  Shrewsbury SY3 ... 124 D6
Kingswood Sch WV7 ... 157 F2
Kinlet Cl DY14 ... 210 B6
Kinlet CE Prim Sch DY12 ... 210 D2
Kinlet Hall (Moffats School) DY12 ... 210 A8
Kinlet Rd DY12 ... 210 D2
Kinloss Ave SY2 ... 156 D8
Kinnerley CE Sch SY10 ... 96 B6
Kinsley Rd LD7 ... 203 B3
Kinsleys The DY14 ... 199 D1
Kirkland Ave 8 SY3 ... 124 A7
Kirkwood Cl 2 SY1 ... 113 C1
Kitchen Hill Rd SY8 ... 212 D1
Kittyoak La SY5 ... 169 B4
Knighton Hospl LD7 ... 203 B2
Knighton Rd 8 LD7 ... 203 E3
Knighton Sta LD7 ... 203 B3
Knighton VP Sch LD7 ... 203 B2
Knights Way
  1 Oswestry SY11 ... 40 F1
  Shrewsbury SY4 ... 125 C2
Knightsbridge Cl SY2 ... 126 A2
Knightsbridge Cres 8 SY3 ... 144 B1
Knolls The 5 SY3 ... 124 A7
Knowle Wood View 3 TF3 ... 144 D4
Knowles La 3 SY1 ... 29 B3
Knowsley Dr 8 SY3 ... 124 A7
Knucklas Rd LD7 ... 203 A3
Knucklas Sta LD7 ... 202 E4
Kynaston Dr SY4 ... 66 B8
Kynaston Pl 1 LL14 ... 6 C8
Kynaston Rd SY1 ... 113 E4
Kynaston's Cave* SY4 ... 170 E6
Kynnersley Dr 4 TF10 ... 109 E3
Kynnersley La SY5 ... 150 C7
Kyreside WR15 ... 220 D4

L
Laburnum Cl SY11 ... 24 F6
Laburnum Dr 6 SY12 ... 27 A2
Laburnum Ct
  1 Market Drayton TF9 ... 36 D2
  7 Shifnal TF11 ... 145 F5
Laburnum Dr
  Madeley TF7 ... 153 B4
  Oswestry SY11 ... 58 F7
Laburnum Mdws 1 SY22 ... 167 A8
Laburnum Rd 8 TF2 ... 132 A4
Lackstone La SY8 ... 208 A6
Lacon Cl 8 DY14 ... 209 D2
Lacon Dr SY4 ... 66 C6
Lacon St SY3 ... 49 E7
Ladbroke Dr SY3 ... 124 C5
Lady Leasow 8 SY3 ... 124 F3
Ladycroft TF1 ... 131 A3
Ladycroft 5 SY3 ... 124 F3
Ladygrove Cty Prim Sch TF4 ... 143 E5
Ladymas La SY4 ... 102 B6
Ladymas Rd SY4 ... 102 C6
Ladywell 4 SY7 ... 204 C5
Lagden La SY9 ... 181 F5
Lake End Dr TF2 ... 153 D8
Lake View LL12 ... 221 F6
Lakelands SY12 ... 27 A1
Lakes Rd The 8 DY12 ... 211 C2
Lambert Rd 9 SY21 ... 170 B6
Lambert Cl 8 SY7 ... 195 E5
Lambeth Dr 10 TF3 ... 144 B1
Lambourn Dr SY3 ... 124 B6
Lambourne Dr 4 DY12 ... 221 C2
Lambpit St 5 LL11 ... 221 D3
Lamledge La TF11 ... 146 B3
Lancaster Ave TF4 ... 143 F4
Lancaster Cl WV7 ... 156 F8
Lancaster Ct 3 TF4 ... 143 F4
Lancaster Pl TF4 ... 143 F4
Lancaster Rd
  2 Bewdley DY12 ... 211 D2
  Shrewsbury SY1 ... 113 E3
Landy Cl TF2 ... 120 C2
Lane End LL13 ... 10 F4
Lanes Cl 27 WV5 ... 190 F3
Lanesfield 3 SY3 ... 124 F3
Laneside 21 TF2 ... 120 F1
Langford Ave SY3 ... 136 E6
Langford Dr SY8 ... 217 F4
Langford Gn 2 SY1 ... 113 C4
Langland Rd
  1 Cleobury Mortimer DY14 ... 209 E3
  Oswestry SY11 ... 58 F8
Langley Cres TF4 ... 143 F3
Langley Dale TF4 ... 70 C5
Langley Dr SY3 ... 136 F5
Langley Fold TF4 ... 143 F3
Langley plum Sch TF3 ... 144 A5
Langley Rd TF4 ... 190 F7
Langley St SY1 ... 113 D3
Lansdowne Cres TF4 ... 136 F7
Lansdowne Rd SY3 ... 124 A4
Lanwood Rd 2 TF3 ... 144 D3
Lapwing Gate 8 TF2 ... 144 C8
Lapwood Dr 9 SY3 ... 113 C2
Lapworth Way 3 TF10 ... 110 A3
Larch Cl 1 SY12 ... 27 A2
Larch Rd SY1 ... 113 C4
Larch Wood 23 TF3 ... 144 D3
Larches The 12 TF10 ... 109 E2
Larchwood Rd LL12 ... 221 F7
Lark Rise TF2 ... 132 C4
Larkey La 2 LD7 ... 203 B3
Larkhill Rd
  Gobowen SY11 ... 41 A4
  6 Shrewsbury SY1 ... 124 D6
Larksie Rise SY4 ... 124 C6
Larksgor Glade 12 TF3 ... 144 D3
Latchford La SY1 ... 114 B4
Laundry La SY2 ... 125 E3
Laurel Dr 4 TF1 ... 109 F3
Laurel La 3 TF3 ... 143 C8
Laurels Cl SY2 ... 27 B1
Laurels Mdws 15 LD7 ... 203 B3
Laurels The LL12 ... 221 E6
Lavender Bank 1 SY3 ... 181 E3
Lavender Way 3 SY3 ... 125 D3
Lavington View 1 WV15 ... 219 A4
Lawford Cl TF4 ... 152 F8
Lawley Cl 3 SY6 ... 216 D7
Lawley Cty Prim Sch TF4 ... 143 C7
Lawley Dr TF3 ... 143 C8
Lawley Gate TF4 ... 143 C5
Lawley Gdns 3 SY2 ... 126 A4
Lawn Central TF3 ... 144 B7
Lawn La TF9 ... 54 F1
Lawns The 4 TF1 ... 130 E4
Lawnswood 2 SY1 ... 124 A4
Lawns Wood TF1 ... 130 C4
Lawson Cl LL12 ... 221 D5
Lawson Gdns 2 SY1 ... 114 B4
Lawton Cl 3 TF1 ... 131 A6
Lawton Farm Rd 8 TF1 ... 131 A6
Lawtons La TF8 ... 152 B7
Laxton Dr 2 DY12 ... 211 C2
Lea Cl 3 TF1 ... 131 A6
Lea Rd LL13 ... 221 C3
Lea The 3 WV15 ... 201 B3
Leabank Cl 10 SY11 ... 113 C2
Leadon Cl TF4 ... 152 F8
Leafields SY1 ... 113 C5
Leamoor Cres SY1 ... 125 E4
Leasow Flag TF4 ... 152 F4
Leasowe Gn TF4 ... 152 E8
Leasowes Cl 22 WV16 ... 218 D5
Leasowes Pk 8 SY4 ... 103 D6
Leaton Dr TF1 ... 130 C5
Ledwyche Ct SY8 ... 207 C1
Lee Dingle TF7 ... 153 A7
Leegomery Ave Jun Sch TF1 ... 131 B5
Leegomery Rd TF1 ... 131 A5
Lees Cl TF5 ... 130 B8
Leeswood Cl 7 SY8 ... 124 B6
Leg St SY11 ... 58 E8
Legge's Hill TF12 ... 152 C1

Legges Way TF7 .....153 B5
Leicester Way 2 TF1 .....131 A5
Leigh Mdws 6 SY2 .....94 A1
Leigh Rd
 Minsterley SY5 .....172 D3
 7 Newport TF10 .....109 E2
Leighton CP Sch
 SY21 .....170 D5
Leighton La TF6 .....142 B2
Leighton Rd
 Shrewsbury SY1 .....113 D3
 Liverpool St SY1 .....170 C6
Leighton View 5 SY3 .....170 B6
Leintwardine Endowed Prim
 Sch SY7 .....205 B5
Lennock Rd TF2 .....132 B7
Leonard Cl 8 TF2 .....132 C7
Leonard St TF2 .....132 A3
Lesley Owen Way SY1 .....113 F2
Lessar Ave 5 SY3 .....125 A6
Letchmere Cl WV6 .....166 C3
Letchmere La WV6 .....166 C2
Leuchars La WV7 .....156 D8
Levens Dr SY11 .....113 E3
Leveson Cl 8 TF2 .....132 C3
Levins Ct TF7 .....153 C5
Lexington Ave SY2 .....126 A2
Ley Brook 2 TF2 .....131 F2
Leyburn Ave SY1 .....124 B6
Leys La HR6 .....212 C1
Lichfield Cl 1 TF2 .....133 A1
Lidgates Gn TF1 .....131 B2
Lighteach Rd SY13 .....32 B2
Lighmoor Rd TF4 .....152 D7
Lilac Cl 8 TF3 .....143 F8
Lilac Dr 22 WV5 .....190 F3
Lilac Dro SY11 .....59 A7
Lilac Way LL11 .....221 B4
Lilleshall National Sports Ctr
 TF10 .....121 C4
Lilleshall Prim Sch
 TF10 .....121 C4
Lilyhurst Rd
 Lilleshall & Donnington
 TF10 .....121 B1
 Sheriffhales TF10 .....133 E8
Lilyvale Cl 9 TF2 .....133 F2
Lime Cl 2 Alveley WV15 .....201 B3
 2 Ellesmere SY12 .....27 A2
 4 Ludlow SY8 .....217 D6
Lime Gr
 Market Drayton TF9 .....52 F7
 7 Oswestry SY11 .....58 F7
Lime Kilns La SY21 .....170 A4
Lime St SY1 .....125 C4
Lime Tree Way TF1 .....109 E5
Limekiln Bank 1 TF2 .....132 E2
Limekiln Cl 2 TF2 .....132 E2
Limekiln La
 Lilleshall TF10 .....121 C5
 Little Wenlock TF1 .....130 F1
Limes Paddock 1 SY5 .....178 C6
Limes Rd 1 TF2 .....132 B2
Limes The WV7 .....157 A4
Lincoln Cres
 Kidderminster DY11 .....211 F3
 8 Oakengates/Donnington
 TF2 .....132 B4
Lincoln Fields WV16 .....200 C2
Lincoln Hill TF8 .....152 C4
Lincoln Rd TF2 .....132 B4
Lindale Cl 2 SY3 .....125 A6
Lindale Dr 5 WV5 .....190 F3
Linden Ave Chirk LL14 .....6 E3
 Much Wenlock TF13 .....159 D5
 Wellington TF1 .....130 D3
 Whitchurch SY13 .....14 F7
 Wrexham LL11 .....221 E2
Linden Gdns 6 SY3 .....125 D4
Linden Gr TF1 .....130 D3
Lindens The TF1 .....145 E4
Lindfield Dr 3 TF1 .....130 A7
Lindley St 8 SY1 .....125 D7
Lindridge CE Prim Sch
 WR15 .....136 F6
Lineton Cl 4 TF2 .....132 B6
Lingen Cl SY1 .....125 E8
Lingen Rd SY8 .....217 F4
Lingfield Rd 7 DY12 .....211 E5
Links Rd
 Church Stretton SY6 .....216 C2
 Shrewsbury SY3 .....125 D3
Linley Ave 4 SY5 .....173 B4
Linley Dr Dawley TF3 .....144 C1
 More SY5 .....175 F2
Linley Pl LL11 .....221 C8
Linley Terr SY3 .....173 B4
Linley View Dr WV16 .....218 D7
Linnet Cl SY1 .....114 B3
Linnet Gate 1 TF1 .....130 C7
Linney SY1 .....217 B4
Lintin Cl 1 SY5 .....113 E6
Lion La
 Cleobury Mortimer DY14 .....209 E2
 Coreley SY8 .....208 C1
 Ellesmere Rural SY12 .....10 C3
Lion Mdw 8 SY6 .....216 C6
Lion St TF2 .....132 B2
Lions Bank 8 SY5 .....174 B3
Lisburne Gr LL12 .....221 F8
Listley St WV16 .....218 E5
Little Acton Dr LL12 .....222 D7
Little Barnyard SY5 .....173 E5
Little Eyton Fold TF4 .....143 F4

Little Harlescott La 3
 SY1 .....113 E5
Little Henfaes Dr
 SY21 .....170 C6
Little London La SY10 .....57 C2
Little Mdw Cl 5 SY5 .....130 A7
Little Ness Rd SY4 .....80 B1
Little Oxton La SY3 .....124 B7
Littlehales Rd TF10 .....121 F4
Littleover Ave 8 SY1 .....113 D5
Littleside Dr SY3 .....125 A1
Liverpool Rd
 Oswestry SY11 .....40 E1
 Whitchurch SY13 .....40 E1
Liverpool Rd W 6 SY11 .....40 D1
Livesey Ave SY8 .....217 D5
Livesey Rd SY8 .....217 D4
Lizard La TF11 .....134 F6
Llanforda Cl 2 SY11 .....58 C7
Llanforda Mead SY10 .....58 C7
Llanforda Rise 1 SY11 .....58 C8
Llanmynech Rocks Nature
 Reserve* SY22 .....93 F8
Llansantffraid CIWA
 SY22 .....92 C5
Llanshay La LD7 .....203 D2
Lletty La SY22 .....92 B3
Llewellyn Roberts Way
 TF9 .....36 D3
Lloyd St SY11 .....40 E1
Lloyd's La LL14 .....6 E1
Lloyds Head TF8 .....152 E3
Lloyds The TF8 .....152 F3
Llwyn Cres SY10 .....58 C4
Llwyn Fields 4 SY11 .....40 E1
Llwyn Rd Clun SY7 .....193 C3
 Oswestry SY11 .....40 E1
Llynclys Comm Nature
 Reserve* SY10 .....76 A6
Llys Ave SY11 .....59 A7
Llys Cl SY11 .....59 A7
Llys Ct SY11 .....59 A7
Llys David Lord LL13 .....221 B3
Llys La SY11 .....59 A7
Llys Rd SY11 .....59 A7
Load St DY12 .....211 D2
Loak Rd WV7 .....156 E5
Lockside 11 WV5 .....190 F4
Lockwood Dr 4 SY1 .....113 D3
Lodge Cl
 8 Beverley DY12 .....211 E2
 Shifnal TF11 .....145 F3
Lodge Cres SY3 .....137 A6
Lodge La Barrow TF12 .....163 B7
 Bridgnorth WV15 .....219 A4
 The Gorge TF8 .....152 C4
Lodge Pk 6 WV5 .....189 E4
Lodge Rd
 Oakengates/Donnington
 TF2 .....132 D2
 4 Wrexham LL11 .....221 B6
Lodmore La SY11 .....117 C6
Lon Brynfa-Brynfa Ave 1
 SY3 .....170 B7
London Rd (Emstrey)
 SY2 .....126 B2
London Rd
 Bridgemere CW5 .....4 E5
 Loggerheads TF9 .....21 B5
 Oakengates/Donnington
 TF2 .....132 D2
 4 Shrewsbury SY2 .....125 F4
 Whitchurch Urban SY13 .....21 C8
 Woore CW3 .....21 C8
Long Bank DY12 .....211 B1
Long La
 Albrighton WV7 .....113 C8
 Bronington SY13 .....13 D4
 Hodnet TF9 .....69 A8
 Longden SY5 .....173 F4
 Sibdon Carwood SY7 .....195 C2
Long La Dr TF7 .....152 D6
Long Length SY7 .....183 E1
Long Mdw
 Bayston Hill SY3 .....136 F6
 Telford Dawley TF3 .....144 C3
Long Mdw CE Prim Sch
 TF3 .....136 F6
Long Mynd Cl 9 SY6 .....216 C7
Long Pack SY11 .....116 B4
Long Row 8 SY1 .....113 E1
Longbridge Cl 18 SY2 .....126 B7
Longden Ave SY1 .....125 C3
Longden CE Prim Sch
 SY5 .....173 E5
Longden Cl 1 SY11 .....125 C3
Longden Coleham
 SY1 .....125 C4
Longden Comm La
 SY5 .....173 A4
Longden Gdns 8 SY3 .....125 C4
Longden Gn SY3 .....125 B3
Longden Rd
 Longden SY5 .....173 A4
 Shrewsbury SY3 .....125 B3
Longfield LL14 .....6 E1
Longford Cl 10 WV5 .....190 F3
Longford Rd TF10 .....109 A1
Longford Rise 1 TF1 .....130 E5
Longhills Rd SY6 .....216 C7
Longhirst Gdns 3 SY2 .....124 C7
Longlands La 3 TF9 .....36 D1
Longlands Prim Sch
 TF9 .....36 D2
Longleat Cl 4 SY11 .....172 E3
Longmeadow Dr 5
 WR15 .....220 D6

Longner St SY3 .....125 B6
Longnor CE Sch SY5 .....178 E3
Longnor La TF11 .....130 C6
Longslow Cl 1 TF9 .....36 B1
Longslow La SY13 .....36 B1
Longthorpe Dr TF3 .....131 C6
Longueville 1 LL13 .....221 C1
Longueville Dr SY11 .....59 B8
Longville Rd 8 SY11 .....113 D4
Longwithy La TF10 .....108 F4
Lonsdale Dr SY3 .....125 A1
Lord Murray Dr TF7 .....152 E7
Lord Silkin Sch TF3 .....144 D2
Lord St 8 Oswestry SY11 .....58 D8
 1 Wrexham LL11 .....221 C3
Lords Dr 1 TF2 .....132 E3
Lordstone La SY5 .....172 A1
Lorne St 8 Oswestry SY11 .....40 E1
 1 Wrexham LL11 .....221 C4
Lostford La TF9 .....51 E4
Loton Butts 9 SY2 .....125 F8
Loughton La WV16 .....198 D1
Lovatt Cl SY2 .....126 A7
Love La
 Bishop's Castle SY9 .....181 F3
 Bridgnorth WV16 .....218 F6
 Cleobury Mortimer DY14 .....209 E2
 Lydham SY9 .....182 A4
 Wem SY4 .....66 B8
Lovell Cl TF11 .....146 A6
Low Valley Cl TF1 .....131 D3
Low Croft 8 SY7 .....205 B5
Low Hill Gdns SY4 .....65 F7
Low Hill Rd SY4 .....65 F6
Lowa La Alveley WV15 .....201 B1
 Upper Arley DY12 .....201 B1
Lower Bar TF10 .....109 E3
Lower Broad St 4 SY8 .....217 C3
Lower Brook St 1 SY8 .....58 D7
Lower Claremont Bank 10
 SY7 .....197 F4
Lower Cross Lanes
 SY7 .....197 F4
Lower Dingle 8 TF7 .....152 F4
Lower Galdeford SY8 .....217 E4
Lower Hafod 8 SY11 .....58 C8
Lower Heath CE Prim Sch
 SY13 .....50 A6
Lower Inhedge DY14 .....209 F3
Lower La SY7 .....183 E1
Lower Mint
 Oswestry SY11 .....58 C8
 Wrexham LL11 .....221 E8
Lower Pk Pk DY12 .....211 D2
Lower Pk 6 SY7 .....130 C7
Lower Pulley La SY3 .....137 B7
Lower Raven La 1 SY8 .....217 C3
Lower Rd
 Myddle & Broughton SY4 .....82 E4
 7 Pontesbury SY5 .....173 A4
Lower St DY14 .....209 E2
Lower Wood TF3 .....143 E7
Loweswater Cl 1 TF2 .....144 E8
Lowfield 8 SY7 .....125 F8
Lowry Cl 10 TF5 .....130 B8
Loxdale 15 SY3 .....124 F3
Lucerne Cl 2 TF1 .....131 C5
Luciefelde Rd SY3 .....125 B4
Ludford Dr
 18 Dawley TF3 .....144 C1
 Shrewsbury SY3 .....113 D3
Ludford View 4 SY9 .....217 E3
Ludlow Castle* SY8 .....217 D4
Ludlow CE Sch SY8 .....217 A6
Ludlow Coll SY8 .....217 B3
Ludlow Com Hospl
 SY8 .....217 C5
Ludlow Dr TF3 .....144 B2
Ludlow Hts WV16 .....218 D4
Ludlow Inf Sch SY8 .....217 D5
Ludlow Jun Sch SY8 .....217 E5
Ludlow Mus* 5 SY8 .....217 E4
Ludlow Rd
 Aston Eyre WV16 .....187 D5
 Bitterley SY8 .....207 D2
 Bridgnorth WV16 .....218 C3
 Caynham SY8 .....208 B2
 Church Stretton SY6 .....216 A3
 DY14 .....209 D2
 Craven Arms SY7 .....195 C2
 Leintwardine SY7 .....205 C2
 Ludlow Sta SY8 .....217 C5
Ludstone Hall* WV5 .....189 E5
Lurkenhope Wood Nature
 Reserve* LD7 .....203 C6
Lutwyche Cl SY11 .....116 E6
Lutwyche Rd SY6 .....216 C6
Lydbury Cl 8 TF3 .....144 C1
Lydbury N Prim Sch
 SY7 .....194 C8
Lydham Rd SY1 .....113 D4
Lymehurst Ct 7 SY11 .....113 C1
Lymore View SY15 .....174 B3
Lynch La SY9 .....213 D2
Lyncroft WV7 .....157 A5
Lyndale Gr LL12 .....221 D7
Lyndhurst Dr
 1 Bayston Hill SY3 .....137 A5
 8 Oakengates/Donnington
 TF2 .....132 A6
Lyneal La SY12 .....28 D2
Lyneham Ave WV7 .....156 C8
Lyons La SY5 .....173 D4
Lysander Ave WV7 .....156 B7
Lyth Hill Rd SY3 .....136 F4
Lytham Gn TF3 .....133 A8
Lythwood Rd SY3 .....136 F4

Lyttelton Rd DY12 .....211 C2

M

Maddocks TF7 .....153 A5
Madebrook Cl TF7 .....153 D5
Madeira Hill 2 LL13 .....221 D2
Madeira Wlk SY6 .....216 C2
Madeley Cl TF4 .....52 D4
Madeley Rd
 Beckbury TF11 .....164 B8
 Madeley TF7 .....152 D4
Madeley Wood View 10
 TF7 .....152 F4
Madog Pl 18 SY11 .....58 E8
Madras Sch LL13 .....10 E4
Maelor Cl 5 LL13 .....10 E4
Maer La TF9 .....36 D3
Maes Celyn 8 LL13 .....221 C1
Maes Chwarae SY5 .....175 A1
Maes Glas 8 LL13 .....221 C1
Maes Hafren 8 SY5 .....167 F6
Maes Hyfryd 1 LL13 .....221 B8
Maes Uchaf SY22 .....92 B6
Maes Y Foel SY22 .....92 B5
Maes Y Llan SY10 .....56 A4
Maes-yr Ysgol LL14 .....6 E1
Maesbrook Rd 4 SY3 .....125 B1
Maesbury Cty Prim Sch
 SY10 .....77 B8
Maesbury Rd
 Oswestry SY11 .....58 F6
 Oswestry Rural SY10 .....59 A2
Maesgwyn Rd LL13 .....221 B4
Maeshryn Cl SY13 .....13 A3
Maeslwyn La SY13 .....12 F4
Maes-y-Clawdd SY10 .....59 A4
Maesydre Rd LL12 .....221 D5
Maes-y-Felin SY21 .....174 A6
Maes-y-Garreg SY22 .....92 B6
Maes-y-Llan SY22 .....92 B6
Maes-yr-Eglwys SY22 .....92 B6
Mafeking Dr 9 TF2 .....132 C5
Mafeking Rd TF1 .....131 C4
Magister Rd WV7 .....156 B7
Magna Cl Dawley TF4 .....143 F2
 Whitchurch Rural SY13 .....16 A4
Magnolia Cl SY4 .....100 F3
Magnolia Dr
 8 Ellesmere SY12 .....27 A2
 5 The Rock TF3 .....143 E8
Magpie Way 4 TF3 .....153 A8
Main Rd Condover SY5 .....178 C6
 Norton in Hales TF9 .....20 C1
 Oakengates/Donnington
 TF2 .....131 B5
 Pontesbury SY5 .....173 A4
 Wrexham LL11 .....221 B8
Main St 16 SY11 .....189 A6
Maitlands The 6 SY5 .....178 C6
Majestic Way
 Dawley Hamlets TF4 .....144 A1
 8 Wellington TF1 .....130 D1
Malcolm Davies Dr 2
 TF3 .....132 B6
Maldwyn Way 8 SY5 .....174 B3
Malinsgate 7 TF3 .....144 A6
Malinslee Cty Prim Sch
 TF4 .....144 A4
Mall The WV15 .....219 A4
Mallard Cl Dawley TF3 .....144 E8
 8 Shrewsbury SY1 .....114 B4
Mallards Cl 3 WV15 .....201 B3
Malory Dr TF3 .....144 A1
Malory Rd 1 SY1 .....58 F8
Malt Rise 2 SY5 .....167 F6
Malthouse Bank TF6 .....142 D2
Malthouse Cl
 Trefonen SY10 .....57 D2
 7 Whittington SY11 .....41 E3
Malthouse La SY5 .....139 A7
Maltings Cl WV6 .....164 D2
Maltings The
 8 Bayston Hill SY3 .....137 A6
 8 Wellington TF1 .....130 D3
 West Felton SY11 .....78 D7
Maltkiln La
 Whitchurch Rural SY13 .....31 E7
 Whixall SY13 .....30 C2
Malvern Cl 7 SY11 .....125 E2
Malvern Cres TF4 .....143 E1
Mamble Craft Ctr*
 DY14 .....215 F6
Manchester Dr TF1 .....131 A7
Manley Rd LL13 .....221 D3
Mannerley La
 5 Ketley TF3 .....131 E1
 5 The Rock TF3 .....143 E8
Manor Cl Dawley TF3 .....72 A1
 1 Market Drayton TF9 .....36 C1
 Shifnal TF11 .....145 F3
Manor Crest SY15 .....169 C4
Manor Dr
 Oakengates/Donnington
 TF2 .....132 C3
 1 Swindon DY3 .....190 F1
Manor Farm Dr TF3 .....131 B2
Manor Farm La WV16 .....218 D2
Manor Gdns
 8 Albrighton WV7 .....157 A5
 Dawley TF3 .....143 F2
 Market Drayton TF9 .....36 C1
 8 Pontesbury SY5 .....173 B5
Manor House Cl 1
 TF13 .....159 E5
Manor House La SY13 .....32 E3

Manor House National
 Nature Reserve Base*
 SY13 .....100 F4
Manor La
 Bobbington DY7 .....190 B4
 Prees SY13 .....32 F1
Manor Pk 8 SY5 .....173 A4
Manor Rd TF1 .....32 E1
Manor Rd Dawley TF4 .....143 E1
 Edgmond TF10 .....109 A4
 8 Wellington TF1 .....131 A4
Manor Rise TF1 .....131 B8
Manor Way 2 SY5 .....167 A6
Manse Cl TF1 .....131 C1
Manse Rd TF1 .....131 C1
Mansell Rd TF1 .....130 D2
Maple Ave
 4 Ellesmere SY12 .....27 A1
 Oswestry SY11 .....59 A5
 Wrexham LL12 .....221 E8
Maple Cl
 2 Craven Arms SY7 .....195 C8
 2 Ludlow SY8 .....217 D2
 Market Drayton TF9 .....52 F7
 Oakengates/Donnington
 TF2 .....132 A2
Maple Cres 1 WV15 .....201 B3
Maple Dr 5 SY11 .....113 C1
Maple Wood 11 TF3 .....144 C2
Maplehurst Dr 2 SY11 .....41 A3
March Gr 8 DY12 .....211 C2
March Way SY1 .....113 F3
Marche La SY5 .....58 C6
Marches Sch & Tech Coll The
 SY11 .....58 C6
Marchwood Cl 1 WV16 .....218 C7
Marcie Orch 8 SY8 .....213 B1
Mardol 11 SY1 .....125 C4
Mardol Head 10 SY1 .....125 A6
Mardol Quay 4 SY1 .....125 C4
Mardu La SY7 .....193 A4
Margaret Ct 4 TF1 .....131 C1
Marigold Cl 2 TF1 .....131 C4
Market Drayton Cty Jun Sch
 TF9 .....53 F2
Market Drayton Inf Sch
 TF9 .....36 B1
Market Drayton Swimming
 Ctr TF9 .....53 A2
Market La WV4 .....190 A1
Market Mews 5 TF10 .....109 F4
Market Pl 11 TF11 .....145 E3
Market Sq
 8 Bishop's Castle SY9 .....181 D3
 2 Tenbury Wells WR15 .....220 C1
Market St
 6 Craven Arms SY7 .....195 C8
 4 Ellesmere SY12 .....27 A1
 7 Knighton LD7 .....203 E8
 10 Ludlow LD7 .....217 E4
 8 Oakengates/Donnington
 TF2 .....132 C5
 2 Shrewsbury SY1 .....125 C4
 2 Tenbury Wells WR15 .....220 C1
 1 Wellington TF1 .....130 D1
 2 Wem SY4 .....66 C6
 Wrexham LL12 .....221 C2
Marlborough Ct 4 SY3 .....114 A7
Marlborough Rd
 TF3 .....143 E7
Marlbrook La WV6 .....166 C2
Marlburn Way 18 WV5 .....190 F2
Marlcroft 8 SY7 .....66 E6
Marlebrook Way TF6 .....116 A6
Marlow Dr 7 SY2 .....125 C4
Marlpool Cl 3 SY3 .....124 E3
Marne Cl 8 SY4 .....66 E6
Marrion's Hill TF2 .....132 C2
Marsh Cres 1 LL11 .....221 C2
Marsh La
 Ellesmere TF9 .....73 A6
 Hinstock TF9 .....72 A6
 Sheriffhales TF11 .....134 D1
Marsh Mdw Cl 4 TF1 .....130 A4
Marsh Rd
 Edgmond TF10 .....108 A5
 Sheriffhales TF11 .....133 C5
Marshalls Ct 4 SY11 .....125 D5
Marshbrook Way TF2 .....132 B6
Marshfields SY10 .....77 F4
Marshgate 3 SY2 .....124 C5
Marsland Cl 2 SY3 .....124 E3
Mart Ave 4 TF2 .....132 E4
Martin Rd TF1 .....131 C1
Martin Wilson Prim Sch The
 SY1 .....125 A1
Martingale Way 4 TF4 .....143 E3
Martins Fields SY10 .....57 E7
Marton Dr
 Shrewsbury SY1 .....113 C3
 Wellington TF1 .....130 D3
Mary Elizabeth Rd 2
 SY5 .....167 A6
Mary Webb Cl 2 SY3 .....173 A4
Mary Webb Rd SY3 .....125 D3
Mary Webb Sch The
 SY5 .....173 A4
Maryvale WR15 .....220 A4
Masefield Cl 3 TF9 .....53 F1
Masefield Cl 4 SY11 .....58 F8
Maslan Cres TF10 .....107 F2
Mason Ave 18 LL13 .....221 B4
Mason Dr 3 TF7 .....153 A5
Mason's Pl TF10 .....109 E5
Massey Cres SY11 .....113 C1
Matlock Ave 6 TF4 .....144 F5

Maudlins Cl WV16 .....218 C4
Maurice Chandler Sports Ctr TF9 .....70 C8
Maurice Lee Ave 4 TF2 .....132 A3
Mawddwy Ave 1 LL11 .....221 C5
Mawley Cl 2 SY1 .....125 F2
Maws Craft Ctr TF8 .....153 A2
Mayfair Cl 4 WV7 .....157 A5
Mayfair Gr 3 TF2 .....132 F2
Mayfield Ave 3 SY7 .....195 E5
Mayfield Cl 6 SY2 .....123 E4
Mayfield Gr SY3 .....136 E6
Mayfield Pk SY2 .....126 A4
Mayfield Rd 3 WV7 .....156 F5
Mayfields 3 SY8 .....217 C6
Maynards Croft
 4 Newport TF10 .....109 F4
 5 Newport TF10 .....110 A4
Maypole Cl 10 DY12 .....211 E2
Maythorne Cl 2 TF7 .....153 C4
Mayville Ave 3 LL11 .....221 C5
McCormick Dr TF1 .....130 F2
McCredy Dr 3 SY2 .....125 F5
McLean Dr 8 TF2 .....132 F1
Mead Way TF1 .....146 A4
Meadcroft 1 TF1 .....153 A4
Meadlands The 5 WV5 .....190 F3
Meadow Bank TF9 .....19 A4
Meadow Brook 3 SY2 .....136 F6
Meadow Brook Cl TF7 .....153 B5
Meadow Cl
 Aston Eyre WV16 .....187 D5
 Bridgnorth WV16 .....218 E3
 Cressage SY5 .....149 E4
 Market Drayton TF9 .....153 C5
 Oakengates/Donnington TF2 .....131 F6
 6 Oswestry SY11 .....41 A1
 4 Shrewsbury SY3 .....124 A2
 Wem SY4 .....66 A8
Meadow Dale Dr 1 TF5 .....130 A6
Meadow Dr
 8 Gobowen SY11 .....14 A1
 Shifnal TF11 .....146 A6
Meadow Farm Dr SY1 .....130 A2
Meadow Lea
 6 Oswestry SY11 .....41 A1
Meadow Mill SY1 .....220 D3
Meadow Pippins 12 TF3 .....144 D3
Meadow Pk 4 SY1 .....125 C6
Meadow Rd
 Albrighton WV7 .....157 B5
 3 Craven Arms SY7 .....195 E5
 1 Dawley TF4 .....143 E4
 4 Newport TF10 .....109 F3
 Oakengates/Donnington TF2 .....132 E8
 4 Wellington TF1 .....130 C4
Meadow Rise
 8 Bewdley DY12 .....211 E3
 Oswestry SY11 .....41 A1
 4 Tenbury Wells WR15 .....220 D5
Meadow The TF9 .....69 D5
Meadow View
 Albrighton WV7 .....167 B8
 3 Prees SY13 .....49 D8
 6 Westbury SY5 .....169 B1
Meadow View Cl
 Newport TF10 .....110 A3
 Whitchurch SY13 .....14 F7
Meadow Way 7 TF1 .....111 A2
Meadowbrook Cl 12 WV15 .....201 B3
Meadowcroft 3 SY13 .....14 E8
Meadows Prim Sch SY11
Meadows The
 Church Stretton SY6 .....216 E5
 6 Gobowen SY11 .....41 A2
 5 Oakengates/Donnington TF2 .....132 A1
 4 Pant SY10 .....76 A1
Meadowsweet Dr 4 TF2 .....132 E1
Meadway 12 WV15 .....219 A4
Meaton La DY14 .....210 B5
Medlar Cl 3 TF3 .....143 F8
Meese Cl TF1 .....130 D6
Meeson Cl TF1 .....130 D6
Melbourne Cl 2 TF4 .....144 A4
Melbourne Rise 3 SY2 .....124 A7
Mellor Cl 4 TF7 .....152 F4
Melrose Ave 3 TF9 .....53 B8
Melrose Dr 4 SY2 .....125 E1
Melrose Gdns TF1 .....130 C3
Melton Way 11 SY3 .....125 A1
Melverley Craft Ctr* SY22 .....168 A7
Melverley View SY5 .....168 A6
Mendip Cl TF1 .....143 D3
Mentone Cres TF10 .....109 B4
Meole Brace Infants Sch SY3 .....125 A1
Meole Brace Ret Pk SY3 .....125 A1
Meole Brace Sch SY3 .....125 C1
Meole Cres SY3 .....125 B2

Meole Rise 6 SY3 .....125 C3
Meole Wlk SY3 .....125 A2
Merchant Cl 4 WV6 .....166 C3
Mercia Dr 5 TF1 .....131 A5
Mercian Cl SY3 .....124 F1
Mercian Ct 4 TF9 .....36 C1
Mere Cl 2 Newport TF10 .....109 F4
 Shifnal TF11 .....146 A3
 Shrewsbury SY3 .....125 F2
Mere Gr 4 TF5 .....201 F6
Mere La 2 TF7 .....201 F6
Meres Visitor Ctr* SY2 .....27 D2
Mereside SY2 .....125 F2
Merganser Cl 1 TF1 .....131 A6
Merlin Coppice 6 TF1 .....131 A7
Merlin Rd
 Shrewsbury SY3 .....124 D7
 Wrexham LL12 .....221 E8
Merricks La DY12 .....211 C3
Merrington Rd
 3 Oakengates/Donnington TF2 .....120 F1
 Pimhill SY4 .....100 E5
Merry La Grinshill SY4 .....84 A1
 Hadnall SY4 .....85 A1
Merton Cl 6 DY12 .....211 C2
Methodist Hill 4 LL20 .....6 A7
Meyrick Rd 4 TF1 .....130 D5
Mickley La TF9 .....51 C5
Middle Croft Rd TF10 .....107 D5
Middle La TF6 .....105 F7
Middle Rd 3 TF2 .....132 B4
Middle Wood Rd
 Bromfield SY8 .....206 E1
 Ludlow SY8 .....217 A3
Middlegate SY1 .....113 D5
Middleton Rd
 Oswestry SY11 .....58 E7
 Oswestry Rural SY11 .....59 C7
Middleton Sq 3 SY2 .....126 A8
Midland Motor Mus* WV15 .....219 E3
Mile Bank Rd SY13 .....2 B2
Mile Oak Ind Est SY10 .....58 F5
Milford Rd SY4 .....99 A7
Mill Bank 5 SY1 .....125 C5
Mill Cl 3 WV5 .....189 A6
Mill Ct LL13 .....9 C8
Mill Farm Dr TF3 .....144 D4
Mill Field Cl 22 LD7 .....203 B3
Mill Gn 2 SY7 .....203 B3
Mill La
 Blymhill & Weston-under-Lizard TF11 .....135 C2
 Bronington SY13 .....13 A4
 Broseley TF12 .....161 C8
 Doddington WV7 .....196 F4
 Donington WV7 .....147 F1
 Hadnall TF10 .....102 C6
 Hanwood SY5 .....169 F11
 Kemberton TF11 .....154 C6
 Knighton on Teme WR15 .....215 B4
 Kynnersley TF6 .....119 C6
 Leintwardine SY7 .....205 B4
 Madeley TF7 .....153 B5
 Prees Higher Heath SY13 .....32 F3
 Stoke upon Tern TF9 .....88 E3
 Tibberton TF10 .....107 D7
 Tong TF11 .....147 D7
 Uffington SY4 .....126 D8
 Wellington TF1 .....130 D3
 2 Westbury SY5 .....170 B6
Mill Pool Cl 11 WV5 .....190 E3
Mill Pool Hl 7 DY14 .....209 E3
 Hodnet TF9 .....51 E1
 Knighton LD7 .....203 B2
 Newcastle on Clun SY7 .....192 D5
 Shrewsbury SY3 .....125 B2
Mill St Bridgnorth WV15 .....219 A5
 Hopesay SY7 .....195 A4
 Ludlow SY8 .....217 C3
 Prees SY13 .....49 C8
 Wem SY4 .....66 A5
 Whitchurch SY13 .....15 A7
Mill Way 4 SY3 .....141 E1
Millbank Rise LL13 .....221 E1
Millbrook Cl 5 SY3 .....212 E2
Millbrook Dr SY4 .....103 D8
Millbrook Way 3 SY3 .....212 D2
Millers Vale SY3 .....190 E3
Millers Way 4 TF3 .....132 F8
Millfield 7 TF2 .....36 F2
Millfield Grange TF4 .....143 E3
Millford Rd 8 SY1 .....130 E3
Millhay Way 8 WV5 .....190 E3
Millichope Pk* 7 .....197 B7
Millington Cl 1 SY4 .....81 A1
Millmead 6 SY4 .....125 F3
Millmead Dr 4 SY4 .....125 F3
Millpool Way WV5 .....190 C5
Millside 29 WV5 .....190 F3
Millstream Bank 6 SY5 .....171 F3
Millstream Way 8 TF1 .....131 B6
Millward Ct TF7 .....132 B8
Millwood Rise 8 LL13 .....9 C8
Milners Cl 7 TF4 .....143 E6
Milners La TF4 .....143 E5
Milnthorpe Cl 8 SY3 .....125 A1
Milton Cl 5 TF7
Milton Dr
 1 Madeley TF7 .....152 F5
 1 Market Drayton TF9 .....36 C2

Milton Rd 5 SY8 .....217 E4
Mimosa Cl TF7 .....153 B3
Miners Mdw TF12 .....161 D8
Minshall Pl 1 SY1 .....59 B7
Minsterley Prim Sch SY5 .....172 D3
Minsterley Rd SY5 .....173 A5
Minter Kemp Art Gall*
 SY5 .....217 C3
Minton Cl 7 TF2 .....152 F7
Mitcham Cl 5 SY3 .....124 D7
Mitchel Way 2 TF7 .....152 F5
Mitnell La SY3 .....212 E5
Moat Cl 8 TF1 .....130 C7
Moat Croft 1 TF11 .....145 F3
Moat Hill SY4 .....181 C4
Moat St WV16 .....218 F5
Mocktree Turnpike SY7 .....205 D6
Modra Pk SY10 .....58 D5
Mold Rd LL11 .....221 A5
Mole Way TF5 .....130 C7
Monet 6 TF5 .....130 B7
Moneybrook Way SY3 .....125 B1
Monger Rd LL13 .....221 C1
Monkmoor Ave
 6 Oswestry SY11 .....58 F8
 Shrewsbury SY2 .....125 F3
Monkmoor Cl 1 SY11 .....58 F8
Monkmoor Cres SY2 .....125 F2
Monkmoor Ind Est SY2 .....126 A8
Monkmoor Pool Nature Reserve* SY2 .....126 C8
Monkmoor Rd
 7 Shrewsbury SY2 .....126 A8
 Ludlow SY8 .....217 A3
Monks CE 18 WV5 .....190 F3
Monkwood 3 TF3 .....144 D3
Montague Pl SY3 .....125 D3
Montgomery Castle* SY15 .....174 B3
Montgomery Mews 2 SY11 .....131 A7
Montgomery Rd
 1 Wellington TF1 .....130 C4
 Wrexham LL13 .....221 E4
Montgomery Way 5 TF1 .....114 A2
Montgomeryshire Mid Wales Airport SY15 .....170 B3
Moor La WV6 .....166 D2
Moor Pk Sch SY8 .....213 F6
Moor Rd TF4 .....143 F6
Moorfield Foundation Prim Sch TF10 .....109 E1
Moorfield La TF10 .....109 D1
Moorhead Cl 8 LL13 .....221 F4
Moorland Ave LL13 .....221 F4
Moorland Dr 14 TF2 .....132 F1
Moorland Rd 3 TF10 .....109 E2
Moors La Farlow DY14 .....209 C7
 St. Martin's SY11 .....24 D4
Moors The
 Cressage SY5 .....149 E5
 1 Diddlebury SY7 .....196 F4
Moors View The 2 SY7 .....196 F4
Morda Bank SY8 .....58 D4
Morda CE (VC) Sch SY10 .....58 D6
Morda Cl SY11 .....58 D6
Morda Gn SY11 .....58 D6
Morden Cl 8 TF2 .....132 C2
Moreton Bsns Pk 23 E5
Moreton Corbet Castle* SY4 .....82 D4
Moreton Cres 3 SY3 .....125 D4
Moreton Hall Sch SY10 .....23 F4
Moreton Say CE Prim Sch TF9 .....34 F2
Moreton La DY7 .....201 F5
Morfe Rd WV15 .....219 A5
Morgan Ave LL11 .....221 D2
Morgan Way 2 TF1 .....131 D2
Morningside SY3 .....220 C4
Mornington Cl 8 SY3 .....124 D6
Morrellswood La
 Leighton & Eaton Constantine SY5 .....142 A1
 Little Wenlock
Morris Cl SY1 .....113 D5
Morris Dr TF2 .....132 C8
Mortimer 2 TF1 .....113 E4
Mortimer Dr 4 TF1 .....130 D5
Mortimer Dr 4 SY8 .....218 E2
Mortimer Gdns 10 DY12 .....209 E2
Mortimer Gr 22 DY12 .....211 D2
Mortimer Pl 2 SY3 .....217 D4
Mortimer Rd 4 SY8 .....217 D4
Morton Cl 4 TF4 .....143 E4
Morville Dr 1 TF1 .....130 C6
Morville Hall & Gdns (NT)*
Morville Rd 1 .....113 D3
Morville Rd WV16 .....187 E5
Mosclay Rd 6 TF2 .....132 D2
Moss La Bronington SY13 .....13 B3
 Chesworardine TF9 .....66 C6
 Ellesmere Rural SY12 .....26 C6
 Hanmer SY13 .....12 C2
 Norton in Hales TF9 .....36 F6
Moss Rd TF2 .....132 C4
Mossbank Way SY3 .....124 D7
Mossey Gn 5 TF1 .....131 F1
Mossey Gn Way TF2 .....131 F1
Mossfield TF9 .....73 A6
Moston Gn 6 SY2 .....114 A3

Moston Rd SY1 .....114 B3
Mottershead 3 SY1 .....113 D4
Mound Way TF7 .....152 F6
Mount (Day Hospital) The TF1 .....130 D3
Mount Bradford La SY11 .....25 A7
Mount Cl
 2 Pontesbury SY21 .....173 A4
 22 Welshpool SY21 .....170 B6
Mount Cres SY11 .....40 C1
Mount Dr 3 SY11 .....58 D8
Mount Gilbert 11 TF7 .....130 F2
Mount Gilbert Sch TF1 .....130 D5
Mount La
 Market Drayton TF9 .....53 C8
 Stoke upon Tern TF9 .....70 F6
Mount Orch 8 WR15 .....220 C4
Mount Pleasant
 3 Clun SY7 .....193 C3
 4 Oakengates/Donnington TF2 .....132 B1
 4 Tenbury Wells WR15 .....220 C4
 2 Trewern SY21 .....167 D3
Mount Pleasant Ave 10 WV5 .....190 F4
Mount Pleasant Dr TF3 .....153 B8
Mount Pleasant Jun Sch SY1 .....113 D1
Mount Pleasant Rd
 2 Madeley TF7 .....153 C5
 Shrewsbury SY3 .....113 D2
 Dawley TF4 .....144 A4
 2 Oswestry SY11 .....58 D8
Mount Rise 40 C1
Mount Side TF1 .....131 D2
Mount St
 Welshpool SY21 .....170 B6
 Wrexham LL13 .....221 D3
Mount View Rd 2 TF2 .....132 B1
Mount Way 4 SY3 .....173 A4
Mountbatten Cl 1 TF1 .....131 A6
Mounts Cl TF7 .....153 C5
Mountwood Pk SY3 .....124 E7
Mousecroft La SY3 .....124 C7
Much Wenlock Leisure Ctr TF13 .....159 F6
Much Wenlock Mus* TF13 .....159 E6
Much Wenlock Prim Sch TF13 .....159 C6
Much Wenlock Rd TF8 .....151 B4
Muckleton Cl TF6 .....104 F4
Muckleton Rd SY4 .....104 B8
Mulberry Ave 5 SY12 .....27 A2
Mulberry Cl SY8 .....169 C4
Mulliner Dr TF1 .....144 A8
Murivance SY1 .....152 B5
Museum of Iron* TF8 .....152 B6
Museum of the Gorge* TF8 .....152 B5
Musk Rose Cl 12 TF2 .....132 E8
Muskoka 10 DY12 .....211 C2
Musley La LL13 .....9 D6
Muxton Cty Prim Sch TF2 .....132 F8
Muxton La
 Lilleshall & Donnington TF2 .....133 A8
 Oakengates/Donnington TF2 .....120 F1
Myddle CE Prim Sch SY4 .....82 D4
Mynd Cl SY2 .....132 E2
Mynd View 5 SY7 .....195 E5
Myrtle Dr SY2 .....132 E2
Myrtle St SY21 .....170 B6
Mythstories Mus* 66 B6
Mytton Cl 3 SY1 .....41 E3
Mytton Gr 4 SY3 .....124 C6
Mytton Oak Rd SY3 .....124 C5
Mytton Rd SY4 .....103 F7

N

Nabb Cl 5 TF2 .....132 C3
Nabb La TF2 .....132 B3
Naird La Hollinswood & Randlay TF11 .....145 A5
 Stirchley & Brookside TF11 .....144 F2
Nairn Rdbt TF1 .....144 A5
Nanny Murphy's La TF11 .....144 F7
Nant La SY10 .....58 C3
Nantman Bank SY10 .....75 C6
Nantmawr Quarry (Outdoor Activity Centre)* SY10 .....75 F6
Nantwich Rd Whitchurch Urban SY13 .....15 E7
 Woore CW3 .....4 F2
Napley Dr TF9 .....20 D2
Napley Rd TF9 .....20 D1
Napoleon Dr SY3 .....124 C4
Narrow La TF9 .....51 D2
Nash Ct (School) SY8 .....214 D6
Neachley La
 Donington WV7 .....156 C8

Neachley La continued
 Tong TF11 .....147 A3
Near Vallens TF1 .....131 D4
Nefod La SY11 .....24 B6
Nelson Cl 2 TF11 .....146 A6
Nelson St LL13 .....221 E2
Nelson Way 8 TF2 .....120 F1
Nesscliffe Hill Ctry Pk* SY4 .....97 F4
Nether Way 5 SY3 .....124 F4
Netherfield 8 WV16 .....200 E3
Netherton La
 Bewdley DY12 .....211 E1
 Highley WV16 .....200 E2
Netley Rd SY3 .....125 B1
Nettles La 3 SY3 .....125 D7
Neufchatel Cl SY13 .....15 B7
Nevil Rd 2 TF1 .....131 D3
Neville Cres 2 LL12 .....221 D5
New Bridge Rd 8 .....152 D4
New Church Rd TF1 .....130 F3
New Coll TF1 .....130 F3
New Forest Cl DY14 .....210 C1
New Hall La SY13 .....13 B4
New Hall Rd TF1 .....130 E3
New Houses SY4 .....169 D6
New Mills La SY5 .....173 B6
New Options Coll TF11 .....164 A6
New Pk Cl 3 SY3 .....125 D8
New Pk Rd
 8 Oswestry SY11 .....41 A1
 3 Shrewsbury SY3 .....125 D2
New Pk St SY3 .....125 E3
New Rd 7 Bewdley DY12 .....211 A3
 Bridgnorth WV16 .....218 F4
 8 Cleobury Mortimer DY14 .....209 E4
 Dawley TF4 .....143 F2
 Farlow DY14 .....209 B6
 7 Gobowen SY11 .....41 A8
 Hanley WR6 .....215 E1
 Hanmer SY13 .....12 B2
 Ironbridge TF8 .....152 C4
 Loggerheads TF9 .....54 F8
 Ludlow SY8 .....217 C5
 Madeley TF7 .....153 A5
 Montgomery SY15 .....174 B4
 Much Wenlock TF13 .....159 E5
 6 Oakengates/Donnington TF2 .....132 C5
 Rock DY14 .....210 D1
 Swindon DY3 .....190 D1
New River Cl 2 TF1 .....130 C7
New St
 8 Bishop's Castle SY9 .....181 E3
 Clive SY4 .....84 A5
 1 Dawley TF4 .....143 E3
 Ford SY5 .....169 C4
 Ludlow SY8 .....217 C6
 Newport TF10 .....109 F2
 Oakengates/Donnington TF2 .....132 A3
 15 Oswestry SY11 .....58 E8
 Shrewsbury SY3 .....125 A6
 1 Welshpool SY21 .....170 B6
 Wem SY4 .....66 A7
New Town TF4 .....143 F4
New Trench Rd
 Lilleshall & Donnington TF2 .....120 E2
 Oakengates/Donnington TF2 .....132 C8
New Works La TF6 .....143 A6
Newbridge Rd LL14 .....6 C8
Newbrigg Rd 10 LL12 .....221 D8
Newbrook Dr 2 SY3 .....137 A5
Newcastle CE Prim Sch SY7 .....192 D5
Newcastle Rd
 Market Drayton TF9 .....36 F2
 Woore CW3 .....5 D2
Newcomen Way TF7 .....152 D5
Newent Cl 2 TF1 .....131 A5
Newfield Cl 2 TF1 .....145 F5
Newfield Dr
 Oakengates/Donnington TF2 .....132 A5
 Shrewsbury SY3 .....125 D7
Newgate SY6 WV6 .....166 C3
Newhouse La
 Albrighton WV7 .....157 A4
 Church Pulverbatch SY5 .....173 F2
 Condover SY5 .....178 A6
Newill Gr 1 TF5 .....130 B7
Newington Way SY5 .....195 E6
Newlands Rd
 8 Oakengates/Donnington TF2 .....132 B1
 12 Oakengates/Donnington TF2 .....132 B2
Newport CE Jun Sch TF10 .....109 F2
Newport Cottage Care Ctr TF10 .....109 F2
Newport Cres TF11 .....145 F5
Newport Cty Inf Sch TF10 .....109 F2
Newport Dr SY2 .....125 F1
Newport Girls High Sch TF10 .....109 E2
Newport Rd
 Albrighton WV7 .....156 E8
 Donington TF10 .....147 D1
 Edgmond TF10 .....109 C4
 Gnosall ST20 .....111 E5

Newport continued
Hinstock TF9 ....71 F3
Perton WV7 ....157 F2
Shifnal TF11 ....145 F5
Sutton upon Tern TF9 ....53 E7
Tong TF11 ....147 D3
Whitchurch SY13 ....15 A7
Newport St SY7 ....193 D4
Newton 14 SY7 ....195 E5
Newton Cl
 Albrighton WV7 ....156 E7
 Bewdley DY12 ....211 C2
Newton St
 12 Craven Arms SY7 ....195 E5
 Wrexham LL11 ....221 E2
Newtonmere Dr
 Shrewsbury SY3 ....113 D2
 Wellington TF1 ....130 C5
Newtown
 Market Drayton TF9 ....53 D8
 Newport TF10 ....109 E1
 Whitchurch SY13 ....15 A8
Newtown CE Prim Sch
 SY4 ....46 F4
Newtown Gdns SY4 ....99 A8
Nickless Way 4 TF4 ....143 E5
Nightingale Way 2 TF1 ....130 F6
Nightingale Wlk SY1 ....113 D5
No Man's Gn La SY7 ....201 F3
Noble St SY4 ....66 A6
Nobold SY4 ....99 A8
Nobold Cl SY4 ....99 A8
Nobold La SY5 ....124 E1
Noel Hill Rd SY5 ....138 F4
Noneley Rd SY4 ....64 E7
Nook La Bronington SY13 ....1 C1
 Prees SY4 ....49 F3
Norbroom Ct TF10 ....110 A4
Norbroom Dr TF10 ....110 A4
Norbury Prim Sch
 SY9 ....182 D7
Norbury Rd SY20 ....111 E8
Norfield View 3 TF4 ....144 D4
Norfolk Rd LL12 ....221 F7
Norman Rd LL13 ....221 D1
Normandie Cl 6 SY8 ....217 E4
North Cl 3 SY3 ....125 C4
North Dr SY10 ....41 B5
North Gate 1 WV16 ....218 F5
North Hermitage
 SY3 ....125 C4
North Rd Pant SY22 ....93 F7
 Wellington TF1 ....130 D5
North St
 TF2 Oakengates/Donnington....132 C2
 Shrewsbury SY1 ....125 D7
North Wales Sch of Art &
 Design LL11 ....221 B4
Northgate Mus* ....
 WV16 ....218 E5
Northlands CW3 ....5 A1
Northleigh Ct LL11 ....221 C7
Northside Cl 3 SY3 ....114 C3
Northumberland Pl 8
 SY1 ....125 D8
Northwood 3 LL12 ....221 F7
Northwood Halt Sta
 DY12 ....211 C4
Northwood La
 Kidderminster Foreign
 DY12 ....211 D3
 Stottesdon WV16 ....199 F3
Northwood Rd SY2 ....126 B6
Northwood Terr TF3 ....144 B3
Norton Dr 1 Dawley TF3 ....144 B1
 Wroxeter & Uppington
 SY5 ....127 C1
Norton in Hales CE Prim Sch
 TF9 ....20 C1
Norton St 4 LD7 ....203 B3
Norwich Dr TF3 ....144 D3
Novers The 6 SY9 ....181 E3
Nurseries The Chirk LL14 ....
 Llanymynech & Pant SY10 ....76 B2
Nursery Cl SY3 ....78 D8
Nursery Dr 2 SY5 ....190 F2
Nursery Rd 7 DY12 ....211 D2
Nurton Hill Rd WV6 ....166 E5

O

Oadby Way 1 SY3 ....124 C6
Oak Ave Newport TF10 ....109 F1
 Penley SY13 ....10 F3
Oak Cl Llandysilio SY22 ....94 A1
 Madeley TF7 ....153 C6
 Weston Rhyn SY10 ....23 D4
Oak Dr 10 Ellesmere SY12 ....172 E3
 2 Minsterley SY5 ....134 F4
 Oswestry SY11 ....58 F6
 Shawbury SY4 ....103 D7
 Trysull & Seisdon WV5 ....190 C5
 Whitchurch SY13 ....14 E4
 Wrexham LL12 ....221 E6
Oak Farm La SY11 ....78 E8
Oak La
 Oswestry Rural SY10 ....75 D8
 6 Shrewsbury SY3 ....124 B6
Oak Mdw SY4 ....181 F4
Oak Rd 2 Hanwood SY5 ....173 F8
 The Rock TF3 ....143 E8
Oak Ridge 6 SY21 ....170 B7

Oak St Highley WV16 ....200 E3
 Oswestry SY11 ....58 D8
 Shrewsbury SY3 ....125 C3
Oak Tree Cl 3 SY3 ....136 C6
Oak Tree Ct 7 WR15 ....220 D6
Oak Tree Cres SY7 ....194 B8
Oakapple Cl 18 SY19 ....148 E8
Oakcroft LL14 ....23 D8
Oakengates Rd TF2 ....132 C6
Oakengates Sta TF2 ....132 C6
Oakengates Theatre* ....
 TF2 ....132 B3
Oakfield 3 LL13 ....221 E1
Oakfield Cl
 3 Shrewsbury SY3 ....124 F5
 St. Martin's SY11 ....25 A6
 Worthen with Shelve
 SY5 ....171 E3
Oakfield Dr 3 SY3 ....124 E5
Oakfield Rd TF13 ....159 E3
Oakfields
 4 Market Drayton TF9 ....36 B1
 Shifnal TF11 ....145 F5
 Shrewsbury SY3 ....124 E5
 Wellington TF5 ....130 C8
Oakfields SY22 ....92 D6
Oakhurst Ave SY10 ....40 D1
Oakhurst Rd SY10 ....40 D1
Oakland Cty Prim Sch
 SY3 ....137 A6
Oakland Pk SY6 ....216 E6
Oaklands WV15 ....219 B4
Oaklands Ave 1 LL12 ....221 F5
Oaklands Dr
 Oakengates/Donnington
 TF2 ....132 A7
 Whittington SY11 ....41 E2
Oaklands Rd LL14 ....23 D8
Oakleaf Rise DY14 ....210 E1
Oakley Ave SY3 ....125 C3
Oakley Cl SY4 ....63 B1
Oakley La TF9 ....37 A6
Oakley St SY3 ....125 C4
Oaks Cres TF1 ....130 A5
Oaks Dr SY5 ....216 E6
Oaks Rd
 Church Stretton SY6 ....216 E6
 1 Craven Arms SY7 ....195 D5
Oaktree La WV16 ....198 F4
Oakvale Ct 2 SY5 ....178 C6
Oakwood Cl 1 SY5 ....41 F2
Oakwood Dr
 3 Oakengates/Donnington
 TF2 ....132 A6
 Shrewsbury SY3 ....113 D3
Oakwood Pk LL14 ....10 F4
Oakwood Rd
 2 Bewdley DY12 ....211 C2
 Cleobury North WV16 ....198 E6
Oatfield Cl 3 SY3 ....15 A6
Occupation La WV16 ....200 D6
Oerley Cl 1 SY10 ....58 C8
Oerley Way SY10 ....58 C8
Offa LL14 ....6 E3
Offa Dr SY11 ....40 F1
Offas Cl SY10 ....75 D7
Offas Dyke Rd SY22 ....94 A1
Office La SY3 ....208 A2
Offoxey Rd TF11 ....147 E5
Okehampton Rd TF1 ....131 B7
Old Armoury The 2 TF9 ....53 D8
Old Bedstone Rd 3
 SY7 ....204 C5
Old Bell Mus The* ....
 SY15 ....174 B3
Old Bowling Gn Cl
 WR15 ....220 C6
Old Chads La SY13 ....1 C8
Old Chirk Rd SY11 ....23 F1
Old Coach Rd SY19 ....148 F7
Old Coleham SY3 ....125 B1
Old Coppice Grange 7
 ....143 F8
Old Farm La TF11 ....121 C3
Old Farm Rd
 8 Esclusham LL14 ....221 A1
 Hadnall SY4 ....102 C4
Old Fort Rd SY11 ....40 E1
Old Hall Cl
 Albrighton WV7 ....156 F5
 1 Wellington TF1 ....130 F2
Old Hall Sch The TF1 ....130 F2
Old Heath SY11 ....113 E2
Old Mill Cl 3 SY3 ....124 E5
Old Mill La WV16 ....218 E2
Old Nursery Cl TF7 ....153 B6
Old Office Cl TF4 ....143 E5
Old Office Rd TF4 ....143 E5
Old Oswestry (Hillfort)* ....
 SY10 ....58 D7
Old Pk Rd 5 TF2 ....132 B1
Old Pk Way TF3 ....143 F7
Old Post Office La
 ....57 D2
Old Potts Way SY3 ....125 D5
Old Roman Rd 3 SY3 ....125 A3
Old Sch Cl 6 WV16 ....200 F2
Old Sch La
 Tenbury Wells WR15 ....220 D6
 Westbury SY5 ....128 E1
Old Sch Mews 1 LL13 ....9 C8
Old Shackerley La
 WV7 ....148 A8
Old Smithy Cl 3 WV6 ....166 C3
Old Smithy Rd TF10 ....107 E5
Old St SY8 ....217 C4
Old Vicarage Rd TF4 ....143 F1

Old Weston Rd ST19 ....148 E8
Old Wharf TF3 ....144 A5
Old Worcester Rd
 Albrighton WV7 ....156 D6
 Bridgnorth WV15 ....219 B3
Oldbury Rd WV16 ....218 E3
Oldbury Wells WV16 ....218 E4
Oldbury Wells Sch E
 WV16 ....218 E4
Oldbury Wells Sch W
 WV16 ....218 E4
Oldcroft TF2 ....132 A3
Olden La Ruyton SY4 ....80 A1
 Ruyton-xi-Towns SY4 ....79 E1
Oldfield Rd 3 TF4 ....144 A2
Oldford Cl 27 SY21 ....170 B6
Oldford La 12 SY21 ....170 B6
Oldford Rise 170 B5
Oldford View 20 SY21 ....170 B6
Oldwood Rd WR15 ....220 B1
Oleander Cl 6 TF3 ....131 E1
Oliver Cl 1 TF1 ....130 E4
Ollerton La
 Child's Ercall TF9 ....70 F1
 Stoke upon Tern TF9 ....88 E8
Onny CE Prim Sch
 SY7 ....206 A6
Onny Gr TF2 ....132 D4
Onnybrook Dr SY7 ....195 E6
Onslow Dr
 Shrewsbury SY1 ....113 D2
 8 Wellington TF1 ....130 C5
Orchard Cl
 Adforton SY7 ....205 A1
 6 Claverley WV5 ....189 E4
 Cressage SY5 ....149 E5
 4 Eardington WV16 ....188 C1
 Hadley TF1 ....131 D2
 Little Wenlock TF6 ....142 D2
 Pattingham WV6 ....166 F4
 Waters Upton TF6 ....106 B4
Orchard Dr
 Bridgnorth WV16 ....218 D6
 1 Minsterley SY5 ....172 E3
 5 West Felton SY11 ....78 E8
Orchard End 1 DY14 ....209 E3
Orchard Fields SY4 ....84 B5
Orchard Gdns 4 LL11 ....221 C7
Orchard Gn SY22 ....93 E6
Orchard Holmes 5
 WV15 ....201 B3
Orchard La
 Great Hanwood SY5 ....173 E8
 The Gorge TF8 ....152 D4
Orchard Lea 5 WR15 ....220 A4
Orchard Rd
 6 Eardington WV16 ....188 C1
 6 Shifnal TF11 ....145 F5
Orchard Rise
 15 Bewdley DY12 ....211 D2
 2 Market Drayton TF9 ....53 A8
Orchard St
 6 Highley WV16 ....200 F2
 1 Oswestry SY11 ....58 E8
Orchard The
 Albrighton WV7 ....157 A5
 7 Clungunford SY7 ....211 C2
Orchard Way
 Wellington TF1 ....130 F3
 Wem Albion SY4 ....66 B6
Orchards The LL13 ....222 F1
Orchid Cl 8 TF7 ....132 E7
Oreton Rd DY14 ....209 C7
Oriel Way 3 SY3 ....124 E3
Orleton CE Prim Sch
 SY8 ....212 E2
Orleton La
 Eastham WR15 ....215 E3
 Wellington TF1 ....130 C4
Orleton La Inf Sch
 TF1 ....130 B4
Orleton Rd SY8 ....217 F3
Orleton Terr TF1 ....130 C3
Ormsdale Cl 8 TF2 ....132 F8
Orsons Mdw 15 SY3 ....124 A7
Orton La WV14 ....190 F6
Osborne Cl
 8 Oswestry SY11 ....59 B8
 3 Wrexham LL11 ....221 C6
Osmere Cl 3 SY13 ....2 B1
Osprey Gr 3 TF2 ....131 A7
Osterley Gr 3 TF2 ....132 F8
Oswald Pl 3 SY7 ....58 D7
Oswald Rd 3 SY7 ....58 D7
Oswald Way 8 LL2 ....221 E5
Oswald's Well La SY7 ....58 C7
Oswell Rd SY3 ....125 A2
Oswestry Heritage &
 Exhibition Ctr* SY11 ....58 D7
Oswestry Inf Sch SY11 ....58 F8
Oswestry Leisure Ctr
 SY11 ....58 D8
Oswestry Rd
 3 Ellesmere SY12 ....27 A2
 Oswestry Rural SY10 ....57 E2
 Whittington SY11 ....41 E3
Oswestry Sch SY11 ....58 D8
Oswestry Sch Bellan House
 SY11 ....58 D7
Oswestry Transport Mus*
 SY11 ....58 D7
Oteley Rd Atcham SY2 ....126 A1
 Shrewsbury SY2 ....125 F2
Otley Way TF1 ....52 E5
Oulton La TF10 ....111 A8
Oundale Rd WV5 ....190 F4

Our Lady & St Oswalds Cath
 Prim Sch SY11 ....58 D7
Outwood 1 SY11 ....113 D5
Oval Cl 2 TF2 ....132 E3
Oval The
 Albrighton WV7 ....156 E8
 Bicton SY3 ....112 A2
 Market Drayton TF9 ....53 C8
Overdale
 8 The Rock TF3 ....131 E1
 The Rock TF3 ....143 E8
Overdale Rd SY3 ....136 E6
Overley Hall Sch TF6 ....129 C2
Overstone 3 SY1 ....113 D5
Overton Cl SY1 ....114 C2
Overton Rd
 Ludford SY8 ....217 C1
 St. Martin's SY11 ....24 E6
Overton View 3 SY8 ....217 B3
Overton Way LL2 ....221 E6
Owen Cl TF3 ....144 B3
Owl's La SY15 ....181 F6
Oxford Rd 3 Dawley TF4 ....144 A4
 Great Dawley TF4 ....143 F3
Oxford St
 4 Oakengates/Donnington
 TF2 ....132 B2
 3 Wrexham LL13 ....221 E3
Oxlip Cl 18 TF2 ....132 E8
Oxon Bsns Pk SY3 ....124 C7
Oxon CE Prim Sch
 SY3 ....124 B6

P

Packwood Haugh Sch
 SY4 ....80 A3
Paddock Cl TF1 ....130 C5
Paddock Ct TF4 ....143 F3
Paddock La TF11 ....146 A6
Paddock The
 3 Church Stretton SY6 ....216 D7
 7 Claverley WV5 ....189 E4
 Much Wenlock TF13 ....159 E4
 10 Oakengates/Donnington
 TF2 ....120 F1
 1 Shifnal TF11 ....145 F2
 4 Wem SY4 ....66 B8
 22 Wombourne WV5 ....190 F3
Paddocks The
 Baschurch SY4 ....48 A6
 2 Cleobury Mortimer
 DY14 ....209 E3
 16 Knighton LD7 ....203 B3
 4 Ludlow SY8 ....217 C5
 3 Shrewsbury SY3 ....124 B6
Padmans Alley 1 TF12 ....152 C1
Pageant Dr
 Dawley TF4 ....144 A3
 1 Telford TF3 ....143 F1
Painsbrook La SY4 ....102 E6
Painswick Cl 2 SY3 ....124 B7
Painters La SY13 ....50 D6
Painters Pl 10 SY3 ....124 C4
Pale Mdw Rd 2 WV15 ....219 A4
Palmer St 4 LL13 ....221 E3
Pandy La 2 LL12 ....221 D8
Panorama 2 TF2 ....132 B3
Pant La SY12 ....44 A4
Pantulf Rd SY4 ....66 B8
Parade The TF1 ....130 D8
Paradise TF8 ....152 B4
Parc Caradog SY21 ....147 F6
Parc Offa SY21 ....94 A2
Pargeter Cl 11 TF3 ....144 A1
Parish Cl TF4 ....143 F4
Parish Dr TF1 ....131 D5
Park Ave Madeley TF7 ....153 B8
 Oswestry SY11 ....58 D8
 Shawbury SY4 ....103 D7
 Whitchurch SY13 ....15 A7
 Wrexham LL12 ....221 D8
Park Bank SY4 ....80 A2
Park Cll 6 Bewdley DY12 ....211 D2
 Kinlet DY12 ....210 C7
Park Cres SY11 ....58 E8
Park Ct TF7 ....152 E6
Park Dingle 1 DY12 ....211 C1
Park Dr SY11 ....40 D1
Park Fechan Gdns 6
 SY11 ....58 E8
Park Hall Working Farm
 Mus* SY11 ....41 B4
Park Issa Gdns 2 SY11 ....58 E8
Park Jun Sch TF1 ....130 D5
Park La Bewdley DY12 ....211 D3
 Craven Arms SY7 ....195 C4
 Ercall Magna TF6 ....116 D7
 Leintwardine SY7 ....205 B5
 Loggerheads TF9 ....52 C5
 Madeley TF7 ....152 E6
 Munslow SY7 ....197 B6
 Richard's Castle (Shropshire)
 SY8 ....212 F4
 Shifnal TF11 ....145 F2
 The Rock TF3 ....143 F8
 24 Welshpool SY21 ....170 B6
 Whittington SY11 ....41 B3
Park La Ave TF7 ....152 E6
Park Rd Cefn-mawr LL14 ....6 C8
 Dawley TF4 ....143 F6
 3 Much Wenlock TF13 ....159 F4

Park Rd continued
 Oakengates/Donnington
 TF2 ....132 C6
 Wem SY4 ....66 A7
 Whitchurch SY13 ....14 F7
Park St Madeley TF7 ....153 A5
 Oswestry SY11 ....58 E8
 Shifnal TF11 ....145 F3
 Wellington TF1 ....130 E4
 Wrexham LL11 ....221 C5
Park View
 Broseley TF12 ....161 C8
 1 Highley WV16 ....200 F2
 14 Worfield WV15 ....189 A6
Parkdale TF1 ....131 C5
Parker Bowles Dr 1 TF9 ....52 F8
Parker's Ct TF13 ....170 B6
Parkers Cl LL11 ....221 C6
Parkhill La SY7 ....193 A1
Parklands TF1 ....130 D5
Parklands The SY12 ....63 C7
Parkleigh Ct 3 LL12 ....221 E4
Parks The SY1 ....114 B3
Parkway TF7 ....152 F5
Parrs La SY3 ....136 E7
Parson's La SY22 ....93 F2
Partridge Cl
 Shrewsbury SY1 ....114 C4
 1 Wellington TF1 ....130 F6
Parys Rd SY8 ....217 B3
Pasmore Cl 3 TF3 ....153 A8
Pastour Dr 1 TF1 ....130 F6
Patricia Dr 3 SY2 ....126 A5
Patshull Rd
 Albrighton WV7 ....156 F3
 Pattingham & Patshull
 WV6 ....166 B3
Pattingham La WV7 ....157 E1
Paulbrook Rd WV16 ....218 E5
Pauls Moss Ct LL13 ....15 A6
Pavilion Cl 8 TF2 ....132 E3
Paxton Pl 11 SY3 ....124 B6
Peace Dr SY2 ....126 A5
Peacehaven 4 SY1 ....114 B4
Pear Tree La
 Claverley WV5 ....190 A2
 Whitchurch Urban SY13 ....1 D1
Pearl Yd SY13 ....145 F2
Pearson Cl SY4 ....11 D7
Pecknall La SY5 ....168 B4
Peel Cl 5 LL13 ....9 C8
Peel St LL13 ....221 B3
Peever Cl SY22 ....26 A7
Pel La SY8 ....197 F2
Pelham Rd SY4 ....127 D6
Pemberton Rd 5 TF5 ....130 A6
Pemberton Way SY3 ....125 D4
Pembridge Cl
 3 Newport TF10 ....121 E8
 2 Oakengates/Donnington
 TF2 ....120 D1
Pembroke Ave 6 WR15 ....220 D5
Pembroke Dr TF1 ....130 D5
Pen Y Vawn LL14 ....6 E1
Penda's Pk LL13 ....10 F4
Pendil Cl TF1 ....130 D2
Pendle Way SY3 ....125 A1
Pendragon Ct 7 LL13 ....221 D1
Pengrove TF9 ....52 E5
Pengwern Cl 13 SY3 ....125 A6
Pengwern Rd SY3 ....125 A6
Penistone Cl TF2 ....132 D6
Penleigh Gdns 2 WV5 ....190 F4
Penley Hospl LL13 ....10 F5
Penllys Rd WR15 ....220 D6
Penmarsh La TF4 ....104 E3
Pennwell 3 SY3 ....124 D7
Pensfold SY3 ....124 B6
Penstone La WV4 ....190 F6
Pentre Church in Wales
 Controlled Prim Sch
 ....6 E6
Pentre Felin 17 LL11 ....221 C3
Pentre Gwyn SY12 ....60 C1
Penybont Rd LD7 ....203 B2
Pen-y-bryn LL13 ....221 C2
Penybryn Ave SY11 ....41 F4
Penycae Ave SY10 ....24 A1
Penycae Cl SY10 ....24 A1
Pen-y-maes La SY22 ....92 F2
Pepper La 3 SY8 ....217 C4
Pepper St 6 SY13 ....15 A8
Percy Rd LL13 ....221 C1
Percy St SY1 ....125 C8
Percy St N SY1 ....125 C8
Peregrine Way TF1 ....131 A7
Perivale Cl 3 SY3 ....124 F4
Perivale Rd SY3 ....124 F4
Perry Rd SY10 ....24 B1
Peter's Cl 3 TF4 ....143 F2
Peveral Dr 4 SY1 ....41 E3
Peverill Bank TF4 ....143 F5
Pewit La CW5 ....6 A6
Rezenas Dr 3 TF9 ....36 B1
Pheasant Cl SY3 ....49 B8
Philips Cl LL12 ....221 F6
Phoenix Bank 9 TF9 ....36 D1
Phoenix Ct TF4 ....143 E2

Phoenix Sports Ctr
TF4 ....143 F2
Picasso Dr 5 TF5 ....130 B7
Pickhill SY4 ....82 A8
Pickstock Cl 7 SY12 ..144 C1
Pickwick Cl 8 TF1 ...145 F5
Picton Cl 4 TF2 .....132 C4
Pierce's Sq 12 LL13 ..221 C5
Pigeon La SY13 ......11 C6
Pimhill La SY4 ......101 B8
Pine Cl 3 Ellesmere SY12 ..27 A2
  Market Drayton TF9 ....36 B1
Pine Cres 3 SY5 ....172 E4
Pine Gr SY11 ....58 F7
Pine View 10 TF2 ...132 E8
Pines The 1 LL12 ...221 D5
Pinetree Rd 4 SY12 ..211 C2
Pineway WV15 ......219 B4
Pinewood Ave TF2 ...132 A6
Pinewood Cl SY11 ...94 F4
Pinewood Dr SY13 ...32 E5
Pinewood Rd SY4 ...103 F7
Pinewoods 2 TF10 ..121 E8
Pinfold TF11 ....134 C5
Pinfold Croft TF6 ...106 A3
Pinfold La
  Ellesmere SY12 .....27 C2
  Loggerheads TF9 ....37 C2
Pinfold The SY13 ...49 D8
Pinkham DY14 ......209 E2
Pinkham La 5 DY14 ..209 E2
Pintail Dr TF1 ....130 F7
Piper's La TF10 .....108 F3
Pitchcroft La TF10 ..121 E7
Pitchford Dr TF2 ....144 F8
Pitchford Rd
  Albrighton WV7 ....156 F4
  7 Shrewsbury SY1 ..113 D4
Pitts La LD7 ....203 E2
Pixley La TF9 ....71 F1
Planks La WV5 .....190 F3
Plash Cl TF4 ....143 E6
Plas Acton Rd 1 LL12 ..221 D8
Plas Cerrig Cl 3 SY11 ..41 F2
Plas Coch Rd LL11 ..221 B5
Plas Darland 6 LL11 ..221 D5
Plas Ffynnon Way 5
  SY11 ....58 F7
Plas Gwyn LL12 ....221 E5
Plas Madoc 2 LL13 ..9 C8
Platt La SY11 ....31 A5
Plealey La SY5 .....173 B5
Plealey Rd SY5 .....173 C6
Pleasant View SY10 ..23 C4
Plex La SY4 ....101 E2
Plex Rd SY4 ....101 E5
Plough La
  1 Newport TF10 ....109 F5
  Rock DY14 ....210 E1
Plough Rd
  12 Knighton LD7 ...203 B3
  Oakengates/Donnington
  TF2 ....132 C5
  5 Wellington TF1 ...130 E4
Ploughmans Croft 9
  TF10 ....110 A4
Plover Gate 3 TF1 ..130 C7
Plox Gn Rd SY5 ....172 D2
Poachers Gate 5 TF4 ..144 A2
Podmore Rd TF9 ...72 F8
Police Dr 6 TF9 ....53 C8
Pont Wen LL13 ....221 E2
Pontesbury CE Prim Sch
  SY5 ....173 B4
Pontesbury Hill Rd
  SY5 ....173 A4
Pontfaen Cl LD7 ....203 C2
Pool Cl TF2 ....131 F6
Pool Dr
  Bridgnorth WV16 ...218 E5
  Hadnall SY4 ....102 C4
Pool Farm Ave TF4 ..131 A6
Pool Hill TF4 ....143 E2
Pool Hill Rd TF4 ....143 E3
Pool House Rd WV5 ..190 E3
Pool Mdw TF1 .....191 A4
Pool Rd Hadnall SY4 ..102 C4
  Montgomery SY15 ..174 B3
  8 Oakengates/Donnington
  TF2 ....131 F6
Pool Rise SY2 ......125 F2
Pooley La TF10 .....123 C7
Poolside SY3 ....136 E7
Poor House La TF7 ..70 D7
Poplar Ave WV7 ....156 F8
Poplar Cl
  4 Church Stretton SY6 ..216 D4
  5 Wellington TF1 ...130 C4
Poplar La TF9 ......19 F5
Poplar Rd LL13 ....221 C2
Poplars Ave 1 SY5 ..173 F8
Poppy Dr 1 TF2 ....132 E7
Porchester Cl 7 TF1 ..131 C7
Porchfield SY2 .....125 F7
Port Way TF7 ......153 C6
Port Way The SY6 ..177 C1
Portal Ave LL13 ....221 E3
Portcullis La 4 SY8 ..207 C5
Porthill Cl SY3 .....124 F5
Porthill Dr SY3 ....124 F6
Porthill Gdns SY3 ..125 A6
Porthill Rd SY3 ....124 F5
Portland Cres 2 SY2 ..125 F5

Portland Dr
  Market Drayton TF9 ....36 A1
  6 Much Wenlock TF13 ..159 F4
  The Rock SY13 .....143 F7
Portley Rd TF4 ....143 E3
Portman's Way WV16 ..218 C5
Portobello 1 SY2 ...125 D6
Portobello Cl 3 TF3 ..143 F8
Post Office La
  Gnosall TF10 ......123 D7
  3 Longden SY5 ....173 B8
  Wem SY4 ....31 C1
Post Office Rd WV5 ..190 C6
Postern 4 WV15 ...218 F5
Potter Cl 7 SY8 ....217 D6
Pound Cl
  1 Bishop's Castle SY9 ..181 F3
  4 Shrewsbury SY3 ..125 D5
Pound La
  Broseley TF12 .....161 E7
  Pontesbury SY5 ...173 E8
  Ruyton SY4 ....80 A1
Pound St
  Bridgnorth WV16 ...218 E5
  Claverley WV5 ....189 D4
Pountney Gdns 3 SY3 ..125 D4
Powder La TF1 ....130 C3
Powell Pl 6 TF10 ..109 F3
Powell Rd Dawley TF2 ..132 F1
  4 Wrexham LL12 ...221 D4
Powell's La 11 SY21 ..170 B6
Powells La 3 SY7 ..193 D3
Powis Ave SY11 ....58 F8
Powis Castle & Gdn (NT)*
  SY21 ....170 A5
Powis Cl SY10 ....76 B1
Powis Ct 3 SY21 ...170 B5
Powis Dr
  Shrewsbury SY1 ...113 D1
  7 Wellington TF1 ...130 D5
Powis Pl Dawley TF4 ..143 E5
  10 Oswestry SY11 ..58 E8
Powysland Mus & Canal Ctr*
  SY21 ....170 C6
Poyner Rd SY8 ....217 D5
Poynton Dr TF1 ....113 E3
Poynton Rd TF1 ....103 D6
Poyser St LL13 ....221 C2
Prees Branch Canal Nature
  Reserve* SY4 .....47 D8
Prees CE Prim Sch
  SY13 ....49 D7
Prees Ind Est SY13 ..49 C7
Prees Sta SY13 ....48 F8
Preeshenlle La SY10 ..24 B2
Prescott Cl 6 SY2 ..125 F2
Prescott Fields 7 SY4 ..99 B8
Prestage Cl TF12 ..161 E7
Prestbury Gn TF4 ..143 F4
Presteigne Rd LD7 ..203 B2
Prestfelde Prep Sch
  SY2 ....125 F4
Preston Gr 7 TF2 ..132 A7
Preston Gubbals Rd
  SY4 ....101 A4
Preston Hall* SY4 ..84 F6
Preston Montford La
  SY4 ....169 A4
Preston St SY2 ....125 F5
Price's La LL11 ....221 C5
Pride Hill 1 SY1 ...125 C6
Primmer Rd TF2 ...120 C2
Primrose Dr
  Newport TF10 ....109 F1
  Shrewsbury SY1 ...125 D3
Primrose Gr 3 TF1 ..130 F2
Primrose La 4 SY11 ..49 E8
Primrose Way 11 LL13 ..221 B4
Prince Andrew Way 2
  TF4 ....143 F6
Prince Charles Cres 4
  TF3 ....144 A6
Prince Charles Rd
  7 Oswestry SY11 ...59 A8
  Wrexham LL13 ....221 F3
Prince Edward Cres 3
  TF3 ....144 A6
Prince of Wales Dr 8
  SY21 ....170 B5
Prince St Madeley TF7 ..153 C6
  1 Wrexham LL13 ...221 C2
Prince William Ct SY4 ..66 B6
Prince's St 8 TF1 ...130 F3
Princes Cl LL11 ....221 C7
Princes End TF4 ...143 E6
Princes St SY15 ...174 B3
Princess Ave Chirk LL14 ..6 E2
  1 Wellington TF1 ...131 A2
Princess Dr WV16 ..218 D6
Princess Gdns 4 TF10 ..109 F1
Princess Royal Hospl (RHS
  Trust) The TF1 ....130 F7
Princess St
  8 Shrewsbury SY1 ..125 C5
  Wrexham LL13 ....221 B2
Priors Cl 5 WV16 ..198 D8
Priors Gate 3 TF2 ..144 E8
Priors La TF9 ......36 A1
Priorslee Ave
  Dawley TF2 ....132 F1
  St. Georges & Priorslee
  TF2 ....144 D8
Priorslee Prim Sch
  TF2 ....144 E8

Priorslee Rd
  Oakengates/Donnington
  TF2 ....144 D8
  Shifnal TF11 ......145 C5
Priory Cl
  2 Bridgnorth WV15 ..219 A3
  Wellington TF1 ....130 E2
Priory Ct 18 TF9 ...36 A1
Priory Dr SY3 .....125 A3
Priory Rd
  Bridgnorth WV15 ...219 A4
  Oakengates/Donnington
  TF2 ....132 A4
  Shrewsbury SY1 ...125 B6
Priory Ridge SY3 ..125 A2
Priory Sch The SY3 ..125 A3
Priory St 10 LL11 ..221 C3
Pritchard Cl 17 DY12 ..211 D2
Pritchard Way SY3 ..125 E3
Proctors Pl TF2 ...132 C4
Prospect Rd
  Market Drayton TF9 ....36 B1
  Wellington TF1 ....130 F4
Puddle La SY11 ...24 E5
Pulley La SY3 .....136 F7
Pulrose Wlk 8 SY3 ..125 E3
Pump La SY21 ....124 B7
Pump Rd SY4 .....100 E4
Pump Rms* WR15 ..220 D5
Punta Verde Dr TF7 ..153 B3
Purton Wood View 5
  TF3 ....144 D4
Puzzle Sq 16 SY21 ..170 B6

Q

Quail Gate TF1 ....130 C7
Quail Ridge SY5 ...169 C4
Quarry Bank Rd TF9 ..53 B7
Quarry Gdns 3 SY8 ..217 C5
Quarry House La 3 TF9 ..53 A7
Quarry La TF1 ....131 E2
Quarry Mdws 17 SY7 ..195 C5
Quarry Pl
  Great Dawley TF4 ..143 E3
  6 Shrewsbury SY1 ..125 B5
Quarry Rd TF12 ...152 C2
Quatford Cl 7 SY11 ..114 C3
Queen Elizabeth Ave
  SY3 ....144 C5
Queen Elizabeth Cl 5
  SY11 ....40 F1
Queen Elizabeth Dr
  SY11 ....40 F1
Queen Elizabeth Way 1
  TF3 ....143 F5
Queen St
  Broseley TF12 .....152 C1
  Madeley TF7 ......153 C5
  3 Market Drayton TF9 ..36 D1
  Much Wenlock TF13 ..159 E5
  Shrewsbury SY1 ...125 E7
  4 Wellington TF1 ...130 D4
  7 Wrexham LL11 ...221 C3
Queen's Cl SY11 ..58 E6
Queen's Dr
  Oswestry SY11 ....58 E6
  8 Whitchurch SY13 ..15 B7
Queen's Pk SY8 ..58 E6
Queen's Rd
  Bridgnorth WV16 ...219 B4
  Oakengates/Donnington
  TF2 ....132 D7
Queen's Way 2 TF12 ..211 E2
Queens Croft TF9 ..72 F8
Queens Ct 7 TF7 ..153 C5
Queens Dr 8 TF10 ..109 F1
Queens Rd
  Bridgnorth WV15 ...219 B4
  Oakengates/Donnington
  TF2 ....132 D7
Queensway
  Dawley TF3 ....144 D6
  Dawley Hamlets TF7 ..153 B7
  Hadley TF1 ....131 C8
  Oakengates TF2 ...132 B1
  Shrewsbury SY1 ...113 D2
  Stirchley & Brookside
  TF7 ....153 D7
  Wem SY4 ....66 B7
  Whitchurch SY13 ...15 A6
  Wilcott SY4 ....97 C2
  Wrexham LL13 ....221 E3
Queensway Dr WV16 ..218 D6
Queenswood Cl 2 TF2 ..144 B8
Queenswood Prim Sch
  TF7 ....144 B8
Quines Cl 9 TF7 ...132 E8
Quinta Terr LL14 ...23 D5
Quinton Cl 11 SY3 ..124 C7
Quorn Dr 2 TF11 ..52 F8

R

Raby Cres SY3 ....125 C4
Racecourse Ave SY2 ..125 E6
Racecourse Cres SY2 ..125 F6
Racecourse Dr WV16 ..218 D5
Racecourse La SY2 ..125 F6
Racecourse La SY3 ..124 B6
Racecourse Rd TF13 ..159 E4
Rack La SY13 .....30 F1
Rad Valley Gdns SY3 ..124 E5
Rad Valley Rd SY3 ..124 E5
Radbrook Cty Prim Sch
  SY3 ....124 C4
Radbrook Rd SY3 ..124 C4
Radford La WV4 ...190 F7

Radfords Field SY11 ..58 F6
Radmore La ST20 ..111 C7
Radnor Ct 3 TF1 ..131 A4
Radnor Dr 3 LD7 ..203 B3
Raf Tern Hill TF9 ..52 C2
Ragged Robins Cl 2
  TF3 ....132 D3
Ragleth Gdns SY6 ..126 A6
Ragleth Rd SY6 ...216 D5
Railway La 2 SY2 ..125 D6
Railway St 11 WV16 ..218 F4
Ramsay Mdws 3 SY1 ..114 B4
Ramsey Mdws 8 SY1 ..114 B4
Randlay Ave TF3 ..144 C3
Randlay Fields TF3 ..144 D3
Randlay Intc TF3 ..144 C3
Randlay Prim Sch TF3 ..144 C3
Ranford Way SY4 ..66 B7
Range Rd 18 LL13 ..221 E1
Ranscombe Cres 2
  TF3 ....221 E8
Raven La 14 SY8 ..217 C4
Raven Mdws 1 SY1 ..125 C6
Raven Sq 2 SY21 ..170 A6
Raven St SY21 ....170 A6
Ravenhill Dr 6 TF2 ..131 F1
Ravensdale Dr 18 TF2 ..132 F8
Rays Farm* WV16 ..200 C2
Rea Dr TF1 ....130 D6
Rea St SY11 ......58 C6
Reabrook Ave SY3 ..125 E4
Real Art Gall The*
  ....125 C6
Rectory Dr TF1 ...135 F2
Rectory Gdns
  Church Stretton SY6 ..216 C6
  3 Worthen with Shelve
  ....171 F3
Rectory La Adderley LD7 ..19 B4
  Pant SY22 ....93 F6
Rectory Rd WV7 ..156 F6
Red Bank
  Market Drayton TF9 ..53 B8
  Welshpool SY21 ...170 B7
Red Barn La SY3 ..125 B4
Red Hall La LL13 ..9 F3
Red Hill DY12 ....211 D2
Red Kite Cl TF1 ..131 B6
Red La Broseley TF12 ..162 A7
  Hopesay SY7 .....195 A6
Redgate Ave WR15 ..220 C4
Redhill Dr SY5 ...136 D7
Redhill Prim Sch TF2 ..132 F2
Redhill Way TF2 ..132 E4
Redlake Mdw 5 SY7 ..204 C5
Rednal Ind Est SY11 ..61 B4
Redstone Dr 18 WV16 ..200 E2
Redwing Cl 3 TF1 ..130 F5
Redwood Cl 3 TF5 ..130 A8
Redwood La SY7 ..194 D1
Reed Cl 8 TF2 ....132 C3
Reedham Rd SY1 ..113 C2
Reet 8 LL13 ......221 B2
Reeves La SY7 ....203 F1
Regent Dr 9 TF2 ..132 C2
Regent St
  Wellington TF1 ....130 F3
  6 Wrexham LL11 ...221 C3
Regents Dr SY11 ..125 E8
Rembrandt Dr 4 TF5 ..130 B7
Renshaw Wood La
  WV6 ....148 F2
Rest The SY4 .....6 C8
Retreat Gdns The 4
  WV6 ....166 C3
Reynards Coppice
  TF7 ....153 B3
Reynards Mdw TF7 ..153 B4
Reynauds Cl 47 SY2 ..126 A5
Reynolds Cl
  12 Ditton Priors WV16 ..198 D8
  8 Swindon DY3 ....190 F1
Reynolds Dr 9 TF2 ..132 B2
Rhallt La SY21 ....170 C7
Rhew Level La SY10 ..94 A8
Rhewl La SY10 ...24 B1
Rhiw Refail 3 SY10 ..94 A8
Rhodes Ave
  3 Dawley TF4 .....143 F5
  4 Dawley TF3 .....144 A5
Rhos Ddu Rd 5 LL11 ..221 C5
Rhosddu Cty Prim Schools
  LL11 ....221 C5
Rhosddu Ind Est LL11 ..221 B7
Rhosnesni La LL12 ..221 E5
Rhosrobin Rd LL11 ..221 B8
Rhyd Broughton La
  LL11 ....221 A4
Rhyd Galeo SY10 ..24 A1
Rhyd-esgyn La SY21 ..167 A5
Rhyn La SY11 .....7 C1
Richards Rd TF2 ..120 C2
Richmond Ave TF2 ..132 A6
Richmond Cl 3 TF1 ..130 D5
Richmond Dr SY3 ..124 F6

Richmond Gdns
  Bridgnorth WV16 ...218 E6
  3 Chirk LL14 ......6 E3
Richmond Rd
  Bewdley DY12 ....211 C2
  Wrexham LL13 ....221 D8
Richmond Terr 2 SY13 ..15 B7
Riddings Cl
  2 Bewdley DY12 ...211 E3
  3 Broseley TF12 ...161 E7
  Hadley TF1 ....131 D1
Riddings La WV16 ..199 E3
Riddings Mdw 3 SY8 ..217 E4
Riddings Rd SY8 ..217 E5
Riders Lea 9 SY3 ..124 C4
Ridge The
  8 Bishop's Castle SY9 ..181 C3
  SY4 ....94 A8
Ridgebourne Rd SY3 ..124 F4
Ridgway TF6 ......116 E8
Ridings Cl 1 TF9 ..36 B1
Ridings The 8 SY3 ..124 B6
Ridley Cl WV16 ...218 C5
Ringers Way 5 TF5 ..130 A6
Ripley Cl 1 TF1 ...131 C5
Ripple Cl 3 SY2 ..125 F2
Rise La Rochford WR15 ..214 E3
  Tenbury WR15 ....220 F6
Rise Orch SY8 ....212 E4
River Cl LL13 .....221 F1
River Gdns SY4 ...103 E7
River La TF6 ......106 A3
River Side WV16 ..218 F5
Riverside WR15 ...220 C5
Riverside Ave TF8 ..153 B1
Riverside Dr 8 SY7 ..193 D3
Riverside Dr DY12 ..211 D2
Riverway Dr 6 DY12 ..211 D2
Rivington Ave 3 SY2 ..125 A1
Rivulet Rd LL13 ...221 D2
Robert-Jones & Agnes Hunt
  Orthopaedic Hospl
  SY10 ....41 B5
Robert Jones Cl 3 SY9 ..98 B8
Roberts Rd TF7 ...152 D5
Robertson Way SY2 ..125 F6
Robin Cl
  Ellesmere Urban SY12 ..27 B3
  Shrewsbury SY1 ...114 C4
Robin La TF10 ....109 A3
Robins Dr TF7 ....152 D6
Robinsford Cl 6 SY3 ..124 B6
Rochester Cl 10 TF3 ..144 D3
Rock Cl 1 SY1 ....182 F8
Rock La Edgmond TF10 ..108 F3
  Hanmer LL13 .....11 B8
  3 Ludlow SY8 .....217 D4
Rock Rd TF3 .....143 E7
Rock The
  Sheriffhales TF11 ..134 B4
  The Rock SY13 ...143 E8
Rockall Way TF3 ..143 F7
Rockside SY8 ....125 E4
Rocke's Mdw LD7 ..203 C2
Rockhill 3 TF5 ...125 C3
Rockwell La SY10 ..76 A1
Roddam Ct 2 TF10 ..109 E2
Roden Cl TF1 .....130 D5
Roden Gr SY4 ....66 F5
Rodenhurst La SY4 ..116 D2
Rodney Cl 6 TF11 ..146 A6
Rodney View SY10 ..76 C5
Rodney's View 1 SY2 ..94 A1
Roft St SY11 .....58 C7
Roman Gr 3 TF2 ..132 C2
Roman Rd SY3 ...125 A3
Roman Way
  Hinstock TF9 .....72 A2
  Whitchurch SY13 ..14 F8
Romsley Dr 2 SY3 ..125 E3
Romsley View 6 WV15 ..201 B3
Ronhill Cres 4 DY14 ..209 E3
Ronhill La DY14 ..209 E3
Rookery La SY4 ..50 F2
Rookery Rd 2 TF2 ..132 C4
Rookery The 2 TF7 ..153 B5
Rose Cres TF1 ...130 E3
Rose Gr TF1 .....130 E3
Rose Hill Rd TF9 ..70 F6
Rose Mount Dr 1 SY3 ..76 A1
Rose Tree Cl 4 TF3 ..143 F8
Rose Way 1 SY5 ..171 F3
Rosebury Gr WV5 ..190 F3
Rosedale 2 SY1 ..113 A1
Roselyn SY11 .....113 F3
Rosemary 12 SY7 ..205 B5
Rosemary La
  Leintwardine SY7 ..205 B4
  Whitchurch SY13 ..15 A7
Rosemary Way 8 SY5 ..173 B4
Rosemede 8 SY11 ..113 F3
Rosemount Gdns
  WV6 ....164 D2
Rosenhurst Dr 17 DY12 ..211 D2
Roseway
  Shrewsbury SY1 ...113 F3

Roseway continued
Wellington TF1 . . . . 130 E3
Rosewood Ave 9 LL13 . . . . 221 E4
Roslyn Rd TF1 . . . . 130 E4
Rossett Way 4 LL12 . . . . . . 221 D8
Rosthwaite TF1 . . . . 130 E3
Rotherfield SY1 . . . . 113 F1
Rothesay Cl 6 LL11 . . . . . . 221 C6
Rothesay Gr 5 SY3 . . . . 124 E4
Rothley Cl SY3 . . . . 124 F4
Rothley Dr 5 SY3 . . . . 124 A6
Rough La TF12 . . . . 161 E7
Round Hill Cl SY1 . . . . 125 B8
Round Hill Gn SY1 . . . . 125 B8
Round Hill La SY1 . . . . 125 B8
Round Oak Dr 4 TF1 . . . . . 130 E7
Roundwood Cl 9 SY4 . . . . . 59 A8
Roushill SY1 . . . . 125 C6
Row The SY6 . . . . 184 A6
Rowallan Way 4 TF2 . . . . . 132 F1

Rowan Ave
5 Dawley TF4 . . . . 144 A2
Great Dawley TF4 . . . . 143 F2
Rowan Cl
4 Ellesmere SY12 . . . . 27 A2
2 Gobowen SY11 . . . . 41 A7
2 Llandysilio SY22 . . . . 94 A1
Rowan Dr 7 TF10 . . . . 109 F1
Rowan Rd TF9 . . . . 36 D2
Rowe La
Maelor South SY12 . . . . 29 A4
Munslow TF13 . . . . 185 E1
Welshampton & Lyneal
SY12 . . . . 28 C2
Rowland Gate 6 TF1 . . . . . 130 D4
Rowley Cl 5 TF7 . . . . 152 F4
Rowley Ct 5 SY2 . . . . 125 F2
Rowton Cl 8 SY1 . . . . 130 F5
Rowton Rd SY2 . . . . 125 F2
Royal Air Force Mus The*
WV7 . . . . 156 C7
Royal Oak Dr
2 Brewood ST19 . . . . 148 E8
6 Hadley TF1 . . . . 131 A6
Royal Shrewsbury Hospl
SY3 . . . . 124 C5
Royal Way Dawley TF3 . . . . 144 A6
1 Great Dawley TF3 . . . . . 143 F6
Ruabon Rd LL13 . . . . 221 A1
Rubery Way 8 LL13 . . . . . . 221 F2
Rudge Heath Rd
WV15 . . . . 189 C6
Rudge Rd
Pattingham & Patshull
WV6 . . . . 166 B1
Rudge WV6 . . . . 190 A8
Rudge The SY1 . . . . 141 B1
Ruewood Mdw Nature
Reserve* SY4 . . . . 65 D4
Ruith Field TF5 . . . . 130 B8
Rural Cotts SY1 . . . . 141 A2
Rush La TF9 . . . . 36 A2
Rushbrooke Way 1
SY2 . . . . 126 A8
Rushbury CE Prim Sch
SY6 . . . . 185 A2
Rushbury Rd
Rushbury SY6 . . . . 185 A3
1 Wellington TF1 . . . . 130 C5
Rushey La WV7 . . . . 165 D8
Rushmoor La TF5 . . . . 117 E1
Rushton Rd 8 SY2 . . . . 125 F8
Rushwater Cl 7 WV15 . . . 190 F3
Ruskin Way 7 TF3 . . . . 144 A1
Russell Cl WV15 . . . . 219 E4
Russell Field 3 SY3 . . . . . . 124 F5
Russell Gr LL12 . . . . 221 E5
Russell Rd TF7 . . . . 153 B5
Russell Ridge SY3 . . . . 124 F4
Russell St 8 LD7 . . . . 203 B3
Russett Way 2 LL12 . . . . . 211 C2
Rushall Cl 4 WV6 . . . . 198 D8
Ruthin Rd LL13 . . . . 221 A3
Rutland SY1 . . . . 113 E5
Rutland Gn 1 TF1 . . . . 131 A4
Rutland Rd LL13 . . . . 221 E2
Ruyton Castle (remains of)*
SY4 . . . . 80 A1
Rydal Ave
Shrewsbury SY1 . . . . 113 F3
Whitchurch SY13 . . . . 175 C8
Rydal Cl 8 LL13 . . . . 221 E5
Ryebank Rd TF2 . . . . 131 F1
Ryefield Way 2 SY1 . . . . . . 15 A6
Ryelands SY3 . . . . 124 E4
Ryelands Gdns 5 SY8 . . . . 218 D5
Ryton Cl 5 SY2 . . . . 125 B1
Ryton Rd
Beckbury TF11 . . . . 164 C8
Ryton TF11 . . . . 155 C1
Ryton Way TF3 . . . . 144 B1

S

Sabrina Dr 6 DY12 . . . . . . 211 D2
Sabrina Rd 5 WV15 . . . . . . 218 F4
Sadlers Fold 1 TF2 . . . . 132 A1
Saggars Cl TF7 . . . . 152 E4
St Agathas Cl TF1 . . . . 130 C7
St Alkmond Mdw 3
SY13 . . . . 14 F8
St Alkmond's Pl 6 SY1 125 C5
St Andrew's Way 4
TF10 . . . . 121 E8

St Andrews CE Prim Sch
Great Ness SY4 . . . . 97 E4
Shifnal TF11 . . . . 145 F2
St Andrews Cl
Hope Bowdler SY6 . . . . 184 C3
6 Shifnal TF11 . . . . 145 F2
St Andrews Rd 3 SY3 124 E3
St Anne's CE Fst & Mid
Schools SY12 . . . . 211 C1
St Anne's RC Prim Sch
LL13 . . . . 221 F3
St Anne's Rd 7 SY3 . . . . . 124 E3
St Antony's Rd 10 SY3 124 E3
St Aubin Dr 2 TF4 . . . . . . 143 E6
St Austin's Friars 9
SY1 . . . . 125 B6
St Austin's St 14 SY1 125 B6
St Barbaras Pl 6 SY11 . . . 41 C4
St Catherine's Dr 1
SY3 . . . . 124 E4
St Catherines Cl TF1 . . . . . 130 E6
St Chad's Cl 6 TF1 . . . . . . 130 D5
St Chad's Terr 2 SY1 125 B5
St Chads CE Prim Sch
WV6 . . . . 166 C2
St Chads Cl WV6 . . . . 166 C2
St Chads Way TF9 . . . . 20 C2
St Christophers Sch (Ysgol
Sant Christopher)
LL13 . . . . 221 C3
St Christophers Way 3
TF4 . . . . 143 F6
St Cuthbert's Cres
WV7 . . . . 156 E5
St David's Cres LL13 . . . . . 221 E4
St Davids Cl
5 Dawley TF4 . . . . 143 F6
6 Gobowen SY11 . . . . 41 A7
St Davids' Ct 3 SY3 . . . . . 221 F5
St Dunstan Cl 8 SY6 . . . . 216 C6
St Dunstan's La WR15 . . . 215 A2
St Eatas La SY5 . . . . 139 A7
St George's By-pass
TF2 . . . . 132 D2
St George's Cres 3
TF2 . . . . 132 D2
St George's Cres 5
LL12 . . . . 221 D3
St George's Jun Sch
SY3 . . . . 124 F6
St George's St 1 SY3 . . . . 125 B7
St George's CE Prim Sch
SY7 . . . . 193 C3
St Georges Gdns 2
SY5 . . . . 173 B4
St George's Rd TF2 . . . . 132 D5
St Giles CE Prim Sch
SY1 . . . . 126 A5
St Giles Cl 2 TF1 . . . . 131 A2
St Giles Cres LL13 . . . . 221 C3
St Giles Jun & Inf Sch
LL13 . . . . 221 D2
St Giles' Rd 2 SY2 . . . . 127 C2
St Giles Way 1 LL13 . . . . . 221 C3
St Gregorys Cl WV16 . . . . . 187 E5
St Helens Cl TF1 . . . . 130 E6
St Helier Dr TF4 . . . . 143 E6
St James Cl 8 SY11 . . . . . . 59 A8
St James Cres 3 TF3 . . . . 144 B1
St James Ct
6 Wellington TF1 . . . . 130 D3
1 Wrexham LL11 . . . . 221 C5
St James Dr 3 WV15 . . . . 219 A3
St James Rd SY2 . . . . 126 B6
St John St TF1 . . . . 130 E3
St John the Baptist CE Prim
Sch SY4 . . . . 80 A2
St John's CE Prim Sch
DY3 . . . . 190 F2
St John's Cl
4 Ellesmere SY12 . . . . 27 C2
Swindon DY3 . . . . 190 E1
St John's Cres 4 SY7 195 D5
St John's Ct 4 WV16 . . . . 198 D8
St John's Dr TF2 . . . . 132 A6
St John's Hill
3 Shrewsbury SY1 . . . . . . 125 B5
St John's La
Bewdley DY12 . . . . 211 A1
Ludlow SY8 . . . . 217 C3
St John's Pk 8 SY13 . . . . . 15 A8
St John's Rd 2 SY8 . . . . . . 217 C3
St John's St
4 Whitchurch SY13 . . . . . . 15 A8
Wrexham LL13 . . . . 221 C3
St Johns CE Fst Sch
ST19 . . . . 148 E7
St Johns RC Prim Sch
WV16 . . . . 219 A4
St Johns St 1 WV15 . . . . . 219 A4
St Joseph's Coll SY4 . . . . . 48 D7
St Joseph's RC High Sch
LL13 . . . . 221 C1
St Julian's La 1 SY8 . . . . . 217 D4
St Julian's Friars 1 SY1 . . 125 C5
St Julians Cl 9 TF1 . . . . . . 130 C7
St Lawrence CE Prim Sch
TF6 . . . . 119 D4
St Lawrence Prim Sch
SY6 . . . . 216 D7
St Leonard's CE Prim Sch
WV16 . . . . 218 E6

St Leonard's Cl 5 WV16 218 F5
St Leonard's Cty Infants' Sch
TF3 . . . . 144 A5
St Leonard's Rd 2 TF4 . . . 143 F5
St Leonard's Rd 8 TF4 . . . 143 F6
St Leonard's Way CW3 . . . 5 A2
St Lucias CE Prim Sch
SY4 . . . . 127 C5
St Luke's Rd TF8 . . . . 152 C4
St Lukes Prim Sch
TF2 . . . . 132 A6
St Lukes Rd TF4 . . . . 143 D1
St Margaret Rd SY8 . . . . . . 217 E5
St Margaret Way LL12 . . . 221 D6
St Margarets Dr SY2 . . . . . 127 C2
St Mark's Rd 6 SY11 . . . . 41 A7
St Marks Cl 1 TF1 . . . . 130 D7
St Marks Dr TF1 . . . . 130 D6
St Martin's Rd
Gobowen SY11 . . . . 41 A8
Selattyn & Gobowen SY10 . 24 C3
St Mary's Ave LL13 . . . . 9 C8
St Mary's Cath Prim Sch
TF7 . . . . 153 B6
St Mary's Cl SY5 . . . . 172 C8
St Mary's Cl
1 Albrighton WV7 . . . . 157 A5
Broseley TF8 . . . . 152 C2
Chirk LL14 . . . . 23 E8
Knockin SY10 . . . . 78 A1
Tenbury Wells WR15 . . . . . 220 C5
St Mary's Ct SY11 . . . . 125 C6
St Mary's La
1 Ludlow SY8 . . . . 217 C5
2 Much Wenlock TF13 . . . 159 E4
St Mary's Mews 2 SY8 217 C5
St Mary's Pl
1 Cleobury Mortimer
DY14 . . . . 209 E2
6 Shrewsbury SY1 . . . . . . 125 C2
St Mary's Prim Sch
WV7 . . . . 157 B5
St Mary's RC Prim Sch
LL13 . . . . 221 C3
St Mary's Rd 2 SY13 159 E4
St Mary's St
1 Market Drayton TF9 . . . 36 D1
4 Newport TF10 . . . . 117 C2
2 Shrewsbury SY1 . . . . . . 125 C6
3 Whitchurch SY13 . . . . . . 15 A8
St Mary's Wr La SY1 . . . . . 125 C6
St Marys Bluecoat Prim Sch
WV15 . . . . 219 A5
St Marys Cath LL11 . . . . . . 221 C4
St Marys CE Prim Sch
SY11 . . . . 125 C5
St Marys RC Prim Sch
SY1 . . . . 125 C6
St Marys St WV16 . . . . 218 E5
St Matthew's CE Aided Prim
Sch TF2 . . . . 132 E7
St Matthew's Rd 2 TF2 132 D6
St Michael's Cl
Lilleshall TF10 . . . . 121 B3
Madeley TF7 . . . . 153 B4
St Michael's Cl SY11 . . . . . 78 C7
St Michael's Dr 7 TF2 . . . 132 A6
St Michael's Gate SY8 . . . 213 B2
St Michael's La SY12 . . . . . 28 C2
St Michael's Rd TF7 . . . . . . 153 A5
St Michael's St SY1 . . . . . . 125 C4
St Michael's Terr 5
SY1 . . . . 125 C8
St Michael's Wlk 4 SY7 . . 153 A5
St Michaels Cl
Lydbury North SY7 . . . . . . 194 C8
Welshampton & Lyneal
SY12 . . . . 28 C2
St Michaels Gate 2
SY1 . . . . 125 D7
St Milburga Row 1
TF13 . . . . 159 F4
St Nicholas Cres 4
WV15 . . . . 219 A4
St Nicholas Rd WV15 . . . . 219 A4
St Oswald's Cl SY12 . . . . . 44 B7
St Oswalds View TF9 . . . . . 72 B1
St Owen's Rd 1 TF13 . . . . 159 E4
St Patrick's RC Prim Sch
TF1 . . . . 130 C5
St Pauls Dr TF1 . . . . 130 E6
St Peter & St Paul Cath Prim
Sch SY4 . . . . 109 A4
St Peter's Cl TF10 . . . . 109 A4
St Peter's Way TF10 108 F3
St Peters CE Prim Sch
SY4 . . . . 66 B7
St Peters Prim Sch
TF5 . . . . 130 B8
St Quentin Gate TF3 . . . . . 144 C6
St Saviour Cl TF4 . . . . 143 E6
St Stephen's Cl 3 SY8 . . . 217 C4
St Stephens Pl 4 WV15 . . 218 F4
St Thomas & St Anne CE
Prim Sch SY5 . . . . 173 E8
Salamanca Ave 3 SY2 . . . 124 E6
Salcombe Dr 2 SY2 . . . . . 126 A2
Sale La SY21 . . . . 167 A1
Salendine SY9 . . . . 133 A1
Salisbury Ave 7 TF3 . . . . . 133 A1
Salisbury Cl 4 LL11 . . . . . 221 D2
Salisbury Dr DY11 . . . . 221 F3
Salisbury Hill View TF7 . . 53 B7
Salisbury Rd
Market Drayton TF9 . . . . . . 53 A8

Salisbury Rd continued
5 Whitchurch SY13 . . . . . . 15 B8
Wrexham LL13 . . . . 221 C2
Salop Rd Oswestry SY11 . . 58 E7
Overton LL13 . . . . 9 C7
Welshpool SY21 . . . . 170 C6
Wrexham LL13 . . . . 221 D2
Salop St
3 Bishop's Castle SY9 . . . 181 F4
Bridgnorth WV16 . . . . 218 E5
Saltbox La WV15 . . . . 219 A5
Saltdean Cl 8 SY2 . . . . 126 A2
Salter's La TF10 . . . . 109 D2
Salters La
Loppington SY4 . . . . 64 F6
Shrewsbury SY3 . . . . 125 D5
Salthouse Rd TF8 . . . . 153 A2
Saltney Cl SY2 . . . . 126 A2
Saltwells Dr TF2 . . . . 120 E1
Sambrook Cl
1 Telford TF3 . . . . 144 C1
6 Shrewsbury SY1 . . . . . . 113 C2
Sambrook Cres TF9 . . . . . . 36 E2
Sandal Cl TF1 . . . . 131 C7
Sandbourne Dr 19 DY12 . . 211 E2
Sandbrook TF1 . . . . 131 C3
Sanderville Cl 5 TF3 . . . . 144 D1
Sandford Ave
Church Stretton SY6 . . . . . 216 F5
Shrewsbury SY1 . . . . 113 E1
Sandford Cl 1 SY1 . . . . . . 113 E1
Sandford Dr SY6 . . . . 216 E5
Sandford Ind Pk SY13 . . . . 33 B1
Sandford Rd 8 SY8 . . . . . . 217 E4
Sandford Cres TF10 . . . . . . 109 E2
Sandino Rd TF3 . . . . 144 D1
Sandiway SY3 . . . . 124 E4
Sandown Cres SY5 . . . . 124 B5
Sandpiper Cl 8 TF1 . . . . . . 130 F6
Sandpit La WV15 . . . . 189 C6
Sandpits Ave SY8 . . . . 217 D4
Sandpits Rd SY8 . . . . 217 D5
Sandringham Ave 4
SY1 . . . . 41 A1
Sandringham Cl 8 TF9 . . . 36 E2
Sandringham Rd
Pattingham WV6 . . . . 166 C2
2 Wombourne WV5 . . . . . . 190 F3
5 Wrexham LL11 . . . . 221 C7
Sandrock La SY10 . . . . 57 C2
Sandway Rd LL11 . . . . 221 C6
Sandy La Abdon SY7 . . . . . 197 D6
Alberbury with Cardeston
SY5 . . . . 169 B4
Donington WV7 . . . . 156 A4
Ellesmere Urban SY12 . . . . 27 C1
Grinshill SY4 . . . . 84 C2
Hinstock TF9 . . . . 72 B5
Loggerheads TF9 . . . . 37 C3
Stoke upon Tern TF9 . . . . . 70 E7
Sutton upon Tern TF9 . . . . 53 C7
Sandy Lane TF10 . . . . 109 F3
Sansaw Rd Grinshill SY4 . . 84 A4
Hadnall SY4 . . . . 102 B8
Sapcote La 3 SY3 . . . . 124 A7
Saplins La TF8 . . . . 151 A7
Savannahs The 6 TF1 . . . . 130 D7
Sawston Cl 3 SY1 . . . . 124 A7
Saxon Ct 8 Hadley TF1 . . . 131 A7
Shrewsbury SY3 . . . . 124 C5
Saxon St LL13 . . . . 221 D1
Sceptre Cl 4 TF4 . . . . 152 F8
Scholars La SY4 . . . . 64 E7
School Bank
Hinstock TF9 . . . . 72 A2
Hopesay SY7 . . . . 195 A5
3 Montgomery SY15 . . . . 174 B3
School Cl
Marbury cum Quoisley
SY13 . . . . 2 E8
Shifnal TF11 . . . . 145 E3
Trysull & Seisdon WV5 . . . 190 E1
School Ct TF12 . . . . 130 F3
School Field Cl 2 TF7 . . . . 62 A7
School Gd La 6 TF10 . . . . 110 A3
School Gdns 2 SY1 . . . . . . 125 C6
School House La SY2 . . . . . 132 A2
School La
5 Bishop's Castle SY9 . . . 181 F3
Blymhill & Weston-under-Lizard
TF11 . . . . 135 F5
Brinfield SY8 . . . . 213 B2
Bronington SY13 . . . . 13 B3
Clungunford SY7 . . . . 195 B1
Gobowen SY11 . . . . 24 A1
Hadley TF1 . . . . 131 D2
Leighton & Eaton Constantine
SY5 . . . . 150 C8
3 Llangollen Rural LL20 . . 6 A7
Marbury cum Quoisley
SY13 . . . . 2 E8
Market Drayton TF9 . . . . . . 53 A8
Overton LL13 . . . . 9 C8
Pant SY10 . . . . 76 E3
St Martin's SY11 . . . . 24 B3
Trefonen SY10 . . . . 57 E2
6 Wellington TF1 . . . . 130 F3
West Felton SY11 . . . . 78 C8
School Rd 2 Clun SY7 . . . 173 E2
Cranwell Arms SY7 . . . . . . 195 E5
Edgmond TF10 . . . . 109 A3
Ironbridge TF8 . . . . 152 B6
Oakengates/Donnington
TF2 . . . . 120 D1
Ruyton SY4 . . . . 80 A2

School Rd continued
Trysull & Seisdon WV5 . . . 190 D4
School St TF2 . . . . 132 D2
Schoolhouse La SY9 . . . . . . 181 F4
Scirmidge La SY8 . . . . 197 E1
Scotland Pl 1 WR15 . . . . . 220 D5
Scotland St
Ellesmere SY12 . . . . 27 B2
5 Whitchurch SY13 . . . . . . 15 A7
Scots La TF12 . . . . 161 D3
Scott Cl 3 TF7 . . . . 153 C3
Scott St SY3 . . . . 125 C3
Scotts La 1 SY8 . . . . 208 A1
Seabright Way 10 WV15 . 201 B3
Seabury Cl SY3 . . . . 125 E4
Second Ave TF2 . . . . 132 A6
Secret Hills Discovery Ctr
The* SY7 . . . . 195 E5
Sedgeford SY13 . . . . 15 A6
Sedgeford Dr SY2 . . . . 126 A1
Sefton Pl 11 SY11 . . . . 40 D1
Sefton La SY8 . . . . 196 D2
Seisdon Comm Rd
WV5 . . . . 190 B4
Seisdon Rd WV5 . . . . 190 D5
Selattyn CE Prim Sch
SY10 . . . . 39 F8
Selba Dr DY11 . . . . 211 F3
Selbourne TF7 . . . . 153 C4
Selkirk Dr TF7 . . . . 153 D4
Selley Cross LD7 . . . . 202 F7
Selwyn Cl 9 SY3 . . . . 124 E3
Seven Acres LD7 . . . . 203 C2
Seven Hills Pl 3 TF1 . . . . . 131 C3
Seven Stars Rd 13 SY21 170 B6
Severn Bank
Shrewsbury SY2 . . . . 125 D7
The Gorge TF8 . . . . 152 C4
Severn Cl TF1 . . . . 130 D6
Severn La SY21 . . . . 170 C5
Severn Rd SY8 . . . . 170 B6
Severn Side 5 SY3 . . . . 124 D3
Severn Side N 1
TF8 . . . . 152 C5
Severn Side S
1 Bewdley DY12 . . . . 211 D2
3 Bridgnorth WV15 . . . . . 218 F4
Severn St
Bridgnorth WV15 . . . . 219 A4
Shrewsbury SY1 . . . . 125 D7
Welshpool SY21 . . . . 170 B6
Severn Terr TF8 . . . . 152 B4
Severn Valley Ctry Pk*
WV16 . . . . 200 C1
Severn View Dr 2
WV16 . . . . 188 C1
Severn Way
8 Bewdley DY12 . . . . 211 C2
Cressage SY5 . . . . 149 C4
Dawley TF4 . . . . 143 E1
Llandysilio SY22 . . . . 94 A2
Severn Wynde SY7 . . . . 167 A2
Severndale Sch (Lower Site)
SY2 . . . . 125 F8
Severndale Sch (Upper Site)
SY2 . . . . 126 A8
Severnmeade 1 WV15 . . . 188 C1
Sgwir Heulwen 8 SY21 . . 170 B5
Shackerley La WV7 . . . . 148 B1
Shackleton Way SY3 . . . . . 124 B5
Shaftesbury Cl 2 TF2 . . . . 132 F2
Shakespeare Way
Madeley TF7 . . . . 153 C3
Whitchurch Urban SY13 . . 15 C3
Shales The 18 WV5 . . . . . . 190 F3
Sham La WV15 . . . . 201 C2
Shamrock Way 2 TF3 . . . . 144 A6
Sharps Dr SY13 . . . . 14 F7
Sharpstone La SY3 . . . . 137 B6
Shatterford Lakes Wildlife
Sanctuary* DY12 . . . . 211 E8
Shaw Croft TF11 . . . . 134 C5
Shaw Hedge Rd DY12 . . . . 211 E2
Shaw La
Albrighton WV7 . . . . 157 B5
Shifnal TF11 . . . . 145 D1
Shraleybrook ST7 . . . . 1 F1
Shaw Rd 4 SY2 . . . . 126 A7
Shawbirch Rd TF5 . . . . 130 A7
Shawbury Airfield SY4 . . . 85 C1
Shawbury Prim Sch
SY4 . . . . 103 D6
Shawbury Rd SY4 . . . . 66 A5
Shawfield Cl TF7 . . . . 153 C4
Shay La TF10 . . . . 110 A8
Shearman Rd 10 SY8 . . . . 217 E4
Sheepwalks La SY7 . . . . 201 F3
Sheepwell Ct 4 TF2 . . . . . 131 F1
Sheet Rd Ludford SY8 . . . . 213 C8
Ludlow SY8 . . . . 207 C1
Sheinton Rd SY5 . . . . 149 E5
Sheinton St TF13 . . . . 159 E5
Shelf Bank Cl 6 SY11 . . . . 40 F1
Shelduck Dr 2 TF1 . . . . . . 131 A6
Shelley Dr TF7 . . . . 153 C3
Shelton Fields SY3 . . . . 124 E7
Shelton Gdns 2 SY3 . . . . . 124 C7
Shelton Hospl SY3 . . . . 124 C7
Shelton La SY3 . . . . 124 D7
Shelton Pk 6 SY3 . . . . 124 D7
Shelton Rd SY3 . . . . 124 C6
Shepherd's La
Bicton SY3 . . . . 112 A1
Chirk LL14 . . . . 23 E8
Hadley TF1 . . . . 131 D2
Shrewsbury SY3 . . . . 124 A8
Shepherds Ct 1 TF1 . . . . . 110 A3
Shepherds Fold 8 TF4 . . . 143 E5
Sherbourne Cl 2 TF2 . . . . 132 D4
Sherbourne Rd SY3 . . . . . . 124 E7

Sheridan Way TF7 ....153 D3
Sheriffhales Cl TF11 .134 B7
Sheriffhales Prim Sch
  TF11 .....134 B4
Sherlock Hoy Cl 6
  TF3 ....161 C8
Sherrymill Hill SY13 ...14 F8
Sherwell Ave 3 LL12 ..221 E8
Sherwood Cl 1 TF5 ...118 C1
Sherwood Cres TF9 .....52 F7
Shetland Gr TF1 .....143 D3
Shields Cl 1 LL11 ....221 E1
Shifnal Ind Est TF11 .146 C3
Shifnal Prim Sch
  ....146 A5
Shifnal Rd TF2 .....144 D8
Shifnal Sta TF11 ....145 F4
Shifnal Sports Ctr
  TF11 ......145 F4
Shillingstone Dr SY1 .114 B5
Shipton Cl 1 TF3 ....144 C1
Shipton Hall* TF13 ...185 E3
Shire Fields Way 2
  TF4 ....143 C3
Shomere Cres SY3 ...125 B1
Shop La High Ercall TF6 .116 F7
  Perton WV6 .....190 D8
  Waters Upton TF6 ..106 A7
  Worthen with Shelve
  SY5 ......172 E1
Shoplatch 1 SY1 ....125 C5
Shore La SY5 .....149 A3
Shorncliffe Dr 3 SY3 ..124 E6
Shorncliffe Way SY3 ..124 E6
Short La 1 LL14 ....6 D8
Shotton Hall Sch SY4 .101 D8
Shotton La SY4 ......83 C1
Shrawardine Castle*
  SY4 ......169 B6
Shrewsbury Abbey*
  SY2 ......125 D6
Shrewsbury Bsns Pk
  SY2 ......126 B2
Shrewsbury Castle*
  SY2 ......125 D5
Shrewsbury Coll of Arts &
  Tech. SY2 .....126 A3
Shrewsbury Dr 1 TF1 .135 E2
Shrewsbury Fields
  TF11 ......145 F5
Shrewsbury High Sch
  SY3 ......125 A4
Shrewsbury Mus & Art Gall
  (Rowley's House)*
  ....125 C6
  SY1
Shrewsbury Sch SY3 ..125 A5
Shrewsbury Sixth Form Coll
  SY1 ......125 B6
Shrewsbury St
  Hodnet TF9 .....69 C6
  Prees SY13 ......49 C7
Shrewsbury Sta TF1 ...181 F3
Shrewsbury Way 9
  TF10 ......109 E2
Shropshire & W Midlands
  Agricultural Show Gd*
  SY1 ......125 B7
Shropshire La SY13 ....3 E1
Shropshire Nuffield Hospl
  SY3 ......124 F2
Shropshire Regimental Mus
  The* SY2 .....125 D6
Shropshire St
  1 Market Drayton TF9 ..36 D1
  Market Drayton TF9 ..52 D8
Shropshire Way 12 SY8 .217 E4
Shropshire Wildlife Trust
  Ctr* SY1 .....125 C5
Shrubbery Gdns SY4 ...66 B7
Shrubbery Rd TF1 ...131 E2
Shuker's Cl TF10 ...110 A2
Shuker's La TF7 .....87 F5
Shutfield Rd 5 TF4 ..152 F8
Sidbury Cl TF1 .....144 C2
Sidney Betts Cl 6 SY5 .178 E5
Sidney Cotts TF6 ...118 F5
Sidney Rd 18 SY8 ...217 E4
Silk Mill La 2 SY8 ..217 C3
Silken View TF3 ....144 B2
Silkin Way
  1 Wrockwardine TF5 ...130 A8
  Wrockwardine Wood & Trench
  TF2 ....132 B5
Silver Birch Dr 4 SY3 .124 F2
Silver Hill TF6 .....116 F8
Silverdale 4 SY2 ...124 A6
Silverdale Cl
  Newport TF10 .....109 E1
  2 Trefonen SY10 ....57 D2
Silverdale Dr 1 SY10 ..57 D2

Silverdale Terr 5 WV16 .200 F2
Silvermere Cl TF3 ...132 E1
Silvermere Pk 8 TF11 .145 F3
Silverstone Cl TF3 ...124 C5
Silvington Cl 2 TF3 ..144 C1
Simon Cl TF1 ......130 D3
Simon Evans Cl 6 DY14 .209 E2
Simons Rd TF9 ......53 B8
Simpson's La TF12 ...152 C2
Simpsons Wlk TF4 ...143 C3
Sinclair Gr TF1 ....131 C2
Singleton 7 TF3 ....153 D5
Singleton Ave 3 SY1 .125 A1
Sion Dr 2 SY3 .....124 C4
Sir John Talbot's Sch &
  Talbot Coll LL13 ....15 B5
Sitwell Cl SY7 ....204 C4
Six Acres 12 SY3 ...124 F3
Six Ashes Rd DY7 ...189 F1
Sixth Ave TF2 .....144 A8
Slade La
  Eardington WV16 ...188 D1
  Much Wenlock TF13 ..159 E8
Slaney La TF2 .....116 E8
Smale Rise SY11 .....59 B8
Smallbrook 8 TF3 ...143 E7
Smallbrook Rd SY13 ..14 E7
Smallwood TF2 .....153 B3
Smarts Way 8 TF3 ...132 C3
Smelt House La SY5 ...76 B1
Smestow La WV5 ...190 E3
Smith Cres TF2 .....132 C5
Smithfield Cl 8 TF9 ...36 D2
Smithfield Rd
  1 Market Drayton TF9 ..36 D1
  Much Wenlock TF13 ..159 E4
  1 Oswestry SY11 ....58 E7
  Shrewsbury SY1 ...125 C6
  25 Welshpool SY21 ..170 B6
  Wrexham LL13 ....221 D3
Smithfield St 5 SY1 ..58 E7
Smithy Bank 4 TF12 .161 C8
Smithy La
  Loggerheads TF9 ....21 B5
  Wrexham LL12 ....221 D8
Smoke Alley 18 WV16 .200 F2
Smokey La SY13 ....3 B7
Snatchfields La 2 SY6 .216 D5
Snedshill Trad Est
  ....144 C8
Snedshill Way
  Oakengates/Donnington
  TF2 ....132 D1
  St. Georges & Priorslee
  TF2 ....144 C8
Snitton La SY8 ....207 E2
Snow Hill TF2 .....132 D2
Snowdon Dr LL11 ...221 D8
Snowdon La WV6 ...164 F7
Snowdon Way TF4 ...165 B6
Snowdrop Cl 8 SY3 ...125 D3
Snowdrop Mdw 11 TF1 .131 E2
Snuff Mill Wlk 2 SY11 .211 D1
Solway Dr TF7 .....153 D4
Somerby Dr SY3 ....124 C7
Somerset Cl 2 TF7 ..152 F4
Somerset Way SY4 ...65 F8
Sommerfeld Rd TF1 ..131 F4
Songthrush Cl 2 TF1 .130 F5
Sontley Rd LL13 ...221 C1
Sorrel Cl 4 TF7 ....132 E7
Soulton Cres 4 SY4 ...66 C6
Soulton Hall* SY4 ...49 A1
South Cl SY3 .....125 B3
South Dr TF7 .....153 A5
South Hermitage SY3 .125 C4
South Rd WV16 ....198 D7
South Shropshire Leisure Ctr
  SY8 ......217 A6
South View 1 TF4 ...143 E1
South View Rd TF4 ..143 E1
Southall Rd
  5 Dawley TF4 .....144 A1
  Dawley Hamlets TF3 .153 B8
Southall St TF4 ....153 C3
Southfield TF7 .....153 C3
Southfield Rd TF13 ..159 E8
Southgate TF7 .....153 B4
Southgate Cl 8 SY1 ...58 F7
Southlands Ave TF4 ...41 B7
Southleigh 9 LL11 ...221 C6
Southville Cl SY3 ...124 C7
Southwater Way TF3 .144 A6
Southwell Cl 3 TF2 ..133 A1
Southwell Riverside
  WV16 ......219 A6
Sovereign Cl 4 SY3 ..154 F8
Spa St SY3 ......125 E4
Spaceguard Ctr The*
  LD7 ......203 D1
Spafield Cl 8 TF5 ...130 B8
Span Mdw 2 TF5 ...130 C8
Sparkham Cl 7 SY3 ...89 C2
Sparrow La 4 SY7 ...125 C5
Sparrowhawk Way
  TF6 ......130 C7
Speedwell Ridge 4
  ....144 D3
Spencer Ave 9 DY12 ..211 E2
Spencer La 5 TF5 ...130 C8
Spicer's Cl 4 SY5 ...159 E4
Spinners Cl 2 TF5 ...130 A8
Spinney The
  Newport TF10 .....121 F8
  6 Oakengates/Donnington
  TF2 ....132 E8

Spitfire Ave WV7 ...156 A7
Spout La Barrow TF12 .152 B2
  Dawley TF3 .....144 A1
  Leighton & Eaton Constantine
  SY5 ......141 E2
  Little Wenlock TF6 ..142 B3
Spout Way TF3 ....144 A1
Spring Bank SY10 ....57 D2
Spring Cl 2 WR15 ...220 D6
Spring Gdns
  5 Shrewsbury SY1 ...113 E1
  Shrewsbury SY3 ...125 C1
  4 Tenbury Wells WR15 .220 D5
  Wrexham LL11 ....221 C5
Spring Gr La WR15 ..220 C2
Spring Hill Dawley TF4 .143 E3
  Wellington TF1 ...130 C4
Spring Hill La WV4 ..190 F7
Spring Mdw TF7 ...153 C4
Spring Rd LL11 ....221 C5
Springfield 8 WV15 ..219 A4
Springfield Ave TF10 .109 E1
Springfield Cl
  1 Dawley TF4 .....143 E3
  Ludlow SY8 .....217 D4
Springfield Gdns SY11 ..78 D8
Springfield Gn 2 TF2 .125 F2
Springfield Infants Sch
  Atcham SY2 .....126 A2
  Shrewsbury SY2 ...125 F2
Springfield Pk
  5 Clehill SY8 ....208 C2
  Overton LL13 ......9 C7
Springfield Rd 8 TF1 .144 E1
Springfield Way SY1 .125 F3
Springfields TF10 ...109 F1
Springhill Cl 1 TF7 ..153 C5
Springhill Cres 8 TF7 .153 C5
Springhill Rd TF4 ...143 E3
Springhill Rise 2 SY1 .114 B3
Springs The 2 SY1 ..114 B3
Spruce Cl 8 SY12 ....27 A3
Spruce Dr 8 TF1 ...130 F5
Square The 8 SY1 ..125 C5
Squires Cl SY8 ....152 F4
Squirrel La 1 SY8 ..207 C1
Squirrel Mdw TF5 ..130 B8
Squirrel View SY8 ..207 C1
Squirrel Wlk 2 SY1 ..124 A6
Stable La 8 TF8 ....36 B1
Stableford Rd WV6 ..164 D2
Stables The 11 TF2 ...132 F8
Stableyard Cl TF4 ...143 D6
Stackyard La TF8 ...108 F4
Stadium Way 2 TF1 ..131 D5
Stafford Ave 1 TF11 .145 F3
Stafford Ct TF3 ....144 D7
Stafford Pk 1 TF3 ...144 D6
Stafford Pk 2 TF3 ...144 E7
Stafford Pk 3 TF3 ...144 E6
Stafford Pk 4 TF3 ...144 E6
Stafford Pk 5 TF3 ...144 F6
Stafford Pk 6 TF3 ...144 F7
Stafford Pk 7 TF3 ...144 F7
Stafford Pk 9 TF3 ...144 F6
Stafford Pk 10 TF3 ..144 E6
Stafford Pk 11 TF3 ..145 A5
Stafford Pk 12 TF3 ..144 E6
Stafford Pk 13 TF3 ..144 F5
Stafford Pk 15 TF3 ..144 D5
Stafford Pk 16 TF3 ..144 E5
Stafford Pk 17 TF3 ..144 E5
Stafford Pk 18 TF3 ..144 D5
Stafford Rd
  Newport TF10 .....109 F3
  5 Oakengates/Donnington
  TF2 ....132 B3
Stafford St
  4 Market Drayton TF9 ..36 D1
  Newport TF10 .....109 F3
  Oakengates/Donnington
  TF2 ....132 C1
Stags Leap SY13 .....14 E8
Stallion La 2 SY5 ...173 B4
Stanall Dr 8 TF7 ...120 E1
Stanborough Rd WR15 .220 D6
Stanham Cl 8 SY12 ...27 B2
Stanham Dr SY12 ....27 B2
Stanhill Rd 19 SY3 ..124 F3
Stanier Dr TF7 ....153 C3
Stank La SY9 .....182 B2
Stanley Dr 2 DY3 ...190 F1
Stanley La
  Astley Abbotts WV16 .188 D6
  Shrewsbury SY3 ...124 C4
Stanley Rd TF3 ....130 F4
Stanley St 8 SY3 ...221 D2
Stanmore Dr TF2 ...132 A7
Stanmore Hall*
  WV15 ......219 E3
Stanmore Ind Est
  WV15 ......219 F4
Stansty Chain Rd
  LL11 ......221 A7
Stansty Cl 8 LL11 ..221 B6
Stansty Dr 8 LL11 ..221 B6
Stansty Lodge La
  LL11 ......221 A7
Stansty Rd LL11 ...221 B6
Stanton Cl 8 SY8 ...217 C6
Stanton Dr 8 SY8 ..217 C6
Stanton Gn SY1 ....114 A3
Stanton Rd Ludlow SY8 .217 C6
  Shifnal TF11 .....146 C4

Stanwyck TF7 .....153 D5
Stanyeld Rd SY6 ...216 C7
Stapleton Rd SY3 ...125 B1
Starcross Cl 8 SY3 ..124 C6
Stargarreg La SY10 ...94 A8
Starr La TF5 .....184 A6
Startleword La SY4 ...98 A8
Station App 1 LL11 .221 C4
Station Ave LL14 ....23 D8
Station Cres SY7 ...195 E6
Station Ct 8 TF10 ..109 F1
Station Dr SY8 ....217 C4
Station Fields 2 TF2 .132 A2
Station Hill TF2 ...132 B2
Station La WV16 ...218 E4
Station Rd Adderley TF9 ..19 A5
  Admaston TF5 .....130 A6
  Albrighton WV7 ...157 A5
  Baschurch SY4 .....81 B1
  10 Bewdley DY12 ...211 E2
  11 Cleobury Mortimer
  DY14 ......209 E3
  Clive SY4 ......83 F5
  Condover SY5 ....137 B1
  Dawley TF4 .....143 E3
  Ditton Priors WV16 ..198 E8
  Hadley TF1 .....131 C3
  Hadnall SY4 .....102 C4
  Highley WV16 ....109 F2
  Hodnet TF9 ......69 D5
  Knighton LD7 ....203 B3
  Lawley & Overdale TF3 .143 D6
  Leebotwood SY6 ..178 C1
  Madeley CW3 ......5 E2
  Madeley TF7 ....153 B5
  Minsterley SY5 ...172 E4
  Montgomery SY15 ..174 A6
  Much Wenlock TF13 .159 E5
  Newport TF10 ....109 F2
  Oakengates/Donnington
  TF2 ....120 D2
  6 Shrewsbury SY11 .113 D8
  Overton LL13 .....9 D8
  Pant SY10 ......76 B1
  Pontesbury SY5 ...173 A5
  Richard's Castle (Shropshire)
  SY8 ......213 A3
  Rock DY14 .....210 D2
  Shrewsbury SY3 ...125 A2
  Stottesdon DY14 ...190 D1
  18 Wellington TF1 ..144 C8
  Wem SY4 ......66 E7
  Weston Rhyn SY10 ...23 D4
  Whitchurch SY13 ...15 B7
  Wrockwardine TF6 .129 F5
Station Rd Junc TF4 ...69 F4
Station St SY1 ....181 F3
Station Wharf 2 TF1 .159 E5
Stebbings TF1 .....153 D4
Steel Rd SY13 .....32 A6
Steeple Cl 9 DY14 ..209 E2
Steepside SY3 ....124 E3
Stephenson Dr SY4 ..125 E4
Steppes Way TF4 ....89 B6
Stersacre 2 SY1 ...113 D4
Steventon Cres 8 SY8 .217 D3
Steventon Gdns 8 SY8 .217 D3
Steventon New Rd
  SY8 ......217 D3
Steventon Rd
  Ludlow SY8 .....217 E1
  Wellington TF1 ...130 C3
Stewardstone Gate 9
  TF2 ....132 F2
Stewart Rd
  4 Oswestry SY11 ...58 E7
  Stanmore WV15 ...219 E4
Stile Rise 8 TF5 ...130 C8
Stilton Cl 2 SY3 ...124 E4
Stiperstones CE Prim Sch
  SY5 ......176 D7
Stiperstones Nature
  Reserve* SY5 ...176 D6
Stirchley Ave 8 TF3 .144 E4
Stirchley Cty Prim Sch
  TF3 ......144 D2
Stirchley Intc TF7 ...144 E4
Stirchley La TF4 ...144 A2
Stirchley Rd TF3 ...144 B1
Stirling Ave LL11 ..221 C7
Stirling Dr TF7 ....153 C3
Stirling Rd WV7 ...156 F8
Stockford Cl 11 TF2 .132 F1
Stockhall La DY14 ..209 A4
Stocking La WV16 ..187 F8
Stocks La SY12 ....88 A4
Stockton Cl 8 TF3 ..144 C1
Stockwell Gr LL13 ..221 D1
Stoke Bank SY8 ...197 F1
Stoke Dr SY8 ....213 E5
Stoke on Tern Prim Sch
  TF9 ....70 C6
Stokesay Ave SY1 ..113 D4
Stokesay Cl 18 SY3 ..154 F8
Stokesay Fore TF7 ..153 C5
Stokesay Gn SY1 ...113 D4
Stokesay Link SY7 ..153 C3
Stokesay Pl 7 TF3 ...52 D4
Stokesay Prim Sch
  SY7 ......195 E6
Stokesay Rd
  Clive Barracks TF9 ..52 D4
  Wellington TF1 ...130 C6
Stokesay Way TF3 ..153 C2
Stone Cres 3 TF1 ..131 B4

Stone House Ct 2
  SY21 ......170 D1
Stone House Dr SY11 ..78 D7
Stone House Hospl
  SY9 ......181 F3
Stone Row TF3 ....144 A5
Stonebridge Cl 11 TF4 .153 A8
Stonechat Cl 7 TF1 ..130 F6
Stonedale TF7 ....153 C4
Stonehurst Dr 6 SY2 .125 F7
Stoneleigh Gr TF2 ..132 F7
Stoney Brook Leys 18
  WV5 ......190 F3
Stoney Rd SY10 ....75 D6
Stoneyhill TF4 ....152 F7
Stottesdon CE Prim Sch
  DY14 ......199 E1
Stour Wlk 8 TF7 ...132 D4
Stourbridge Rd WV15 .219 A4
Stourport Rd DY12 ..211 D2
Stowe Cl 9 TF3 ....144 C1
Stratford Cl 3 LL12 .221 E6
Stratford La WV15 ..189 C7
Stratford Pk TF2 ...132 B7
Street The SY22 ....93 F3
Strethill Rd TF8 ...152 A4
Stretton Ave 8 TF10 .109 E2
Stretton Cl
  Bridgnorth WV16 ...218 D4
  Madeley TF7 ....153 C3
  Shrewsbury SY2 ...125 E5
Stretton Farm Rd SY6 .216 C5
Stretton Rd 8 SY3 ..159 B3
Strickland 8 SY3 ...113 D4
Striga Bank SY13 ...12 B4
Striga La SY13 ....12 B4
Strine Cl TF1 .....130 D5
Strine Way TF10 ...109 F4
Stryt Y Venti LL20 ...6 A6
Stuart St LL13 ....221 D1
Stump La TF11 ....134 D7
Suffolk Way TF4 ...143 D3
Sugdon La TF6 ....117 B3
Sulby Dr 2 TF1 ...130 F5
Sultan Rd SY1 ....125 D8
Summer Cres TF2 ..132 C4
Summer House Dr 8
  TF1 ....131 B4
Summerfield Cl SY11 ..59 A8
Summerfield Rd SY6 ..66 C6
Summerfields 8 SY8 .217 C6
Summerhill TF7 ....53 B7
Summerhill Gdns TF9 ..53 B7
Summerhill Rd LL11 .221 A6
Summerhouse Gr 6
  TF10 ......109 E2
Summerhouse La SY5 .173 F4
Summit Cl SY3 ....125 D2
Sunbury Dr TF2 ...132 B6
Sunderland Dr 8 TF1 .131 A7
Sundorne 4 LL13 .....9 C8
Sundorne Cl TF1 ...113 F2
Sundorne Cres SY1 .113 F2
Sundorne Rd SY1 ..114 A3
Sundorne Sch SY1 ..114 A3
Sunfield Gdns SY3 ..136 E6
Sunfield Pk SY2 ...126 A4
Sunflower Cl 8 TF1 .113 E1
Sungrove SY4 .....65 F5
Sunniside TF8 ....152 A7
Sunny Gdns 8 TF10 ..109 E2
Sunnybank Rd SY2 ..125 E2
Sunnycroft (NT)*
  ....130 E2
Sunnyfields SY4 ...128 B7
Sunnymead TF4 ...153 B7
Sunnyside Rd TF2 ..133 C3
Sunset Dr SY2 ....125 D3
Sussex Dr SY3 ....125 D2
Sussex Gdns 8 LL11 .221 D7
Sutherland Ave TF1 ..130 F5
Sutherland Rd TF1 ..120 F1
Sutherland Way 8 TF2 .132 B6
Sutton Cl SY2 ....125 D2
Sutton Grange Dr
  SY3 ......125 D2
Sutton La
  Shrewsbury SY3 ...125 D4
  Sutton upon Tern TF9 .53 D4
Sutton Rd
  Admaston TF5 .....130 A6
  Shrewsbury SY2 ...125 D2
Sutton Way
  Madeley TF7 ....153 C5
  Market Drayton TF9 ..53 B7
  Shrewsbury SY2 ...125 D4
Swain's Mdw 8 SY6 .216 C5
Swallow Dr 8 SY1 ..114 B4
Swallowfield Cl 12 TF2 .132 F1
Swan Cl 8 WR15 ...220 D6
  4 Tenbury Wells WR15 .220 D6
Swan Farm La CW3 ...4 F1
Swan Gate TF1 ...130 C2
Swan Hill
  Ellesmere SY12 ....27 C3
  Shrewsbury SY1 ...125 B5
Swan Hill Ct 11 SY1 .125 B5
Swan Hill Gdns 10 SY1 .125 B5
Swan La 6 Oswestry SY11 .40 E1
  Shrewsbury SY1 ...125 B5
  6 Tenbury Wells WR15 .220 D6
Swan Mdw TF13 ...159 D4
Swan Mere Pk SY12 ..27 C3
Swan St TF1 .....161 C8
Swanmere 7 TF10 ..109 F5

Swansmede Way TF3 ....144 C2
Sweeney Fen Nature
  Reserve* SY21 ......76 B7
Sweep's La SY21 ......170 A3
Sweet Chestnut Gr
  TF3 ....143 F7
Sweetbriar Cl TF2 ...120 F1
Sweetlake 1 SY3 ....124 F1
Swift Cl SY1 ....114 B4
Swift Gate 2 TF11 ...65 C2
Swin Forge Way 2 DY5 ..190 F1
Swinburne Cl TF7 ...153 C3
Swinderby Cl 1 WV7 ..156 E8
Swinford Leys 1 WV5 ..190 E3
Swiss Farm Rd SY3 ...124 D5
Sycamore Cl
  3 Llandysilio SY22 .....94 A1
  5 Ludlow SY8 ......217 D6
  6 Shifnal TF11 ......145 E5
  7 St. Martin's SY11 ....24 F6
  Wellington TF1 ....130 B5
Sycamore Cres 7 SY2 .27 B2
Sycamore Dr 5 Chirk LL14 ..6 C3
  Oswestry SY11 ......58 F7
  4 Wem SY4 .....66 A7
Sycamore Gr SY8 .....208 A1
Sycamore Rd TF12 ...152 C2
Sycamore Way WV16 ..200 E3
Sydnal La WV7 ......156 F8
Sydnall La TF9 ......53 E1
Sydney Ave SY2 .....125 E7
Sydney Cottage Dr
  WV16 ......218 D6
Sylvan Cl
  Lilleshall TF10 ......121 C6
  Prees Higher Heath SY13 ..32 E5
Sylvester Ct 2 LL13 ...221 E1
Symons Way TF1 .....72 F8
Sytche Cl TF13 ......159 E6
Sytche La TF13 ......159 D5

T

Tadorna Dr TF3 .....144 D1
Tag La TF9 .....55 A3
Tag's Gutter SY5 ....173 D6
Talbot Cl
  Church Aston TF10 ...109 D1
  2 Oakengates/Donnington
  TF2 .....132 C5
  Shifnal TF11 .....145 E4
Talbot Cres 3 SY11 ...15 B8
Talbot Ct 4 LL13 ....221 C2
Talbot Fields TF11 ...116 E7
Talbot Rd
  Albrighton WV7 ....156 E5
  3 Oakengates/Donnington
  TF2 ......132 C5
  4 Wrexham LL13 ....221 C2
  Whitchurch SY13 ....15 B8
Talbot Way 2 TF9 ...36 C2
Talcott Dr SY3 .....137 B8
Talisman Dr 4 SY2 ..125 F6
Tamarisk Cl 2 TF3 ...143 E8
Tan Bank
  2 Newport TF10 ....109 E3
  Wellington TF1 .....130 E3
Tan Y Mur 2 SY5 ....174 B3
Tanfield Cl 2 SY1 ...113 C1
Tanglewood Cl 4 TF11 ..145 F3
Tankerville Pottery & Gall*
  SY5 .....176 C6
Tankerville St 2 SY2 .125 E6
Tanners Hill DY12 ...211 B2
Tannery Ct 1 SY4 ....66 A6
Tannery La 2 SY13 ...124 E4
Tan-y-foel Dr 2 SY22 ..93 F6
Tapley Ave LL12 ....221 F6
Tar Tunnel Mus* TF8 .153 A2
Tarbach Cl 4 TF12 ...161 E7
Tarporley Rd SY13 ...1 F2
Tarvin Rd 2 SY1 ....125 E7
Tasley Cl WV16 .....218 D5
Tavern La WR15 .....215 A4
Tayleur Dr TF9 .....131 F5
Teagues Bridge Prim Sch
  TF2 .....131 F5
Teagues Cres TF2 ...131 F6
Teal Cl TF1 .....153 C8
Teal Dr SY12 .....200 E3
Teawell Cl TF3 .....143 E7
Tedsmore Rd SY11 ...79 A7
Tee Lake Bvd TF1 ...130 C7
Teece Dr TF2 .....144 F8
Telford Ave
  Albrighton WV7 ....157 A6
  Weston Rhyn LL14 ...23 E6
Telford Bridge Ret Pk
  TF3 ......144 A7
Telford Central Sta
  TF3 ......144 C7
Telford Coll of Arts & Tech
  (Walker Annexe)
  TF1 ....131 E2
Telford Coll of Arts & Tech
  TF1 ......131 B3
Telford Dr 10 DY12 ..211 D2
Telford Ice Rink &
  Superbowl* TF3 ....144 B6
Telford Int Ctr* TF3 .144 C5
Telford Rd
  1 Dawley TF4 .....144 A4
  Wellington TF1 .....130 D2

Telford Ski Ctr* TF7 .153 B6
Telford Town Pk*
  TF3 ....144 B3
Telford Way SY11 ...113 E1
Teme Ave 5 Ludlow SY8 .217 D3
  Wellington TF1 .....130 C6
Teme St WR15 .....220 D6
Tenbowell Ave SY11 ...217 E3
Temeside Cl 10 WR15 .220 D6
Temeside Est SY8 ...217 E3
Temeside Gdns 6 SY8 .217 E3
Tenbury & District Hospl
  WR15 ......220 D6
Tenbury CE Prim Sch
  WR15 .....220 D6
Tenbury Dr
  2 Oakengates/Donnington
  TF2 ......132 A6
  Shrewsbury SY2 ....126 A7
Tenbury High Sch
  WR15 ......220 C3
Tenbury Mead 11 DY14 .209 E2
Tenbury Mus* WR15 ..220 D5
Tenbury Rd
  Caynham SY8 .....208 C1
  Cleobury Mortimer
  DY14 ......209 D2
  Hope Bagot SY8 ...214 C8
Tenbury Swimming Pool
  WR15 ......220 D5
Tenbury Wells Bsns Pk
  WR15 ......220 D3
Tennyson Cl 5 TF9 ...53 A7
Tenters La 1 LL13 ...221 C2
Teresa Way TF1 ....130 F6
Tern Cl 7 TF4 .....152 E8
Tern Valley Bsns Pk
  TF9 ......36 B2
Tern View TF9 .....53 A7
Tern Way TF1 .....130 D6
Terrick Rd SY13 .....2 A2
Terrills La WR15 ....220 D5
Theatre on the Steps*
  WV16 ......218 F5
Thieves' La SY21 ...126 B2
Thimble La SY11 .....24 F6
Third Ave 6 TF2 ...132 B1
Thirlmere Gr 6 TF2 .132 D1
Thistle Cl 11 TF9 ....144 D3
Thomas Adams Sch
  SY4 ....65 F7
Thomas Ct 8 LL13 ...221 E1
Thomas Telford Sch
  TF3 ......144 A6
Thompson Dr SY13 ...14 E7
Thorn La WV13 .....198 C1
Thornhill Dr 8 LL13 ...221 D1
Thornhill Rd SY3 ...124 E7
Thornhurst Ave 2 SY11 .40 D1
Thorns Gr 1 SY3 ....124 A7
Thornton Pk Ave 9 TF2 .120 F1
Thornton Rd 8 SY11 .113 A6
Threadneedle St SY11 .78 C7
Three Ashes Rd WV16 .218 C5
Three Crosses 1 SY8 .208 C2
Three Gates SY4 .....66 C6
Three Oaks Prim Sch
  SY9 ....144 D2
Three Tuns Brewing Mus*
  SY9 ....181 F4
Threlfall Dr 8 DY12 .211 E3
Thriftwicket La SY8 .207 A7
Tibberton CE Prim Sch
  TF10 ......107 E5
Tilbrook Dr SY1 ....125 E7
Tilley Rd Wem SY4 ...66 A5
  Wem Rural SY4 .....65 F4
Tilstock CE Prim Sch
  SY13 ......32 A8
Tilstock Cl 2 SY13 ...32 A8
Tilstock Cres SY2 ...125 F2
Tilstock La 3 SY13 ...15 C1
Tilstock Rd
  Whitchurch Rural SY13 .15 A3
  Whitchurch Urban SY13 .15 A5
Timbers The TF7 ....132 D3
Tindale Pl 2 SY3 ...124 D6
Tining Cl 9 SY4 ....218 C5
Tinker's Castle Rd
  WV5 ......190 B5
Tipton's La 2 SY7 ...205 B5
Titterstone Cl 5 SY8 .208 C2
Titterstone Rd 6 WV16 .200 E3
Toll Rd TF1 ......131 A2
Tollgate Rd SY4 ....107 B6
Tollhouse Way 1 WV5 .190 F4
Tom La DY7 .....190 B3
Tom Morgan Cl TF4 ..143 C6
Tomkinson Cl 7 TF10 .148 E8
Tong Cl ST19 .....148 E8
Tong Dr TF11 .....135 F1
Tong Rd ST19 .....148 F7
Tontine Hill TF8 ....152 C3
Top Rd SY5 .....152 C4
Topham Dr 2 SY2 ...125 F3
Torrin Dr SY3 .....124 F4
Tower Cl 7 TF9 .....36 B1
Tower St 4 SY8 ....217 C4
Tower View LL13 ...221 F4
Town St SY3 .....32 E4
Town Hill 18 LL11 ...221 C3
Town Walls SY1 ....125 B5
Townsend Croft TF2 .130 D8
Trafalgar Cl
  1 Oakengates/Donnington
  TF2 ......120 E1
  2 Wrexham LL13 ...221 D1

Trafalgar Pl SY2 ....125 E6
Trederwen La SY22 ...167 A7
Treflach Rd SY10 ....57 D1
Trefonen CE Prim Sch
  SY10 ......57 E2
Trefonen Rd SY10 ...58 C6
Tregarthen La SY10 ...76 A1
Trehowell Ave SY10 ...65 F8
Trem Dyffryn 8 SY21 .23 D5
Trem Eryri 2 LL11 ...221 C7
Trem Hafren 7 SY21 .170 B7
Trem-yr-eglwys 6
  SY21 ......221 C1
Trench Cl TF2 .....131 F6
Trench Hall Residential Specl
  Sch SY4 ......66 A2
Trench Lock 1 TF1 ..131 E5
Trench Lock 2 TF1 ..131 E5
Trench Lock 3 TF1 ..131 E5
Trench Lock 5 TF1 ..131 E5
Trench Lock 6 TF1 ..131 E5
Trench Rd TF2 .....131 E6
Treowen Gdns TF2 ...132 A5
Trentham 12 SY4 ....66 A7
Trentham Rd Wem SY4 .66 A8
Tresta Cl 13 SY11 ...124 F3
Trevithick Cl TF7 ...152 E6
Trevor Ave SY11 .....24 E5
Trevor Hill SY6 ....216 C7
Trevor St (Stryt Trefor) 8
  LL13 ......221 C2
Trewern Ave 6 SY11 .41 A7
Trimpley Ct 8 SY22 ...27 B2
Trimpley La SY12 ...211 E3
Trimpley St SY22 ....27 B2
Trinity CE Prim Sch
  SY5 ......169 C4
Trinity Rd TF1 .....143 E1
Trinity St
  Shrewsbury SY3 ....125 D4
  Wrexham LL11 .....221 C3
Troon Way TF7 .....153 C3
Trysull Holloway SY5 .190 E6
Trysull Rd WV5 ....190 F4
Tudor Cl
  Berrington SY5 .....138 F3
  11 Newport TF10 ...110 A4
Tudor Dr LL13 .....10 E1
Tudor Mdw TF2 ....131 F6
Tudor Rd
  6 Bewdley DY12 ...211 C2
  Shrewsbury SY2 ...125 E3
  Wrexham LL13 ....221 D1
Tugford Rd 4 TF3 ...144 A1
Tunnel La SY6 .....212 E1
Turbervill Cl TF2 ...132 E4
Turners La
  Edgmond TF10 .....109 A3
  Llanyblodwel SY10 ...76 B4
Turnstone Dr TF1 ...131 A5
Turreff Ave TF2 ....132 D7
Tuttle St LL13 .....221 D2
Tweedale Cl TF7 ...153 C6
Tweedale Ct TF7 ...153 C6
Tweedale La TF7 ...153 C7
Tweedale Wharf TF7 .153 C6
Twemlows Ave SY13 ..32 E5
Twemlows Wlk SY13 .32 D6
Twiney La TF6 .....105 D5
Twitchen Rd TF2 ...194 D3
Two Ashes SY3 ....136 F6
Twyford La SY11 ....60 D1
Twyfords Way 5 SY2 .124 A2
Ty Gwyn La LL11 ...221 C8
Ty Mawr Cty Pk* LL20 ...6 C7
Tynsley Ct 1 TF7 ...153 B5
Tynsley Terr TF7 ...153 B5
Tyrley Rd
  Loggerheads TF9 ....54 A6
  Sutton upon Tern TF9 .53 F5

U

Ullswater Cl
  10 Dawley TF2 .....132 D1
  Shrewsbury SY3 ...144 D8
Under Ffrydd Wood
  LD7 ......203 B2
Underdale Ave SY2 ..125 E7
Underdale Rd SY2 ..125 E7
Underhill Cl TF10 ...109 C7
Underhill Cres 8 LD7 .203 B3
Underhill La SY10 ..218 F4
Undertrees Cl 5 TF1 .130 D7
Underwood TF12 ...152 D1
Unicorn Rd SY1 ....40 F1
Union La WV5 .....190 E5
Union Rd
  8 Oakengates/Donnington
  TF2 ......132 B4
  Wellington TF1 .....130 D3
  3 Wrexham LL11 ....221 B2
Union St
  9 Bishop's Castle SY9 .181 F3
  Hadley TF1 ......131 D5
University of Wolverhampton
  (Shropshire Campus)
  TF2 ......144 E8
Uplands Ave 2 TF2 ...132 A3
Uplands Dr
  Bridgnorth WV16 ...218 D4
  7 Shrewsbury SY3 ..125 E3
Upper Arley CE Fst Sch
  DY12 ......211 B7

Upper Ashj Rd 7 SY11 ..40 D1
Upper Bar TF10 ....109 F2
Upper Brook St SY11 .58 D7
Upper Church St SY11 .58 D7
Upper Dingle 6 TF7 .152 F4
Upper Galdeford 2
  SY8 ......217 C4
Upper Gunnas Cl 3
  SY7 ......195 A1
Upper Linney 5 SY8 .217 C4
Upper Lord St 9 SY11 .40 D1
Upper Rd Madeley TF7 .153 A4
  Shrewsbury SY3 ...125 B2
Upper Wood TF3 ...143 E7
Uppington Ave 4 SY3 .125 C4
Upton La 5 SY2 ....125 F3
Upton Magna Bsns Pk
  SY4 ......127 D6
Urban Gdns 4 TF1 ..130 F3
Urban Rd TF2 .....132 B4

V

Val View SY21 .....43 F5
Valencia Rd 3 WV7 .156 E7
Valeswood La SY4 ...98 A5
Valiant Rd WV7 ...156 E7
Valley Cl DY11 .....211 F4
Valley Rd The Rock SY3 .143 D8
  Wellington TF1 .....131 A1
Valley View
  2 Bewdley DY12 ...211 C1
  3 Highley WV16 ...200 E2
  Market Drayton TF9 ..53 A7
Valley Way LL13 ...221 D1
Van Diemans Rd 43
  WV5 ......190 F3
Vane Rd SY3 .....125 B4
Vashon Cl 2 SY8 ...217 E4
Vaughan Rd 7 DY14 .209 D2
Vauxhall Cres 1 TF10 .109 A6
Vennington Wlk 8 SY2 .126 A6
Verbena Way TF7 ...153 B3
Verlon Cl SY11 ....174 B4
Vernon St LL11 ....221 C4
Vicar St TF2 .....132 D1
Vicarage Bank WV15 .201 A3
Vicarage Dr
  4 Oswestry SY11 ...58 D7
  Shifnal TF11 .....145 F3
Vicarage Gr TF4 ...143 E3
Vicarage Hill 10 LL11 .221 C3
Vicarage La
  11 Highley WV16 ...200 E3
  Sutton Maddock TF11 .163 A7
  Much Wenlock TF13 ..23 D4
Vicarage Rd 20 Clun SY7 .193 D3
  Ditton Priors WV16 ..198 D8
  Shrewsbury SY3 ...125 B2
Victor Cl WV7 .....156 E7
Victoria Ave
  Hadley TF1 ......131 C3
  Shrewsbury SY3 ...125 B6
  Wellington TF1 .....130 E4
Victoria Cl 9 SY11 ..58 E7
  8 Whitchurch SY13 ...15 A7
Victoria Ct 1 TF1 ..131 D5
Victoria Fields 6 SY3 .125 B6
Victoria Jun & Inf Schools
  SY3 ......221 C3
Victoria Meml Hospl
  SY21 ......170 B6
Victoria Rd
  2 Albrighton WV7 ..156 E8
  4 Albrighton WV7 ..156 E7
  Bridgnorth WV16 ...218 D6
  3 Knighton LD7 ....203 B3
  Madeley TF7 ......36 B1
  Much Wenlock TF13 ..159 D4
  Oswestry SY11 .....58 E7
  Shifnal TF11 .....145 F4
  Wellington TF1 .....130 E3
  Wrexham LL13 ....221 B2
Victoria St
  Ellesmere SY12 .....27 B2
  Oswestry SY11 .....58 D7
  Shrewsbury SY3 ...125 D6
Viewlands Dr TF2 ...132 A7
Village Cl TF2 .....132 A3
Village Ct Dawley TF2 .144 D8
  Wellington TF1 .....221 D7
Village Rd
  Child's Ercall TF9 ...89 A7
  Stockton TF11 ....163 B5
Village Way TF2 ...132 A3
Villiers St LL13 ....221 B3
Vincent Cl 4 WV7 ...156 E7
Vine Cl SY5 .....173 F8
Vineyard Cotts SY5 .178 D3
Vineyard Dr
  Newport TF10 .....109 F3
  2 Wellington TF1 ..130 D4
Vineyard Pl 1 SY11 .130 D4
Vineyard Rd
  Much Wenlock TF13 .159 D6
  Newport TF10 .....109 F3
  Wellington TF1 .....130 D4
Violet Cl 6 TF1 ....132 E8
Viols Wlk 8 DY14 ...209 E2
Virginia Rd WV7 ...156 F7
Viscount Ave TF4 ...153 A8
Vyrnwy Pl SY11 ....40 D1
Vyrnwy Rd SY11 ....40 D1

W

Waddington Rd WV7 .156 D7
Wade Rd 1 TF2 ....132 C5
Wadham Cl 10 TF1 ..130 F5
Waggoner's Fold 6
  TF3 ....144 A5
Wagtail Dr 6 TF4 ...153 A8
Waincott 4 SY7 ....153 A8
Wains Cl 5 TF1 ....130 A4
Walder Cl 3 TF4 ...143 E4
Walford & N Shropshire Coll
  Oswestry SY11 ....58 D7
  Whitchurch Urban SY13 .15 C6
Walford Coll of Ag SY4 .99 C6
Walford Rd 6 SY11 ..58 D7
Walker Cl 9 SY13 ...219 A4
Walker Cres TF2 ...132 D1
Walker St 3 TF1 ...130 D3
Walkers Bank 4 TF3 .144 A3
Walkley Bank TF10 ..110 C4
Walkmill Dr TF9 ....53 C8
Walkmill Rd TF9 ...53 C8
Wallshead Way TF10 .109 F1
Walney Ct TF7 ....152 F4
Walnut Cl 10 Dawley TF4 .153 A8
  6 Newport TF10 ....109 F1
  Pant SY10 ......76 A1
Walnut Dr
  1 Shrewsbury SY1 ..113 D3
  Whitchurch SY13 ...14 F6
Walnut St 2 LL11 ...221 C5
Walnut Tree La TF10 .123 B7
Walsh Cl 8 TF2 ....132 F1
Walsham Ave 9 SY11 .41 E3
Walsham Cl SY3 ...124 F3
Walton Ave TF13 ...159 F4
Walton Rd SY3 ....124 D5
Waltondale TF7 ....152 F4
Wantage TF7 .....152 F6
Wardens La 5 SY7 ..205 B5
Wardle Cl 4 WV15 ..219 F4
Waring Cl 9 LL13 ...221 E1
Warings The 8 WV5 .190 F2
Warrant Rd TF9 ....52 D1
Warrenby Cl 9 SY11 .113 E1
Warrensway SY7 ...152 D5
Warrenwood Rd 1
  LL12 ......221 F6
Warstone Hill Rd WV6 .166 E3
Warwick Ave LL13 ..221 E2
Warwick Cl 8 TF9 ...36 E2
Warwick Way TF1 ...131 C6
Washbrook Rd 8 WV15 .219 A4
Washford Rd SY3 ..125 A1
Wassell Dr 3 WV12 ..161 E3
Wat's Dyke SY11 ....40 E1
Wat's Dyke Prim Sch
  LL11 ......221 C7
Watchcote 2 SY1 ...113 D1
Water La Emville DY7 .190 B3
  Newport TF10 .....109 F3
  7 Shrewsbury SY1 ..125 B6
Waterdale 10 WV5 ..190 E4
Waterford Dr TF10 ..109 D1
Watergate St 3 SY1 .15 A7
Watergate St 2 SY12 .27 C2
Waterloo Cl
  Hadley TF1 ......131 D4
  6 Wrexham LL13 ...131 D4
Waterloo Fields 2
  SY21 ......170 C1
Waterloo Pl 2 SY21 .170 C1
Waterloo Rd
  6 Bewdley DY12 ...211 C2
  Edgmond TF10 ....109 A6
  Hadley TF1 ......131 D2
  Lawley & Overdale TF3 .143 D8
  Wellington TF1 .....130 F4
Waterloo St 2 TF2 ..133 A1
Waterside Cl 13 SY13 .14 F8
Waterside Dr TF9 ...36 E2
Waterside Mews TF10 .109 E3
Watery La 1 SY21 ...167 A2
Watery Rd LL13 ....221 B3
Watkin Dr SY11 ....58 C7
Watling St
  Craven Arms SY7 ...195 D6
  4 Leintwardine SY7 .205 B5
  Wellington TF1 .....131 A3
Watling St N SY6 ...216 C6
Watling St S SY6 ...216 C5
Wattisham Way WV7 .156 D8
Wavell Ave 2 LL11 ..221 E3
Waverley 7 TF3 ....152 F6
Waverton Way 88 SY3 .132 C2
Wavertree Cl 7 TF2 .132 C2
Waxhill Cl 8 TF2 ...132 C2
Wayford Cl 2 SY3 ..125 B1
Wayhill 1 SY11 ....113 E5
Wayland Cl SY13 ...15 B6
Wayland Rd SY3 ...15 B7
Waymills SY13 .....219 A1
Wayside Clive SY4 ...83 F4
  Wellington TF1 .....130 C2
Weald Dr 83 SY2 ...152 F6
Wealdstone TF4 ...152 D6
Weale Ct 7 LL13 ...221 D1
Weavers Ct 5 TF2 ..132 A1
Weavers Rise TF2 ..133 F1
Webb Cres TF4 ....143 E2
Websters La TF9 ....69 E4
Wedgefields Cl SY4 .102 C4
Wedgewood Cres TF1 .130 C5
Wedgwood Cl 7 WV5 .190 F4

Weeping Cross La SY8 ......217 D3
Weir La SY4 ......66 C5
Weir Rd SY5 ......173 F8
Well La Great Ness SY4 ......97 E5
　Pontesbury SY5 ......125 B1
Well Mdw Gdns SY3 ......124 E6
Well Mdw Rd SY3 ......124 E6
Well Mead La SY5 ......173 F5
Well Pl 15 LL11 ......221 C3
Well St 14 SY15 ......174 B3
Welbury Cl SY3 ......137 A5
Wellfield Way SY13 ......1 F1
Wellgate SY4 ......A6
Wellington & District Cottage
　Care Ctr Trust 11 ......130 C3
Wellington C & Leisure Ctr
　TF1 ......130 D3
Wellington Cl 6 SY1 ......114 A2
Wellington Cres 1
　SY21 ......170 C6
Wellington Rd
　Albrighton WV7 ......147 F1
　Church Aston TF10 ......121 D8
　Dawley Hamlets TF4 ......143 B4
　Ironbridge TF8 ......152 B6
　Lilleshall & Donnington
　TF10 ......121 B4
　Little Wenlock TF6 ......142 D3
　Newport TF10 ......109 C1
　5 Oakengates/Donnington
　TF2 ......120 D1
Wellington Ret Pk
　TF1 ......131 B2
Wellington Sta TF1 ......130 E4
Wellmeadow WV15 ......219 A4
Wells Cl WV16 ......218 E4
Wellsfield TF7 ......152 F6
Wellswood Ave TF2 ......144 B8
Wellswood Rd 5 LL12 ......221 C2
Wellwood Cl 3 SY3 ......124 C6
Welsh Harp Hollow
　SY21 ......171 A6
Welsh St SY1 ......181 E4
Welsh Walls SY1 ......58 D8
Welshampton CE Prim Sch
　SY12 ......28 C3
Welshpool Ind Est
　SY21 ......170 C6
Welshpool Rd SY3 ......124 A7
Welshpool Sta SY1 ......170 C6
Wem Ind Est SY4 ......48 D1
Wem Moss Nature Reserve*
　SY13 ......29 E1
Wem Rd Clive SY4 ......84 A6
　Myddle & Broughton SY4 ......83 C1
　Shawbury SY4 ......103 D8
Wem Sta SY4 ......66 B6
Wemsbrook Dr 2 SY4 ......66 A8
Wemsbrook Rd SY4 ......66 A8
Wendsley Rd 3 SY1 ......113 D4
Wenlock Abbey TF13 ......159 F5
Wenlock Cl TF7 ......152 E6
Wenlock Dr 11 TF10 ......100 C2
Wenlock Edge (NT)*
　TF13 ......159 C4
Wenlock Rd
　Bridgnorth WV16 ......218 C5
　3 Shrewsbury SY2 ......128 E1
Wentworth Cl 1 SY3 ......136 F6
Wern LL14 ......6 D3
Wern Y Wiel SY10 ......75 E6
Wesley Cres TF11 ......145 F3
Wesley Dr 5 TF2 ......132 A2
Wesley Rd TF8 ......152 E3
West Ave TF2 ......132 C7
West Castle St 3 WV16 ......218 F4
West Circ SY3 ......221 E4
West Cir Way SY14 ......143 F6
West Edge 5 SY3 ......124 A6
West Felton CE Prim Sch
　SY11 ......78 E8
West Hermitage 6 SY3 ......125 C4
West Midland Saf Pk*
　DY12 ......
West Pl SY11 ......41 A8
West Rd
　Newcastle on Clun SY7 ......192 D5
　1 Oakengates/Donnington
　TF2 ......131 F1
　1 Oakengates/Donnington
　TF2 ......132 A1
　Wellington TF1 ......130 C3
West St Knighton LD7 ......203 B3
　Oakengates/Donnington
　TF2 ......132 C2
　Oswestry SY11 ......58 D7
　4 Shrewsbury SY1 ......125 D7
　Wrexham LL11 ......221 B5
West View Terr 5 TF7 ......152 F5
West Way LL13 ......10 E3
Westbeech Rd WV6 ......166 D5
Westbourne 7 TF1 ......131 A3
Westbourne Rise 3 TF6 ......136 F7
Westbourne St 12 DY12 ......211 E2
Westbrook Ave 2 SY3 ......14 F8
Westbury Rd SY4 ......113 D4
Westcott La TF9 ......72 E6
Westcroft Wlk 4 TF2 ......132 C2
Westerdale Cl 3 TF4 ......143 D2
Westerkirk Dr 6 TF7 ......152 F5

Western Ave
　Albrighton WV7 ......156 E6
　Whittington SY11 ......41 E2
Western Dr SY11 ......40 F1
Western Rise TF1 ......131 B3
Westfield Prim Sch
　WV5 ......190 F3
Westfields SY4 ......216 E5
Westfields Ct SY4 ......81 A1
Westfields Rise CW3 ......5 A1
Westfields The 1 TF9 ......72 F7
Westgate WV16 ......218 D5
Westgate Dr WV16 ......218 D5
Westland Dr 4 WV16 ......218 D5
Westland Rd SY7 ......204 D6
Westlands Rd 2 SY3 ......124 D6
Westleigh Rd 11 WV5 ......190 F3
Westminster Cl
　3 Shrewsbury SY1 ......125 C8
　Wrexham LL12 ......221 D5
Westminster Dr
　1 Market Drayton TF9 ......53 A7
　Wrexham LL12 ......221 D5
Westminster Way 1
　TF2 ......133 A1
Westmoreland Mews 2
　SY1 ......125 D8
Westmorland Mews 6
　SY1 ......131 A5
Weston Ave SY3 ......58 D6
Weston Cl
　5 Brewood ST19 ......148 E8
　Oswestry SY10 ......58 D4
Weston Ct Mews 2 SY13 ......15 A7
Weston Dr
　Shrewsbury SY1 ......113 E2
　Wellington TF1 ......130 C5
　1 Wrexham LL11 ......221 B6
Weston La SY11 ......58 E5
Weston Lullingfield CE Prim
　Sch SY4 ......81 A8
Weston Rd
　Albrighton WV7 ......157 A5
　Bucknell SY7 ......204 B4
　Oswestry SY10 ......58 D4
Weston Rhyn Prim Sch
　SY10 ......23 D5
Westune SY13 ......14 F6
Westwood Dr SY3 ......124 E6
Westwood Pk 5 SY21 ......170 B6
Westwood Rd 4 SY21 ......170 B6
Wetmore La
　Bromfield SY8 ......206 A3
　Leintwardine SY7 ......205 F7
Weymore La SY7 ......204 E4
Weybourne Wlk TF1 ......132 F7
Weybridge TF7 ......152 D6
Weyman Rd
　Ludlow SY8 ......217 D6
　2 Wellington TF1 ......130 D5
Wharfage The
　Ironbridge TF8 ......152 B4
　4 Whitchurch SY13 ......130 D5
Wharf Cl 4 TF7 ......132 C3
Wharf Rd 1 SY21 ......27 B2
Wheatcommon La SY8 ......212 F5
Wheatland Dr TF11 ......145 F5
Wheatlands 11 SY21 ......78 E7
Wheatlands The
　5 Baschurch SY4 ......99 B8
　Bridgnorth WV16 ......218 D5
Wheatley 6 SY1 ......113 F2
Wheatley Cres 13 TF11 ......131 B6
Wheatsheaf Dr SY13 ......15 A6
Wheeldale Cl 4 TF4 ......143 D2
Wheeler Orch WR15 ......220 C3
Wheeler Rd 3 SY8 ......217 E5
Whimbrel Cl 4 TF1 ......131 B5
Whinchat Cl TF1 ......130 F6
Whip La SY10 ......77 D3
Whiston Cl
　10 Albrighton WV7 ......157 A5
　3 Shrewsbury SY2 ......124 E3
Whitbatch Cl 4 SY8 ......217 C6
Whitbread Rd 2 SY8 ......217 D5
Whitburn St WV16 ......218 E5
Whitchurch Bsns Pk
　SY13 ......15 C7
Whitchurch CE Infants Sch
　SY13 ......15 B7
Whitchurch Com Hospl
　SY13 ......15 B8
Whitchurch Dr TF1 ......130 F5
Whitchurch Hr Ctr*
　SY13 ......15 A8
Whitchurch Rd
　Prees SY13 ......32 C1
　1 Shrewsbury SY1 ......113 F3
　Wem SY4 ......114 A4
　3 Whitchurch SY13 ......130 D7
　Wem SY4 ......66 B8
　Wem Urban SY4 ......48 B1
Whitchurch Sta SY13 ......15 C7
Whitchurch Swimming Ctr
　SY13 ......15 A7
Whitcliffe Rd 4 SY8 ......217 B3
Whitcomb's Orch 13
　DY14 ......209 E2
White Bank 5 SY8 ......124 B7
White Cross DY7 ......190 A1
White Hart 4 SY15 ......125 D2
White Heart Cl 10 DY12 ......211 C2
White Horse Cl 1 SY4 ......143 E4

White House (Mus) The*
　SY7 ......196 F5
White House Gdns 2
　SY1 ......113 E1
White House La DY3 ......190 D1
White House Sch SY13 ......15 B5
White Ladies Cl 1 WV7 ......156 E6
White Lodge Pk SY4 ......103 D6
White Mdw Cl 2 SY1 ......113 D1
White Minst SY1 ......58 C7
White Row WV5 ......190 E5
Whiteacre Cl 8 TF3 ......143 F8
Whitebrook Mdw SY1 ......49 B8
Whitechapel Way TF2 ......144 D8
Whitecote Dr 11 SY3 ......124 A7
Whitecott Rd SY3 ......125 E3
Whitefriars
　8 Oswestry SY11 ......41 A1
　10 Wrexham LL11 ......221 E8
Whitegate Rd 6 LL13 ......221 E4
Whitehall Gdns TF12 ......161 D8
Whitehall St SY1 ......125 E6
Whitehorse Pas 5 SY3 ......125 B6
Whitehouse La SY4 ......100 C3
Whitemeadow Cl 4
　SY5 ......195 E5
Whitemere Rd
　Shrewsbury SY1 ......113 E2
　7 Wellington TF1 ......130 C5
Whiteoaks Dr 3 SY19 ......148 C8
Whiteway Dr 4 TF5 ......130 A8
Whitewayhead La SY8 ......208 A1
Whitewell Rd SY13 ......13 C8
Whitfield Cl 8 SY11 ......59 B8
Whitley Rd WV7 ......156 B7
Whitmore Cl
　1 Bridgnorth WV16 ......218 D6
　5 Broseley TF12 ......82 F5
Whitmore La SY4 ......99 A8
Whittal Cl 12 WV15 ......203 B3
Whittington Castle (remains
　of)* SY11 ......41 E3
Whittington Bsns Pk
　SY11 ......41 B2
Whittington CE Prim Sch
　SY11 ......41 F2
Whittington Rd LL14 ......114 C2
Whittington Rd SY11 ......41 B6
Whittington Cl 5 SY2 ......125 F2
Whitwell La SY5 ......173 A4
Whitworth Dr TF3 ......144 C3
Whixall CE Prim Sch
　SY13 ......30 E3
Wicket Cl 4 TF2 ......132 E3
Widewaters Cl 3 TF4 ......152 F8
Wigeon Gr TF1 ......130 F7
Wigmore La SY5 ......168 C2
Wigmore TF1 ......152 F6
Wilcot Ave SY3 ......97 C2
Wild Thyme Dr 4 TF2 ......132 E8
Wilderhope Manor*
　TF13 ......185 D3
Wilderley Cres
　2 Shrewsbury SY3 ......125 B1
　Shrewsbury SY3 ......137 B8
Wildings The 3 SY8 ......217 C5
Wildon Way 13 SY3 ......124 E4
Wildwood TF7 ......152 E6
Wildwood Ct 3 SY21 ......170 B5
Wilfred Owen Ave 2
　SY11 ......59 A7
Wilfred Owen Cl
　7 Market Drayton TF9 ......53 A7
　3 Oswestry SY11 ......59 A7
Wilfred Owen Prim Sch The
　SY2 ......126 A8
Wilkins Cl 1 WV16 ......200 E3
Wilkinson Ave TF12 ......161 D7
Willets Way SY13 ......33 E4
Willetts Way TF4 ......143 E4
Willeymoor La SY13 ......17 A7
William Brookes Sch
　TF13 ......159 E6
William Reynolds Cty Infants
　& Jun Schools TF2 ......152 E5
Williams Rd TF2 ......120 C3
Willington Cl 7 SY1 ......113 E5
Willmoor La TF10 ......121 C4
Willow Bank 4 TF4 ......153 A8
Willow Cl
　Llandysilio SY22 ......94 B1
　6 Market Drayton TF9 ......52 F8
　St. Martin's SY11 ......24 F6
　Worfield WV15 ......189 C6
Willow Cres 3 SY12 ......27 B2
Willow Ct SY4 ......102 C4
Willow Dr
　8 Gobowen SY11 ......41 B8
　4 Hanwood SY5 ......173 F8
　1 Highley WV16 ......200 E2
Willow Pk 3 SY5 ......172 E3
Willow Pl
　Shawbury SY4 ......103 F7
　1 Shrewsbury SY4 ......124 E6
Willow St
　Ellesmere SY12 ......27 B2
　Oswestry SY11 ......58 D8
　Overton LL13 ......9 C8
Willowdale Gdns 5
　SY21 ......113 D1
Willowfield TF1 ......152 F7
Willows Cres 3 SY21 ......27 B2
Willows Rd TF2 ......132 B3
Willows The
　8 Welshpool SY21 ......170 B5
　8 Wombourne WV5 ......190 F3
　3 Wrexham LL12 ......221 D5

Wilmore St 2 TF13 ......159 E4
Wilmot Dr SY11 ......58 C5
Wilson Ave LL13 ......221 C4
Winbrook SY12 ......211 D2
Winchester Dr 18 TF2 ......132 F8
Windermere Dr 3 TF2 ......144 D8
Windermere Rd
　5 Shrewsbury SY1 ......113 F3
　Wrexham LL12 ......221 E8
Windle Hill SY6 ......216 E5
Windmill Cotts SY13 ......31 C3
Windmill La
　Shrewsbury SY1 ......156 E5
　Stockton TF11 ......163 B6
　Welshpool SY21 ......170 A7
Windrush Cl 4 LL13 ......221 E1
Windsor Cres TF11 ......152 C1
Windsor Dr
　Market Drayton TF9 ......36 E2
　Oswestry SY11 ......221 A4
　Wellington TF1 ......130 E5
Windsor La SY4 ......100 F4
Windsor Pl Dawley TF4 ......143 E3
　5 Shrewsbury SY1 ......125 C6
Windsor Rd
　Albrighton WV7 ......157 A5
　Dawley TF4 ......143 E3
　Oswestry SY11 ......41 A1
　6 Pattingham WV6 ......166 C2
　Wellington TF1 ......131 A2
Wingfield Cl SY1 ......113 E1
Wingfield Gdns 4 SY1 ......113 E1
Winifred Cl 2 SY2 ......126 A5
Winifred's Dr TF2 ......132 C7
Winlan La SY22 ......94 B4
Winlan Rd SY22 ......92 B6
Winston Dr TF2 ......132 D8
Winston Rd SY3 ......124 A7
Winston Rd DY3 ......190 F1
Winterton Way SY3 ......124 A7
Wirswall Rd SY13 ......2 C8
Wistanstow CE Prim Sch
　SY7 ......195 E8
Witchwell La TF6 ......142 D4
Withies Bank DY14 ......209 D6
Withington Cl 1 TF2 ......132 B3
Withy Ave 1 SY11 ......170 D1
Withy Ct 11 SY21 ......170 B5
Withybrook TF7 ......152 D6
Withywood Dr TF3 ......144 A5
Witley Gdns 12 WV16 ......200 E2
Wittering Rd WV7 ......156 C8
Wodehouse Cl 11 WV5 ......190 F4
Woden Cl 13 WV5 ......190 F4
Wold The 4 WV5 ......189 E4
Wolmore La WV5 ......190 B5
Wolverhampton Rd
　Bridgnorth WV15 ......219 A5
　Pattingham & Patshull
　WV6 ......166 D3
Wolverley Ct
　8 Albrighton WV7 ......157 A5
Wombourne Enterprise Pk
　TF2 ......132 A2
Wombridge Prim Sch
　TF2 ......132 A2
Wombridge Rd TF2 ......131 F3
Wombridge Rd WV12 ......131 F4
Wombrook Dale 4
　WV5 ......190 B3
Wonderland* TF3 ......144 C5
Wood Cl TF1 ......131 A6
Wood Hill Dr 10 WV6 ......190 F3
Wood La Cressage SY5 ......149 C1
　Harley SY5 ......158 C3
　Hinstock TF9 ......72 A4
　Hodnet TF9 ......51 C3
Wood Rd SY4 ......101 F4
Wood St SY1 ......125 C8
Woodbank Rd 1 SY3 ......124 F5
Woodbatch Rd 2 SY9 ......181 E3
Woodberry Cl
　Bridgnorth WV16 ......218 D5
　2 Wrexham LL13 ......221 A2
Woodbine Cl 5 SY5 ......171 F3
Woodbine Dr 5 TF9 ......36 F4
Woodbury 2 SY11 ......24 F7
Woodcock Cnr TF11 ......146 E8
Woodcote Edge SY6 ......216 B5
Woodcote Way SY21 ......125 F8
Woodcrest 13 SY3 ......124 A6
Woodcroft TF7 ......152 F6
Woodfield Ave SY3 ......124 C5
Woodfield Cty Infants Sch
　SY3 ......124 F6
Woodfield Rd SY3 ......124 F6
Wooford Gn 4 SY5 ......130 B8
Woodford La WV5 ......190 A4
Woodford Way 2 WV5 ......190 E3
Woodhall Cl 1 SY3 ......124 A6
Woodhall Dr SY5 ......173 E7
Woodhill Cl 14 WV5 ......190 F3
Woodhill Rd WV16 ......200 D3
Woodhouse Central
　TF3 ......144 B6
Woodhouse Cres TF12 ......132 B6
Woodhouse Dr 11 SY11 ......61 A5
Woodhouse La
　Aymestrey SY8 ......212 C4
　Boningale WV7 ......157 C3
　Buerton CW3 ......19 D8
　3 Dawley TF2 ......132 E1
　Knighton LD7 ......203 A1
　Lilleshall & Donnington
　TF11 ......133 B3
Woodhouse Rd TF2 ......161 C8
Woodland Cl WV7 ......157 A6
Woodland Rise 2 DY14 ......209 E3

Woodland View SY10 ......57 E2
Woodlands Ave
　6 Hanwood SY5 ......173 F8
　Wellington TF1 ......130 C4
Woodlands Cl
　Broseley TF12 ......152 C2
　2 Oswestry SY11 ......58 F7
　Withington SY4 ......128 B4
Woodlands Dr 6 TF2 ......132 B4
Woodlands Gr
　5 Llangollen Rural LL20 ......6 A7
　Prees Higher Heath SY13 ......32 E5
Woodlands La TF4 ......143 C1
Woodlands Pk 1 SY2 ......125 C3
Woodlands Rd
　Broseley TF12 ......152 C2
　Llangollen Rural LL20 ......6 A7
　The Gorge TF8 ......
Woodlands The 5 TF2 ......132 B4
Woodlark Cl 5 SY1 ......114 C3
Woodlea 5 SY2 ......125 C3
Woodpecker Cl
　6 Hadley TF1 ......131 B7
　1 Shrewsbury SY1 ......114 B4
Woodridge Cl TF10 ......109 A4
Woodrows TF7 ......152 F6
Woodrush Heath TF3 ......143 F7
Woodside Bicton SY3 ......132 B6
　Ironbridge TF8 ......152 B6
　3 Oswestry SY11 ......40 E1
Woodside Ave TF7 ......152 D5
Woodside Dr 7 TF4 ......131 D2
Woodside Cty Infants & Jun
　Sch TF7 ......152 F5
Woodside Rd SY3 ......124 C5
　4 Shrewsbury SY11 ......40 E1
Woodside Rd TF1 ......131 D2
Woodspring Gr TF2 ......132 F7
Woodthorpe Dr 1
　DY12 ......211 D2
Woolams The 6 SY4 ......124 B7
Woollam Rd TF1 ......131 A2
Woolpack Cl 5 TF11 ......145 F5
Woolpack Rd SY10 ......77 D6
Woore Prim Sch CW3 ......5 A1
Woore Rd CW3 ......4 A2
Worcester Rd
　Dawley TF4 ......143 F4
　Shrewsbury TF1 ......156 D7
　3 Shrewsbury SY1 ......113 E4
Wordsworth Dr TF1 ......131 C5
Wordsworth Way 8
　TF2 ......132 D1
Worfe Cl 2 TF3 ......144 D4
Worfe Rd TF11 ......145 F6
Worfield CE Prim Sch
　WV15 ......189 B6
Worrow Dr 3 SY3 ......124 A7
Worthen CE Prim Sch
　SY5 ......171 F3
Worthington Dr
　Albrighton WV7 ......156 E6
　3 Shrewsbury SY3 ......124 E4
Worthington St 5 SY3 ......15 B8
Wrekin Ave TF10 ......109 C2
Wrekin Cl 2 TF2 ......131 F6
Wrekin Coll TF1 ......130 F4
Wrekin Course TF6 ......141 E6
Wrekin Ct SY5 ......138 F3
Wrekin Dr TF2 ......132 C7
Wrekin Rd
　8 Bridgnorth WV16 ......218 C6
　Wellington TF1 ......130 D3
Wrekin Ret Pk TF1 ......131 B1
Wrekin View TF1 ......152 E4
Wren's Nest La 5 TF1 ......131 D2
Wrexham Central Sta
　LL11 ......221 C3
Wrexham Cty Borough Mus*
　LL11 ......221 C2
Wrexham General Sta
　LL11 ......221 C4
Wrexham Maelor Hospl
　LL13 ......221 A3
Wrexham Rd
　Marchwiel LL13 ......221 A1
　Overton LL13 ......9 C8
　4 Whitchurch SY13 ......14 E7
　Wrexham Urban SY13 ......14 87
Wribbenhall Cof Sch
　DY12 ......211 E3
Wrockwardine Rd 1
　TF1 ......130 D3
Wrockwardine Wood CE Jun
　Sch TF2 ......132 B6
Wrockwardine Wood
　Infants Sch TF2 ......132 B6
Wrockwardine Wood The
　TF2 ......132 A4
Wroxeter Roman Site & Mus
　(English Heritage)*
　SY5 ......139 E6
Wroxeter Roman Vineyard*
　SY5 ......139 D6
Wroxeter Way TF3 ......144 D1
Wych Elm Dr TF5 ......130 D8
Wyebourne Rd 10 SY3 ......124 F3
Wyke La Barrow TF12 ......160 F8
　Much Wenlock TF12 ......161 E1
Wyke Rise 7 TF11 ......
Wyke Way TF11 ......145 E4
Wylcwm St 12 LD7 ......203 B3
Wyle Cop SY1 ......125 C5

Wyndham Gr **4** TF2 .....**132** F2
Wynn Ave LL11 ....**221** C6
Wynn Cl **8** DY12 ....**211** E3
Wynnstay Ave LL13 ....**221** F4
Wyre Cl **7** WV16 ......**200** E3
Wyre Forest Nature
  Reserve* DY12 ....**211** A3
Wyre Hill DY12 ....**211** C1
Wyrebrook Gdns
  WR15 ....**215** A4
Wyson Ave SY8 ....**213** B3
Wyson La SY8 ....**213** A2
Wytheford Rd SY4 ....**103** F6
Wyton Ave WV7 ....**156** D8
Wyvern TF7 ....**152** D5

Y

Y Bwthyn the Cottage **21**
  LD7 ....**203** B3
Yale Coll (Coleg Ial)
  LL12 ....**221** C4
Yale Gr LL12 ....**221** D5
Yale Pk LL11 ....**221** A4
Yardington **5** SY13 ......**14** F8
Yarwood Dr **4** LL12 ....**221** E8
Yates Way TF2 ....**144** A8
Yeld Bank SY6 ....**216** C8
Yeld The **2** SY3 ....**124** A6
Yellowstone Cl **1** TF2 ..**132** D3
Yeomanry Rd SY4 .....**113** E6
Yeomans The WV16 ....**200** D6
Yew Tree Ave SY11 ......**41** E2
Yew Tree Bank SY4 ....**100** E4

Yew Tree Cl
  11 Bewdley DY12 ....**211** C2
  Whittington SY11 ....**41** E2
Yew Tree Dr TF10 ......**121** B2
Yew Tree Gr **4** WV16 ...**200** E3
Yew Tree La
  Bewdley DY12 ....**211** C2
  Bridgemere CW5 ....**4** E6
Yew Tree Rd
  Madeley TF7 ....**152** F4
  Pattingham WV6 ....**166** C3
Yewtree Dr SY3 ....**136** F5
Yockleton Rd SY5 .....**169** A3
York Rd
  14 Bewdley DY12 ....**211** C2
  4 Shrewsbury SY1 ......**113** E4
St. Georges & Priorslee
  TF2 ....**133** A2
York St SY11 ....**40** D1

Yorke St LL11 ....**221** D3
Yorton Sta SY4 ....**83** E4
Yr Helfa LL14 ....**6** E3
Ysgol Bro Cynllaith
  SY10 ....**56** A5
Ysgol Ceiriog Jun Sch
  LL14 ....**6** E1
Ysgol Dewi Sant (St David's
  High School) LL13 ....**221** F5

Any feature in this atlas can be given a unique reference to help you find the same feature on other Ordnance Survey maps of the area, or to help someone else locate you if they do not have a Street Atlas.

The grid squares in this atlas match the Ordnance Survey National Grid and are at 500 metre intervals. The small figures at the bottom and sides of every other grid line are the National Grid kilometre values (**00** to **99** km) and are repeated across the country every 100 km (see left).

To give a unique National Grid reference you need to locate where in the country you are. The country is divided into 100 km squares with each square given a unique two-letter reference. Use the administrative map to determine in which 100 km square a particular page of this atlas falls.

The bold letters and numbers between each grid line (**A** to **F**, **1** to **8**) are for use within a specific Street Atlas only, and when used with the page number, are a convenient way of referencing these grid squares.

Example *The railway bridge over DARLEY GREEN RD in grid square B1*

Step 1: Identify the two-letter reference, in this example the page is in **SP**

Step 2: Identify the 1 km square in which the railway bridge falls. Use the figures in the southwest corner of this square: Eastings **17**, Northings **74**. This gives a unique reference: **SP 17 74**, accurate to 1 km.

Step 3: To give a more precise reference accurate to 100 m you need to estimate how many tenths along and how many tenths up this 1 km square the feature is (to help with this the 1 km square is divided into four 500 m squares). This makes the bridge about **8** tenths along and about **1** tenth up from the southwest corner.

This gives a unique reference: **SP 178 741**, accurate to 100 m.

Eastings (read from left to right along the bottom) come before Northings (read from bottom to top). If you have trouble remembering say to yourself "Along the hall, THEN up the stairs"!

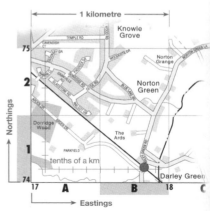

Name and Address	Telephone	Page	Grid reference